MW01506290

America Nuked on 9/11

*Compliments of the CIA,
the Neocons in the DoD
& the Mossad*

Also by Mike Palecek

Fiction:

SWEAT: Global Warming in a small town,
and other tales from the great American Westerly Midwest
Joe Coffee's Revolution
The Truth
The American Dream
Johnny Moon
KGB
Terror Nation
Speak English!
The Last Liberal Outlaw
The Progressive Avenger
Camp America
Twins
Iowa Terror
Guests of the Nation
Looking For Bigfoot
A Perfect Duluth Day
American History 101:
Conspiracy Nation Revolution
One Day In The Life of Herbert Wisniewski
Operation Northwoods: . . . the patsy
Red White & Blue

Non-Fiction:

Cost of Freedom (with Whitney Trettien and Michael Annis)
Prophets Without Honor (with William Strabala)
The Dynamic Duo: White Rose Blooms in Wisconsin (with Chuck Gregory)
And I Suppose We Didn't Go To The Moon, Either? (with Jim Fetzer)
Nobody Died At Sandy Hook (with Jim Fetzer)
And Nobody Died in Boston, either (with Jim Fetzer)
White Rose Blooms in Wisconsin (MRB edition)
America Nuked on 9/11 (with Jim Fetzer)

America Nuked on 9/11

Compliments of the CIA, the Neocons in the DoD & the Mossad

Jim Fetzer and Mike Palecek
Editors

MOON ROCK BOOKS

Save the World/Resist the Empire Series

The Dynamic Duo: White Rose Blooms in Wisconsin
And I suppose we didn't go to the Moon, either?
Nobody Died at Sandy Hook
And Nobody died in Boston, either
White Rose Blooms in Wisconsin (MRB edition)
America Nuked on 9/11

Mike Palecek, Jim Fetzer
Series Editors

America Nuked on 9/11
Compliments of the CIA, the Neocons in the DoD & the Mossad

James H. Fetzer, Ph.D. & Mike Palecek
First edition 4 July 2016

ISBN: 978-0692756102

Ordering more: Order more copies of *America Nuked on 9/11, Compliments of the CIA, the Neocons in the DoD & the Mossad* from

MOON ROCK BOOKS
6256 Bullet Drive, Crestview, FL 32536
www.MoonRockBooks.com

Special Thanks to Sterling Harwood, J.D., Ph.D., for his excellent copy editing of this book, without which it would have had many more minor mistakes, which we shall attempt to fix in future editions.

Cover design and layout by Ole Dammegård

CONTENTS

CONTENTS (continued)

Preface

Why 9/11 Should Matter
by Mike Palecek

So, yeah, we've been waiting months and months to be able to put this book out.

We've lived through years and years of American Life with all its banalities and trivialities and ritual, going through the motions, until this day.

And finally, I am able to say that the whole war on terror is phony. And the whole meme winds up through the fake terror attacks since then and only a scattered few outlaws know where it's leading.

But we are Butch and Sundance, you and I, and we are going to head them off at the goddamn pass.

All of American Life leans on the fake attacks of Sept. 11, 2001. Oh, the killing and dying that day were real, but the rest of our culture, based on that false event, is phony and fake, built in sand, so to speak.

George W. Bush did it. Yep, that stupid idiot knows the truth and he will never tell you. He is as afraid now as he was sitting in front of that second grade class. He knew the material was over his grade level.

You have seen his press conferences where he is asked the questions and he dances around them, saying, there's a time for politics. There's a time for jail cells.

Dick Cheney did it.

You heard the quote from Mineta about the incoming whatever into the Pentagon.

Condoleeza Rice did it. She knows the truth, an actual terrorist.

Karl Rove did it. *We are an empire now and you will be left to study what we have done while we go on to do other evil things.*

Israel did it. The Dancing Israelis on Israeli television saying, "we were only there to film the event."

You saw all that. You know all that. And still you park in your same spot at work, go in at the same, time, go home, come back again.

How much more proof do you need?

Well, there's plenty in this book. If you'll take it to the bank, that is.

My mother once said that when she was young they heard "The War of The Worlds" fake radio broadcast and it scared them. They got into the car and drove, just to be moving, to be doing something, I guess, when the world ended.

I think that we do that every day.

In our case, we know what's going on and we think there is nothing we can do about it, so we just work as hard as we can and shop and drink and get into debt and whatever it takes just to be in motion.

Because if we sit still the world will end and we will just be sitting there.

"So, yeah, actually, how's it going?
How about those ... umm, Cubs.
You goin' out tonight?
How are the kids? How was Florida?
Didja hear what that stupid idiot pro football player did?
Somebody Crowdfunded their what?
Where are you watching *Portlandia* this week?
Jazz hands.
That's so lame.
I know, right?
#don't hate me cause you ain't me.
There's this great group, but you probably haven't heard about them.
Going on YouTube thinking you just want to watch this three-minute music video and five hours later you are watching a tutorial on how to talk to a giraffe.

Used to have a great world, woods, lakes, oceans, animals, people.
Aaaannnd it's gone.

The Greatest Generation, The Silent Generation, The Silent Majority, The Younger Generation, Generation X, Baby Boomers, Millennials, Gen Z: everyone is talking, after church, on the phone, texting, surfing, Facebooking, just all-round communicating, but, so, yeah, nobody is really saying anything.

Not that what you are saying is wrong or you shouldn't talk.

No. I *wish* I could communicate like you. You are doing great things, creating, talking, being good to each other, laughing, being funny, working hard, learning new things, all that.

But that's not enough.

Even all that doesn't get it, go to the root.

All that, ideas, plans, well, it's just ridiculous if we don't even care enough to understand how we are being manipulated by lies. Yes, by the CIA, the rich, the government. All that standard "conspiracy theory" jargon you have learned to mistrust.

If your life is going to make sense, to have worth, don't throw your present

life away, just find room for more, because there is more, so much more.
Just sayin'.

So, yeah, Operation Northwoods was a plan concocted by American
leaders to murder American citizens involving planes and fool the American
people into believing it was done by someone else in order to justify our
military attacking Cuba.

President John Kennedy was informed of the plan and he vetoed it.

They killed him.

President George W. Bush and vice-president Dick Cheney did not turn
down the plan to attack America on Sept. 11, 2001. They went along with it,
perhaps they helped plan it. They live, in big houses, big lives.

We don't know all the details, but we do know they have not told us the
truth. The truth is not important to them and neither are we.

That is our world.

Of course it matters.

Practically everything is connected to that day.

When you go as fast as you can on the elliptical watching the TV in front
of you and you are sweating out your demons with your phone and your water
and your locker key in all the little handy slots on the machine you are not
connected to the TV because you are above that.

You are listening to your music on your iPod and this is your workout
and your world.

You have those ear buds shoved so far into your head they are almost
touching. You will do anything not to have to listen to those two women
talking to your right or those two men to your left or those *god*-damn idiots
in front of you and behind you more idiots. Small talk doesn't only bore you.
It's more than that. It isn't to the point. It's a disruption. It's hesitating. It's
cowardice. You would sooner poke out your eardrums than have to hear the
conversations of the Americans around you. You are not an American. You
are not one of those. You are different. You are better. You are smart. They
are stupid. Stupid idiots.

You cast glances toward CNN on the one TV and there is cooking on
the middle TV, and house shopping on the third, every day all day, the three
choices. You run, run, sweat, the TVs play loop after loop.

You know the truth, but you say … *nothing.*

You know these people. They are Americans and they will kill you.

At the first utterance of "9/11 was an …," they know what you are getting
at and they come toward you. They know your whole argument, your whole
life and they will kill you. You shut your … mouth or we will shut it for you.

On the TV the standard announcers talk about the elections, sometimes
terror, more elections, little more terror. On the cooking shows they compete,
bake, taste, run full-speed around a kitchen. The house shoppers clutch

hundreds of thousands of dollars in tight fists. They seek a nice "space" for their comely lives.

All based on the premise that the attacks of Sept. 11, 2001 were done by "radical Islamic terrorists."

To understand and proclaim the truth would be to topple the turnip truck in the middle of Mayberry, to overturn the piroshky kart right in Red Square, the apple cart in front of the White House, the money changer's tables in the temple.

There would be no more CNN, no more cooking with the chubby Countess, no more biggest house, best bathroom, widest kitchen.

You might not even need to artificially sweat yourself to death every day.

Life would not be fake. It would be interesting. You would talk to your neighbor and not about stupid, idiotic trivialities, but things that matter. You would not want to just die and give up and get it over with. You would want to live.

That's what they have taken from you.

Your life.

It matters.

Think of what could be done with the billions of dollars that are spent for flag napkins at the church fellowship hall, for the little flags for everyone in the crowd at the ballgame, for the flags for each student in the bleachers as they wheel into the gym the last living veteran of the war that killed the Indians, and the flags next to the altar, the flag lapels for the United States Congress, the flags in the cemetery.

Nobody really listens to TV news anymore, just the dumb people. And you are not one of those. Nobody reads newspapers, just the ones with kids in sports. Nobody listens to radio, just the old guy at the post office who has Rush on full blast all afternoon. Everyone is smarter than that.

There's other stuff to occupy our time. We don't have to spend all day plowing fields or killing Indians, or discovering washer-dryers and automatic garage-door openers and security systems, that's all been done.

We really don't have that much to do. This is our Jetsons time, when we can just whooosh around in the air with no roads and have something like fun.

And ... It's not really like that.

So, we imagine. We daydream. We wonder what life would be like ... over there ... or ... if only.

I imagine that when we are not sweating we are studying history.

There is more to it than you know: U.S. History. There are lots and lots of Indians slaughtered, the Ludlow Massacre, Haymarket Square, Palmer Raids, lynchings.

There is so much to know and if you don't know at least some of it, you don't know anything. You don't know what's going on as you watch CNN.

But, surprisingly, CNN does make sense if you know what you are looking at.

You are looking at the culmination of Manifest Destiny, such highly refined sugar-coated superficiality that you can't even see it.

It's kind of fascinating actually. The Soviets drove up to someone on the street and shoved them inside. We have cloaked the Black Maria and made it smell like freshly baked bread, the kind you stick in the oven to try to sell the house.

American History 101

Yeah, history is boring, that's right.

Think of it as a Billy Joel song.

• Oswald didn't do it. James Earl Ray didn't do it. Osama didn't do it. Sirhan didn't do it.

• Oscar Torrijos. John Perkins. Salvador Allende. Jaime Roldos Aguilera. Hugo Chavez. El Salvador. The Phoenix Program. Operation Condor. Commies, Reds. JFK, MLK, RFK, Wellstone, Lumumba, Arbenz, Mossadegh. Cointelpro: The American Indian Movement, The Black Panthers, the '60s anti-war movement.

• Scalia stops the counting of votes in Florida.

• George H.W. Bush smirks at the Ford funeral when he talks about the shooting of John Kennedy.

• The deaths of the Kennedy witnesses, the death of Gary Webb, Michael Hastings, how many more deaths, there are hundreds, thousands, heart attacks, cancer, car crash, plane crash, along with the personal character assassinations, the people driven crazy, MK Ultra, the persons trained to kill, minds altered.

And probably, maybe, more every day, we don't even know. This is the American-Soviet novel we are living in. All we need is more vodka. Somebody inhabiting a novel doesn't freaking realize it. It isn't even real. It's made up.

In the Soviet Union you got disappeared by "they," but the people had a good idea of what was going on.

In America, years later our "they" is so sophisticated we really haven't any idea.

This is America.

You got yer War On Drugs, Panama Just Cause, Gulf Wars, now we're getting somewhere, 9/11, Oklahoma City, Waco, Aurora, Sandy Hook, going too fast here, slow down, can't, no time, there's more, Tucson, Aurora, Boston, Paris, San Bernardino. H. Wayne Carver, Gene Rosen.

Barack Obama buried at sea.

George Bush: there's a time for politics, it's an absurd insinuation.

Dancing Israelis, we were just there to film it.

There's a lot more and still that is just what we know of. Imagine how much is happening that we've never heard of, never had a whiff of the sulfur.

So, that is where we are, and it's very confusing. It's meant to be.

But then again, there is this book you hold in your hands.

Have you ever read a novel where you just really connect? It's like the writer knows your own mind. It's like you could have written this book yourself. This guy is really smart. He thinks just like you do.

I think that you already know what is in this book.

You could have written it yourself.

But you didn't. You were busy sweating and shoving those goddamn earbuds way into your ears so the stupid people would not ruin your workout.

I know. I am you. You are me. We are Americans. Stupid idiots.

I am the person on the elliptical sweating.

I am the Walrus.

And I didn't write this goddamn book either.

But heck, somebody did. All these writers have taken time, not taken time, you don't do something like this as a hobby, it takes your life, you give your life, you don't care about losing your life, because this means something. That's why these writers have done this.

It matters.

And they have done it for us even though we are Americans and we are stupid. Stupid idiots. But they have taken the time anyway. And for that we are grateful and because of that we are not lost completely.

So, yeah, here we go, roll up the windows, don't catch your finger in the door, did we turn off all the burners, too late now, we are good to go, take it to the next level, stay on the same page, it is what it is, bring something to the table, wake up, your toast is ready, the bus is here, the world is on fire.

Contributors

An Aeronautical Engineer graduated from a major university with a Bachelor's degree (with Honors) in Aeronautical Engineering with a major in aerodynamics. A qualified pilot and co-designer of two experimental aircraft, he has been engaged in aviation for over four decades. Many online debates about a "Boeing 757" at the Pentagon confuse the aerodynamic phenomenon known as *Wake Turbulence* (caused mainly by Induced Drag) with *Ground Effect* (caused as a reaction to downwash). Arguments that dispute the official account of a Boeing 757 approaching the Pentagon at 400 mph and taking out a series of lampposts are shown to be well-founded in their conclusion but in need to technical corrections to the explanations that have been advanced in their support, where a Boeing 757 at 400 mph could not have come closer than about 100 feet of the ground.

Joshua Blakeney, a journalist and writer based in Calgary, Alberta, Canada, earned a BA (with distinction) in Sociology from Lethbridge. As a grad student, he received The Queen Elizabeth II Graduate Scholarship. His research on the Origins of the Global War on Terror became national news in Canada, when certain Neoconservatives took issue with his chosen line of academic enquiry. He published *Japan Bites Back: Documents Contextualizing Pearl Harbor* (2015) based upon archival research he conducted at The National Diet Library in Tokyo, Japan. He has published in Global Research.ca, The American Herald Tribune, Voltairenet.org, Coldtype.net, The Canadian Dimension, The Canadian Charger and The Information Clearing House. He recently started blogging about Japanese History at: *https://questioningjapanesehistory.wordpress.com*

Dennis Cimino, who has extensive engineering and support experience with military electronics, predominantly US Navy Combat Systems, was the Navy's top EMI troubleshooter before he went to work for Raytheon in the 1980s. He has collaborated with Jim Fetzer on many articles about "false flag" attacks, including (with regard to Sandy Hook), "The Nexus of Tyranny: The Strategy behind Tucson, Aurora and Sandy Hook" (30 January 2013), "Sent worldwide, Shannon Hicks' 'iconic' photo was faked" (18 July 2014), and "Sandy Hook, Stephen Sedensky, William Shanley and the Elaborate Hoax" (28 July 2014). He has also published extensively on various aspects of 9/11. His articles on the Pentagon, for example, include "The 'official account' of the Pentagon is a fantasy" (2012), "9/11: A World Swirling in a Volcano of Lies" (14 February 2014) and "Reflections on the Pentagon: A Photographic Review" (16 August 2014), and "Limited Hangouts: Kevin Ryan, A&E911 and The Journal of 9/11 Studies" (with Jim Fetzer, 14 August 2014).

Jim Fetzer earned his Ph.D. in the history and the philosophy of science. A former US Marine Corps officer, he has published widely on the theoretical foundations of scientific knowledge, computer science, artificial intelligence, cognitive science, and evolution and mentality. McKnight Professor Emeritus at the University of Minnesota Duluth, he has also conducted extensive research into the assassination of JFK, the events of 9/11 and the plane crash that killed Sen. Paul Wellstone. The founder of Scholars for 9/11 Truth, his latest books include *The Place of Probability in Science* (with Ellery Eells, 2010), *And I Suppose We Didn't go to the Moon, either?* (2015), *Nobody Died at Sandy Hook* (2015) and *And Nobody Died in Boston, either* (2016), which was his 32th. He also hosts the two-hour video show, "The Real Deal", on Media Broadcasting Center M/W/F from 8-10 PM/ET and "The Raw Deal" on *renseradio.com* T/Th from 8-9 PM/ET.

Don Fox has done extensive research on the role of mini-nukes by Dr. Ed Ward and on work by The Anonymous Physicist on the towers and has formulated an account of how it was done and why there is more to this story relative to very low-yield thermonuclear devices. His articles include "Mystery Solved: The WTC was Nuked on 9/11" and "Mini Neutron Bombs: A Major Piece of the 9/11 Puzzle (with Clare Kuehn, Jeff Prager, Jim Viken, Dr. Ed Ward and Dennis Cimino). Don Fox has been among the most successful in conveying the results of this complex and technical research in a fashion that makes it easily accessible to a wide audience. See, for example, "2 + 2 = Israel Nuked the WTC on 9/11" and "Rainbow in the Dark: Powerful Proof of 9/11 Nukes". He maintains a blog at https://donaldfox.wordpress.com.

T. Mark Hightower earned B.S. and M.S. degrees in Chemical Engineering from San Jose State University and over 30 years of engineering experience. He has worked in the chemical industry, the space program and the environmental field. He is a member of the American Institute of Chemical Engineers (AIChE), the American Institute of Aeronautics and Astronautics (AIAA), and the American Water Works Association (AWWA). He became a "born again" conspiracy theorist in January 2004 after stumbling upon Peter Meyer's *Serendipity* web site and learning that controlled demolition was a more likely explanation for the destruction of the Twin Towers than the official government story. He is a member of Scholars for 9/11 Truth, a petition signer at Architects & Engineers for 9/11 Truth, and a member of Pilots for 9/11 Truth. His 9/11 research is done as an exercise of his Constitutional rights as a private citizen, and in no way represents his employers or the professional societies in which he holds membership. He recently retired after 25 years with NASA

Nicholas Kollerstrom, Ph.D., has two history of science degrees, one from Cambridge 1968, plus a Ph.D. from London, 1995. An honorary member of staff of UCL for 11 years, he was in 1999 elected as a Member of the New York Academy of Sciences. A Fellow of the Royal Astronomical Society, he has several dozen articles on the history of astronomy in academic journals. His book, *Terror on the Tube (*3rd edition, 2011), establishes that the accused Islamic youth were innocent of the 2005 London bombings. *Breaking the Spell: The Holocaust, Myth and Reality* (2014), demonstrates that the official narrative of WWII cannot be sustained. He contributed four chapters to *And I suppose we didn't go to the moon, either?* His latest book, *The Life and Death of Paul McCartney 1942-66: A Very English Mystery* (2015), has recently appeared.

Susan Lindauer covered Iraq and Libya at the United Nations, as a U.S. Intelligence Asset and back-door channel on anti-terrorism from 1993 to 2003. Most notoriously, in the summer of 2001, her team warned about a major terrorist attack involving airplane hijackings and a strike on the World Trade Center. Lindauer also campaigned heavily against the War in Iraq, and developed a comprehensive peace framework through her back-channel in the run up to War. Her book, *Extreme Prejudice* (2010), is the true story of what happened when she tried to disclose what she knew personally of Iraqi Pre-War Intelligence and the 9/11 warning to Congress and the American people. Her attempts to bring the truth to the public led to the nightmare of her arrest under the Patriot Act and her imprisonment without trial at the notorious prison inside Carswell AFB in Texas.

Mike Palecek lives in Saginaw, Minnesota, west of Duluth. A writer, he is a former federal prisoner for peace and the Iowa Democratic Party candidate for the U.S. House of Representatives, 5th District in the 2000 election, gaining 65,000 votes on an anti-war platform in a conservative district. A former award winning reporter, editor, publisher in Nebraska, Iowa, Minnesota. The small newspaper that Mike & Ruth Palecek owned and operated in Byron, Minnesota, won the MNA Newspaper of the Year Award in 1993. He co-hosts "The New American Dream" radio show and has published over a dozen books that offer fictional but insightful studies of the American character and the plight in which we lend ourselves in the world today. Mike is the founder of Moon Rock Books and the co-editor of this volume.

Jeff Prager, founder of an award winning magazine for Senior Citizens, set out in 2002 to prove that 19 Muslims had hijacked four airplanes and attacked us. After extensive investigation by 2005, he realized that the official narrative of 9/11 was false, sold his business, left the United States and began to conduct 9/11 research full-time. What he found astonished even himself, because the evidence that the Twin Towers had been destroyed by a sophisticated arrangement of very small nuclear devices became simply overwhelming. He subsequently published an extensive and detailed report about this research in 9/11 AMERICA NUKED! (2012), which is a 500-page book available to the public for free as Part 1 *(http://www.datafilehost.com/ download-79644cfa.html)* and Part 2 *(http://www.datafilehost.com/download-51eec327.html)*.

Mike Sparks is a graduate of Liberty University with a B.S. degree in History/Education. His last assignment in the U.S. Army Reserves was as a MOS 11A5P Airborne-qualified Infantry officer with the rank of 1LT promotable. He leads Military Intelligence Group [00]7 (aka MI7) focusing on how Commander Ian Fleming, creator of the fictional super-spy James Bond (Agent 007), is actually warning us in code of real organized evil entities. He is the editor and co-author of several military reform books, including *Air-Mech-Strike: Asymmetric Maneuver Warfare for the 21st Century* (2002) and *Airborne Warfare: New Edition* (2015), plus several books on American Cultural Reform; *Racket Theory: Why Humans Embrace Problems instead of Solving Them* (2006), *Hive Theory: Why Humans Stay in Destructive Rackets* (2015) and in the military/spy arena with James Bond is REAL: *The Untold Story of the Political & Military Threats Ian Fleming Warned Us About* (2011). More recently, he has published *The Point of Gravity* (2012), *Masquerade: Everything is NOT What it Appears* (2013) and *The Bell Tolls for Thee: The Poppy is Also a Flower* (2014).

Ed Ward, M.D., among the leading experts on the use of nukes on 9/11, maintains an extensive archive about them and other forms of malfeasance by the US at his "Weblog of Tyranny", http://edwardmd.wordpress.com/. He has been among the most brilliant and tenacious investigators of "false flag" attacks by the government and other entities, where his recent publications include "EgyptAir 804: Just another Government Mass Murder" and "Proven 9/11 Nukes = US Government Involvement", where he was among the first to appreciate that the official account of plane impact/jet-fuel fires/collapse was completely preposterous and scientifically indefensible Ward has also appeared as a guest on "The Real Deal", which you can hear at *radiofetzer. blogspot.com.*

PROLOGUE

9/11: The Who, the How and the Why

by Jim Fetzer

"(All) the wise people in the world who are experts on American policy and who analyze the images and the videos [of 9/11] agree unanimously that what happened in the [Twin] Towers was a purely American action, planned and carried out within the U.S"--Saudi Arabian Press

It was only a matter of time. Once the infamous 28 suppressed pages of *The 9/11 Commission Report* (2004), which report on Saudi Arabian funding for several of the 19 alleged 9/11 hijackers--15 of whom were from Saudi Arabia, none of which were from Iraq--became the focus of public attention in the mass media and a bill had been introduced to allow US citizens to sue Saudi Arabia for its complicity in the atrocities of 9/11, it was only a matter of time before Saudi Arabia struck back by revealing that, on 9/11, the US had attacked the US in order to provide the pretext for perpetual war in the Middle East.

Saudi Press Just Accused US Govt Of Blowing Up World Trade Centers As Pretext To Perpetual War

TOPICS: Jay Syrmopoulos Saudi Arabia September 11th
MAY 24, 2016

By Jay Syrmopoulos

In response to the U.S. Senate's unanimous vote to allow 9/11 victims' families to sue Saudi Arabia in federal court, a report published in the London-based *Al-Hayat* daily, by Saudi legal expert Katib al-Shammari, claims that the U.S. masterminded the terror attacks as a means of creating a nebulous "enemy" in order garner public support for a global war on terror.

Saudi Arabia has blown the whistle on the US over 9/11

The plan for 9/11 appears to have originated in the fertile imagination of Benjamin Netanyahu, who was seeking a means for manipulating the United States into attacking the modern Arab states that served as a counter-balance to Israel›s domination of the Middle East, which would pave the way for its eventual expansion to become "the Greater Israel" of historic Zionist aspirations that would extend from the Tigris-Euphrates to the Nile.

He had already organized a conference held in Jerusalem on which *Terrorism: How the West can Win* (1987), long before the concept of terrorism had begun to exert its influence up the American mind. Netanyahu has displayed political genius in bending America to do the dirty work for Israel.

9/11 was brought to us compliments of the CIA, the Neocons in the Department of Defense (most of whom had come from the Project for a New American Century and were dual US-Israeli citizens) and the Mossad, with funding, it turns out, from Saudi Arabia.

It should have struck a nerve in the US when a half-dozen or more of the alleged "hijackers" turned up alive and well the following day, making contact with the media in the UK, which David Ray Griffin, *The 9/11 Commission Report: Omissions and Distortions* (2011), makes the first point in his classic demonstration of the deceit and deception of the 9/11 Commission by suppressing and misrepresenting key aspects of the atrocities of that day.

What this means is that the WHO and the WHY are easier to establish than the HOW, where the HOW becomes enormously important as proof about the WHO and the WHY. There are three major 9/11 research groups active today, including Architects and Engineers for 9/11 Truth, which has long championed the use of nanothemite in the destruction of the Twin Towers) and the Judy Wood DEW group (which focuses on the use of directed energy weapons as the means that was deployed to attack the World Trade Center).

Remarkably, neither A&E911 nor the DEW group has been willing to address the WHO and the WHY--where even their explanations of the HOW appear to suffer from serious inadequacies.

Only those associated with Scholars for 9/11 Truth--and, in the past, with *veteranstoday.com*--have addressed all three with success.

The importance of "the HOW"

The question of HOW it was done has to be the foundation for any serious investigation of the WHO and the WHY for the obvious reason: If the WTC was attacked by 19 Islamic terrorists who hijacked four commercial carriers and brought about the atrocities of 9/11 under the control of a guy in a cave in Afghanistan, as we have been told, then the case is closed! It is because the "official narrative" of 9/11 cannot be sustained that serious students have been driven to search for more adequate accounts of 9/11, which are consistent with the available relevant evidence and do not violate laws of physics, of engineering and of aerodynamics. Indeed, these violations are among the most blatant refutations of *The 9/11 Commission Report* (2004), because they prove that it cannot possibly be true.

The Twin Towers incorporated an innovative "tube within a tube" design, with 47 massive core columns at the center, which were connected to the external steel support columns by steel trusses, which were filled with 4-8" of concrete (where  the variance reflects that the trusses had v-shaped groves that were 4" deep, so in some places, the concrete was 4" thick but in others 8" instead. The buildings were among the most robust in the history of architecture, exceeded perhaps only by WTC-7, the infamous "Building 7", which would undergo a *bona fide* collapse at 5:20 PM/ET, 7 hours after the Twin Towers were demolished, even though it was hit by no plane and endured no jet fuel fires.

In "20 Reasons the "Official Account" of 9/11 is Wrong". *veteranstoday. com*. 10 September 2000), I explained some of the most basic reasons we know that what we have been told is not only false but provably false and, in crucial respects, not even scientifically possible. The impact of the planes, for example, cannot have caused enough damage to bring the buildings down, since the buildings were designed to withstand even multiple impacts by aircraft (as Frank DeMartini, the project manager, has observed), the planes alleged to have hit were similar to those they were designed to withstand, and the buildings continued to stand after those impacts with negligible effects.

Most of the jet fuel, principally kerosene, burned up in those fireballs in the first fifteen seconds or so. Below the 96th floor in the North Tower and the 80th in the South, those buildings were stone cold steel (unaffected by any fires at all other than some very modest office fires that burned around 500 degrees F), which functioned as massive heat sinks dissipating the heat from building up at specific locations of the steel. The melting point of steel at 2,800 degrees F, moreover, is about 1,000 degrees higher than the maximum burning temperature of jet-fuel-based fires, which do not exceed 1,800 degrees F under optimal conditions; but the NIST examined 236 samples of steel and found that 233 had not been exposed to temperatures above 500 degrees F and the others not above 1200.

Underwriters Laboratories, Inc., had certified the steel in the buildings up to 2,000 degrees F for three or four hours without any significant effects, where these fires burned neither long enough or hot enough at an average temperature of about 500 degrees for about one hour in the South Tower and one and a half in the North Tower to weaken, much less melt, any steel.

And if the steel had melted or weakened, then the affected floors would have displayed completely different behavior, with some degree of asymmetrical sagging and tilting, which would have been gradual and slow, not the complete, abrupt and total demolition that was observed. Which means the NIST cannot even explain the initiation of any "collapse" sequence. And their collapse was not even physically possible.

The Destruction of the Twin Towers

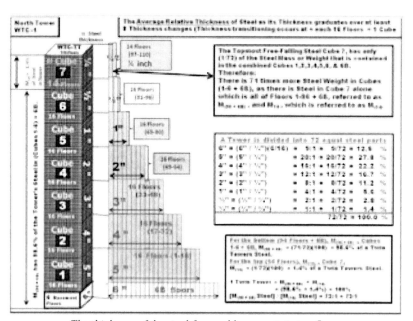

The thickness of the steel from subbasements to top floors

The top 30 floors of the South Tower pivoted and fell to the side, turning to dust before it reached the horizontal. So it did not even exist to exert any downward pressure on the lower 80 floors. A retired high-school physics, chemistry and math teacher, Charles Boldwyn, has calculated that, if you take the top 14 floors of the North Tower as one unit of downward force, there were 199 units of upward force to counteract it. Moreover, the relative thickness of the steel used in the core columns diminishes from 6" thick in the subbasements to 1/4" inch at the top, where the top 14 floors of the North Tower, for example, represented only 1.4% of the mass of the steel, where it is absurd to suppose that 1.4% of the mass of the steel could have caused the collapse of the lower 98.6%.

William Rodriguez, who was the senior custodian in the North Tower and the last man to leave the building, has reported massive explosions in the subbasements that effected extensive destruction, including the demolition of an hydraulic press and the ripping of the skin off a fellow worker, where they filled with water that drained the sprinkler system. Rodriguez has observed that the North Tower explosion occurred prior to reverberations from upper floors, a claim that has now been substantiated in a research by Craig Furlong and Gordon Ross, "Seismic Proof: 9/11 Was an Inside Job", in which they demonstrate that those explosions--both in the North Tower and also in the South--took place as much as 14 and 17 seconds before the presumptive airplane impacts, a point to which I shall return.

Heavy-steel-construction buildings, such as the Twin Towers, are not generally capable of "pancake collapse," which normally occurs only with concrete structures of "lift slab" construction and could not occur in redundant welded-steel buildings, such as the towers, unless every supporting column had been simultaneously removed, floor by floor, as Charles N. Pegelow, who is a structural engineer, has observed. The demolition of the two towers in about 10 seconds apiece is very close to the speed of free fall with only air resistance, which Judy Wood, Ph.D., formerly a professor of mechanical engineering, has observed is an astounding result that would be impossible with extremely powerful sources of energy. If they were collapsing, they would have had to fall through their points of greatest resistance.

Indeed, the towers are exploding from the top, not collapsing to the ground, where their floors do not move, a phenomenon Wood has likened to two gigantic trees turning to sawdust from the top down, which, like the pulverization of the buildings--their conversion into millions of cubic yards of very fine dust--the government's account cannot explain. There were no "pancakes". WTC-7 came down in a classic controlled demolition at 5:20 PM/ET after Larry Silverstein suggested the best thing to do might be to "pull it", displaying all the characteristics of classic controlled demolitions: a complete, abrupt and total collapse into its own footprint, where the floors are all falling at the same time, yielding a stack of pancakes about 5 floors high.

How it was done

Had the Twin Towers collapsed like WTC-7, there would have been two stacks of "pancakes" equal to about 12% the height of the buildings or around 15 floors high. But they were actually reduced to below ground level. Since there were no "pancakes", there cannot have been any "pancake collapse" of either building, where the buildings were destroyed by different modes of demolition.

WTC-7 debris (upper left) vs. WTC-1 (mid-right)

As Fr. Frank Morales of St. Mark's Episcopal Church located near "Ground Zero" and a first responder, explained to me during two interviews on "The Real Deal", both buildings were actually destroyed to or even below ground level, as the photographic evidence confirms. Notice here, for example, that, to the left you can see the 5.5 stories of debris from WTC-7, but in the immediate foreground where WTC-1 had stood, there is nothing comparable--because these buildings did not collapse!

But if the buildings did not collapse but were converted into millions of cubic yards of very fine dust in about 10 seconds apiece (officially, 11 seconds for the North Tower; 9 for the South), how was it done? Judy Wood's comparison to two enormous trees turning to sawdust from the top down gives us some clues.

Blowing them apart from the top down required some form of energy that delivered far more than conventional and that could be directed, where the apparent cause was a very sophisticated arrangement of micro and mini nukes, directed upward, and initiated in a sequence that was intended to simulate the collapse of buildings by another means, one model for which would be to take them out one cube of 10-floors at a time, which, in the case of the North Tower, would have required 11 seconds and, in the case of the South, 9, which corresponds with NIST's own temporal estimates.

Anyone who studies the destruction pattern of the North Tower has to be struck by the complete and total demolition taking place, which proceeded in stages that correspond closely to the model. Here, for example, is a time sequence of the destruction of the North Tower as it took place on 9/11:

Blown apart and converted into millions of cubic yards of very fine dust

While the photographic records prove that the Twin Towers did not collapse, it does not explain HOW it was done, which has been established on the basis of other evidence, including especially the United States Geological Survey (USGS) studies of dust samples taken from 35 locations in lower Manhattan, which record the presence of an array of elements that would only been present in the quantities and correlations found had this been a nuclear event. Consider the following findings:

Indeed, the USGS data has been confirmed by the variety of incapacities incurred by the first responders and others in the vicinity of Ground Zero, which including multiple myeloma at the rate of 18 per 100,000 vs. 3-9 per 100,000 in the general population; non-Hodgkins lymphoma, leukemia, thyroid, pancreatic, brain, prostate,

Barium and Strontium: Neither of these elements should ever appear in building debris **in these quantities**. The levels never fall below 400ppm for Barium and they never drop below 700ppm for Strontium and reach over 3000ppm for both in the dust sample taken at Broadway and John Streets.

Thorium and Uranium: These elements only exist in radioactive form. Thorium is a radioactive element formed from Uranium by decay. **It's very rare and should not be present in building rubble, ever.** So once again we have verifiable evidence that a nuclear fission event has taken place.

Lithium: With the presence of lithium we have compelling evidence that this fission pathway of Uranium to Thorium and Helium, with subsequent decay of the Helium into Lithium has taken place.

Lanthanum: Lanthanum is the next element in the disintegration pathway of the element Barium.

Yttrium: The next decay element after Strontium, which further confirms the presence of Barium.

Chromium: The presence of Chromium is one more "tell tale" signature of a nuclear detonation.

Tritium: A very rare element and should not be found at concentrations 55 times normal the basement of WTC-6 no less than 11 days after 9/11, which is another "tell tale" sign of nukes.

Elements found in USGS 9/11 dust studies

esophageal and blood and plasma cancers, which are highly associated with exposure to ironizing radiation. As of March 2011 no less than 1,003 first responders died from various cancers; more recent estimates put the number close to 70,000.

What about the planes?

Since a half-dozen or more of the alleged hijackers turned up alive and well the following day, it ought to have crossed the mind of Americans that they cannot have died on 9/11 by causing four commercial carriers--two 767s in New York and two 575s in Shanksville and at the Pentagon--to have crashed in suicide missions. in The Pentagon's own videotapes do not show a Boeing 757 hitting the building, as even Bill O'Reilly admitted when one was shown on "The O'Reilly Factor"; at 155 feet, the plane was more than twice as long as the 77-foot Pentagon is high and should have been present and easily visible; it was not, which means that the video evidence also contradicts the official account.

The aerodynamics of flight would have made the official trajectory "flying at high speed barely above ground level" physically impossible, because a Boeing 757 flying over 400 mph could not have come closer than about 60 or even feet of the ground, which means that the official account is not

The clear, green, unblemished Pentagon lawn

even aerodynamically possible, an aeronautical engineer, explains here. Since the laws of aerodynamics, no less than the laws of physics and of engineering, cannot be violated and cannot be changed, we should have known from the beginning that something was drastically wrong with the official story of 9/11. But, as CIT (Citizens Investigative Team) has emphasized, we have multiple reports of a plane approaching the Pentagon on a different trajectory only to swerve over it with no impact.

Flight 93, which is alleged to have crashed in Shanksville, left no obvious aircraft debris. As both the reporters first on the scene reported, the eerie aspect of the crash site is that there was no sign that any plane had crashed there. To cope with the obvious one variation has it that the plane disappeared into an abandoned mine shaft, which is absurd on its face. But then they should have brought out the heavy equipment and the bright lights and dug and dug, 24/7, in the hope that, by some miracle, someone might possibly have survived. But nothing like that was done. Even the singed trees and shrubs were trimmed, apparently to make it impossible to subject them to chemical analysis, which would have revealed that they had not been singed by any jet-fuel based fires.

The fascinating cases, therefore, are not the 757s in Shanksville or at the Pentagon, where the proof no planes crashed is simply overwhelming, but in New York, where we seem to have videos showing Flight 11 hitting the North Tower and Flight 175 hitting the South. Because we have so much more data related to Flight 175, let's take a closer look at what happened there, which appears to be a classic instance of the *propter hoc* fallacy, which maintains that, because one event happened before another, we are entitled to infer that *the second happened because of the first.* As in the case of typical Hollywood special effects (such as Superman in flight or Spiderman spinning webs), things are not always as they appear to be. This may be the most stunning case in history.

Flight 175 and the South Tower

There are some 52 videos of one or another portion of the trajectory of Flight 175 approaching the South Tower, which were broadcast again and again on 9/11 to create the virtually indelible visual impression of the plane hitting the building. It actually requires considerable concentration to see that the plane disappears effortlessly into the building *with no collision effects!* So we are witnessing an impossible scenario in violation of the laws of physics and of engineering. The impact between a 120-ton aluminum aircraft and a massive 500,000-ton steel and concrete building should have caused the plane to crumple against the building, with wings and tail, bodies, seats and luggage falling to the ground. The engines might have entered, but most of it not. Yet none of that appears to have happened. It simply disappears into the building.

We have done frame-by-frame analysis of the two most important videos, the Michale Hezerkhani (taken from the side) and the Evan Fairbanks (taking looking up the side of the South Tower). In both cases, the plane disappears its whole length into the building in the same number of frames it passes its whole length through air. (Try it yourself, if you have any doubt! Do frame-by-frame advance and verify what I am reporting here.) Unless the resistance posed by a massive, 500,000-ton steel and concrete building to the trajectory of an aircraft in flight poses no more resistant than air, we cannot be viewing a real event. We know the formula, $d = r \times t$, where d is the length of the plane and t is the time taken, which yields the rate of travel. They are the same. There is no diminution in velocity.

As if that were no sufficient proof, we know the structure of the facades of the Twin Towers, where Flight 11 was intersecting with seven floors consisting of steel trusses connected at one end to the core columns and at the other to the external steel support columns, filled with 4-8" of concrete. At 208' on a side, that means each floor represented an acre of concrete. The horizontal resistance posed would have been simply enormous. We also have photos of the streets beneath those facades, which are bereft of any aircraft debris. You could have reclined in a lounge chair sipping Mai Tais and been perfectly safe at the times these events took place.

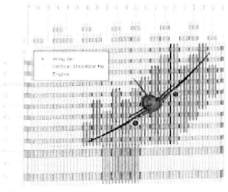

6–8 Orientation and trajectory of UAL 175 that matches the impact (vertical approach angle = 6°, lateral approach angle = 13°).

These were not real collisions with real airplanes, where debates have raged over whether it was done with CGI (computer-generated images), VC (video compositing) or using sophisticated holograms. As if more proof were required, Jack White, legendary photo/film analyst with whom I collaborated in research on JFK, discovered video footage of a white van at the intersection of Church & Murray, where an antiquated engine from a Boeing 767 was found. Several agents wearing FBI vests are in the process of unloading something heavy, but they didn't know enough to get it right. It was under a steel scaffolding and resting on the sidewalk. Had anything so massive hit the sidewalk at high speed, it would have done tremendous damage. But there it sits. They even left a dolly behind! If the crash had been real, they would not have had to fake it.

Why did they have to fake it?

It sounds incredible until you put the pieces together to figure out why they had to fake it. The plan was to have these planes completely enter the buildings before they exploded to create the impression that the Twin Towers had collapsed because of the jet-fuel based fires. We already know that that was simply impossible, but the perps were counting on the media to endlessly repeat the video footage in the expectation that public would believe what it was seeing with its own eyes. The original plan had been to use drones under remote control, until they discovered that the intricate lattice structure of the steel and concrete buildings made that physically impossible. They had to fall back on "Plan B" by faking the images of the planes and using prepositioned explosives to simulate those explosions.

An intense fire in the North Tower in 1975 had tested Underwriters Laboratories certification, burning at an estimated 2000 degrees F for four hours without causing the steel to weaken, much less melt. At that time the decision was made to install sprinkler systems in both of the towers, which would have extinguished the very modest fires that remained after the prepositioned jet fuel or napalm had been consumed in those spectacular fireballs.

In order to nullify their effect and preserve the illusion that the buildings had collapsed because of the fires--where no steel structure high-rise has even collapsed from fire before or after 9/11, much less on 9/11 itself--they had to neutralize the sprinklers. Massive explosions were set off in the subbasements of both buildings in order to drain them of water.

The problem was to "explain away" those explosions, which were timed to coincide with the apparent impact of the planes with the buildings, where they would be attributed to jet fuel falling through the elevator shafts. That was implausible, since the buildings had staggered elevators that ran for 30 floors, where you had to exit and take the next for another 30 to reach the ground. There were only a few maintenance elevators that went from the subbasements to the top. But who would even notice? It required precise timing, however, which made it all the more imperative that the planes should appear to impact with the buildings at just the right time to be responsible for the explosions in the subbasements. It did not work out as planned.

Explosions drained the water from the sprinklers

As Gordon Ross and Craig Furlong, "Seismic Proof: 9/11 was an 'Inside Job'", have shown, there were hand/eye coordination discrepancies of 14 and 17 seconds in the detonation of the explosions in the subbasements and the apparent impacts of the planes--*where the*

Original seismic and Commission times.

Table 1				
AA Flt 11				
	2001	LDEO	8:46:26	Original seismic
	2004	Commission	8:46:40	(14 seconds difference)
UA Flt 175				
	2001	LDEO	9:02:54	Original seismic
	2004	Commission	9:03:11	(17 seconds difference)

14 seconds too early at the North Tower; 17 at the South explosions occurred before the plane impacts! They have reviewed the data repeatedly, but have been unable to eliminate the time differential, which makes their research one more decisive proof that 9/11 was indeed "an inside job"--where this one does not depend upon any violations of the laws of physics, of engineering or of aerodynamics, which are, if anything, even more conclusive. They simply screwed up the timing, which, all by itself, proves that 9/11 was, indeed, "an inside job".

Where do things stand with 9/11?

There is more, especially about the alleged Islamic hijackers, including that they were not competent to fly these planes and that their names are not on any original, authenticated passenger manifest.

But it's hard to defeat the fact that several of them turned up alive and well the following day, which ought to have raised suspicions in the minds of Americans that, if the hijackers did not die, then the planes cannot have crashed; and if the planes did not crash, then the passengers aboard them did not die because they had been hijacked and forced to crash by the 19 Islamic fundamentalists--which means that the entire "War on Terror" was based upon a lie by the American government to the American people.

The American government has not even produced their tickets as evidence that they were even aboard the aircraft that they are alleged to have hijacked, which would have been easier to create than faking all four of the alleged aircraft crash sites. (For more of the evidence that supports this conclusion, see "The Real Deal Ep #100 The 9/11 Crash Sites" with Maj. Gen. Albert Stubblebine (USA, ret.), who was formerly in charge of all US military signals and photographic intelligence, who not only agrees but offers some additional substantiation.)

As Wesley Clark informed us during his speech to The Commonwealth Club in San Francisco in 2007, when he returned to the Pentagon from serving as Supreme Commander, Allied Forces Europe (the Commanding General of NATO), he learned of a plan to take out the governments of seven countries in the next five years, beginning with Iraq and Libya and ending with Syrian and Iran.

The Russians have put an end to that by intervening at the request of the Syrian government, but it has not been for lack of trying. What most Americans do not appreciate to this day is that the plan Gen. Clark was outlining was not a

Wesley Clark
October 3, 2007
Commonwealth Club of California
San Francisco, CA
Courtesy of Commonwealth Club of CA

response to 9/11 but the motivation for 9/11 by annihilating each of the nations that posed the least threat to Israel and its future aspirations.

When the 28 pages of *The 9/11 Commission Report* (2004) that have been suppressed became the inspiration for Congress to pass a bill that would allow American citizens to sue the Saudi Arabian government for its complicity in 9/11, the families and survivors of the victims of 9/11 were livid that the President of the United States would side with Saudi Arabia and lobby for its defeat.

But Barack Obama is simply carrying out the policies and positions that he inherited from the previous administration of George W. Bush and Dick Cheney, who directed the CIA, the Neocons in the Department of Defense (most of whom had come from the Project for a New American Century and were joint US-Israeli citizens) and Mossad to conduct the operation to transform US foreign policy from one in which we, at least officially, never attacked any other nation that had not attacked us first to one in which we, to benefit our "ally" in the Middle East--have now become the greatest aggressor nation that the world has ever known.

The truth would have emerged by now but for the influence of 9/11 organizations that are functioning as gatekeepers by offering limited hangouts in lieu of the truth, the whole truth and nothing but about 9/11. A&E911, for example, continues to focus on nanothermite, even though it cannot possibly have been responsible for blowing the Twin Towers apart from the top down. They claim they know that other explosives may have been involved, but refuse to identify what they could possibly be.

And, like Judy Wood and DEWs, they refuse to discuss WHO was responsible and WHY. Unfortunately, they do not even do an adequate job of explaining HOW it was done, where the nanothermite theory was inspired by the study of dust samples from an apartment near Ground Zero, which has now been superseded by the far more extensive research of the USGS. What lives by the dust, dies by the dust.

You are not going to like what you read here, but it is your duty as an American/World citizen to absorb it.

Part I

Who was Responsible
and Why 1

1

9/11 was Created by CIA, Neocons and the Mossad

by Jim Fetzer (Interview by Javad Arab Shirazi)

"9/11 was brought to us by the CIA, the Neocons in the Department of Defense (most of whom were from Project for the New American Century), which believed that, with the collapse of the Soviet Union, there was a unique historical opportunity for the US to build a world-wide empire that would endure for the next 100 years, if only we would move aggressively into the Middle East and project military and diplomatic influence outward from that geopolitically sensitive region, and the Mossad.

"It hasn't played out that way, but that was the plan. The chaos with Iraq, Syria and Afghanistan continues unabated with Iran as the ultimate objective," James Henry Fetzer said in an exclusive interview with FARS News Agency on the advent of the 13th anniversary of 9/11 attacks.

"We have massive proof that the Twin Towers were blown apart and did not collapse, which appears to have been done using a sophisticated arrangement of mini or micro nukes. It was not even possible that It could

have collapsed, given its design and construction. WTC-7 came down in a classic controlled demolition.

"All four of the airplane "crash sites" were faked or fabricated, albeit each in its own way. None of them actually crashed, which means that no passengers abroad died in crashes. And no "suicide

hijackers" were aboard them to cause them to crash, which means that the whole "War on Terror" was based on a false premise. 9/11 was staged to create a pretext for wars of aggression," he added.

What follows is the full text of the interview:

Q: As you know 9/11 conspiracy theories attribute the planning and executions of the September 11 attacks to certain parties or claim there was an advance knowledge of the attacks among high-level government officials. Possible motives claimed by conspiracy theorists of such actions include justifying the invasions of Afghanistan and Iraq as well as geostrategic interests in the Middle-East. What's your take on that?

A: To understand 9/11, we must return to the dissolution of the USSR in 1990-91, which left the US military-industrial-intelligence complex without an international boogeyman to motivate the American people to continue to support vast expenditures on bombs, planes and tanks. A shadowy and elusive "terrorist organization" in the Middle East was the perfect replacement, especially since "terrorist attacks" could be arranged almost anywhere at almost anytime and, if the government declared that it was the work of "terrorists", who would be in the position to contradict them?

The master plan was to draw the United States into endless wars in the Middle East on behalf of Israel, where no American interests were at stake. In the past, the stability of the region was viewed as paramount to guarantee the uninterrupted flow of oil from stable but despotic regimes. Indeed, no rational soul today would claim that Iraq, for example, is better off now than it was under Saddam Hussein, whose blunder may have been to abandon the petro-dollar. Gaining a foothold for international bankers in a region dominated by Islam, which tends to eschew usury, was another powerful motive.

Q: As we approach the 13th anniversary of the September 11th attacks, there still exists an almost complete blackout in mainstream media of the voluminous forensic evidence that demands an immediate and independent new investigation of that determining day. If the American people were to demand a new investigation into the 9/11, a common criticism would be that the government is not very good at investigating itself and when it does so, historically it usually either absolves itself of any alleged crimes or finds convenient scapegoats in the form of either patsies or CIA sponsored boogeymen. What in your mind would

be required for a new investigation to be successful and to actually lead to some type of reform of the system?

A: The desire for a "new investigation" of 9/11 sounds like a great idea, but we could expect exactly the same outcome as the "new investigation" of JFK conducted by the House Select Committee on Assassinations in 1977-78, which led to its Final Report in 1979. In many ways, it was redoing the cover-up but doing it better than had the original Warren Report of 1964. By ignoring the massive blow-out at the back of the head reported by the Parkland physicians (which was fist-sized) and even the much larger wound at Bethesda (enlarged with a cranial saw to make it look more like a shot from behind) and reducing it to a small entry wound at the top of the head, they replaced a bad investigation with one that was even worse.

We have massive proof that the Twin Towers were blown apart and did not collapse, which appears to have been done using a sophisticated arrangement of mini or micro nukes. It was not even possible that it could have collapsed, given its design and construction. WTC-7 came down in a classic controlled demolition. All four of the airplane "crash sites" were faked or fabricated, albeit each in its own way. None of them actually crashed, which means that no passengers aboard died in crashes.

And no "suicide hijackers" were aboard them to cause them to crash, which means that the whole

19

"War on Terror" was based on a false premise. 9/11 was staged to create a pretext for wars of aggression.

Q: The US authorities described the event as coordinated terrorist attacks launched by Al-Qaeda and later claimed that Osama Bin Laden was the mastermind behind the attacks. Then American intelligence forces purportedly carried out a mission codenamed "Operation Neptune Spear" which led to Osama's death. What do you think? Who did really orchestrate the 9/11?

A: 9/11 was brought to us by the CIA, the Neocons in the Department of Defense (most of whom were from Project for the New American Century), which believed that, with the collapse of the Soviet Union, there was a unique historical opportunity for the US to build a world-wide empire that would endure for the next 100 years, if only we would move aggressively into the Middle East and project military and diplomatic influence outward from that geopolitically sensitive region, and the Mossad. It hasn't played out that way, but that was the plan. The chaos with Iraq, Syria and Afghanistan continues unabated with Iran as the ultimate objective.

The changes in US foreign policy were complemented by subversion of the Constitution in implementing the misnamed PATRIOT Act, which has profoundly altered American society into a surveillance state in which freedom of speech and of expression has been severely constrained. History will record its gross misadventure into the Middle East as the last dying gasps of an empire that has depleted its military and expended its treasury for an unattainable goal, leaving an enormous swath of death and devastation in its wake. I wish the situation was more promising, but nothing good for human beings is about to emerge.

Osama bin Laden had nothing to do with 9/11 as he observed at the time. He was "our man in Afghanistan" and was visited by a CIA agent when hospitalized in Dubai not long before he died on 15 December 2001, which has been addressed by Nicholas Kollerstrom, "Osama bin Laden: 1957-2001" and David Ray Griffin, OSAMA BIN LADEN: DEAD OR ALIVE? It was politically beneficial to Barack Obama to

9/11 was 'massive deception, deliberate hoax' by US and Israel: Scholar

resurrect him and kill him again, as I have explained in "Zero Dark Thirty; The deeper, darker truths". American politics, sad to say, has become little more than a theater of the absurd.

Q: Do you believe there is a connection between 9/11 attacks and appearance of the so-called Islamic State of Iraq and the Levant (ISIL)? Is ISIL an offshoot of the 9/11?

A: The ISIL phenomenon, which includes fake beheadings of journalist with real destruction of religious icons, has been astonishing in its apparent rapidity. Recent reports that its leader is an agent of the Mossad are illuminating, since, given the Assad government's success in routing the rebels there, suggests that the forces who want to create instability in the region by removing secular leaders and allowing ancient and deep faith-based antagonisms to reassert themselves can only work to the benefit of Israel. New claims from the American government (that it might take three years to suppress ISIL) hint that we are being taken for a ride to create an excuse to use NATO forces to depose Assad and perform other mischief there.

So this appears to be one more ruse to destabilize the Middle East for the benefit of Israel. It is stunning how much terror and destruction has been wrought by that small state and its advocates, going back to the bombing of the King David Hotel in 1946 by Irgun terrorists dressed as Arabs, the air attack on the USS Liberty, the false flags on the Israeli Embassy and the Jewish Community Center in Buenos Aires in 1992 and 1994, and even attempts to blame the Palestinians for the atrocities of 9/11.

The world has now been reminded of the savage nature of its government by the recent slaughter of the Palestinian people, which destroyed 40% of the land they control. Aggression by the US and Israel justifiably deserves the world's condemnation.

Source note: This chapter originally appeared as "9/11 was Created by CIA, Neocons and Mossad", *FARS News Agency* (13 September 2014).

2

9/11: Confessions of
a former CIA Asset
by Susan Lindauer (with Jim Fetzer)

It was my great pleasure to invite Susan Lindauer, a former CIA asset, who had extraordinary experiences conducting back channel talks with Saddam Hussein about resuming UN weapons inspections during negotiations prior to the invasion of Iraq, to speak at The Vancouver Hearings.

She had served as a conduit in communications between the US and Saddam, who had been cooperating with the United States and even offered to purchase 1,000,000 new cars from Detroit per year for the next ten years or, if that were not enough, for the next twenty, if the US would not attack his country.

Imagine what an impact that would have made on our economy if Bush and Cheney had not been dedicated to the invasion of Iraq?

We were told that Saddam had been involved in 9/11, that Iraq and al Qaeda were in cahoots, and that he was out to develop nuclear weapons and had attempted to purchase yellowcake from Niger, a fraud that was exposed by US Ambassador Joe Wilson, in retaliation for which his wife, Valerie Plame, was outed as an undercover CIA agent who was managing the most important intelligence operation in the world at the time to prevent the proliferation of nuclear weapons in the Middle East.

Dick Cheney and his minions did not take that kindly and revealed that Valerie was conducting this operation, which not only decimated the task on which it had embarked but no doubt led to the deaths of those who had placed their lives at risk by cooperating covertly with Plame and her associates.

This is only one of many crass and corrupt acts by our own Vice President, who was running an assassination ring out of his office in the White House itself, which appears to have been responsible not only for the death of Sen. Paul Wellstone(D-MN) for opposing the administration on Iraq but also Cpl. Pat Tillman, who had become disillusioned with the war and — in a fatal error of judgment — appears to have confided in Noam Chomsky, who in turn appears to have advised the White House that they had a problem, which they resolved by taking him out and fabricating a story of his death as a tragic and fateful "accident".

While Chomsky has been lionized by the left for his courageous and outspoken criticism of one administration after another and has done brilliant work exposing the use of propaganda and disinformation in instances of intermediate significance, when it comes to major events, such as the assassination of JFK and the atrocities of 9/11. He has become an apologist, even dismissing the idea of conspiracy in the case of JFK on the grounds that, even if there had been collusion between parties, it was of no significance, since his death did not involve any major policy issues.

We are left to believe as though not invading Cuba, signing an above ground test ban treaty with the Soviet Union, withdrawing from Vietnam, shattering the CIA into a thousand pieces, cracking down on organized crime, cutting the oil depletion allowance, and abolishing the FED were not major policy issues! Chomsky's theories of linguistics are as impoverished as his political stance on issues of this magnitude.

Chomsky may be doing the most damage to the 9/11 Truth movement, but others are playing subsidiary roles, even if they may have different reasons for doing so. Dan Rather would prefer the world would forget that, on 9/11, he broadcast a report about the arrest of two suspects in a van with enough explosives to do "great damage to the George Washington Bridge", which has been confirmed by other sources. See, for example,

BILL HEMMER, CNN CORRESPONDENT: Thank you. Again, our apologies to our viewers about five minutes ago, but we do have an established connection now with CNN's Deborah Feverick. The reports we're getting now, two or three men arrested on the New Jersey Parkway. Deborah, can you hear me now?

DEBORAH FEVERICK, CNN CORRESPONDENT: Yes, I can. That is the information that I am getting from two sources, that there was a van either on the New Jersey Turnpike or the Garden State Parkway, and that it was near the George Washington Bridge.

There were two or three men who were in the van that was pulled over. It is not clear why the van was pulled over, but when it was, law enforcers found tons of explosives inside of the van.

That is, right now, all I am hearing. But again, two to three people in custody, and we are trying to get more information on that right now.

HEMMER: Deborah, I don't mean to put you on the spot here. Do you know where on the Jersey Turnpike this was? How far from New York City?

FEVERICK: We do not know that. We are looking into that. There is one report that it was on the New Jersey Turnpike. There is another report that it was very close to the bridge, if not on the bridge. So again, these details are emerging. We're trying to piece them together. But that's what we have so far, two to three people in custody, found with a van filled with explosives.

Even web sites that attempt to debunk these reports inadvertently confirm them, where, although Dan Rather opined that it wasn't clear whether this van-load of explosives was related to the other events of 9/11, it is not rocket science to appreciate that they were connected. Indeed, we have a great deal of information that links Israel to 9/11 via the transfer of the WTC to Larry Silverstein, "the Dancing Israelis", Urban Moving Systems, ICTS, and much, much more.

We know that Israel was complicit in the crimes of 9/11. Susan reports that a series of vans was also used to visit the Twin Towers late in the evening to prep the buildings for destruction. Even though some have continued to entertain the possibility US intelligence was incompetent and that 9/11 was simply "allowed to happen", we now have persuasive information from an informed source, who should enable even the most naive to better understand that 9/11 was "an inside job" and that, as many of us have pieced together from other sources, where the US government attacked the US to promote a political agenda.

For her attempts to expose the truth about 9/11, Susan was arrested and prosecuted under the PATRIOT ACT, only the second US citizen to endure such a fate. She was incarcerated and tortured for five years and denied the right to legal counsel, even though she was innocent of any crime. This is a stunning indictment of what the United States has become, which our

Founding Fathers would not recognize: a neo-fascist, militaristic police state, where surveillance is ubiquitous.

The Department of Homeland Security has now acquired more than a million rounds of .40 hollow-point ammunition, which is not even permissible in times of war under the Geneva Conventions. We know there are hundreds of FEMA campsaround the country and that Congress has authorized the use of 30,000 drones to track American civilians. What she has to tell us should disturb every American, indeed, every citizen of the world who cares about human rights, due process, and simple decency.

AFFIDAVIT BY
SUSAN LINDAUER
VANCOUVER
HEARINGS ON 9/11
August 13, 2012

My name is Susan Lindauer. I was one of the very few U.S. Intelligence Assets covering Iraq and Libya at the United Nations in New York from 1995 to 2003. As a back channel, I started talks for the Lockerbie Trial with Libya's senior diplomats. I also conducted preliminary talks to resume weapons inspections with Iraq's Ambassador Dr. Saeed Hasan, as part of a larger, comprehensive peace framework.

I submit this sworn affidavit as evidence of criminal actions by President George Bush, Vice President Richard Cheney, Attorney General John Ashcroft, Attorney General Alberto Gonzales; Secretary of Defense Donald Rumsfeld and National Security Adviser, Condoleeza Rice.

This affidavit will prove beyond any shadow of doubt that those officials in the Bush Administration knowingly and deliberately practiced "command failure" to thwart the 9/11 attack. It will prove that those officials hyped a War with Iraq as a probable outcome of the attack, exciting motive and opportunity for an orphan intelligence team to lay explosives through the Towers to maximize damage and guarantee the outcome.

After the attack, White House officials compounded the crime of mass murder with perjury and obstruction of justice in the Federal Courts and the 9/11 Commission to a degree that would be punishable offenses for ordinary citizens.

I also accuse Larry Silverstein of profiteering from government lies about 9/11 to a degree that qualified as insurance fraud. Together with government officials, Silverstein committed multiple acts of perjury in the Federal Court of Chief Justice Michael B. Mukasey, the Southern District of New York — and obstruction of justice to protect the financial profits of his insurance scam.

This was done with full knowledge of the consequence — that a fellow American was subjected to false arrest, false imprisonment on a military base without trial or hearing, and threats of forcible drugging in prison, as a judicial effort to destroy knowledge of the CIA's advance knowledge of 9/11 — thus safeguarding Silverstein's profits. I know, because I was that American.

Any ordinary citizen would face prison for Silverstein's crimes — and their attorneys would face disbarment —whereas Silverstein and White House officials got off "scott free".

Above all, to understand why 9/11 was an "inside job," it's critical to understand that its completion resulted from opposing forces colliding against each other — one side working aggressively to stop the attack, and the other undercutting every proactive move.

This affidavit exposes their legacy.

I, Susan Lindauer, hereby swear under oath that I first learned of the 9/11 Conspiracy from my CIA handler, Dr. Richard Fuisz, in mid-April, 2001.

In April, I received a summons to visit Dr. Fuisz at his office in Great Falls, Virginia. We met weekly anyway. On this occasion, he rang my home and asked me to come straight away. He inquired when I planned my next trip to the Iraqi Embassy at the United Nations in New York. He wanted to talk before I left, and he wanted me to go soon.

This does not strike me as unusual. My back channel to Iraq and Libya existed to communicate messages back and forth from Washington, because those countries had no official ties with the United States. Most significantly, my team kept a special line open for intelligence on terrorist activities that Tripoli or Baghdad might need to share with the West.

Even under sanctions and global isolation, the importance of intelligence to block terrorism was recognized as a necessary exemption to U.S. foreign policy isolating Iraq.

And so I visited Dr. Fuisz immediately. He instructed me to demand that Libya and Iraq must hand over any intelligence regarding conspiracies involving airplane hijackings and/or airplane bombings. He insisted that I must warn Iraqi diplomats Baghdad would suffer a major military offensive— worse than anything Iraq had suffered before— if the U.S. discovered Saddam's government had possessed such intelligence on airplane hijackings and failed to notify us through my back channel.

Admittedly, I was reluctant to deliver such a harsh message. I have always been an anti-war activist. So on my next trip to New York, I soft pedaled Dr. Fuisz's message. I asked diplomats to send cables to Baghdad and Tripoli, watching for possible airplane conspiracies. But I made no threats of violent reprisal against Iraq or Libya.

When I got home to Washington, I met with Dr. Fuisz, who demanded to know how Iraqi diplomats (only) had responded to his threat. I admitted that I stopped short of delivering his full message. But I assured him that I had requested Iraq's cooperation.

At that point, Dr. Fuisz became enraged. In all of our years together, I recall no other time that he lost his temper and shouted at me. He stormed up and down the conference room, letting loose a tirade punctuated with colorful obscenities. Dr. Fuisz demanded that I must return to New York immediately. I must not be polite. I must tell Iraqi diplomats exactly what he said.

"The United States would bomb Baghdad back into the Stone Age, worse than they've ever been bombed before, if they discovered a terrorist conspiracy involving airplane hijackings or airplane bombings and failed to notify us. They would lose everything. We would destroy them."

There was one more point that Dr. Fuisz was adamant I must communicate: "Those threats originated at the highest levels of government," and I quote, "above the CIA Director and the Secretary of State."

Those were his exact words. And it was not ambiguous. It could only mean President George Bush, Vice President Richard Cheney or Secretary of Defense Donald Rumsfeld.

As of that conversation, there was no doubt in my mind that the President's Office and the CIA were fully cognizant of the existence of the conspiracy. Dr. Fuisz claimed the CIA lacked "actionable intelligence" to stop the attack. (That's nuts and bolts—who, day, flight #, airport hub). But the conspiracy itself was known.

Dr. Fuisz was not pacified until I promised to deliver his message with all the force that he communicated. He expressed tremendous satisfaction that I would make sure Iraqi diplomats understood the warning came from above the CIA itself—not from him or me— but from the highest levels of government "above the CIA Director and Secretary of State."

In early May, 2001, I returned to New York and delivered that message exactly as he dictated.

Tension built throughout the summer of 2001. Practically every week, we discussed the 9/11 strike. By June, our focus turned to the World Trade Center. Our belief in that target was very precise. We believed the attack would finish the cycle started by Ramzi Youssef in the 1993 World Trade Center attack. And we fully expected that airplanes would be seized by hijackers and used as trajectory weapons to strike the Towers. No other target was ever discussed — not the Pentagon or the White House, only the World Trade Center.

We also discussed the possibility that a miniature thermo-nuclear device might raze the buildings. Throughout the summer of 2001, we were convinced the Twin Towers would be demolished, using a combination of explosives with the airplanes. That's why Dr. Fuisz warned me to stay out of New York in August. Nobody worried that I might get hurt if the Towers collapsed. The CIA worried about exposure to military grade contaminants in the dust or air, including possible radiation.

Throughout June and July of 2001, Dr. Fuisz continued to push hard for any fragment of actionable intelligence from Iraq. After our first conversation in April, he never asked about Libya at all. Over and over again, Dr. Fuisz demanded that I threaten Baghdad — not Libya — if the strike occurred.

Every police officer will tell you a crime requires motive and opportunity. I know from direct conversations with Dr. Fuisz that six (6) months before 9/11, a cabal of pro-War neoconservatives at the top of the government was already prepping the Intelligence Community to accept War with Iraq as the inevitable consequence of the strike. That created "motive" and plenty of advance opportunity for any pro-War intelligence team to do the unthinkable — wire the Towers with explosives, to guarantee maximum destruction and secure the desired outcome of War. That's what I'm convinced happened. The evidence certainly supports that conclusion.

As of May, 2001, Iraqi diplomats proposed an immediate solution to the 9/11 conspiracy. As of February, 2001, Baghdad agreed to allow an FBI Task Force into Iraq — to monitor radical Jihadis who might attempt to exploit Baghdad's weakened central authority to launch terrorist strikes on its neighbors. The CIA made this demand through my back channel following the bombing of the U.S.S. Cole in Yemen, in October, 2000. From the opening days of the Bush Administration, Iraq agreed to show good will towards Saudi Arabia and the Gulf States.

When confronted with the 9/11 scenario, Iraq placated the U.S. masterfully: "Perhaps this would be the appropriate moment for the FBI to start its work —" the diplomat suggested. "If the United States is very worried, the FBI should come right away."

The world knows that never happened. Over the summer, Iraq continued to invite the FBI, as U.S. warnings about 9/11 persisted. And I expressed frustration for the slow learning curve of the Bush Administration, which felt unnatural after eight years of rapid and decisive policy-making by the Clinton White House.

The 1990s have been called the Halycon Years of U.S Intelligence. From my perspective as an Asset, the arrival of George Bush felt like driving a high performance Maserati after some fool pours lower grade oil into the engine— and it starts clunking and sputtering and seizing up. You don't know if the car will keep running until the

mechanic's ready to work on the problem— or if the car will die on the street.

That was Republican Policy on anti-terrorism before 9/11. Our problem was the CIA had to keep driving that car no matter what. And we had to block terrorist threats against the U.S, regardless of whether the White House was responsive to warnings about those threats— or not.

Before 9/11, the answer was "not." I was not alone in feeling frustrated Throughout June and July, Dr. Fuisz beseeched me not to filter intelligence on the impending aerial strike on the World Trade Center. During our meetings, he would painstakingly explain how urgently he needed to collect even fragments of actionable intelligence on these airplane hijackings, whether it made sense to me or not. He begged me to hold nothing back. He appeared to be frantically searching for anything to pre-empt the strike. In fairness, a significant faction of CIA and Defense Intelligence urgently tried to stop 9/11.

Tensions accelerated to a head on August 2nd, the day of the Senate hearings on Robert Mueller's nomination to head the FBI.

My heated conversation with Dr. Fuisz about Mueller's confirmation accounts for why I recall the timing of events so precisely in the weeks before 9/11. I can pinpoint my actions to the day of the week because of this hearing.

In our opinion, Robert Mueller was such a political animal that we argued he would throw the FBI investigation into this future attack on airplane hijackings used to strike the World Trade Center! He'd do whatever was most helpful to politicians!

"You want me to crash the nomination hearings this afternoon? Lay a little truth on Congress?" I said to Dr. Fuisz.

"No. No, it's too late for that."

"Too late for the hearings? Or too late to stop the attack?"

"Both, I think."

"You think it's that soon???"

"I think it could be."

I was aghast. The phone got quiet for a moment.

"We can't do nothing, Richard."

"Of course not."

"I'm going to New York," I said. "I'll ask the Iraqis again. I'll push them hard."

"What? When are you going?" I recall vividly the alarm saturating his words.

"I'm going this weekend."

"No, no. This weekend? Don't go to New York, Susan. Don't go. It's too dangerous."

"It's just the weekend. The day after tomorrow. I'll be up and back. I'll stop by your office on Monday. I understand what you guys want. I've been pushing Iraqi diplomats all summer for any fragment of intelligence on this attack. They know what's up. I will check if something's come in from Baghdad."

August 4th would be my last trip to the Iraqi Embassy and the Libya House before that fateful September morning. That's something I deeply regretted for many years.

As it happens, there were extraordinary reasons for Dr. Fuisz's concern. The "chatter" between terrorist cells monitored by the National Security Agency reached unprecedented levels by May 2001, which accelerated until September 11, 2001.

The U.S. Intelligence Community buzzed with warnings. On July 10, 2001, CIA Director, George Tenet, was so alarmed by a classified debriefing on the threat from Al Qaeda that he marched straight to the White House.

A top CIA analyst suggested a major attack was coming in the next few weeks.

George Tenet

Apparently Tenet wasted no time alerting Condoleezza Rice in writing. He also brought along one of the CIA officers tracking Bin Laden, who gave Rice an oral debriefing. Former Anti-Terrorism Czar, Richard Clarke strongly endorsed the importance of the report. The CIA officer who gave the briefing said the nation had to "go on a war footing now."

On Friday, Sept. 7, the State Department issued a worldwide alert— "American citizens may be the target of a terrorist threat from extremist groups with links to [Osama bin Laden's] al Qaeda organization." That report cited intelligence from May, 2001 as suggesting an attack was imminent. The State Department bulletin warned "Al Qaeda does not distinguish between official and civilian targets."

As one of the participants in those discussions, I am ready to swear under oath that U.S. Intelligence anticipated the attack in all of its precise detail.

Intelligence predicted airplane hijackings and a strike on the World Trade Center—not the Pentagon or the White House.

What was missing was actionable intelligence to stop the conspiracy — who were the terrorists, how many, which airport, what airlines, what flight numbers. I was looking for a name. A number. A fragment. All summer Dr. Fuisz pleaded with me exhaustively to bring him anything at all. He swore that if I could get it, the NSA and CIA would bust overtime to flesh it out, and make sense of it, so that we could stop the attack.

I will prove now why action in August, 2001 (to maximize or stall the attack) was so much bigger than ever reported. .

Proof of a Second Team

By August, our hunt was becoming frenetic. I have physical proof that a second intelligence team was also ferreting for intelligence on the 9/11 conspiracy the weekend of August 4-5. During a speaking tour through Japan before the release of my book, "Extreme Prejudice," I spoke extensively about our team's aggressive actions in the critical week after Robert Mueller's Senate nomination hearing.

Low and behold, when I returned from Japan, I discovered a copy of the original newsprint edition of the Wall Street Journal dated July 30, 2001— pinned by a rose quartz paper weight on my desk next to my computer, so that it would not get thrown away. The faded 10 year old newspaper was addressed to my boss at the street address of my consulting job in Silver Spring, Maryland during the summer of 2001.

That's where I was working on August 2nd when I phoned Dr. Fuisz on the day of Robert Mueller's nomination hearing. The Wall Street Journal proves that several weeks before 9/11 somebody had gone to the trouble of tracking down where my phone call to Dr. Fuisz originated.

That individual "visited" my office, no doubt seeking any scribbles or papers that I might have left around my desk, which might provide clues of what our team had discovered about the conspiracy so far. It's standard practice to grab a newspaper off a desk in situations like that, as an accurate snapshot with the company's name, address and date, etc. It's a "proof of life."

The July 30, 2001 edition of the Wall Street Journal would have been tossed in the trash weeks before the official 9/11 investigation kicked off. Ergo, it could only have been grabbed the week of Robert Mueller's nomination hearing.

Yes, it indicates another intelligence team picked the locks to get into the office — (and tapped our phones). There's a time when that sort of thing is necessary. And this would be it! I'm grateful for it. Our team urgently desired as much help as we could get.

This was a race to stop massive violence against the United States — not a competition. All of us gravely worried over what we all knew was coming. Intelligence teams are structured to function independently and overlap, but (most of the time) we're on the same side, with the same shared goals.

Rober S. Mueller

On that note, I take umbrage at the lies that were invented by The 9/11 Commission over our so-called intelligence failures. Prior to 9/11, the Intelligence Community was accustomed to functioning on a superior and pro-active footing. U.S. Intelligence had rapid fire reflexes, and a reputation for attracting brilliant case officers. These were creative strategists and problem solvers. They were the best and the brightest.

The Intelligence Community was at the top of its game. It's just not monolithic, like most civilians imagine. Teams are separate and joined to different factions, with different objectives and motivations.

That's where 9/11 went to hell.

9/11 was not the result of mistakes. It was a deliberate execution. Though 90 percent of U.S. Intelligence tried to stop the attack, the compartmentalized structure of the intelligence community made it possible for a minority 10 percent to undercut all the good work and proactive planning of the others.

That's what I believe happened on 9/11.

9/11 was an Inside Job that played a magician's trick on the American people. All eyes were on the left hand — that would be airplanes crashing into the Towers — But the real action was done by the right hand. The controlled demolition of the Towers using a combination of military grade explosives.

There, I bow to explosives experts on the type of explosive devices and materials. There has been some excellent research on thermatic bombs, which produce such heat intensity as to melt steel, and create dust from a sulfur compound. [More recent research, however, especially by T. Mark

Hightower, suggests that thermite / thermate / nanothermite could not have been the principal cause of the destruction of the Twin Towers.] Throughout the summer, we discussed the use of a miniature thermo-nuclear device. It could have been a combination.

The point I must underscore is that our discussions from June, July and August always presumed explosives would be used in combination with the airplane hijackings to destroy the Towers. I recall conversations where and how somebody could locate the necessary explosives inside the United States—even a nuke. How those explosives could be stolen from a military base in driving range to New York City. We always forecast the total destruction of the Towers in the attack, and predicted "mass human casualties."

9/11 fit our scenario in all detail. And so, I insist, 9/11 was not an intelligence failure. There was active concern. Despite those efforts, it succeeded because a minority decided to smash any progress by the majority to thwart the attack. They were incited to act by wild leadership pronouncements that maximum destruction would provoke War with Iraq. Threats of war created motive for a second team to do the unthinkable.

The leadership egged them on. There are so many fail-safes and trip wires in place to trigger pre-emptive responses that it required a leadership decision to subvert the process.

Deliberate Command Failures in August

On my last trip to New York on August 4, 2001, Iraqi diplomats threw up their hands. They'd been warned of the consequences for months if something awful happened. Retribution would be swift and severe. Nevertheless, even with his ear to the ground, Saddam and his vast network of Iraqi Mukhabarat could locate no actionable intelligence to give us. Saddam could not find it!

Instead, diplomats insisted the U.S. was the only source chattering about this airplane hijacking conspiracy. All intelligence reports originated from us, they claimed! Diplomats protested that Washington was demanding cooperation from Baghdad, yet took no action to send the FBI. If the CIA believed the conspiracy was real, we had options. Baghdad locked on to Washington's failure to act as undercutting our sincerity.

My next face meeting with Dr. Fuisz took place on August 6, 2001. At the same hour of the same day, down at Crawford Ranch in Texas, President Bush was handed a memo from the CIA outlining the severe threat of a terrorist attack by Osama bin Laden's network on the United States. I'm told

President Bush tossed aside the CIA's Presidential Briefing Memo: "Now you've covered your ass. Let's go shoot some golf balls."

Unaware that President Bush had just blown off the CIA's explicit warnings about the airplane hijackings and the planned aerial strike on the World Trade Center, Dr. Fuisz and I decided to request emergency assistance from the Justice Department.

At the instructions of Dr. Fuisz, I telephoned the private office of U.S. Attorney General John Ashcroft, consisting of about 20 senior staff. (Having worked in anti-terrorism for almost a decade, our team had all the correct phone numbers to raise the alarms in any terrorist crisis.)

Quickly I identified myself as the chief U.S. Asset covering Libya and Iraq at the United Nations. That way I could make sure the bureaucrat on the other end of the phone recognized my special access to high level intelligence on terrorism as a primary source, which should be weighed before disregarding my call.

Once I had the staffer's attention, I made a formal request for Attorney General Ashcroft's office to "broadcast an emergency alert through all agencies, seeking any fragment of intelligence pertaining to possible airplane hijackings or airplane bombings."

John Ashcroft

I explained that we believed "a major attack on the United States was imminent, with a high probability of mass casualties." I expressly stated that we believed "the target was the World Trade Center, which would suffer some sort of aerial strike, using hijacked airplanes." I provided as many specific details as possible to help focus the investigation.

Given the dangers and timing of the attack, I asked that "our request for emergency cooperation should be given the highest priority."

Immediately Attorney General Ashcroft's private staff gave me a phone number at the Office of Counter-Terrorism at the Justice Department, and urged me to repeat my message. I did so without delay. I repeated the warning in full detail, and requested that any possible information should be submitted immediately to all agencies.

With those phone calls to the Attorney General's private staff and the Office of Counter-Terrorism, the U.S. government lost its cover of deniability. If I testified before the 9/11 Commission or any congressional inquiry—the Justice Department would have been forced to admit that some of its very own top staff received formal warning about the conspiracy by early August, when there was still time to coordinate a response, and thwart the demolition of the Towers.

I didn't stop there. Most Americans would be stunned to know that in mid-August, our team was so convinced a 9/11 style attack was "imminent," that I visited my second cousin, Andy Card, Chief of Staff to President Bush, requesting his intervention at the Justice Department, too.

I parked on the street outside his house in Arlington, Virginia, chain smoking for almost two hours. (I quit in 2005!) Occasionally, I could see neighbors peering out of their windows and frowning at me.

In my head, I rehearsed what I would tell Virginia State Police or the Secret Service, if they showed up to investigate this strange car parked outside the home of the Chief of Staff to the President of the United States.

Unhappily, Andy did not return that afternoon. I finally left without sharing our fears. Driving away, I distinctly recall asking myself if I might be making the greatest mistake of my life. Throughout all these years, it is one of my few regrets.

Andrew Card

What I could not know, is that another intelligence faction was working aggressively opposite us—anticipating all of the protocols to stop the strike, and sabotaging our best efforts to activate the warning system.

Like the copy of the Wall Street Journal that appeared on my desk after my Japanese book tour, a trustworthy source revealed this to me after the first edition of my book, Extreme Prejudice had gone to galleys. The new second edition includes this information.

Security Cameras Capture Mysterious Vans

Late on the night of August 23, 2001, at about 3 a.m. security cameras in the parking garage of the World Trade Center captured the arrival of three or four truck vans. Visual examination determined the vans were separate and unique from trucks used by janitorial services, including different colors and markings. More curious, all the janitorial trucks had pulled out of the Towers by about 2:30 a.m — half an hour before the second set of vans arrived.

According to my source, who saw the tapes, no vans matching that description entered the parking garage at that extraordinary hour in any of the weeks or months prior to August 23. It was a unique event.

Security cameras caught the vans leaving the Towers at approximately 5 a.m — before the first wave of Wall Street tycoons arrived to track the Asian markets.

For the next 10 to 12 nights, the same mysterious vans arrived at the World Trade Center at the same mysterious hour — after the janitorial crews had left the building and before the robber barons on Wall Street started their work day. The vans clocked into the parking garage from approximately August 23, 2001 until September 2 or 3, 2001.

After that last night, they never appeared at the Towers again. The vans were never heard of again, either. The 9/11 Commission was never informed of their surprising presence on 10 consecutive nights up to the week before the 9/11 strike.

Were the vans transporting explosives into the Towers — or transporting gold reserves out? Or possible some combination of the two? We cannot be certain.

Video from those security cameras in the parking garage could be the most significant missing evidence of the 9/11 puzzle. My source was convinced those mysterious trucks transported explosives into the Towers, so that this unidentified orphan team could finish wiring the World Trade Center for a controlled demolition.

My source has stayed quiet to protect his government job, his retirement pension and his reputation — knowing that others who spoke up have gotten fired or thrown in prison.

Like me.

Confirmation by a Civilian Witness

Unlike others who could be bullied into silence (or bought off), I was adamant that I wanted to talk. I made one fatal mistake. I requested to testify through proper channels. I declared my intention to show how 9/11 intersected with Pre-War Intelligence. My testimony before a blue ribbon Presidential Commission on Pre-War Intelligence would have disclosed the existence of a comprehensive peace framework — and Baghdad's eager efforts to cooperate with the 9/11 investigation.

My testimony would have put 9/11 into a larger global perspective — which most Americans still don't understand to this very day.

It's greater insight as to why the Pro-War Cabal urgently required a Pearl Harbor Day, in order to overcome international loathing of another War in Iraq.

I should have known better than to trust Congress. Thirty days after I phoned the Offices of Senator John McCain and Senator Trent Lott, I woke to find the FBI pounding on my front door. At that point, I gained a new distinction as the second non-Arab American arrested on the Patriot Act, facing secret charges, secret evidence and secret grand jury testimony. I was held under indictment for five years without a Trial—and thrown in prison on Carswell Air Force Base in Texas for a year, without a hearing.

To Washington's greatest shame, the Patriot Act, which Congress proclaimed a key judicial weapon to break up terrorism in the United States, was first used to stop a whistle blower from telling the truth about 9/11 and Iraqi Pre-War Intelligence.

Uniting and Strengthening America by Providing Appropriate Tools Required to Intercept and Obstruct Terrorism Act of 2001

USA PATRIOT Act, also Patriot Act

107th United States Congress

Over my fiercest objections, on Carswell Air Force Base, I was declared "incompetent to stand trial" — and threatened with forcible injections of Haldol, a zombie drug that imitates the stone-like effects of Parkinson's Disease.

That's an old intelligence tactic from the Cold War, designed to scare Assets into silence. Believe me, the threat can be very effective.

All the while, the Justice Department aggressively lied to the Court about my team's 9/11 warnings.

That subterfuge was no accident (as the corporate media would like the public to believe). Chief Justice Michael Mukasey was also hearing the financial lawsuit brought by Larry Silverstein, owner of the World Trade Center, and his insurance claims for 9/11.

I recall distinctly Silverstein's high-priced New York attorneys strutting into Court, while I got shackled and marched off to my cell, and my public attorney chatted.

Silverstein's attorneys could not have been ignorant of the ferocity of our debate. The Courtroom was abuzz with my outrage and urgent pleas that my Intelligence team had full knowledge of the 9/11 Conspiracy, and tried to warn the Bush Administration officials about the dangers of the impending attack.

Silverstein's attorneys heard it all — including my frantic appeals not to be forcibly drugged without a hearing to prove that I had warned about 9/11.

It was a tangled web of deceit from start to finish. Even the bailiffs looked at me with eyes filled with horror.

The pretense of my "incompetence" was an outrage to protect White House and Congressional leaders.

Unhappily for Silverstein's attorneys and the Bush Administration, they quickly discovered that I warned civilian friends about the 9/11 style of attack, too — particularly friends with family or professional ties to New York City.

That's where the Feds got crossed up.

Four years almost to the day before my sworn testimony at the Vancouver Tribunal on 9/11 — on June 17, 2008, a Canadian Resident named Parke Godfrey, who lives in Toronto, was sworn in to testify at the Federal Courthouse of Manhattan. The Courthouse stands 1,000 feet from Ground Zero, where the World Trade Center once graced the New York skyline.

Godfrey's testimony was a watershed moment for the 9/11 community. For 4 ½ years prior to that day, the U.S.

Justice Department had fought savagely to stop his testimony from reaching public ears.

Despite the public's ignorance, Godfrey's revelations were already notorious to the U.S. Attorney General's office, the Office of Counter-

Phil Berg, Susan Lindauer, and Parke Godfrey

Terrorism, the FBI, the Royal Canadian Mounted Police, and the U.S. Bureau of Prisons — not to mention top officials at the White House, CIA and Defense Intelligence Agency.

Parke Godfrey was one of my closest friends in Maryland, working on his Ph.D. in computer science at the University of Maryland in College Park.

His family lived in the Connecticut suburbs of New York City. We spoke frequently by phone, socializing a couple of times a week, and shared much of the same political outlook.

Godfrey has a distinguished career as a tenured Professor of Computer Science and Technology at York University in Toronto, Canada. He presents a calm, studied demeanor. He speaks precisely and methodically, choosing his words carefully — what some friends have teasingly compared to Mr. Spock of Star Trek. During difficult courtroom questioning, he would frequently pause and take his time to give an accurate, thoughtful response. He proved a superior witness by any measure.

In shattering testimony, Godfrey told the Court how several times in the spring and summer of 2001 I warned him that we expected a major terrorist strike that would encompass the World Trade Center.

BRIAN SHAUGHNESSY, Attorney for My Defense: "Did there come a time when she was concerned about a possible attack on the United States?"

GODFREY: "She had described that."

SHAUGHNESSY: "What did she describe?"

GODFREY: "In particular, she warned me when I was job hunting and considering potential work in New York— because I liked New York City– that New York City was dangerous. In particular she was predicting that there was going to be a massive attack here. In southern Manhattan. This was before 9/11."

"So when I was looking for the job at William and Mary, which was late 2000 – I was at York University, but looking at other universities [for a sabbatical] – she warned [me] not to consider New York because she thought an attack was imminent here."

SHAUGHNESSY: "Continue, please."

GODFREY: "I asked her about the nature of it. She said that she thought it would be something very, very big. I asked her, "Well, what do you mean?" She said that it would involve airplanes and possibly a nuclear weapon. She said that what was started in '93, she thought was going to come back."

SHAUGHNESSY: "What was that she referenced as having started in '93?"

GODFREY: "Well, the attempt on the World Trade Center at the time."

SHAUGHNESSY: "Did she believe, or was she telling you that very shortly there was likely to be another attack of that nature?"

GODFREY: "She did. She said that it would complete the cycle of the 1993 attack. And she said that there would be an attack in late summer, early fall."

"In August, she told me that she thought it was some time imminent."

SHAUGHNESSY: "Now, did you know any of the things that she was doing that might have given her access to information, that might lead to a prediction of that nature?"

GODFREY: "Well, I had known that she was active in trying to prevent escalation with what turned out to be the war in Iraq."

At another point, Godfrey detailed the Justice Department's knowledge of my 9/11 warnings.

GODFREY: "In September, 2004— I was interviewed by the FBI in Mississauga [adjacent to Toronto], in the presence of the Royal Canadian Mounted Police. The RCMP insisted on this, as the interview was in Canada, and I was a Canadian resident. I spoke with FBI special agent Suzan LeTourneau."

"While the interview focused on mundane details of Ms. Lindauer's life, I told {Special Agent] LeTourneau that Ms. Lindauer had predicted the 9/11 attack throughout the spring and summer of 2001, and that her prediction was very specific. It involved airplane hijackings and a strike on the World Trade Center."

Parke Godfrey's testimony sworn under oath in the Federal Courthouse in Manhattan provides irrefutable proof that the FBI received confirmations of my 9/11 warnings by September, 2004 — a few months after my arrest — and before the 9/11 Commission issued its report.

In truth, the FBI and the U.S. Attorney's Office in Manhattan had time to alert the 9/11 Commissioners about this shattering revelation.

Instead, they made a decision to withhold exculpatory knowledge from the Court of Chief of Justice Michael B. Mukasey — who was hearing arguments from Larry Silverstein's attorneys seeking a massive insurance settlement. Twelve months later, I got shipped off to Carswell Prison, while the Justice Department vigorously denied all knowledge of my 9/11 warnings. Once I

Michael Mukasey

was in prison on Carswell Air Force Base, the Justice Department argued vigorously that I should be forcibly drugged with Haldol, Ativan and Prozac until I stopped claiming to have warned about the attack.

Godfrey's testimony proves the Cover-Up Conspiracy was widespread throughout the Justice Department.

GODFREY: "In early December 2005, a few months after Ms. Lindauer had been sent to Carswell Prison, I spoke with the psychologist handling her competence evaluation for the Court. I attempted to confirm that Ms. Lindauer had made predictions of a terrorist attack in Manhattan to me and others prior to the 9/11 attack. He seemed to have no interest in hearing this. Our conversation was brief."

"While she was still detained in prison, I offered to travel from Toronto and testify at any hearing on her mental competence, on what I knew of her political activities before her indictment, about warnings of terrorist attacks, and other aspects which might interest the Court."

"I attended the hearing on forcible drugging in May, 2006. In fact, I arrived at Court, assuming that I was to testify. Her attorney, Sam Talkin, did not call me. In conversation that day, I told him that she made warnings of a terrorist attack to me and others, in advance of 9/11. I told him that I was mortified by what the Court seemed to be doing."

He expressed concern for the legal competence of my attorney, Mr. Talkin as well.

GODFREY: "I made myself available to speak with the investigator working for her defense attorney. I was prepared for a lengthy conversation, including a discussion of Ms. Lindauer's 9/11 warning. I was surprised when the investigator cut short the conversation after only five to ten minutes. His questions seemed far inadequate for the scope of the indictment against Ms. Lindauer, and for what I felt I had to share with her Defense Attorney."

GODFREY: "Several months later, I contacted Ms. Lindauer's uncle, Ted Lindauer, and spoke with him at greater length about several issues in her case, including her 9/11 warnings. I can verify that Ms. Lindauer felt compelled to seek her uncle's assistance interviewing witnesses for her case, before she got sent to Carswell."

Godfrey's cross-examination with the Prosecutor on 9/11 was aimed at sowing confusion. The Prosecutor tried to dismiss my 9/11 warning as "a premonition."

Godfrey adamantly corrected him that it was "a prediction— not a premonition."

And he stuck by it, never deviating from the word.

For the sake of further clarity, he submitted an affidavit on my team's 9/11 warnings, which cuts through the Prosecutor's attempts to deflect the impact of my warning.

GODFREY: "Ms. Lindauer's original warning to me in 2000 was somewhat vague, describing her opinion that a terrorist attack would occur in New York City. I recall that by the spring and summer of 2001, her warning became much more emphatic and explicit. She got much more agitated about the likelihood of the attack."

"Ms. Lindauer confided on several occasions that the next terrorist attack would involve airplane hijackings and/or airplane bombings."

"In the spring and summer of 2001, she claimed it would reprise the 1993 attack on the World Trade Center. She described it as completing the cycle started in that first attack."

"She definitely tied the threat of airplane hijackings to some sort of strike on the World Trade Center—and the possible use of a miniature nuclear bomb. That's what she was predicting."

"In August, 2001, Ms. Lindauer told me the attack was "imminent. She warned me to stay out of New York City. She told me the situation was very dangerous, and that a lot of people would get killed in this attack. She expected heavy casualties."

Godfrey disputed the notion of my incompetence whole heartedly, and roundly castigated the Justice Department.

GODFREY: "In my opinion, contrary to the Justice Department lawyers, Ms. Lindauer is now, and always was, competent to stand trial. The decision to accuse her of incompetence was baffling to myself and many others. I was forced to conclude that it was likely politically motivated to block her request for a trial."

"Throughout this entire ordeal, Susan Lindauer suffered harassment. She faced inexcusable delays in setting a trial date, (or dropping the charges). She was repeatedly questioned in court over the reliability of her terrorist warnings, despite that her warnings had been corroborated by me and by many others in affidavits, and under oath in spoken testimony. She was incarcerated in a mental facility, within a federal prison for 7 months,

1,600 miles from her home for supposed observation. And then held in confinement for months afterwards."

"The FBI and the US Attorneys Office's behavior in Ms. Lindauer's case were abhorrent. It is quite clear that much more was going on."

At the defendant's table, I recall a grim satisfaction of triumph. My mind flashed back to those terrified nights at Carswell Air Force Base and the Metropolitan Correctional Center in Manhattan, writing frantic, tearful letters to Judge Mukasey at 2 in the morning.

Everything I said was truthful always. Within a few months of my arrest, the FBI, the US Attorneys Office in Manhattan — even the Royal Canadian Mounted Police — were fully aware that a private citizen outside the Intelligence Community stood ready to authenticate my 9/11 warning in a Court of Law.

Notably, Godfrey's testimony could not be suppressed by secrecy laws. His revelations would have created serious blowback for Congress. Politicians, pundits and the 9/11 Commission strongly denounced "conspiracy theorists" who believed action should have been possible to prevent the strike, or substantially cripple its impact.

The 9/11 Commission Report would have been exposed as an egregious public fraud on so many levels. The truth would be out in the open. That provided a strong motivation for the Justice Department to fight my demands for a trial, or even a hearing.

This affidavit proves that 9/11 was an Inside Job. There were countless ways to stop the attack, which were defeated systematically. Afterwards, the 9/11 investigation was crafted to hide shocking decisions by White House leaders and Attorney General John Ashcroft, which enabled the attack to go forward as planned. And profits were shoveled out to Larry Silverstein, at the expense of freedom, and the lives of our fellow Americans.

Shame on the White House and Congress! Shame on the Justice Department! Shame on the greed of Larry Silverstein! Shame on the CIA for saving the politicians! They don't deserve praise for their national security policy!

If you want to know who committed 9/11, turn on the television or look in the mirror!

The enemy is Us. It was always Us.

Sworn by
Susan Lindauer,
Former U.S. Intelligence Asset

Source note: This chapter originally appeared as "9/11: Confessions of a former CIA Asset, *veteranstoday.com* (30 August 2012).

3

Peeling the 9/11 Onion:
Layers of Plots within Plots
by Jim Fetzer with Preston James

One of the primary means of immobilizing the American people politically today is to hold them in a state of confusion in which anything can be believed and nothing can be known... nothing of significance, that is.

Martin Schotz, HISTORY WILL NOT ABSOLVE US (1996)

9/11 appears to have been a classic "false flag" operation in which an attack is planned by one source but blamed upon another. In this case, the evidence suggests Neocons in the Department of Defense and their allies in the Mossad were actually responsible for the execution of the atrocities of 9/11. That story was buried, however, in a surfeit of alternative explanations for which the evidence was far more tenuous but which were of much greater political utility. And in each case, qualified experts uncovered evidence that induced sincere but false beliefs that they were "the real deal".

The situation encountered with regard to 9/11 turns out to be far more sophisticated than the efforts that were made to divert attention from the conspirators in the case of the assassination of JFK, where "Track #1", as we might call it, implicated Lee Harvey Oswald as "the lone assassin". Track #2 suggested that he working for Fidel Castro and that Cuba had done it. Track #3 was redirected domestically to encompass the mob, while Track #4 targeted the Soviet Union. But these were superficial distractions for which most of the evidence was flimsy and inconclusive. 9/11 presents a greater challenge to unpack, because in this case, planted evidence was more extensive and appeared to be real.

Deep black covert operations, of course, are by their very nature shrouded in layers of secrecy, protected by the "need to know" and sensitive compartmented information (SCI). Since WWII, however, major covert operations have become increasingly sophisticated and new models have been developed which take full advantage of the extensive national security laws and practices guaranteed under the National Security Acts of 1947 and 1952. The experts who create these plots are specialists in PSYOPS, which entails accessing, stimulating and manipulating the subconscious minds of the target population as a single unit in order to create beliefs and instill motivations in the public mind that are necessary to support of their actions but would normally be viewed as unacceptable.

When basic primal survival fears are activated in the "group mind" of the masses, this fear induces the motivation for a population willingly to give up their rights and liberty even for merely the promise of more protection from the boogeymen. This principle is the basis for successful PSYOPS. The use of multi-track intermeshed, deep-black covert operations also creates massive cognitive dissonance among federal investigators, private researchers and the public, which typically eventually results in folks abandoning the issue and going away in "quiet desperation", which is the actual intended result of those who plan and activate them. This is related to Maslow's "hierarchy of needs".

Deep Black/False Flag Ops

The "shroud of secrecy" they afford provides perfect cover to plan and carry out these sophisticated multi-track deep black covert operations and keep them secret–even from those operatives who are involved as well as the government's own agents who do the investigations. The "national security" cover can be dropped on any matter that is at risk of being disclosed to the public and then can be invoked again at any time. Thus, alphabets who discover what really happened can be silenced and the media can be gagged with the delivery of a "national security letter".

One of the greatest advances in deep black, false flag/stand-down covert operations has been the development of a new, more complex design, best referred to as "multi-track, enmeshed". This involves using a complicated design with independent covert operations, each of which could individually do the job if they were actually "taken live". These operations, however, are designed to be enmeshed at the nexus of the actual target, at which point some are de-activated and one or more taken live.

This can completely confound even the most seasoned investigators, thus creating so much conflict among researchers that these emergent conflicts between them provide the best cover possible for what was actually done and how it was done. Multi-track and interwoven deep black covert operations are therefore designed from the very start to obfuscate the actual operation that is selected and taken live, thereby denying most intel and government officials as well as the public any real knowledge of the actual operational purpose and information about the covert operation or why a particular covert operation was taken live as the predominant op.

As an illustration, when we attempt to peel the 9/11 onion, we discover there are at least five different alternative theories for which evidence has emerged, where each of them has sincere supporters who falsely believe that they have found critical evidence about that happened on 9/11. Each of these is actually one plot of many plots, which were deliberately contrived to creating sufficient confusion that everything about 9/11 turns out to be believable and nothing is knowable. Such deep black covert op designs can thereby provide sufficient "after the fact" cover to keep the truth buried in confusion forever.

Palestinians Did It

Cover Story #1: Palestinians Did It! Efforts were being made before the Twin Towers were destroyed to imply Palestinian responsibility for commandeering those planes and committing those crimes, which may have taken the lives of as many as 3,000 citizens and employees. Those who were watching closely saw archival footage of Palestinians rejoicing on a festive occasion being broadcast as though it were contemporaneous to convey the impression—meant to be indelible—that the Palestinian people had taken pleasure at inflicting misery on America.

An early report from CNN even asserted that the Democratic Front for the Liberation of Palestine had claimed responsibility for 9/11—and that was before Flight 175 had hit the South Tower! So during that brief interval between the first hit on the North Tower at 8:46:40 and the second on the South Tower at 9:03:11, a propaganda operation to implicate the Palestinians was well under way. The immediate availability of this report and video footage indicates the direction in which responsibility for these attacks was originally intended to be cast.

And that might have become the official cover story, were it not for observant residents near Liberty State Park in New Jersey who watched as five young men, dressed in Arab garb, filmed the destruction of the Twin Towers, cheering and celebrating, which came across as odd behavior,

under the circumstances. When they were apprehended in a white van from Urban Moving Systems, the driver would inform the arresting officer that they were not the problem: "We are Israelis. We are not your problem. Your problems are our problems. The Palestinians are your problem."

They were found to have $4,700 in cash, box cutters, and foreign passports in their possession. Urban Moving Systems would subsequently be identified as a Mossad front. After 71 days of incarceration, the Dancing Israelis would be released and return to Israel, where three of them would go on TV there and explain that their purpose had been to document the destruction of the Twin Towers. Once they had been arrested, however, the story was quietly dropped. It was just too revealing that Israel had been profoundly involved in the events of 9/11.

Arab Hijackers Did It

Cover Story #2: 19 Arab Hijackers Did It. If these attacks could not be blamed on the Palestinians without revealing Israeli complicity, the fall back was effortless. We know "the official account"—that nineteen Islamic terrorists hijacked four commercial carriers, outfoxed the most sophisticated air defense system in the world and perpetrated these atrocities under the control of a guy in a cave in Afghanistan. It would turn out that 15 of the 19 alleged terrorists were from Saudi Arabia and none were from Iraq.

But that would not matter in the grand scheme of things, where Bush/Cheney/Rumsfeld would push 9/11 as a justification for attacking Iraq. Not only was the public being fed false information about weapons of mass destruction and collusion with al Qaeda, but the national press was oblivious to the obvious question that remained unaddressed by government officials or the main stream media: If 15 of 19 hijackers were from Saudi Arabia, two from the UAE, one from Lebanon and Egypt, then why were we attacking Iraq?

Even our own FBI would eventually acknowledge that it had no "hard evidence" that Osama bin Laden had had anything to do with 9/11. But the range of evidence that exonerates al Qaeda and implicates the Bush/Cheney administration in these crimes has become as broad as it is deep. Elias Davidsson, for example, has shown that the US government had never produced evidence that the alleged (Muslim) "hijackers"

were even aboard those four planes. David Ray Griffin, the leading expert on 9/11 in the world today, has shown that the alleged phone calls from those planes were faked, where even our own FBI has confirmed that Barbara Olsen never spoke to her husband, Ted.

Leslie Raphael has offered reason after reason for concluding that the Jules Naudet film was staged. The evidence that no planes crashed in Shanksville or hit the Pentagon is beyond reasonable doubt, where others have shown that the videos of Flight 175 hitting the South Tower are fake, which may have been a brilliant stroke to generate dissension within the 9/11 Truth movement, since the truth of video fakery has proven to be politically divisive. The scientific evidence disproving the official account is also abundant and compelling. Given what we know now, anyone who continues to believe the "official account" of 9/11 is either unfamiliar with the evidence or cognitively impaired.

Pakistan/Turkey/Saudi Arabia

Cover Story #3. The Pakistanis Did It. This track was based upon the supposition that well-financed Pakistani intel were able to buy expensive "K Street" lobbyists and gain influence with high officials in the government and Department of Defense, who had much to gain from a "staged terror attack" such as 9/11.

It was the next layer of the onion to be peeled when and if the Arab hijackers story wouldn't work any longer and was initiated by the revelation that Omar Sheikh, a British-born Islamist militant, had wired $100,000 before the 9/11 attacks to Mohammed Atta, allegedly the lead hijacker, at the direction General Mahmoud Ahmed, the then head of Pakistan's Inter-Services Intelligence (ISI).

As Michael Meecher has observed, it is extraordinary that neither Ahmed nor Sheikh have been charged and brought to trial on this count. It certainly raises the prospect that the ISI was deeply involved and possibly responsible for the events of 9/11. Even if it were true, however, it cannot begin to account for the causal nexus that brought about 9/11 or identify those who were "pulling the strings".

"Ahmed, the paymaster for the hijackers," Meecher writes, "was actually in Washington on 9/11, and had a series of pre-9/11 top-level meetings

General Mahmoud Ahmed

in the White House, the Pentagon, the national security council, and with George Tenet, then head of the CIA, and Marc Grossman, the under-secretary of state for political affairs. When Ahmed was exposed by the Wall Street Journal as having sent the money to the hijackers, he was forced to "retire" by President Pervez Musharraf. Why hasn't the US demanded that he be questioned and tried in court?"

Although a number of reasons have been advanced for not taking this story seriously, Meecher mentions a number of sources who have information that might or might not implicate the ISI and expose those who were behind 9/11, the most important of whom appears to be former FBI translator, Sibel Edmonds, who has recently been speaking out.

Edmonds, a 33-year-old Turkish- American linguist, who is fluent in both Turkish and Azerbaijani, has tried to blow the whistle on the cover-up of intelligence that names some of the culprits who orchestrated the 9/11 attacks. While Sibel has been under gag orders forbidding her from testifying in court or mentioning the names of the people or of the countries involved, she has said. "My translations of the 9/11 intercepts included [terrorist]  money laundering, detailed and date-specific information … if they were to do real investigations, we would see several significant high-level criminal prosecutions in this country [the US] … and believe me, they will do everything to cover this up".

Revelations claimed to emerge from her case have been described as being explosive, including "that foreign operatives who were working in the translation department been tried to recruit her for their operations; that there exists a nuclear spy ring aided and abetted by high ranking US government officials who have been selling America's nuclear secrets on the black market; that foreign language intelligence directly pertaining to 9/11 was deliberately withheld from FBI agents in the field; that Osama bin Laden had an 'intimate relationship' with the United Stages government right up until 9/11."

While most of this is probably true, the theory of the case that she appears to imply—that Turkey (with assistance from actors from Pakistan, and Afghanistan and Saudi Arabia) had been using Bin Laden and the Taliban as a proxy terrorist army to promote its own agenda—may be true in its own right, but based upon the totality of what we know now, does not begin to approach an explanation for the stand-down by NORAD, for example, or of how the demolitions were situated or the post-attack cover-ups.

The US "Let it Happen"

Cover Story #4: It was allowed to happen. The distinction between "LIHOP" (let it happen on purpose) and "MIHOP" (made it happen on purpose) has been powerfully reinforced by the "Able Danger" contretemps. As a highly classified, anti-terrorist intelligence operation, Able Danger fell under Special Operations (SOCOM) and Defense Intelligence Agency (DIA) control. When claims arose that the US had had advanced knowledge of 9/11 and had allowed it to happen, a 16-month investigation by the Senate Intelligence committee reported in December 2006 that there had been no knowledge of the 9/11 attacks by US authorities.

The evidence, however, indicates that was not the case—and, indeed, that the events of 9/11 were orchestrated and staged by elements within the Department of Defense with help from their friends in the Mossad. As the 10th observance of 9/11 approaches, we know that there were a minimum of two independent deep cover covert operations which were operating on dual track, parallel and also interwoven. The first one was the creation and tracking—principally by the Mossad—of some "low tech" terrorist cells, which were set up, financed, and trained by US and other intelligence agencies.

"Able Danger" discovered this low-tech terror cell sub-track, which we can call "Track A". The operation was designed to be discovered to create false cover, so that when 9/11 succeeded, it could be shown by information discovered by a bona fide intelligence group that this terror cell was responsible.

That would be the role played by Lt. Col. Anthony Shaffer, other members of the "Able Danger" team, and Coleen Rowley of the FBI in Minneapolis. Track A, however, was designed to be discovered and then the

Coleen Rowley (center)

investigation stopped, creating the image of high-level US incompetence that had allowed this terror cell to succeed in hijacking aircraft with box-cutters and then flying those aircraft into the Twin Towers and the Pentagon.

When the folks from "Able Danger" swear that they uncovered "a real terrorist cell plot", they are telling the truth. It was set up this way as a false track. When Coleen Rowley expresses frustration because she could not obtain a search warrant for the hard drive of Zacarias Moussaui because he was involved in this terror cell, she was telling the truth. But Track A was set up as a false track to be terminated before the 9/11 attacks to provide a convincing cover story for the highest levels of US intelligence and make the government appear to be merely hugely incompetent. After all, how could government officials of this incompetence have staged a successful and effective covert operation?

The US "Made it Happen"

Actual Story: The US "Made it Happen". Track B, by comparison, was a high-tech track designed to use readiness exercises on 9/11, including some 17 anti-terrorist drills on 9/11 that disrupted communication and coordination between NORAD and the FAA, by taking some of them live and substituting high-tech weapons in order to target the Twin Towers and the Pentagon by that means. Track B involved the use of numerous different demolition means, including incendiaries and multiple modes of destruction, most of which alone would be insufficient cause for the detonation of the Twin Towers, which was arguably used to induce false leads confusing investigators and researchers.

A perfect example turns out to be the "hard science" 9/11 Truth group's insistence that nanothermite was the principal element used in the demolition of the Twin Towers. This position, which has assumed a status akin to that of a dogma within the 9/11 movement, turns out to be unsustainable in light of research that has established that nanothermite is non-explosive—or, at best, a feeble explosive—and cannot have been responsible for blowing the towers apart, for ejecting massive steel assemblies hundreds of feet, or for the pulverization of concrete or the destruction of steel by means of shockwaves.

To a bona fide explosives expert, the claim that nanothermite provided the explosive energy or enough shockwave velocity to perform these tasks had to be an obvious deception. If it was deliberately planted to divert research on 9/11 along an ultimately unproductive line, it may have succeeded beyond the wildest intel dreams as a classic "red herring".

Another example, surprisingly, is the Pentagon attack, where some of those within the 9/11 community have argued strenuously for not going there, because the Department of Defense might spring a new video on the public that proves a Boeing 757 actually did hit the building. The evidence contradicting that contention is abundant and compelling, however, including the expert assessment of Major General Albert N. Stubblebine, USA (ret.), perhaps the world's leading expert on image analysis and interpretation, who has concluded that no plane hit the Pentagon. When you take all the evidence into account, the case against a plane is staggering, but internal dissension has precluding using it— and other powerful proofs of governmental fakery —

The clear, green Pentagon lawn: Where's the plane?

and has taken this evidence out of the public domain:

"From the photographs I have analyzed very, very carefully," Stubblebine has explained, "it was not an airplane." During an interview in Germany, he explained that there should have been wing marks on the façade of the Pentagon. "If it had wings, it would have left wing marks. [There are] those who claim that the plane tilted and hit the ground first and lost a wing. But airplanes have two wings, and he could not find indications of any wing in any of those photographs."

Regarding the Twin Towers, he added, "Look at the buildings falling— they didn"t fall down because of an airplane hit them. They fell down because explosives went off inside. Demolition. Look at Building 7, for God's sake."

Whistleblowing as Deception

The politics of 9/11, however, are far more murky than the science. So when folks from Able Danger swear that they uncovered a real terror cell plot, they are telling the truth. It was set up this way as a false track. When a Colleen Rowley expresses frustration because she could not get a search warrant for Moussaui's hard-drive because he was involved in this terror cell, she is telling the truth. When a Sibel Edmonds is gagged by court order and tries to tell how certain how administration officials were communicating with this terror cell, she is telling the truth.

Indeed, the effort to mislead our own experts even extended to Richard Clarke, who has explained that he himself had been given the false impression that, apart from a few analysts, the CIA had been unaware of what was going on prior to 9/11, which was intended to support the theory of US incompetence.

Clarke, who was the nation's leading anti-terrorism expert, recently observed, "It's not as I originally thought, which was that one lonely CIA analyst got this information and didn't somehow recognize the significance of it," Clarke said during an interview. "No, fifty, 5-0, CIA personnel knew about this. Among the fifty people in CIA who knew these guys were in the country was the CIA director. ... We therefore conclude that there was a high-level decision inside CIA ordering people not to share that information. ... It is also possible, as some FBI investigators suspect, the CIA was running a joint venture with Saudi intelligence in order to get around that restriction ... These are only theories about the CIA's failures to communicate vital information to the bureau ... Perhaps the agency decided that Saudi intelligence would have a better chance of recruiting these men than the Americans. That would leave no CIA fingerprints on the operation as well."

Indeed, as Ian Henshall has observed, if you substitute the Mossad for the Saudis, you have the explanation for the dancing Israelis, who were apprehended for filming and celebrating during the destruction of the Twin Towers and were released later under orders from Michael Chertoff, then an advisor Attorney General John Ashcroft and a dual US-Israel citizen, who would become Director of the new Department of Homeland Security—which leads directly to reports like those from Dr. Steve Pieczenik that 9/11 was indeed "an inside job" and studies like those from Alan Sabrosky, Ph.D., who has explain that 9/11 involved complicity between Neocon Zionists in the Department of Defense and the Mossad, where Israel had very powerful motives for 9/11 and, along with the Bush/Cheney administration, has been its primary beneficiary.

But Israel cannot have done this alone. The NORAD "stand down" and the attack on the Pentagon required complicity at the highest levels of the Department of Defense. And the benefits to the Bush/Cheney administration have likewise been enormous. As Patrick Martin has observed, "Without 9/11, there would be no US occupation of Iraq, putting an American army squarely at the center of the world's largest pool of oil. Without 9/11, there would be no US bases across Central Asia, guarding the second largest source of oil and gas. And without 9/11, the Bush administration would have been unable to sustain itself politically, faced with a deteriorating economy and widespread opposition to its tax cuts for millionaires and social measures to appease the fundamentalist Christian Right."

The Fourth Reich

Indeed, the extreme motivation of a small number of radical Israelis and their lobbies like AIPAC to manipulate US foreign policy in the Mideast may have created a huge future trap for them in their role as "classic cutouts", which can be later exposed in a limited hangout admission in order to direct blame toward the Mossad and the small number of radical Jews involved, who do not represent most Jewish folks at all, thus directing blame away from from those who used them in their cutout role and who were actually at the top of the command structure.

Richard Clarke, anti-terrorism czar

This limited hangout disclosure could then later be used to blame all Jews and add them to the large and growing Homeland Security watch-list list of possible domestic terrorists such as Muslims, fundamentalist Christians, returning veterans, Ron Paul supporters, Constitutionalists and tax protestors, and member of any current social group that is trying to gain exposure and cessation of rampant government corruption and creeping tyranny of the government at all levels, which of course encompasses those dedicated to 9/11 Truth.

It does not take a PSYOPS expert to discern the pattern here when Richard Clarke resuscitates the incompetence theory, according to which the US "let 9/11 happen". Even on the assumption that he is sincere, we have a fall-back position intended to minimize concern for complicity by the Bush/Cheney administration and its friends in the Mossad—who, moreover, do not necessarily represent the highest level of control over the atrocities of 9/11.

Because Clarke was in the crucial position of being the nation's anti-terrorism czar, his affirmations about incompetence between agencies, such as the CIA and the FBI, come across to the public and can be widely promoted as admirable and courageous acts of whistle blowing, when their role in deceiving the public drowns amidst the anguish and concern that "if only we had done better" and "we must not let this happen again", oblivious of the role that his reports are playing in burying the truth about 9/11.

We have now reached the point in America where any citizen or group wanting to obtain needed social justice, or the cessation of undeclared, unprovoked, and unConstitutional wars, in violation of international law and the UN Charter, are now placed on a secret watch list and considered as "potential domestic terrorists" by Homeland Security, which some—with ample justification—view as "The New American Gestapo."

If the US has been hijacked by offshore corporate and banking interests, which have their own anti-American agenda and are now in the process of Nazifying America, as some astute researchers have suggested, then certainly this could lead to a "Fourth Reich" run by offshore banks and large international corporations and we could see a replay of the unlimited persecution of minorities and special scapegoats such as specific groups such as Muslims, Jews and Christians who dissent from The New Tyranny.

So if you have wondered why covert operations like 9/11 are so difficult to unravel or why it is all but impossible to convince the feds who investigated it that this was actually a US false flag/stand-down/inside-job, deep-black covert operation, the answer to that question appears to be that the plan was designed from conception to obfuscate what happened, not only regarding the public but also the government's own experts, who would be assigned to investigate them—and even to keep most of those who had an actual part in those operations in the dark, so only those at the highest levels of the government knew what happened and, even among them, only a few probably knew the full dimensions of the plan.

The objective throughout, accordingly, has always been to keep the public in a state of uncertainly, where everything about these events is believable and nothing is knowable—which is the ultimate objective of disinformation.

Source note: This chapter originally appeared as "Peeling the 9/11 Onion: Layers of Plots within Plots", *veteranstoday.com* (14 August 2014).

Part II

Who was Responsible and Why 2

4

9/11 and Zion:
What was Israel's Role?
by Nick Kollerstrom

A nation can survive its fools, and even the ambitious, but it cannot survive treason from within. An enemy at the gates is less formidable, for he is known and he carries his banners openly. But the traitor moves among those within the gate freely, his sly whispers rustling through all the alleys, heard in the very halls of government itself.
— Marcus Cicero, to the Roman Senate, 42 BC

One may feel shocked by this title. Zionists have such a grip upon "The Guilt Industry", virtually a monopoly, politically speaking. Was 9/11 an inside job? America was in some degree seeded with the perpetration of this event, from outside, and various echelons of its security services and military then responded by co-operating and then weaving a Muslims-did-it story. That is the hypothesis we will here examine.

So when Netanyahu said the very next day, *'This is very good for Israel"*, he wasn't just blurting out something indiscreet, he was publicly congratulating the various agents who had worked so hard.

The smooth integrity which the official story soon acquires, is an expression of the nation's will-to-survive: an event has taken place and been covered up, where the Truth cannot come out without effectively disintegrating the nation, in its present form. Aye, there's the rub.

Benjamin Netanyahu

That is the sense of fun which the Chief Operators derive, as they see all the media, who may not particularly like them, compelled to endorse and weave out of their own accord, the fabricated tale. Here are the "Seven Pillars" of the argument.

I. Silverstein and the WTC

The private property developer, billionaire Larry Silverstein, acquired the WTC complex off the New York Port Authority (founded and owned by the Rockefeller family), two months before 9/11 – the first time in its 33-year history the complex had ever changed ownership. Silverstein was formerly a chairman of the United Jewish Appeal, the largest Zionist organization dedicated to raising money and support for Israel.

Lewis Eisenberg, former chairman of The New York Port Authority and the man who personally supervised the negotiations that delivered the 99-year lease to Silverstein, is also a former leader of the United Jewish Appeal. His first order of business as the new owner was to change the company responsible for the security of the complex: the new security company he hired was Securacom (now Stratasec). George W. Bush's brother, Marvin Bush, was on its board of directors, and Marvin's cousin, Wirt Walker III, was its CEO. According to public records, not only did Securacom provide electronic security for the World Trade Center, it also covered Dulles International Airport and United Airlines — two key locations in the 9/11 attacks.

Silverstein personally ordered WTC-7 to be demolished ("pulled") around noon of 9/11 and has never been cross-examined by any enquiry over this. His firm had built that very building in the mid-1980s! In 1980, Silverstein Associates won a bid to lease and develop that portion of the WTC, and to build the 47-story "Building 7".

Despite being a mere leaseholder of the buildings, he was the sole beneficiary of the insurance payouts. He increased the insurance policies, when he signed the lease two months before the catastrophe happened. The insurance was for 3.6 billion dollars, but he found an obscure clause in the insurance policy which enabled him to claim twice, one for each "attack!" "Larry Silverstein, since July landlord of the towers, demands from the insurers $7,2 billion compensation. His speaker Steve Solomon, said that with help from New York's Jewish mayor, Michael Bloomberg, he found investments to rebuild the WTC.

A good chunk of the seven billion insurance went to Israel, so God once more helped out His chosen people, financially" [1]. Ground Zero is being rebuilt by Daniel Liebeskind, the Jewish architect of Berlin's "Jewish Museum". The person said to be Silverstein's closest friend — one with whom he speaks almost daily by phone — is the former Israeli Prime Minister, Benjamin Netanyahu. For financial reasons (chiefly involving asbestos problems) the WTC complex was no longer viable and needed to be demolished, but the costs of doing this legally were prohibitive.

In the early 1990s, a group of leading U.S. Jewish businessmen formed a company that was to become the Israel Export Development Company, as a way to make it easier for foreign investors to trade with Israel. It never quite worked out (for complex reasons), despite the best efforts of Benjamin Netanyahu, but following that struggle gives us the impression of Silverstein as possibly the most distinguished US financier assisting Israel. Thus, David Yerushalmi, who had led the IEDC effort since its inception, was asked to turn over the leadership of the company to Silverstein, an accomplished real estate developer and ardent fundraiser for the Jewish Federation of New York, itself a big contributor to Israel. Perhaps, had it worked out, events would not have let to the donation which he made to Israel, following the insurance claim from the WTC-7 collapse.

WTC-7 appeared as the only steel framed building in history for which fire was the sole cause of its collapse. Any building that was not owned by Silverstein Properties that day strangely remained upright, despite being a lot closer to the two towers that collapsed onto them. Let's quote what Lucky Larry said on acquiring the leasehold: *"This is a dream come true, we will be in control of a prized asset, and we will seek to develop its potential, raising it to new heights"*.

II. Zakheim and his Missing Trillions

Ordained Rabbi, Zionist and citizen of Israel, Dov Zakheim served as Comptroller of the Pentagon, i.e. he was in charge of its finances, from May 2001 to March 2004. While Bush was still Governor of Texas, Zakheim became one of his closest advisers, counseling him on defense technology and strategic aspects of Middle Eastern affairs, and was Bush's senior foreign policy advisor during the 2000 campaign. Dov had earlier held the position of Chief Executive Officer at Systems Planning Corporation (SPC), then he became the Undersecretary of Defense and Comptroller (head money man) of the Pentagon in May 2001, appointed by Bush. He was sworn in as the Under-Secretary of Defense and Chief Financial Officer for the Department of Defense on May 4, 2001. Since then over three trillion dollars has gone unaccounted-for.

Dov Zakheim's SPC offers the appropriately named "'Flight Termination System' for remote control and flight termination of airborne test vehicles" [2]. It consists of a Command transmitter system plus custom control, interface and monitoring systems.' The system can be configured to operate from a single local site, or with several remote sites. It does sound useful.

System Planning Corporation, of which he had been Corporate Vice-President, is a high-tech, research and manufacturing firm based in Arlington, Virginia, a major player in the "Homeland Security" industry and a leading designer of airborne remote control technology. It makes the Command Transmitter System, a remote control system for planes, boats, missiles and other vehicles, which can be configured to interface with all sorts of vehicle types.

He is Chief Executive Officer of SPC International Corporation, a subsidiary of SPC that specializes in political, military, and economic consulting. A subsidiary of this firm, Tridata Corporation, oversaw the investigation of the first "terrorist" attack on the World Trade Center in 1993, which would have provided vital first-hand knowledge of the security systems and structural blueprints of the World Trade Center.

Zakheim has close ties to the Israeli government, holding dual Israeli-American citizenship [3]. As a member of the Council for Foreign Relations, and founding member of the Neocon cult, he co-authored the Heritage Foundation's infamous tract, "Rebuilding America's Defenses: Strategy, Forces and Resources for a New Century" published by The American Enterprise's "Project for a New American Century", in which the Bush

Administration's entire design for renewed global conquest was laid down, exactly a year prior to 9/11. It called for "some catastrophic and catalyzing event – like a new Pearl Harbor" as necessary to foster the frame of mind needed for the American public to support a war in the Middle East. As a respected and established voice in the intelligence community, his views were eagerly accepted.

In 2004, an article entitled The Mastermind Behind 9/11? on the 'Truthseeker' website [4] expressed the view that:

Considering his access to Boeing 767 tankers, remote control flight systems, and his published views in the PNAC document, it seems very likely he is in fact a key figure in the alleged terrorist attacks in New York City on September 11, 2001. Rabbi Zakheim had access to things like structural integrity, blueprints and any number of important facets of information about the WTC through his work with Tridata Corporation in the investigation of the bombing of the WTC in 1993. That he had access to remote control technology through his work at System Planning Corporation (SPC); that he had access to Boeing aircraft through a lease deal he brokered while working at the Pentagon; and finally, that he was part of a group of politically radical Straussian Neoconservatives, who, through their association with PNAC, called for restructuring of the Middle East.

In response, the Truthseeker was threatened with prosecution by Zakheim's lawyers in 2005 and had to remove the article. However, the insightful articles, "Dov Zakheim and the 9/11 Conspiracy" and also "The Mastermind Behind 9/11" can still be viewed [5].

The planes that purportedly slammed into the Towers that morning were supposed to be Boeing 767s, and Zakheim had contracted and sent a number of these to Florida-MacDill Air Force Base before the event. The Flight Termination System produced by his SPC does somewhat resemble the object visible in photographs under the fuselage of flight 175, just prior to its impact into the South Tower [6].

This plane is suspected to have been a KC-767, the military tanker version of the Boeing 767. As the Truthseeker observed, the remote-control technology whereby those specially-prepared planes impacted the Towers, was probably made and managed by Zakheim's company. In addition he has enabled substantial support for Israel over the years: thanks to him, Israel is awash in F-15's, F-16's, and the latest in offensive and defensive missile systems – sold to Israel at a fraction of their value. Zakheim had a central role in the perpetration of 9/11.

III. Israeli Intelligence-Espionage Companies

The airline security company responsible for the shocking security lapses at both the Boston and Newark airports on 9/11 is a wholly-owned subsidiary of an Israeli company (ICTS) headed by men with clear ties to Israel's military intelligence agency, Mossad: Huntleigh, USA is a subsidiary of International Consultants on Targeted Security, headed by "former [Israeli] military commanding officers and veterans of government intelligence and security agencies. It sells security, ticketing, check-in and passenger screening services to Boston's Logan airport and New Jersey's Newark airport.

Menachem Atzmon, convicted in Israel in 1996 for campaign finance fraud, and his business partner Ezra Harel, took over management of security at the Boston and Newark airports when their company ICTS bought Huntleigh USA in 1999. UAL Flight 175 and AA 11, which allegedly struck the Twin Towers, both originated in Boston, while UAL 93, which purportedly crashed in Pennsylvania, departed from the Newark airport.

Atzmon just happens to be a good friend of current Israeli Prime minister, Ehud Olmert. In fact, Atzmon is such a good friend of Almert that he was involved in a financial scandal involving forged receipts for donations to the Likud campaign with Olmert back in 1997 when Atzmon was co-treasurer of the Likud party [7].

Does this at last explain how those "Muslim hijackers" could appear as getting on the planes, with no CCTV pictures of them anywhere in the airports, no Arab names on any flight lists, no boarding staff prepared to testify to having seen any Arab-looking guys mount the planes, nor any post-mortems indicating any Arab bodies anywhere?

That phantasm could be woven, and sustained, with the aid of Israeli intelligence agents handling security and passenger screening at just those very airports [8].

Two Israeli-based companies Amdocs and Comverse have wiretapping technologies, which tend to have a back door built in to overhear monitored conversations [9]. In January 2001, Comverse purchased a large stake in the

company Odigo, 'giving it access to Odigo's operations, accounting and technologies.' In 1999, the NSA issued a top secret report on how US phone records were getting into 'foreign' i.e. Israeli hands, concerning Israeli-linked drug-crime mafia rings.

A revealing, four-part investigative series was aired by Fox News in December 2001, by Carl Cameron. This outlined how the Israeli-controlled company Amdocs had installed new White House communications system during the mid-1990s. This stimulated FBI probes into the extent of Israeli eavesdropping on calls to and from the White House, NSC, Pentagon and State Department. Clearly, Amdocs was spying on the White House [10]. Cameron and Fox News were told, 'Evidence linking these Israelis to 9/11 is classified, we cannot tell you about evidence that has been gathered' [11].

An Israeli government run company called Zim Israel Navigational commands over 80 vessels, is the 9th largest shipping company in the world, and had 200 employees in the North tower. One week before 9/11, Zim moved out of its World Trade Center offices with over 200 workers, paying a $50,000 fine for breaking its lease. Its decision to move had been announced six months earlier. The reason given was, to save on rent.

IV. The Dancing Israelis

As the towers crumbled, five young Israelis, who turned out to be Mossad agents, were caught doing the 'happy dance' while videotaping the event. Police ascertained that their van contained $4,700 in cash, plus 'box cutters', and some photographs, showing their smiling faces in front of the smoldering wreckage, and one showing a hand flicking a lighter open in front of the Towers!

The van tested positive for explosives. There were "maps of the city in the car with certain places highlighted ... It looked like they're hooked into this. It looked like they knew what was going to happen." When the five returned to Israel, one of them brazenly explained on Israeli TV, "The fact of the matter is that we have been in a country that experiences terror daily.

Our purpose was to document the event," showing that they knew what was going to happen.

They set up their cameras on banks of the Hudson River, trained them onto the Twin Towers, and congratulated each other when the crashes occurred, according to The New York Times. A witness noted: 'They seemed to be taking a movie. They were like, happy, you know … they didn't look shocked to me. I thought it was strange.' The company they worked for, 'Urban Moving Systems', had few discernible assets. It closed up shop immediately afterward as its owner fled to Israel. In the weeks and months following 9/11, numerous cells of other Mossad "moving" agents were arrested across the nation, and then in December 2001, Fox News reported that U.S. authorities had detained 60 such "movers."[12]

The revealing, four-part investigative series was aired by Fox News in December, 2001, dealing with the arrests of several hundred Israeli nationals as well as some of the incriminating circumstances surrounding their activities in the United States. In response, every major media outlet in America received a visit from Abraham Foxman, the head of the Anti-Defamation League. A phrase he used was, "What are you doing putting this stuff out there? You're killing us!" Executives at the highest levels of the various networks were inundated with phone calls, letters and emails. Members of the most powerful Jewish groups in the country – ADL, AIPAC with its 60,000 members, and the misnamed Committee for Accuracy in Middle East Reporting in America CAMERA – visited the White House and petitioned officials at the highest levels to close down investigations of the Israeli spies.

V. Israeli Spy Ring

At least 120 Israeli intelligence operatives entered America and posed as art students, with door-to-door sales of artwork. "Many of the ring's activities seemed to run parallel with the movements of several of the 9/11 hijackers. A group of about 140 Israeli spies were arrested and US government documents alluded to this ring as having 'organised intelligence-gathering operations designed to penetrate government facilities." The Fox News program revealed documents indicating that these art students had targeted and penetrated military bases, no mean achievement for art students [13].

Other reports speak of two hundred Israeli spies being uncovered, among them military members, electronics experts, wiretapping and phone tapping specialists, and explosives experts with the skill to bring down tall buildings. [14] They were arrested for trying to sneak into secured US Federal buildings and staking out 36 Department of Defense sites. Some of these suspicious "art students" showed up at the homes of Federal employees.

An investigative report concluded that: "'A former Defense Department analyst, Hatchett believes groups may be gathering intelligence for possible future attacks. Some organization, thinking in terms of a potential retaliation against the U.S. government could be scouting out potential targets and looking for targets that would be vulnerable." Another federal memo stated that, besides Houston and Dallas, the same thing has happened at sites in New York, Florida, and six other states, and, even more worrisome, at 36 sensitive Department of Defense sites. "One defense site you can explain," says Hatchett, "well that was just a serendipitous, … Thirty-six? That's a pattern." [15]

Between December 12-15th, 2001, the FBI, the DEA and the INS informed Fox News that there were no connections between the "art students" and the incidents of 9/11, and that continuing to pursue this topic would be a form of "career suicide."

On December 16, 2001, Fox News pulled the information regarding the "art student spy ring" from its website. Jane's Intelligence Digest commented, "It is rather strange that the US media seems to be ignoring what may well be the most explosive story since the 11 September attacks—the alleged breakup of a major Israeli espionage operation in the USA." The Palm Beach Post alluded to a DEA report on the Israeli "art students," saying it had determined that all of the students had "recently served in the Israeli military, the majority in intelligence, electronic signal intercept or explosive ordnance units." [16]

The story of the largest spy ring ever discovered inside the United States was soon hushed up: "Evidence linking these Israelis to 9/11 is classified. I cannot tell you about evidence that has been gathered. It's classified information," explained a US official, on Cameron's Fox News Report on the Israeli spy ring and its connections to 9/11. The Israeli national Michael Chertoff, who would become the first head of the Department of Homeland Security, was responsible for letting them off and making sure they got safely back to Israel.

The Florida flight school president Rudi Dekkers recalled of 'Mohammed Atta': "Well, when Atta was here and I saw his face on several occasions in the building, then I know that they're regular students and then I try to talk to them, it's kind of a PR – where are you from? I tried to communicate with him. I found out from my people that he lived in Hamburg and he spoke German so one of the days that I saw him, I speak German myself, I'm a Dutch citizen, and I started in the morning telling him in German, "Good morning. How are you? How do you like the coffee? Are you happy here?" and he looked at me with cold eyes, didn't react at all and walked away. That was one of my first meetings I had."'[17]

Atta's German may not have been up to much, but he could speak Hebrew! The 'Mohammed Atta' of Florida loved eating pork chops, had various different passports and IDs, according to his lingerie-model and stripper girlfriend Amanda Keller, and could speak Hebrew. She challenged him when he claimed the latter, and then by demonstrating his skill in Hebrew, he convinced her! He loved partying, strip-clubs, fast cars, casinos and snorting cocaine (not quite the suicidal type, maybe?).

The real Mohammed Atta, who lived in Hamburg as an architecture student, had his passport stolen in 1999 [18], which presumably enabled the identity-theft to take place. Austere, silent and devout, he avoided women and hated flying so much that his sister had to give him special medicine to enable him to do it!

There could not be two more opposite characters. The Hamburg Atta was about three inches shorter. One presumes he was killed after September 11th after he spoke to his Father on the 12th over the phone. The Florida Atta lived on the same street as one of the groups of the Israeli "art students."[19] The Israeli-art group leader, Hanan Serfati, had rented several dwellings in the neighborhood, and he stayed next to the post office where the Huffman Aviation flight-students had their mailbox. Mohammed Atta's "vital task" on the morning of 9/11 has been well described by Rowland Morgan, and it involved a journey to Portland, in order to have his baggage (complete with Koran, will, etc) delivered to Boston airport, in such a way that it would be retained by the airport, not be put onto a plane. [20] For this, there was no need for him to board one of 'the' planes.

VI. One Israeli Death

Nearly 500 foreign nationals from over 80 different nations were killed in the World Trade Center. The next day, September 12, the Jerusalem Post reported that the Israeli embassy in America was bombarded on 9/11 with calls from 4,000 worried Israeli families. On September 13th, "Four Israelis were almost certainly in the Twin Towers of the World Trade Center when they collapsed, the Israeli consul in New York said this evening." This number dwindled. The Towers specialized in international banking so one might have expected a few more Israeli citizens. One or possibly three Israelis died on 9/11, one in the towers and two on the planes. There is very little on the web.

A week later, President Bush stated that 130 had died, but 129 of these were found to be still alive. The NY times 22 Sept found that 3 Israelis were confirmed dead, two from planes and one from the Towers [21,22]. Of this total the British historian David Irving wrote: "We are happy to report that the 4,000 figure dwindled eventually to three (not three thousand, but three), then two, then one: the unfortunate Daniel Lewin."

Two Mossad agents were present, on Flight UA 175 and Flight AA 11 respectively: the first flight had Danny Lewin, a 28-year old graduate of Israel's elite commando unit, the "World's most elite anti-hijacking team".

He was a captain in this unit, and the story soon developed that he had been shot by Satam Al Suqami, as the four Arabs attempted to storm the cockpit. (Satam was the one whose passport supposedly fluttered down to Ground Zero where the FBI found it). Sayeret Matkal is Israel's elite team that handles aircraft hijackings and assassinations, specializing in aircraft takeovers. During the 1970s and 1980s, this secretive Israeli anti-terrorist unit (akin to the Delta Force) thwarted many attempted hijacking. Members of this unit are trained in looking and thinking like an Arab. Flight UA 175 (Boston to LA, allegedly hijacked to fly into the south tower) had the Israeli citizen and probable Mossad agent named Alora Avraham. This 27 year old was raised in the Israeli settlement of Ashdod. One surmises that Lewin may not have died, but had some key role in … whatever happened.

Daniel Lewin

On the morning of 9/11, a two-hour advance warning to stay out of the towers was received by the Israeli firm of Odigo, [23] whose Research and Development center is in Herzliya, Israel, a town north of Tel Aviv where Mossad is headquartered. This messaging company, with its office a mere two blocks from the former WTC, received a warning originating from an Israeli branch.

One never heard details, but Odigo's vice president Alex Diamandis said, "The messages said something big was going to happen in a certain amount of time, and it did – almost to the minute." Odigo has a feature called "People Finder" which allows a user to send an instant message to a large group based on a common characteristic, such as Israeli nationality, while maintaining user privacy. This is surely the explanation, as to why no Israeli nationals working in the Towers died that morning (there was one who died, but he was just visiting). "Comverse and Odigo have had a long-standing partnership and together have developed instant communications products and services that we have recently begun to offer to operators around the world," declared Zeev Bregman, CEO of Comverse [24].

VII. Zionist Neocons and Straussian Jews

Irving Kristol, 'godfather' of the Neocon movement, founded PNAC, the Project for a new American Century. His son William Kristol, worked closely with Richard Perle, and this Jewish duo achieved more than anyone else in erasing the concept of détente – which had traditionally been the policy of the Council of Foreign Relations – and extinguishing hope of any 'peace dividend' following the Soviet Union's collapse.

In September 2000 PNAC produced 'Rebuilding America's Defences' which famously called for a permanent war philosophy, Empire, the advancing of the cause of Israel, and the catalyzing event of a new Pearl Harbor' to make it all possible. The Kristols used their enormous influence prior to 9/11 to promote the concept of Arabs as potential terrorists, then after the event they ensured that the media focused and stayed focussed on Bin Laden and Muslim guilt. The day before the Iraq war began, Kristol bragged in an editorial of his journal The Weekly Standard, that, "obviously we are gratified that the Iraq strategy we have long advocated ... has become the policy of the US government' and a columnist of The Washington Post had once declared the looming conflict to be 'Kristol's war.'"[25]

The civilian Defense Policy Board wields more control over the military establishment than the Defense Secretary or the generals and admirals. The notoriously belligerent Perle, nicknamed the "The Prince of Darkness", was Chairman of this Board. There are a number of other Zionists who served on the board (Kissinger, Cohen, Schlessinger) as well as non-Jewish members who have always supported Israel and the expansion of the "War on Terror".

Defense Policy Board

- This board was at the heart of the push for war, from the first days after 9/11.

Membership from 8/16/2001 through and beyond the start of the Iraq war:
Richard Perle, Chairman (American Enterprise Institute), Kenneth Adelman, Newt Gingrich, Henry Kissinger, Dan Quale, James Woolsey, many more.

Apart from top Jewish Neocons Henry Kissinger and Richard Perle as Chairman of the Defense Policy Board, Zionist Paul Wolfowitz as

Undersecretary of Defense, and Zionist award winner Douglass Feith as Undersecretary of Defense Policy, the Zionist Pentagon gang controlled 3 of the top 4 civilian leadership positions of America's armed forces. Others such as Condoleeza Rice and Donald Rumsfeld were fairly in accord with their drive for WW III. The Perle-Wolfowitz-Feith gang represent a fanatical "government-within-a-government". And, of course, in league with these Zionist Pentagon conspirators, Jewish Zionist and 2004 Presidential candidate, Senator Joseph Lieberman and his Gentile partner in crime Senator John McCain, would vie for the nation's highest offices.

Top members of the Bush administration had very close ties with the Israeli government. Every one of the following kingpins of the Bush administration were also Israeli citizens: Paul Wolfowitz, Richard Perle, Douglas Feith (undersec of Defense), Michael Chertoff, George Tenet (real name: Cohen), Elliot Abrams (NSC), Donald Kagan, Richard Haas, Kenneth Adelman, Edward Luttwak (National security Study Group), Robert Satloff, David Frum, David Wurmser, Steve Goldsmith, and Marc Grossman. Ari Fleisher, Press Secretary. Concluded Ruppert, 'These and other Israeli-connected experts formed the core group at the Project for a New American Century [26]. These are Zionist warmongers who adore and obey Israel and who view America chiefly as Israel's financial sugar-daddy and mercenary slave. Their aim is global power for the Jews and profits for Jewish bankers and Illuminati-directed oil barons."

Former Israeli Prime-Minister Ehud Barak well expressed the aim of the enterprise when he said in an interview just days after 9/11: "The whole world has now to start a world war against the enemies of Israel."[27] But, World War III was not that easy to start! Soon after, Israel's Prime Minister Ariel 'the Butcher' Sharon bellowed at his Cabinet, "I want to tell you something very clear: Don't worry about American pressure on Israel. We, the Jewish people, control America, and the Americans know it."[28]

On any reasonable analysis, Dick Cheney, Vice-President of America, has to have been a pivotal 9/11 perpetrator. As Mike Ruppert concluded:

"I have absolutely no doubt that on the day of September 11th Richard Cheney was in full and complete control of a properly functioning and parallel command and communications system …"[29].

Richard Cheney

Cheney sat on the board of JINSA the Jewish Institute for National Security, "probably the most important organization, in terms of its influence on Bush administration policy formation."[30] Cheney would take leave from JINSA while serving as VP, where his office was "run by aides known to be very pro-Israel." [31]

The Pentagon set up the Office of Strategic Influence (OSI) for fabricating news [32]. A Zionist Air Force General named Simon P. Worden was chosen to head this, his boss being Douglass Feith, another dedicated Zionist who serves as Undersecretary of Defense for Policy. The Zionist Organization of America (ZOA) honored Feith and his father at an award dinner in 1999. ZOA's 1997 press release explained: "This year's honorees will be Dalck Feith and Douglas J. Feith, the noted Jewish philanthropists and pro-Israel activists. Dalck Feith will receive the ZOA's special Centennial Award at the dinner, for his lifetime of service to Israel and the Jewish people. His son Douglas J. Feith, the former Deputy Assistant Secretary of Defense, will receive the prestigious Louis D. Brandeis Award at the dinner." [33]

As the Mayor of New York, Rudolf Giuliani was told in advance to get out of the WTC towers because they were going to fall, on that morning, which shows very privileged treatment. After the event he declared Ground Zero area a 'crime scene' and was thus able to prohibit any photos from being taken, but then by swiftly removing all of the steel and having it melted down he demolished the primary evidence for the crime. He had a hard struggle with the firemen, most of whom knew that the towers had been taken down.

Rudolf Guiliani

Since retiring as mayor he has been involved with security companies, and his turning up in London on the morning of July 7th 2005, staying in a hotel right next to the Liverpool Street terror-blast (so he 'heard' the blast), is hardly accidental. He is a friend of Benjanmin Netenyahu, whom he welcomed while Mayor of New York, and they both turned up in the same hotel on the same morning [34]. Rudolf Giuliani, of course, was Israel's favorite for the 2008 US presidential election: AIPAC lists and scores all the candidates by their degree of adoration for Israel, and Giuliani was tops – his support for Israel is total and unconditional. Thus, he returned a $10m donation from a Saudi prince, due to the latter making some comment about Israel and 9/11.

In weeks before 9/11, between August 26 and September 11, 2001, a group of speculators, identified by the American Securities and Exchange

Commission as Israeli citizens, sold "short" a list of 38 stocks that could reasonably be expected to fall in value as a result of the pending attacks. These speculators operated out of the Toronto, Canada and Frankfurt, Germany, stock exchanges and their profits were specifically stated to be "in the millions of dollars." [35] Short selling of stocks involves the opportunity to gain large profits by passing shares to a friendly third party, then buying them back when the price falls. Precedings a traumatic event, it indicates foreknowledge.

The Enemy Within

At 9.30 am on the day of September 11th, the White House received a call, saying "Angel is Next." Angel was that day's codeword for Air Force One, then carrying President Bush. The credibility of the message was further established by use of Presidential identification codes [36]. Cheney advised Bush not to return to Washington: "There's still the threat," he said [37].

At this point, argues Tarpley, "the sponsors showed their hand. They were not located in a cave in Afghanistan, but were rather a network located high within the US government and military." [38] The rogue network was then demanding, that a Straussian "war of civilisations" be unleashed: "The principal clue leading us to the existence of the rogue network is the 'Angel is next' threat," which meant it was perpetrated by persons having expertise in, and access, to top military codes.

Who could that be? On the September 12th press briefing, Ari Fleisher confirmed that a coded message had been used in threatening Air Force One carrying the President. No fighter planes to escort Air Force One arrived until noon – it took off from Florida at 9.30 am with no protection, flying alone through the skies over those terrible hours! The purpose here could have been to instill fear into the President.

Sometime after that "Angel is Next" threat, President Bush phoned up Ted Olsen, the US's Solicitor-General, and a few days later Olsen recalled, "We couldn't speak long. This was during the day of the crisis. And I didn't – I hadn't expected him to call, because he is the President of the United States. We know now – he knew then there were thousands of victims and terrible devastation and crisis, and the potential of further dangers to the structure of our government, meaning the institutions of our government and the leadership of our government." [39] Let's conjecture that Ted Olsen may have been telling the truth in some degree. People like Olsen and Bush are totally complicit and so are not at liberty to spill the beans later on. But still, they experienced some external manipulating power, which was a threat, or which was intimidating.

The most secret US-government codes were being used by the perpetrators [40], and we are suggesting that it would have been Israeli-based agencies that could do this, using the advanced Promis software [41]. Air Force One flew on that morning from Florida to the Strategic Command centre at Offut, as Bush's physical presence there was the only way to counteract the evident betrayal of the secret presidential codes.

That morning, while this threat was being made against the President, the name of Osama Bin Laden was already being broadcast across the airwaves, as the official suspect. All around Planet Earth his name was being linked forever to the Burning Towers. In vain – and unheard – were his protestations that he had had nothing to do with it. The press should have been able to eliminate any conjectures about a mastermind in the Tora Bora mountains without further ado. Let's listen now to his rather sensible view of who really perpetrated the event, reported on September 28th, as reported in Ummaut, the Urdu-language, Karachi-based Pakistani daily:

> *'The United States should try to trace the perpetrators of these attacks within itself; the people who are a part of the U.S. system, but are dissenting against it...persons who want to make the present century as a century of conflict between Islam and Christianity ... There are intelligence agencies in the U.S., which require billions of dollars worth of funds from the Congress and the government every year.*

> *This [funding issue] was not a big problem during the existence of the former Soviet Union but after that the budget of these agencies has been in danger. They needed an enemy. So, they first started propaganda against Usama and Taleban and then this incident happened. You see, the Bush Administration approved a budget of 40 billion dollars. Where will this huge amount go? It will be provided to the same agencies, which need huge funds and want to exert their importance.*

> *Now they will spend the money for their expansion and for increasing their importance. I will give you an example. Drug smugglers from all over the world are in contact with the U.S. secret agencies. These agencies do not want to eradicate narcotics cultivation and trafficking because their importance will be diminished. The people in the U.S. Drug Enforcement Department are encouraging drug trade so that they could show performance and get millions of dollars worth of budget. General Noriega was made a drug baron by the CIA and, in need, he was made a scapegoat.*

> *In the same way, whether it is President Bush or any other U.S. President, they cannot bring Israel to justice for its human rights abuses or to hold it accountable for such crimes. What is this? Is it not that there exists*

a government within the government in the United Sates? That secret government must be asked as to who carried out the attacks.

'I have already said that we are not hostile to the United States. We are against the [U.S. Government] system, which makes other nations slaves of the United States, or forces them to mortgage their political and economic freedom. This system is totally in control of the American-Jews, whose first priority is Israel, not the United States. It is clear that the American people are themselves the slaves of the Jews and are forced to live according to the principles and laws laid by them...

'The Western media is unleashing such a baseless propaganda, which surprises us but it reflects on what is in their hearts, and gradually they themselves become captive of this propaganda. They become afraid of it and begin to cause harm to themselves. Terror is the most dreaded weapon in modern age and the Western media is mercilessly using it against its own people.'

The western media have indeed become captive of their own fear-inducing propaganda, as the BBC "Power of Nightmares" series so well documented. How can we break out of this spiral of fear and terror? How can America become aware of its degree of subservience to Israel? There is no more career-terminating topic for US journalists. One could try asking the question, "Is there any criminal act that Israel can do without being protected from criticism from the United States?" [42]

One could discuss the brazen Israeli attack on the USS Liberty in 1967, with planes and torpedo boats, an attempt to start a US war against Egypt, with LBJ's connivance – classic false-flag terror. No official protest has been made, nor have reparations been paid. No other nation can attack an American vessel in international waters, killing 34 US Naval servicemen, with impunity [43].

As Admiral Thomas Moorer, Chairman of the US Joint Chiefs of Staff under Ronald Reagan, stated: "I've never seen a President — I don't care who he is — stand up to them [the Israelis]. It just boggles the mind. They always get what they want. The Israelis know what is going on all the time. If the American people understood what a grip those people have got on our government, they would rise up in arms. Our citizens certainly don't have any idea what goes on." [44]

When looking at the 'likely suspects' CIA, NSA, FBI, etc, one doubts whether any of them would have had the necessary combination of profound intelligence, deep wickedness, capacity for effective action, plus the ability to keep a big secret. One is here reminded of the remark by Richard Clarke in Against All Enemies that it would be 'pure fantasy' to suppose 'that the US government can keep a big and juicy secret' [45] on such an issue.

If it is unthinkable to ordinary Americans that a secret military clique would betray their country in this way, it is doubly unthinkable that a foreign power would be able so to corrupt its centers of power as to mastermind this event: it is this double unthinkability which is the safety-catch, which locks the

Michael Chertoff

secret in place, for long enough to get rid of all the evidence. The Neocon love affair with Israel has allowed them to do this. Maybe some things did go wrong, maybe Flight 93 was meant to strike WTC-7, had it not been delayed half an hour, we'll never know. The 'Axis of Evil' CIA-Mossad-M16 is so interconnected that we can hardly know which part of it is responsible, when something happens. It is dedicated to Eternal War and works though Untruth.

On September 10, 2001, the day before 9/11, The Washington Post would run a story about a report issued by the U.S. Army School for Advanced Military Studies, which had commented thus about Mossad: '"Wildcard. Ruthless and cunning. Has capability to target U.S. forces and make it look like a Palestinian/Arab act."

After the event the intelligence analyst George Freeman observed: 'The big winner today, intended or not, is the state of Israel. There is no question that the Israeli leadership is feeling relief.' [46] The name 'Mossad' does not feature in the index of David Ray Griffin's classic, The New Pearl Harbour, however we may need to understand the Mossad's way with its katsas and sayanim.

It has a mere 30 to 37 case officers called katsas operating at any given time. It is able to function with this low level of core katsas because of a much larger network of volunteer Jewish helpers, the Sayanim, who live outside Israel. Their roles are specific to their professions and they are contacted and activated as required. This system allows the Mossad to work with a skeleton staff. [47] The Mossad has always followed its motto: *"By way of deception shall you make war."*

In January 2001, Lyndon Larouche, a well known economist and political figure with worldwide intelligence connections, issued the following insightful prediction:

"A new Middle East war of the general type and implications indicated, will occur if certain specified incidents materialize. It will occur only if the combination of the Israeli government and certain Anglo-American circles wish to have it occur. If they should wish it to occur, the incidents to 'explain' that occurrence, will be arranged." [48]

Source note: This chapter originally appeared as "9/11 and Zion: What was Israel's Role?", *veteranstoday.com,* (22 August, 2012).

References
1. Lucky Larry – Spiegel online, Hamburg, Sep 19, 2001
2. Mike Ruppert, Crossing the Rubicon, 2004, p.585, quoting SPC's website.
3. Ruppert, p.587.
4. They removed it from here: *http://64.233.187.104/search?q=cache:Y_mUdEMLTYUJ:www.thetruthseeker.c o.uk/articl...*
5. Thanks to webmaster Stuart Rixon for info.
6. For Zakheim and Flight 77, *see www.newsfollowup.com/flight77_32.htm*
7. 19th April 2006, American Free Press.
8. Laura Knight Jadczyk and Joe Quinn, 9/11The ultimate Truth 2006, p.108
9. For July 7th connections, see: *www.nineeleven.co.uk/board/viewtopic.php?t=5003*
10. Webster Tarpley, 9/11 SyntheticTerror Made in the USA, 2006, 329.
11. Tarpley, 327.
12. There seem to have been several groups of these Israelis in vans taking photos, at different parts of NewYork.
13. Cameron, Suspected Israeli Spied held by US, Fox News, Dec 11-14, 2001; Tarpley, 328.
14. FOX News. Massive Israeli Spy Operation Discovered in US. Carl Cameron Investigates. Four Part series. December 2001. Google: Israeli spy carl cameron
15. KHOU, Channel 11 (Houston) Federal Buildings Could be in Jeopardy – in Houston and Nationally October 10, 201. Google users enter: israeli art students federal buildings.
16. Jane's Intelligence Digest, 3/13/02; Palm Beach Post, 3/11/02.
17. ABC Channel 4. (Florida). A Mission To Die For. Rudi Dekkers interviewed by

Quentin McDermott. October 21, 2001 Google users enter: rudi dekkers interview.

18. *Wikipedia.com.* The Free Encyclopedia. Mohammed Atta. Google: atta reported passport stolen

19. A group of Jewish 'art student' double-agents lived at 4220 Sheraden Street, Hollywood, Florida, just down the road from where Atta lived at no. 3389: 'the Israeli network was a nationwide operation based in Florida ... [they] lived on the same street in Hollywood, Florida as Mohammed Atta': Len Bracken, The Shadow government, 9/11 and State Terror, 2004 Ill, p.124.

20. Rowland Morgan, Flight 93 Revealed 2006, p.90.

21. The only site is *http://www.publiceye.org/frontpage/911/Missing_Jews.htm* – and, note how its foreword dissociates itself from any views expressed.

22. CNN. September 11. A Memorial. Google users enter: cnn september 11 memorial

23. Newsbytes/Washington Post. Instant message to Israel warned of WTC attack. September 27, 2001. By Brian McWiliams Google users enter: instant messages Israel warned attack

24. The Jerusalem Post in May 2002, .

25. Michael Collins Piper, The High Priests of War, 2005 Washington DC, p39.

26. Ruppert 254.

27. Le Monde, Sep. 13, 2001.

28. Hebrew Israeli radio station, Kol Yisrael, Oct. 3rd report, during an argument in an Israeli cabinet meeting.

29. Ruppert, 591, also 411.

30. Piper, p.13.

31. Piper, ibid.

32. The New York Times. Pentagon Considers Using Lies. By James Dao & Eric Schmitt. February 18,2001. Google: new york times simon worden osi.

33. Google usues enter: feith zionist organization award

34. wagnews, google: Netanyahu/Giuliani -Same London Hotel on 7/7

35. 'ISRAELIS were 9/11 short sale stock buyers, betting on WTC terror strikes.'

36. According to the *New York Times*: Thierry Meyssan The Big Lie 2002 p.44.

37. Bob Woodward, Bush at War, 2003, p.18. This book evades the simple implication of this fact, only making the bland statement, 'it could mean that terrorists had inside information.'

38. Tarpley, p.286.

39. Olsen interviewed by Larry King, three days after 9/11: Janczyk p131.

40. Thierry Meyssan 9/11 The Big Lie, 2002 (L'Effroyable Imposture), 44.

41. Ruppert Ch 10, re the PROMIS software.

42. Recently-retired U.S. Brigadier General James J. David, in an article entitled "A Passionate Attachment to Israel"

43. On 8 June, during the 6-day War, off the Sinai coast: Peter Hounam, Operation Cyanide, 2003.

44. Google: admiral moorer boggles mind. Paul Findley, They Dare to speak Out, People and Institutions confront Israel's lobby, 2003.

45. Richard Clarke, Against All Enemies, NY 2004, p.126.

46. His internet website *www.stratfor.com*: Jadczyk, 110.

47. Jadzcyk, p.118.

48. *Executive Intelligence Review.* Lyndon Larouche. January 2001. Google: larouche middle east war implications

5

9/11 J'accuse:
Zelikow, Cheney, Rumsfeld,
Bush and O'Brien

by Jim Fetzer

As the founder of Scholars for 9/11 Truth (2005), the editor of THE 9/11 CONSPIRACY (2007), the chair of the Madison conference (2007) and the co-chair of The Vancouver Hearings (2011), it has been astonishing to me to discover that the atrocities of 9/11 were not simply allowed to happen but come closer to having been produced as a Hollywood-style spectacle, with phantom flights, faked phone calls, and fabricated crash sites.

Anyone who wants to continue in a state of naive belief in their government as a nurturing institution that is dedicated to the best interests of the American people and to promoting their welfare should read no further, because 9/11 appears to have been a national security event that was approved at the highest levels of the Bush/Cheney administration, including the CIA, the Pentagon, the NSA and The White House itself. When consideration is given the the totality of the evidence, no alternative explanation is reasonable.

For those who find this difficult to believe, check out "Seismic Proof: 9/11 was an inside job" by Gordon Ross and Craig Furlong, who undertook the systematic study of reports from Willie Rodriquez, who was the senior custodian in the North Tower and

reported that an enormous explosion had taken place in the subbasements even before there were any effects from the impact of a plane.

Original seismic and Commission times.

Table 1				
AA Flt 11				
	2001	LDEO	8:46:26	Original seismic
	2004	Commission	8:46:40	(14 seconds difference)
UA Flt 175				
	2001	LDEO	9:02:54	Original seismic
	2004	Commission	9:03:11	(17 seconds difference)

They used very precise seismic data from a lab run by Columbia University and compared it with very precise FAA and military radar data and discovered that he was right: there had been explosions in the sub-basements of both towers, which occurred 14 and 17 seconds prior to the hits of those planes on either tower.

But this is only the tip of an enormous iceberg, which we can now seen encompasses the faking of the major events of 9/11, including the crash of Flight 93 in Shanksville, the hit by Flight 77 on the Pentagon, and both Flights 11 hitting the North Tower and Flight 175 the South. It seems incredible, I know, but the evidence is there and, as I explain here, we know who the perps were who brought us 9/11. They were among the most familiar faces on our political stage at the time, actors one and all.

(#1) Evidentiary Submission #1 of 5 by James H. Fetzer

At the Vancouver Hearings, held 15-17 June 2012, judges asked participants to write an evidentiary submission of at least two persons regarding their complicity in the 9/11 plot.

I submit the names of *Philip Zelikow, Richard B. Cheney, Donald Rumsfeld, George W. Bush,* and *Lt. Col. Steve O'Brien, MNANG,* based upon the facts as noted and sourced below.

Name: *Philip Zelikow*

Title at the Time of his Offense: *Executive Director, The 9/11 Commission*

Probable Cause: In his capacity as Executive Director of The 9/11 Commission and the principal author of its report, Philip Zelikow caused false claims to be disseminated about the events of 9/11, including the following:

(1) that Flight 11 had hit the North Tower;
(2) that Flight 77 had hit the Pentagon;
(3) that Flight 93 had crashed in Shanksville; and,
(4) that Flight 175 had hit the South Tower.

Information published in THE 9/11 COMMISSION REPORT (2004) regarding (1) though (4) is demonstrably false because:

(a) Bureau of Transportation Statistics (BTS) records show that Flight 11 was not scheduled for 9/11;1

(b) BTS records show that Flight 77 was likewise not scheduled for 9/11;2

(c) FAA Registration Records show that the plane corresponding to Flight 93 was not deregistered (formally taken out of service) until 28 September 2005;3

(d) FAA Registration Records show that the plane corresponding to Flight 175 was likewise not deregistered (formally taken out of service) until 28 September 2005; 4

(e) Pilots for 9/11 Truth has established that Flight 93 was in the air but was over Champaign-Urbana, IL, subsequent to the time it was reported to have crashed in Shanksville,PA ; 5 and,

(f) Pilots for 9/11 Truth has also established that Flight 175 was in the air, but was over Harrisburg and Pittsburgh, PA, long after the time it was reported to have crashed into the South Tower. 6

Summary: Planes that were not even in the air cannot have crashed on 9/11; and planes that crashed on 9/11 cannot have still been in the air four years later. Zelikow appears to have been selected for his appointment as Executive Director of The 9/11 Commission, at least in part, because his area of academic expertise prior to joining the Bush administration turns out to have been "the creation and maintenance of, in his words, 'public myths' or 'public presumptions'".7 In addition to using flights that did not occur and crashes that did not take place, specifically:

(5) contrary to (1), Flight 11 did not hit the North Tower;
(6) contrary to (2), Flight 77 did not hit the Pentagon;
(7) contrary to (3), Flight 93 did not crashed in Shanksville; and,
(8) contrary to (4), Flight 175 did not hit the South Tower;

there is abundant additional proof that what the public was presented in THE 9/11 COMMISSION REPORT (2004) is itself a "public myth", whose framework of four alleged "hijackings" and "plane crashes" is itself a contrived fabrication, which makes the person responsible for that report an accessory after the fact, as a person who assists in the commission of a crime by helping to cover it up.

Further proof that THE 9/11 COMMISSION REPORT was intended to deceive the American people includes that the government has not been able to prove the alleged "hijackers" were aboard any of those planes;8 several of them turned up alive and well after 9/11;9 and the phone calls alleged to have been made from the panes were faked10. Virtually everything it claims about 9/11 is false.

1 Edward Hendrie, 9/11: ENEMIES FOREIGN AND DOMESTIC (2011),
2 Hendrie, p. 9 The BTS would subsequently revise its data base and thus make itself an accessory after the fact. See http://thewebfairy.com/ holmgren/1177.html
3 http://www.911blogger.com/news/2006-08-23/strange-saga-911- planes NOTE: The official FAA site, http://registry.faa.gov/, shows no records for any of the four planes.
4 http://www.911blogger.com/news/2006-08-23/strange-saga-911- planes NOTE: The official FAA site, http://registry.faa.gov/, shows no records for any of the four planes.
5 United 93 Still Airborne After Alleged Crash – According To ATC/Radar http://pilotsfor911truth.org/united-93-still-airborne.html
6 ACARS CONFIRMED – 9/11 AIRCRAFT AIRBORNE LONG AFTER CRASH UNITED 175 IN THE VICINITY OF HARRISBURG AND PITTSBURGH, PA http://pilotsfor911truth.org/ACARS-CONFIRMED- 911-AIRCRAFT-AIRBORNE-LONG-AFTER-CRASH.html
7 http://en.wikipedia.org/w/index.php?title=Philip_D._ Zelikow&oldid=56836687
8 Elias Davidsson, "There is no evidence that Muslims committed the crime of 9/11"http://www.opednews.com/articles/There-is-no-evidence- that-by-Elias-Davidsson-100811-366.html
9 David Ray Griffin, THE 9/11 COMMISSION REPORT: OMISSIONS AND DISTORTIONS (2005), pp. 19-20; sources, p. 298.
10 David Ray Griffin, "Phone Calls from the 9/11 Airliners"http://www. globalresearch.ca/index.php?context=va&aid=16924

(#2) Evidentiary Submission #2 of 5 by James H. Fetzer

At the Vancouver Hearings, held 15-17 June 2012, judges asked participants to write an evidentiary submission of at least two persons regarding their complicity in the 9/11 plot.

I submit the names of *Philip Zelikow, Richard B. Cheney, Donald Rumsfeld, George W. Bush*, and *Lt. Col. Steve O'Brien, MNANG*, based upon the facts as noted and sourced below.

Name: ***Richard B. Cheney***

Title at the Time of his Offense: *Vice President of the United States*

Probable Cause: In his capacity as Vice President of United States, Richard Cheney issued orders that a plane approaching the Pentagon not be shot down, which thus allowed the plane to approach the building unimpeded.

This appears to have been the plane that flew toward and then swerved over the Pentagon, while explosives were set off in the building, in an elaborate charade, which was used as the pretext for the following "declaration of war", and to justify invasions of Afghanistan and of Iraq; and subsequently made false claims about the events of 9/11. Consider the following:

Department of Transportation Secretary Norman Mineta tesified to The 9/11 Commission about his experience in the Presidential Emergency Operating Center with Vice President Richard Cheney, as (what would be identified as) American Airlines Flight 77 approached the Pentagon. According to Mineta, the vice president was asked about orders concerning the approaching aircraft:

> *There was a young man who had come in and said to the vice president, 'The plane is 50 miles out. The plane is 30 miles out.' And when it got down to, 'The plane is 10 miles out,' the young man also said to the vice president, 'Do the orders still stand?' And the vice president turned and whipped his neck around and said, 'Of course the orders still stand. Have you heard anything to the contrary?' Well, at the time I didn't know what all that meant.* 11

Commissioner Lee Hamilton queried if the order was to shoot down the plane, to which Mineta replied that he did not know that specifically.12 That interpretation, moreover, appears to be inconsistent with the aide's concern. Since planes were being used as weapons, an order to shoot it down should not have caused any concern: You lose the pilots and the

passengers, but not the personnel and the property that is being targeted. Instead,125 lives were lost at the Pentagon. 13

Mineta's testimony to the Commission on Flight 77 differs rather significantly from the account provided in the 22 January 2002 edition of *The Washington Post*, as reported by Bob Woodward and Dan Balz in the series "10 Days in September".14 This article reports that the conversation between Cheney and the aide occurred at 9:55 am, about 30 minutes later than the time Mineta cited (9:26 am) during his testimony to the 9/11 Commission. However, Cheney's earlier arrival was independently confirmed both by Condoleezza Rice15 and by Richard Clarke. 16

Cheney's remarks on "Meet the Press" (16 September 2001) support the earlier entry, 17 as does a newly discovered Secret Service document.18 The Woodward and Balz article thus appears to have been an effort to conceal his earlier arrival at the bunker, when the exchange with the aide occurred. Remarkably, the day after I appeared on "Hannity & Colmes" and reported Mineta's testimony on FOX NEWS, 19 The White House announced that he had retired from the government. 20

Summery: News leaks are a tried and true method for disseminating both true information (when it would be helpful) and false (when it would be more helpful). The Woodward and Balz article appears to have been intended to defect public attention from Cheney's presence prior to the alleged hit on the Pentagon, since his order—that it not be shot down—facilitated the fabrication of a fake attack.

It therefore reflects the consciousness of guilt, as did the abrupt "retirement" of the Transportation Secretary immediately after I publicized his story on FOX NEWS.

The Pentagon is among the most heavily defended building in the world. If the order had been to shoot it down, it would have been shot down. The plane now appears to have been a prop in an elaborate charade. This makes Cheney not only an accessory after the fact but an accomplice to the mass murder of 125 persons. While this aircraft itself does not appear to have been their cause of death (because they appear to have been killed by a series of explosions that simulated a plane crash), many of the dead were budget analysts and financial experts attempting to locate the $2.3 trillion Rumsfeld reported missing on 9/10.

11 Mineta's testimony is at http://www.9-11commission.gov/archive/hearing2/9-11Commission_Hearing_2003-05-23.htm

12 http://en.wikipedia.org/wiki/Norman_Mineta#cite_note-Commission_Hearing-4

13 http://libertyforlife.com/eye-openers/911/pentagon_missile_911_vict.html

14 Dan Balz and Bob Woodward, "10 Days in September", The Washington Post,http://www.washingtonpost.com/wp-dyn/articles/A42754-2002Jan26_3.html

15 David Ray Griiffin, "9/11 Contradictions: When Did Cheney Enter the Underground Bunker?"http://globalresearch.ca/index.php?context=va&aid=8788

16 Griiffin,http://globalresearch.ca/index.php?context=va&aid=8788

17 http://www.youtube.com/watch?v=Ibdl2OogFPI

18 http://forums.randi.org/showpost.php?p=6959886&postcount=131

19 22 June 2006, First appearance on "Hannity & Colmes" discussing Mineta's 9/11 testimony:http://www.youtube.com/watch?v=xQInlZvb_E8

20 23 June 2006, Announcement of Mineta's retirement: http://georgewbush-whitehouse.archives.gov/news/releases/2006/06/20060623-9.html

(#3) Evidentiary Submission #3 of 5 by James H. Fetzer

At the Vancouver Hearings, held 15-17 June 2012, judges asked participants to write an evidentiary submission of at least two persons regarding their complicity in the 9/11 plot.

I submit the names of *Philip Zelikow, Richard B. Cheney, Donald Rumsfeld, George W. Bush*, and *Lt. Col. Steve O'Brien, MNANG*, based upon the facts as noted and sourced below.

Name: ***Donald Rumsfeld***

Title at the Time of his Offense: *United States Secretary of Defense*

Probable Cause: In his capacity as the Secretary of Defense, Donald Rumsfeld actively participated in arranging for the occurrence of the Pentagon attack and by making false claims about the events of 9/11, including the following:

(1) The SOP for interdicting hijacked aircraft was change on 1 June 2001 so that it would now require the personal authorization of the Secretary of Defense;1

(2) Rumsfeld claimed to be unaware of any threats to the Pentagon, where he was located during the 9/11 attacks, until Flight 77 crashed into the building;2

(3) Rumsfeld. Condoleezza Rice, and other officials claimed they had no idea that planes could be used as weapons, which is contradicted on many grounds;3

(4) The "official account" of the Pentagon attack is not only wholly unsupported by the available evidence but is neither aerodynamically nor physically possible:

(a) the plane is alleged to have skimmed the lawn at over 500 mph, but that is not aerodynamically possible due to the phenomenon of "ground effect",4 which would preclude the plane getting any closer than 60' of the ground;

(b) the plane is alleged to have taken out a series of metal lampposts without affecting its flight path, which is physically impossible, because they would have ripped the wing off the plane and caused its fuel to have exploded;5

(c) the alleged "hit point" in the building is too small to accommodate a 100-ton airliner, where there is no massive stack of aluminum debris, wings, tail, bodies, seats or luggage, and not even the engines were recovered;6

(d) even though the Pentagon is surrounded by cameras, the only frame that it has released shows the image of a plane far too small to have been a Boeing 757, so the government's own evidence contradicts its own story;7

(e) after the civilian lime-green fire trucks had extinguished the modest fires, the Pentagon lawn was clear, green, and unblemished by any debris from the crash of a large airplane, which should have been widely distributed;8

(f) Major Gen. Albert Stubblebine, USA (ret.), who was formerly in charge of all us military photographic intelligence, confirmed that no large plane had hit the Pentagon based upon his careful study of photographic evidence;9

(g) Other witnesses and evidence, including April Gallup, photographic and video evidence, substantiates that no Boeing 757 hit the Pentagon and that, according to BTS records, Flight 77 was not even in the air on 9/11;10

(5) Secretary Rumsfeld predicts the Pentagon may be hit and is missing in action for at least 20 minutes before emerging on the lawn helping to carry the injured;11

(6) In his first public response, he accents that Secretary of the Army Tom White was responsible for "incidents like this", shrugging off his own responsibility;12

(7) Tom White, a former Enron executive, had been appointed to that position on 31 May 2001, the day before the new hijacking instructions had been issued.13

Summary: Even this brief and partial survey indicates that Donald Rumsfeld was too clever by half, appointing a patsy to take the blame the day before he changed the hijacking SOP, which appears to have been part of the plan to be sure there would be no NORAD response to the alleged hijackings.

The claims made about "the Pentagon attack" are not only provably false but are not even aeronautically and physically possible. No reasonable alternative competes with the conclusion that Rumsfeld was a principal in planning the atrocities of 9/11, which not only caused the deaths of 125 persons who were in the building at the time but betrayed his responsibilities to the people of the United States as their Secretary of Defense, and deserves prosecution to the fullest extent of the law.

1http://911research.wtc7.net/planes/analysis/norad/docs/intercept_proc.pdf
2 http://www.defense.gov/transcripts/transcript.aspx?transcriptid=1886
3 http://911review.com/means/standdown.html
4 http://www.veteranstoday.com/2010/08/13/nila-sagadevan-911-the-impossibility-of-flying-heavy-aircraft-without-training/
5 Nicely illustrated by a Lockeed Constellation hitting wooden telephone poles: http://www.youtube.com/watch?v=p4rYj9UmmE4 (turn down the audio first)
6 http://jamesfetzer.blogspot.com/2010/01/what-didnt-happen-at-pentagon.html
7 http://www.veteranstoday.com/2011/07/05/inside-job-seven-questions-about-911/

8 *http://jamesfetzer.blogspot.com/2012/06/official-account-of-pentagon-attack-is.html*

9 *http://www.youtube.com/watch?v=daNr_TrBw6E*

10 *http://jamesfetzer.blogspot.com/2012/06/official-account-of-pentagon-attack-is.html*

11 *http://www.historycommons.org/timeline.jsp?timeline=complete_911_timeline&day_of_9/11=donaldrumsfeld*

12 *http://www.patriotresource.com/wtc/federal/0911/DoD.html)*

13 *http://911research.wtc7.net/planes/analysis/norad/docs/intercept_proc.pdf*

(#4) Evidentiary Submission #4 of 5 by James H. Fetzer

At the Vancouver Hearings, held 15-17 June 2012, judges asked participants to write an evidentiary submission of at least two persons regarding their complicity in the 9/11 plot.

I submit the names of *Philip Zelikow, Richard B. Cheney, Donald Rumsfeld, George W. Bush,* and *Lt. Col. Steve O'Brien, MNANG*, based upon the facts as noted and sourced below..

Name: ***George W. Bush***

Title at the Time of his Offense: *President of the United States*

Probable Cause: In his capacity as President of the United States, George W. Bush participated in planning the occurrence of and made false claims about the events of 9/11 to conceal their origins, an especially revealing example of which is a statement he made implicating himself.

On 4 December 2001, in Orlando, FL, he said the following about his visit to Booker Elementary School on 9/11:1

> *"I was sitting outside the classroom, waiting to go in, and I saw an airplane hit the tower. You know, the TV was obviously on. And I used to fly myself. And I said to myself, 'Well, there's one terrible pilot.' It must have been a terrible accident."2*

The alleged first hit on the North Tower took place at 8:46 AM/ET to be followed by the alleged second on the South Tower at 9:03 AM/ET.3 Bush's motorcade had left the Colony Beach and Tennis Resort to head to Booker at 8:35 AM/ET.4 He arrived there at 8:55 AM/ET.5 Bush was told of the second hit at 9:06 AM/ET.6

Once he learned there had been two attacks, there was no rational justification to think the first had been "an accident". Bush and Condoleezza Rice would initially feign that of the first hit, but they could not possibly have known.7 And he cannot have seen the Naudet video, which would not be broadcast until 1 AM/ET, 9/12.8

(a) An effort has been made to dismiss Bush's remark about having seen the first hit "on television" as having been a mistake;9
(b) but he would repeat the same story during a town meeting in Ontario, CA, 5 January 2002, including having viewed it on TV;10
(c) a National Geographic Special that almost certainly included his recitation of his television viewing experience has been pulled;11 and,
(d) another—which is an obvious attempt to revise history–has been made available instead, where he recounts his story very differently:12

"I had been notified that a plane had hit the WTC. At first I thought it was a light aircraft. And my reaction was, 'Man, either the weather was bad or something extraordinary happened to the pilot'. I then informed some of my staff members to provide help to New York City—whatever help was needed—and walked into the classroom".

Summary: President George W. Bush committed a gaffe when he spoke about his experiences on 9/11, candidly revealing that he had seen the first hit on TV, which has to have occurred while his motorcade was en route between Colony Beach and Tennis Resort and Booker Elementary School.

This means that the Secret Service had a television camera focused on the North Tower when only those involved in planning the events of 9/11 would have had reason to watch the side of WTC-1. He could not have seen the hit on TV any other way.

Eager to convey the impression he thought it was "an accident", he revealed too much.

Removing "George W. Bush: The 9/11 Interview" and the substitution of another in which he contradicts his previous reports displays consciousness of guilt and the desire to tamper with evidence. But it was a risk that had to be run, because his having watched the first hit on Secret Service television was such an obvious indication of governmental complicity in 9/11. Given our other findings, such as:

(1) the fabrication of the four "crash sites" (see Evidentiary Submission #1);
(2) the failure to prove any of the "hijackers" were aboard any of the planes;13
(3) the faking of the phone calls alleged to have been made from the planes;14

and further forms of proof,15 it becomes increasingly apparent that the atrocities of 9/11 was a national security event that was approved at the highest levels of the American government, including The White House, NSA, CIA, Joint Chiefs and Department of Defense, where even the president appears to have been an accessory to the crime and to have committed treason against the United States.

1 http://www.cwalocal4250.org/news/binarydata/9-11%20Government%20 Inconsitencies.pdf
2 http://www.liveleak.com/view?i=dbc_1188804768
3 THE 9/11 COMMISSION REPORT (2004), for example, p. 285
4 http://www.historycommons.org/timeline.jsp?day_of_9/11=bush&timelin e=complete_911_timeline
5 Ibid.
6 Ibid.
7 Ibid.
8 http://911blimp.net/vid_Naudet.shtml
9 http://www.cwalocal4250.org/news/binarydata/
10 http://web.ebscohost.com/ehost/detail?sid=af92984c-5f77-483d-9a73-4732f3226815%40sessionmgr13&vid=1&hid=10&bdata=JmF1dGh0 eXBlPWdlbyZnZW9jdXN0aWQ9czczMjQ5NjQmc2l0ZT1laG9zdC1sa XZl#db=f5h&AN=6059432
11 "George W. Bush: The 9/11 Interview" (NO LONGER AVAILABLE) http://topdocumentaryfilms.com/george-w-bush-the-9-11-interview/
12 "The President looks back", http://video.nationalgeographic.com/video/ national-geographic-channel/all-videos/ngc-the-president-looks-back/
13 http://www.opednews.com/articles/There-is-no-evidence-that-by-Elias-

Davidsson-100811-366.html
14 http://www.globalresearch.ca/index.php?context=va&aid=16924
15 http://www.veteranstoday.com/2011/09/10/20-reasons-the-official-account-of-911-is-wrong/

(#5) Evidentiary Submission #5 of 5 by James H. Fetzer

At the Vancouver Hearings, held 15-17 June 2012, judges asked participants to write an evidentiary submission of at least two persons regarding their complicity in the 9/11 plot.

I submit the names of *Philip Zelikow, Richard B. Cheney, Donald Rumsfeld, George W. Bush*, and *Lt. Col. Steve O'Brien, MNANG*, based upon the facts as noted and sourced below.

Name: **Lt. Col. Steve O'Brien, Minnesota Air National Guard (MNANG)**

Title at the Time of his Offense: *Pilot of C-130H circling the Pentagon on 9/11*

Probable Cause: Among the most striking and indisputable aspects of 9/11 was the utter failure of NORAD, the NMCC and the FAA to coordinate any military response to (what were alleged to have been the hijacking of four commercial carriers, spanning an interval of time from 8:14 AM/ET, when the first reports of the possible hijacking of Flight 11 surfaced until after the Pentagon had been "hit" by Flight 77 at 9:38 AM/ET, over 1:14 hours later, even though a response to a hijacking should have taken less than 10 minutes.1 The failure to follow SOP is so blatant that there is no reasonable alternative to a deliberate "stand down".2

THE 9/11 COMMISSION REPORT (2004), minimizes the absence of response and the time available to scramble fighters as if it was an innocuous event.3 One of the most peculiar aspects of the Pentagon attack is how our nation's military leaders could not have known that a plane was approaching the building.4 This appears to be untrue on at least two grounds: first, that Vice President Cheney had been informed by an aide that a plane was headed toward the building by an aide and issued an order that the plane not be shot down (see Submission #2).

Another is that Lt. Col. Steve O'Brien was piloting a military C-130H cargo plane (call named, "Gofer 06") in the vicinity of the Pentagon, where he and his crew were reported to have witnessed the crash of Flight 77 into the building as well as the crash of Flight 93 into the ground at Shanksville.5 Since O'Brien is said to have followed Flight 77—and to have identified it as a Boeing 757—it appears to be impossible that Pentagon officials, with whom he was in radio communication, could not have known a plane was approaching.

The "official account" cannot be true, since it violates laws of aerodynamics and of physics (see Submission #3).

At 9:42 AM/ET, the FAA directed that all planes in the air should land6—minutes after the purported plane crash—but Gofer 06 remained airborne, apparently to perform a task essential to the cover-up.

That no Boeing 757 hit the Pentagon is not only established by the impossibility of the official trajectory—just skimming the ground at over 500 mph and taking out a series of lampposts without damage to the plane or affecting its trajectory—but also by the virtual absence of debris appropriate to the crash of 100-ton airliner: no massive pile of aluminum debris, no wings, no tail, no bodies, seats or luggage, such as would be expected.7 Not even the engines, which are virtually indestructible, were recovered from the site.

Photographs of the clear, green, Pentagon lawn—over 30 minutes following the attack, when a section of the building collapsed—display a stunning absence of debris.8 9

As even Jamie McIntrye reported live on CNN, there was no indication that any large plane had crashed anywhere near the Pentagon.10

Pieces of plane fuselage and other debris would show up on the lawn, even though no plane had crashed there, which raises the question of where it came from. It would have been awkward to have officers or enlisted men carry pieces of debris out on the lawn, but it would not have been difficult to have dropped it from the C-130H that O'Brien was piloting.

One especially notable piece of fuselage has been tracked back to the crash of a Boeing 757 that had occurred in Cali, Columbia, in 1995.11

Summary: Debris that appeared on the Pentagon lawn more than 30 minutes after the alleged crash of Flight 77 cannot have come from a non-existent crash and must have been planted by military personnel or dropped from the C-130H that was circling the building. When I explained to the BBC that it had to have come from the plane for its second "Conspiracy Files: 9/11 Ten Years On", they featured Lt. Col. Steve O'Brien, who expressed disgust at the implication that he had participated in faking the plane crash by dropping debris from his plane.12 13

But there is no reasonable alternative. The alleged crash did not occur and any claims to have seen the plane hit the building cannot be true. It would have been impossible for the cargo door of his C-130H to open for the drop and the pilot be unaware of it; moreover, the C-130H is a special version with electronic warfare capabilities and may have played other important roles on 9/11.14 The evidence thus substantiates that Lt. Col. O'Brien remained airborne because he was "on a mission", complicit in the crimes of 9/11, and actively engaged in their cover-up.

1 An excellent discussion is David Ray Griffin, THE 9/11 COMMISSION REPORT: OMISSIONS AND DISTORTIONS (2005), Chapter 11. "NMCC" is the National Military Command Center.
2 Ibid., especially pages 146-153; and http://www.flcv.com/offcom77.html.
3 THE 9/11 COMMISSION REPORT (2004), Chapter 1, especially pages 24-40.
4 David Ray Griffin, 9/11 CONTRADICTIONS (2008), Chapter 11.
5 http://digwithin.net/2011/12/04/gofer-and-trout-questions-on-two-flights-out-of-andrews-afb-on-911/#_edn2 That claim is disputed athttp://www.abovetopsecret.com/forum/thread312008/pg1
6 http://shoestring911.blogspot.com/2008/08/andrews-air-force-base-stand-down-how.html
7 http://jamesfetzer.blogspot.com/2010/01/what-didnt-happen-at-pentagon.html
8 http://jamesfetzer.blogspot.com/2012/06/official-account-of-pentagon-attack-is.html
9 http://www.veteranstoday.com/2011/09/03/the-bbcs-instrument-of-911-misinformation/
10 http://www.youtube.com/watch?v=C02dE5VKeck
11 http://jamesfetzer.blogspot.com/2011/07/seven-questions-about-911.html
12 http://www.bbc.co.uk/programmes/b0148yz5 is as close as I have been able to find it.
13 http://www.veteranstoday.com/2011/09/03/the-bbcs-instrument-of-911-misinformation/
14 Email correspondence with military aircraft expert, Dennis Cimino

Source note: This chapter originally appeared as "J'accuse: Zelikow, Cheney, Rumsfeld, Bush and O'Brian", *veteranstoday.com* (30 August 2012).

6

Is 9/11 Research "Anti-Semitic"?

by Jim Fetzer

A kind of hysteria regarding 9/11 research has surfaced in multiple forms, the most blatant of which has been an assault by FOX host Glenn Beck, who has characterized students of 9/11 as "anarchists", "terrorists" and "Holocaust deniers".

The comparison with Holocaust deniers is patently false, of course, because Holocaust deniers deny that the (German) government committed atrocities, while 9/11 investigators affirm that the (American) government committed them. They could not be more opposite. The use of the phrase can be politically potent, nonetheless, because it subtly conveys the prospect that anti-Semitism may be involved, no matter how faulty the analogy.

This is hardly the first time that students of 9/11 have been accused of that offense. At the "Accountability Conference" held in Chandler, AZ, February 2007, for example, the issue arose repeatedly during a press conference, parts of which are included in a 4:33 minute YouTube piece entitled, "Truthers Defend Holocaust Denier", but none of us was defending Holocaust denial.

Some of us, including me, were defending a scholar's research on 9/11, even though he is very critical of Israel and may even be anti-Semitic, which is not the same thing.

Suppose that is the case. If he were anti-Semitic, which

AZ 9/11 Accountability Press conference

I personally deplore, would that render his 9/11 research, which is principally focused on the physical destruction of the World Trade Center, of no value?

Should it therefore be discounted, discarded, or ignored?

"Anti-Semitism"

That is a rather ironic claim to make, because "anti-Semitism" commits the same offense of discounting, discarding, or ignoring a person, their work or other attainments on the ground of their ethnicity, religion, or race. To contend that a person's research on 9/11, for example, cannot be taken seriously because they are anti-Semitic is parallel to discounting a person's opinions because they are Jewish.

Either way, the conclusion (of dismissing their argument) because of other of their personal traits commits the ad hominem fallacy or, more broadly, the genetic fallacy. An argument can be well-founded regardless of its source, including the characteristics of the individuals who advanced it, who may be lacking in virtue in other respects. Arguments have to be assessed on the basis of logic and evidence, not the personal virtues of those who advance them.

We all have our own intellectual strengths and weaknesses, where we may not be as good in mathematics, for example, as we are in history. Our shortcomings with respect to mathematics do not diminish our excellence in history!

Interestingly, a 9/11 researcher, Gregg Hoover, is filing a lawsuit against Glenn Beck for defamation, which appears to be entirely appropriate. Notice that Beck is not simply attacking specific research on 9/11 but the very idea of research on 9/11. Some of the most prominent students of 9/11 are widely admired scholars, such as David Ray Griffin and Peter Dale Scott. Do their efforts to bring the truth about 9/11 to the American people make them racists?

The issue of anti-Semitism has to be addressed on its own merits. It has been used as a political club to attack research on 9/11 whenever consideration has been given to the possibility of Israeli involvement in the crime.

That is hardly a stretch, since Israel has probably benefited from 9/11 more than any other political entity. 9/11 has been used to justify wars of aggression abroad against Iraq and Afghanistan—which President Obama, alas, seems to be expanding—and to constrain civil liberties at home in the form of the so-called PATRIOT Act, The Military Commissions Act, and the massive illegal surveillance of the American people, which, alas, he has yet to repeal.

9/11 and the
Neo-Con Agenda

by Dr. James H. Fetzer
Founder, Scholars for 9/11 Truth
April 22, 2008

*We cannot support the troops by "staying the
course" when the Commander-in-Chief is
marching them over a cliff.*
　　　—Jim Fetzer (15 April 2008)

There is a crucial link between the anti-war movement and the 9/11 truth movement, because exposing the truth about 9/11 destroys the justification for those wars.

We are told not to discuss conspiracy theories, but if 19 Islamic fundamentalists hijacked four planes, outfoxed the most sophisticated air defense system in the world, and perpetrated these atrocities under the control of a guy off in a cave in Afghanistan, then 9/11 involved a conspiracy.

If we can't talk about conspiracies, we can't talk about 9/11. Why would this administration want to suppress public discussion of 9/11? To conceal the truth about the war or to conceal the truth about 9/11?

I addressed some of these issues during the Ron Paul "Freedom Rally" held on the grass in front of the United States Capitol Building on 15 April 2008. The article I published that laid out what I had said there, "9/11 and the Neocon Agenda", OpEdNews (April 22, 2008), was even featured on the front page of The Daily Paul the same day, 22 April 2008, it appeared here.

During the course of my analysis of who might have been responsible for 9/11, I explicitly addressed the possibility of Israeli complicity in the crime. I wrote, What about Israel?

But could Israel have been involved? There are disturbing indications. The five "dancing Israels" were observed on a roof across the Hudson in New Jersey drinking and celebrating as they filmed the destruction of the Twin Towers. Complaints by neighbors led to their apprehension in a van. The driver told the arresting officer, "We are not your problem. The Palestinians are your problem!" They would be incarcerated for 71 days until an assistant to then-Attorney General John Ashcroft directed their release.

They returned to Israel where three of them appeared on Israeli TV and explained they were there to document the destruction of the Twin Towers. Obviously, they could not have done that without knowing the Twin Towers were going to be destroyed.

"I GOT A MESSAGE ON THAT UH PLANE, IT'S A BIG TRUCK WITH A MURAL PAINTED OF A... OF AN AIR-PLANE DIVING INTO NEW YORK CITY AND EXPLODING"

The man who directed their release was Michael Chertoff, our 2nd Director of Homeland Security, who is a joint US/ Israeli citizen. The Controller of the Pentagon at the time $2.3 trillion went missing was Dov Zokheim, another joint US/Israeli citizen. Others in the administration with dual citizenship include Paul Wolfowitz, Elliot Abrams, Richard Pearle, Douglas Feith, "Scooter" Libby, Eliot Cohen, and John Bolton. Do any of these names sound familiar?

An especially interesting case is Michael Mukasey, our new Attorney General, who was also the judge on litigation between Larry Silverstein and insurance companies over the events of 9/11.

Who runs this country? About two weeks after 9/11, Ariel Sharon said, "We own America, and the Americans know it". If Israel was involved in 9/11, the American people are entitled to know.

I was confident that I would be attacked for being "anti-Semitic" formaking such observations, no matter how factual, so I addressed the issue head-on: I will be accused of anti-Semitism for telling you facts in the public domain. But it is not "anti-Semitic" to criticize the state of Israel, the government of the state of Israel, or the policies and actions of the state ofIsrael.Anti-Semitism involves discounting or belittling persons on the basisof their religious orientation or their ethnic origins.

It is not anti-Semitic to object to the expansion of illegal settlements, the starvation and killing of the Palestinian people, or the butchering of a peace activist with a bulldozer!

For these gross violations of human rights, we have the government of Israel to thank. We need laws to keep dual citizens from decision-making and policy-shaping position in the US government. Who knows whose loyalty they respect? I call upon those with joint citizenship to resign their positions in the interests of the nation—the United States of America!

It was my belief that I had been successful in clarifying the difference between anti-Semitism and research on possible Israeli complicity in the events of 9/11, but I was soon to discover that conveying this to the American people might pose a even greater challenge than I had supposed and that another distinction would require clarification, in particular, the difference between "anti-Semitism" and "anti-Zionism".

The principal problem encountered with 9/11 research is not a lack of data, where disproofs of the official account are virtually boundless—see, for example, more than fifteen key findings in "Why doubt 9/11?"—but reaching the American people with what we have discovered. Thus, when Michael Morrissey, a linguist living in Germany, created a new forum at *911aletheia. ning.com*, therefore, I was delighted, since it offered the promise of interactive research among students of the case and an additional opportunity to convey our findings to the American people through a public (or quasi-public) forum. With Michael's encouragement, therefore, I began posting many of my studies, including "9/11 and the Neocon Agenda".

As the founder of Scholars for 9/11 Truth, whose web site I maintain at 911scholars.org, I have posted links to two version of that article and a clip of my presentation at the Capitol. Both include their own links in t urn to supporting documents. One is a simple text version, while the other is an illustrated version at *americanfirstbooks.com*. I was therefore taken aback when Michael objected to my posting the illustrated version because, he told me, it appears at *americafirstbooks.com*, which he said is an "anti-Semitic" site. He thought there should be no association with such a site and insisted I remove it from 911aletheia, even though it only appeared in my own blog.

In deference to his preferences, I posted a link instead. *Americafirstbooks. com* is maintained by Major William Fox, a former Marine Corps intelligence officer. In collaboration with Capt. Eric May and SFC Donald Buswell, both of whom are former Army intelligence, I, a former Marine Corps officer, had co-authored several "false flag" warnings.

Because we are familiar with the evidence that 9/11 was "an inside job", we have been acutely concerned that Bush/Cheney administration, elements of which—including Dick Cheney, Donald Rumsfeld, and even General Richard Myers—appear to have been profoundly involved in might want to create another pretext for further "false flag" attacks and have issued warnings about them when there were causes for concern. The warnings, principally the product of research by Capt. May and Major Fox, are archived many places More importantly, while I do not believe that either Capt. May or Major Fox is anti-Semitic, I have no doubt that they are "anti-Zionist".

The word "Zionism" was not in my functional vocabulary, I just say, until very recently. It has always been a vague term to me, which led me to feature several guests on my interview program, "The Real Deal", including Steven  Lendman (on March 13, 2009) and Barry Chamish (on March 30, 2009), where our interviews are archived at *radiofetzer.blogspot.com*. I formed the opinion that the concept of Zionism combines a belief in Jewish superiority with the presumption of entitlement to the lands that Jews (presumably) once occupied in Palestine, regardless of the consequences for Palestinians. This is an issue I would subsequently discuss with David Ray Griffin, who is also a professor of religion emeritus and expert in this area.

The differences between Michael Morrissey and me came to a head over a paper by a high-school physics teacher, Charles Boldwyn, in which he uses vector addition to demonstrate that it would have been physically impossible for the Twin Towers to have collapsed from the force of its top floors falling down on the floors beneath them. Chuck fashioned his calculations around the North Tower, assuming that the top 16 floors were falling onto the bottom 94 as a consequence of the damage from the plane and the fires that followed, which ostensibly weakened the steel and caused the upper floors to fall on the lower. This is a fantasy, since neither the damage from the planes nor the subsequent fires could have brought this about (as I explain in "Why doubt 9/11?"), since the fires burned neither hot enough nor long enough to bring this effect about.

Michael, rather to my astonishment, objected to Boldwyn's study on the ground that he personally could not follow his calculations. I have archived it several places, including at Scholars site, 911scholars.org, under "Articles" as the first appeariing under the subheading "General Articles", where anyone can download it to study for themselves. He took a different approach by asking how much energy would have be required for that 16-floor section to have caused the bottom 96 floors to collapse and discovered that it would have been enormous, as I'm going to explain. (The very idea is even more preopsterous in the case of the South Tower, where the top 30 floors pivot and start to fall from the structure, but then turns into very fine dust in mid-air, which has to be the most stunning and anomalous feature of the destruction of the towers—apart from the fact that they are both turned into very fine dust at the rate of free fall!)

Michael had more than one reason for objecting to Boldwyn's work, since it also appeared—or a summary of his findings—on a web site called "Real Zionist News" that is clearly anti-Semitic. I tried to explain that the exclusion of his study on the basis of its origins is an example of the genetic fallacy, which is especially egregious in this instance because mathematics is not amenable to evaluation on the basis of the political orientation of its author. Like deductive arguments generally, if the inference from the premises to the conclusion is valid and the premises are true, it is not possible for the conclusion to be false. And those considerations apply no matter who might have advanced the argument, even if it were Adolf Hitler himself!

Mathematics and Truth

Because Michael insisted that he would not countenance studied he personally could not understand, I responded by offering a translation of Boldwyn's argument in ordinary language that he might be better positioned to appreciate its significance. Here is the content of the post which I advanced, which I subsequently submitted to Boldwyn for confirmation. I asked him if I had understood him properly, to which he replied, "yes your synthesis of my thesis is correct and very [well] put and clearly [expressed]", in the vernacular of Skype "chats". Here is what I wrote translating the argument for Michael's benefit:

About Boldwyn's paper, his thesis is very clear: that it would have taken the equivalent of 48,000 tons of explosives to equal the kinetic energy (energy of motion) that the top 16 floors of the North Tower (taking the plane to have hit at the 94 floor and subtracting 94 from 110 = 16) would have had to exert upon the bottom 94 floors for their "collapse" to have initiated the collapse of those 94 floors. John Skilling, one of the senior engineers of the firm that built the towers, had observed that they could carry 20 times the expected live load" (that is, physical steel and concrete structure plus office furniture and human beings) that they would ever be expected to carry.

Charles believes it was actually much greater than that, but when using Skilling's more conservative figures, he has calculated that the force required to collapse the lower 94 floors (using vector addition and subtraction of forces) which would have required the combined weight of some 588 16-floor equivalents (taking into account that those uppermost 16 floors were not as heavy as lower 16 floor units because the steel was not as thick) before collapse would ensue; or, using the thought of those 16 floors falling through space downward onto the lower 94, that that 16-floor unit would have to be elevated to a height of 120 miles above the remaining 94 for it to possess enough energy of motion to collapse the remaining 94; or, alternatively, that the energy required would be equivalent to that of 2.4 (Hiroshima sized) atomic bombs, which clearly was not available from the miniscule potential energy that was allegedly released by the fires weakening the steel and causing the top 16 floors to collapse on the bottom 94.

This is an impressive argument, which completely vitiates any claim to scientific significance of the claim that the Twin Towers "collapsed". I also told him Michael that I had featured Charles on my radio show on 10 June 2009, which should be posted at radiofetzer.blogspot.com in the next few days. I expressed regret that we are parting ways over this and (what I take to be) his excess of zeal as an anti-anti-Semite, because it functions as basis for excluding arguments from posting and discussion simply on the ground that they are "associated" with "anti-Semitism", in the case of Boldwyn's summary, or anti-Zionism, in the case of my "9/11 and the Neocon Agenda" in its illustrated version by virtue of being posted on *americafirstbooks.com*.

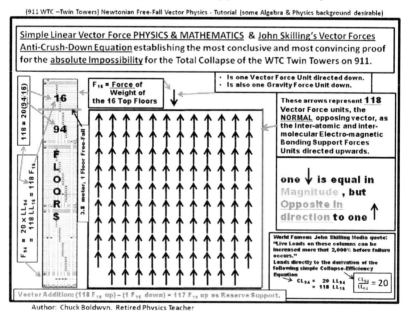

His unwavering attitudes have led me to create an alternative form at *911scholars.ning.com*, where I have posted them and additional studies by Elias Davidsson, David Ray Griffin, and others serious students of 9/11.

The Search for Truth

Michael has expressed disappointment with me because, during a much earlier exchange on the forum for Scholars for 9/11 Truth, I had sided with him in objecting to discussions of Holocaust denial on that site. I was not thereby opposing research on Holocaust, however, but excluding it because it has nothing to do with 9/11 research. The possibility of Israeli complicity in the events of 9/11, however, is within the scope of 9/11 research, and yet Michael wants to exclude it, too. That's just a bit much. We have seen that "anti-Semitism" has been used as a club to thwart and discredit 9/11 research by many, but we have a moral and intellectual obligation to pursue it, nevertheless. If Israel was involved in 9/11, the American people are entitled to know.

I suggested that David Ray Griffin might be an appropriate arbiter of our differences. By sheerest coincidence, he called me a few days ago in relation to his appearance on my program. When I raised the question of whether anti-Zionism was equivalent to anti-Semitism, he told me that, before he became involved in 9/11 research, he had begun drafting an article on the nature of Zionism, where he said he had distinguished between some five different senses, ranging from a generalized desire for a Jewish homeland to the strongest and more commonly used sense of an amalgam of belief in Jewish superiority with an entitlement to the lands of Palestine. He indicated to me that Zionism has a political dimension that makes it distinct from Judaism and that "anti-Zionism" in that sense is distinct from and not a form of anti-Semitism. I dearly hope that he will complete the article that he had only begun.

No one should be afraid of research, even research on complex and controversial subjects, whether it is JFK, 9/11 or the Holocaust. I, like Michael, believe in the historical reality of the Holocaust. Neither he, nor I, nor anyone else, for that matter, should worry about someone wanting to do work in that domain because, if their research is sound they will inevitably be led to conclude that it was real! None of us, for example, would worry about someone doing research on whether or not the Earth is flat. Holocaust deniers are in a similar plight: if they do their homework properly—and, of course, if we are right in our belief in its reality—then they should arrive at the conclusion that it was real. And if we are wrong, we need to know that, too. Either way, there is no moral or intellectual warrant for censoring inquiry.

Research, even on complex and controversial subjects, should be open and unfettered, regardless. There is certainly no good reason to fear research on subjects like these, especially by resorting to the use of elementary fallacies—such as the ad hominem, the genetic fallacy, and guilt by association—that I spent 35-years teaching freshmen to avoid. I believe that every thoughtful person, especially professional scholars, will side with me about these things.

Indeed, it would like to think that every American would recognize that politics should not be put ahead of the search for truth. We have seen too much of that from the last Is 9/11 Research "Anti-Semitic"? administration, which has been doing everything it can to place obstacles in the search for truth about 9/11, especially. It is the highest form of respect for those who died that day to know how and why they died, which, alas, we have certainly not yet been told by our own government.

Source note: This chapter originally appeared as "Is 9/11 Research 'Anti-Semitic'?", *OpEdNews.com* (17 June 2009).

Part III

What Happened on 9/11?

7

Top 10 9/11 Cons:
Fraud Vitiates Everything

by Jim Fetzer, Dennis Cimino and Mike Sparks

"Fraud vitiates every transaction and all contracts. Indeed, the principle is often stated, in broad and sweeping language, that fraud destroys the validity of everything into which it enters"–37 Am Jur 2d, Section 8

"FRAUD VITIATES EVERYTHING" (FVE) is the legal principle that, once it has been shown shown that one party has lied or committed a deliberate misrepresentation, their whole case is thereby compromised and no longer defensible in a court of law.

37 Am Jur 2d, Section 8, states, *"Fraud vitiates every transaction and all contracts. Indeed, the principle is often stated, in broad and sweeping language, that fraud destroys the validity of everything into which it enters, and that it vitiates the most solemn contracts, documents, and even judgments."*

Were that principle applied to the government's case for 9/11, the demonstration of fraud and deliberate deception would warrant its dismissal in it's entirely, since it's entire case has been built upon nothing but fraud and deliberate deception. Here we are going to present ten examples of fraud and deliberate deception in relation to 9/11, five of which derive from the Pentagon, the other five from events in New York City. Given the principle that "Fraud vitiates everything" (FVE), each of these is sufficient, by itself, to warrant the dismissal of the official account of 9/11.

In the case of the Pentagon, they range from the relatively obvious–that the plane seen in the Pentagon frame labeled "plane" turns out to be too small to be a Boeing 757, but could be a Global Hawk delivering a missile to the building–to the far more subtle and complex case of the image that Frank Legge touts as his "conclusive proof", which has been photoshopped–in the case of the Pentagon.

In New York City, they range from the impossible speed and impossible entry of a Boeing 767 to planting an engine component that did not come from the plane to the impossible "collapse" of the Twin Towers and the blatant controlled demolition of WTC-7. These are "ten top" cases, which warrant dismissing the government's case in its totality because of fraud and deliberate deception, where there are many, many more.

At the Pentagon

There are dozens of arguments against the official account that a B-757 hit the Pentagon, which is a fantasy. They include that the "plane" seen in the Pentagon frame is too small to be a Boeing 757; that the "hit point" could not have accommodated a 100-ton airliner with a 125' wingspan and a tail standing 44' above the ground; that debris from a Boeing 757 which should have been present is not there–no wings, no fuselage, no seats, no bodies, no luggage and no tail–where not even the engines, which are made of titanium and steel, were recovered; that one piece of debris, which did come from a Boeing 757, has been traced back to a crash in Cali, Columbia, in 1995; and that the smoke observed by members of Congress rushing out of the Capitol came from a series of enormous dumpsters, a blatant act of fakery.

(1) The Pentagon "plane"

According to the official account, AA Flight 77 approached the Pentagon on an acute north-east trajectory, barely skimming the ground at over 500 mph and taking out multiple lampposts, which would have ripped its wings open and caused the plane to burst into flame. The aerodynamics of flight, including "downwash", moreover, would have made the official trajectory–flying at high speed barely above ground level–physically impossible, because a Boeing 757 flying over 500 mph could not have come closer than 60 or more feet to the ground, which means that the official account is neither physically nor aerodynamically possible. But here is an even simpler disproof:

When the image of a Boeing 757 is sized to the tail of "the plane", it turns out to be more than twice as long as what the frame shows, which means it cannot possibly be a Boeing 757. But, as Dennis Cimino has observed, it could have been a Global Hawk, which may have fired a missile into the building, where the white plume is not from the exhaust of any jet engine but from the solid-propellant engine of a Maverick. The fragile composition of the Global Hawk would have made it an ideal delivery system, since it would have been

obliterated into tiny parts upon impact with the Pentagon.

(2) The lack of debris

Although many Americans are unaware, the hit point on the Pentagon is a hole about 10' high and 16-17' wide, which is surrounded by a chain-link fence, two enormous spools of cable and a pair of cars, where there are unbroken windows beside and above the opening. What we do not see is an enormous pile of aluminum debris, broken wings or the tail, bodies, seats or luggage.

Remarkably, not even the engines were recovered from the crash site—although a part of a compressor, which was too small to have come from a 757 and too large for a cruise missile—was later reported there. Even more striking to me, however, is this photo of the civilian lime-green fire-trucks as they extinguish the fires:

Since these fire trucks arrived after the crash and spent fifteen minutes or so putting it out, I have been struck by the clear, green, unblemished Pentagon lawn. There is no indication that a Boeing 757 hit the building–NONE! Nor in any of the other  photographs we have featured about the Pentagon. And, as Dennis Cimino has observed, if a plane had flown into the building, then why are these supports blown outward? No plane hit the building.

(3) The planted fuselage

Later, of course, debris would start showing up. Since there was none even as the fire trucks were extinguishing the fires, it has to have come from somewhere. It would have been difficult to have had officers and enlisted men carry pieces of debris out onto the lawn without being observed, so it has occurred to me that perhaps it was dropped from a C-130, which was circling the Pentagon that morning. That's my best guess. I am open to other possibilities, but I haven't been able to think of real alternatives. One piece of debris has been used to cement the case for the crash of Flight 77, where Frank Legge, for example, has argued that no one has been able to show it did not come from a 757:

One of the oddities about this debris is that it shows no signs of having been involved in a violent crash or exposed to the intense heat of those fireballs–and it includes a piece of vine. Another student of the Pentagon, James Hanson, a newspaper reporter who earned his law degree from the University of Michigan College of Law, has traced that debris to an American Airlines 757 that crashed in a rain forest above Cali, Columbia in 1995. "It was the kind of slow-speed crash that would have torn off paneling in this fashion, with no fires, leaving them largely intact." That this piece was on the Pentagon lawn is an obvious case of fraud and deliberate deception vitiating the official account.

(4) The dumpster fires

As though that were not disturbing enough, I was also puzzled why, later in the day, when rumors were circulating that the Capitol might be next and the members of Congress rushed out onto the steps of the building, when they looked across the Potomac, they witnessed billowing black clouds of smoke.

That struck me as rather odd, since the lime green fire trucks had put out the modest fires long ago. When I took a closer look, I discovered that these black clouds of smoke were not coming from the Pentagon itself but from a series of enormous dumpsters in front of the building:

When I was still living in Duluth before my retirement in June of 2006, another student of the Pentagon came by and showed me forty-four (44) more frames of the same thing, where you could actually see light

between the dumpsters and the building. If a plane has actually crashed there, it would not have been necessary to fake fires coming from the Pentagon, which appears to have been contrived to induce members of Congress to support requests for new funding Donald Rumsfeld would present the next day–another instance of fraud and deception vitiating the official account.

(5) The photoshopped images

When we turn to the photograph that Frank Legge cites as "proof positive" of the presence of an airliner, a B-757, specifically, inside the Pentagon, not only do you not notice no debris associated with an airliner, but it turns out that the photo has been altered extensively–it has been photoshopped!–to obfuscate details in it (see the next photo with the cyan marking and the magenta bottom line) In this photograph, the cyan area (expanded in the final photo) clearly reveals that photoshopping was crudely used to add the extremely lighter area into the image:

Even closer examination in the debris field mostly in the upper half shows demarcation lines of cut and paste having been performed in more than one area inside it. In his original upper ceiling beam (left-hand side), you can see where they pasted in over the beam to obfuscate something that happened on the beam itself in an attempt to hide that from us. The shading of the reverse "E" area shows, beyond any doubt, that this photo was heavily retouched and altered.

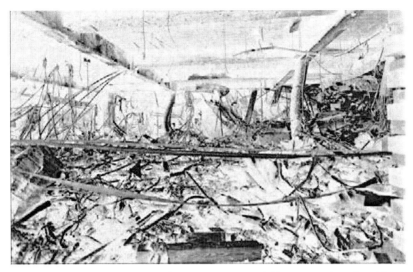

However they were not able to paste any airliner parts into it without having issues with perspective and sizing very obvious to the naked eye. This photo, which Legge himself emphasizes, is bogus and hence "non-authentic". He thus picked a very sad and poor choice from Jim Hoffman's web site.

A very good question to ask Frank Legge, therefore, is, *"Why did you pick a photograph that had been altered and is also bereft of any sign of aircraft wreckage?"*

That this photo was shopped may or may not have been something of which the Journal of 9/11 Studies was aware when it accepted his article for publication. But that means its vaunted "peer-review" process, upon which Steven Jones has placed so much emphasis, failed in this instance. As I have explained elsewhere, Jones also advocates an inadequate mode of scientific reasoning, which means that the procedures he endorses as "scientific" are not those that properly qualify. But something is terribly wrong when a faked photo appears in the Journal of 9/11 Studies.

In New York (6) The Impossible speed

Indeed, as John Lear, perhaps our nation's most distinguished pilot, has observed, the plane in these videos does not even have strobe lights, which are required of every commercial carrier.

But how can a Boeing 767 possibly travel at an impossible speed (as Pilots for 9/11 Truth has confirmed), where the estimates of its speed run as high as 560 mph or more, which is aerodynamically impossible at the altitude of 700-1,000' at which this flight trajectory was taking place?

(7) The Unreal entry

The footage of the South Tower hit exemplifies several anomalies, including a Boeing 767 flying at an impossible speed, an impossible entry into the building (in violation of Newton's laws), and even passing through its own length into the building in the same number of frames it passes through its own length in air—which is impossible, unless this 500,000 ton, steel and concrete building posed no more resistance to its trajectory in flight than air.

Some have claimed that this was a "special plane" that could fly faster than a standard Boeing 767, but no real plane could violate Newton's laws. The structure of the building, moreover, meant that it actually intersected with eight different floors. Each of those floors

consisted of steel trusses connected at one end to the core columns and at the other to the steel support columns.

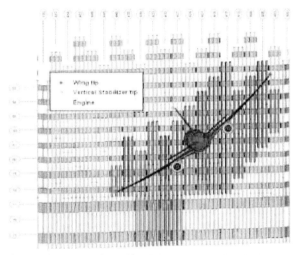

Figure 6–8. Orientation and trajectory of UAL 175 that matches the impact pattern (vertical approach angle = 6°, lateral approach angle = 13°).

They were filled with 4-8" of concrete (deeper in the v-shaped grooves) and posed enormous horizontal resistance. (Imagine what would happen to a plane encountering one of them suspended in space!) The windows were 18" wide and the support columns one meter apart, while there were no windows between floors, which means far less than 50% if the plane should have entered via them. But as Jack White has shown on the next page, that is not what the videos display:

No real plane–commercial, military or otherwise–could enter a steel and concrete building in violation of Newton's laws, pass through its own length into the building in the same number of frames that it passes through its own length in air, and not have its fuel explode as it makes contact with

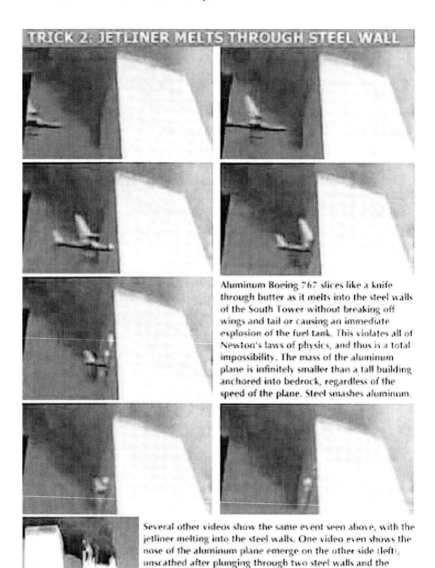

TRICK 2: JETLINER MELTS THROUGH STEEL WALL

Aluminum Boeing 767 slices like a knife through butter as it melts into the steel walls of the South Tower without breaking off wings and tail or causing an immediate explosion of the fuel tank. This violates all of Newton's laws of physics, and thus is a total impossibility. The mass of the aluminum plane is infinitely smaller than a tall building anchored into bedrock, regardless of the speed of the plane. Steel smashes aluminum.

Several other videos show the same event seen above, with the jetliner melting into the steel walls. One video even shows the nose of the aluminum plane emerge on the other side (left), unscathed after plunging through two steel walls and the building's interior core. An aluminum plane cannot penetrate a steel building undamaged. Unless you're a magician.

that massive edifice. Even the frames from the Pentagon show a huge fireball upon impact. If that was true of the 757 there, why is it not also true of the 767 here? And no real plane could have passed through and its nose come out the other side. It looks as though the fabrication of Flight 77 fakery was just a bit better than the fabrication of Flight 175 fakery. But both involved massive fraud and deception.

(8) The planted engine

Notice that the plane completely enters the building before its jet fuel explodes, when one would have thought that, insofar as most of its fuel is stored in its wings, they should have exploded on entry—which is comparable to the failure of the 757 at the Pentagon to have its fuel explode when its wings hit those lampposts. And while some have sought to support the claim that this was a real 767 based upon the engine found at Church & Murray Streets, those who were fabricating evidence in this case did not get it right: what we have is a JTD9 engine with a cooling duct assembly from a Boeing aircraft manufactured in the 1970s, not the plane allegedly used for Flight 175:

Pickup or delivery?

Newsworthy things were happening on 9-11 at Church and Murray, so Fox News was there. An FBI van is parked on Murray at the Church intersection, door open. An FBI agent stands guard over something not seen in other photos at this location. Blue-clad FBI agents appear beside the van and seem to struggle with something heavy. There appear to be six FBI agents and a photographer in the video frames. Another image taken at the deserted corner, right, shows a dolly used for moving something. What does the complete video show...a pickup or delivery?

Since this is the wrong engine component and was off-loaded as a prop, how can anyone be so gullible as to believe that it supports the official account, especially when its under a steel scaffolding and sitting on a sidewalk, where if something that massive had hit there at high velocity (having come from the South Tower as alleged), it would have been buried half-way into the concrete, not sitting on top of it? There is even a dolly present, which–although not heavy-duty–may have played a role in moving it from the white van to its location on the sidewalk. This a blatant case of deliberate deception and fakery that completely vitiates the official account.

(9) The impossible collapse

The Twin Towers were masterpieces of architecture and engineering, which received multiple awards at the time. By using an innovative design known as "a tube within a tube"–which was innovative with regard to the elevator systems (using a combination of express and local elevators) and by adopting 47 massive core columns at the center connected to 238 external steel support columns by steel trusses–the architect, Minoru Yamaski, created enormous open space unobstructed by walls and support columns. Here you can see the 47 core columns at the center, where the external steel support columns–which would be added to what is shown–created the equivalent of "a steel beam 209' deep":

As Chuck Boldwyn has shown, the thickness of the steel varied from six inches thick in the subbasements to a quarter-inch thick at the top, which meant that the overwhelming mass of the steel was below the level at which "the plane" is alleged to have hit the North Tower. By his calculation, the fourteen floors above the "hit point" represented 1.4% of the mass of the steel, where it is preposterous to suppose that its collapse could have overcome the 98.6% of the mass of the steel below it. Indeed, as John Skilling observed, the towers were build with a safety factor of 20, which means that each floor could support 20 times its expected live load (dead load + furniture, facilities and human personnel) (see next page).

The claim that the jet fuel from the plane strikes burned so intensely it caused the steel to weaken cannot withstand critical scrutiny. The steel used in the building was certified by Underwriters Laboratories, Inc., to 2,000*F for three to four hours without suffering any adverse effects. NIST studied 236 samples of steel and found that 233 had not been exposed to temperatures above 500*F and the other three not above 1,200*F. Plus the fires in the South

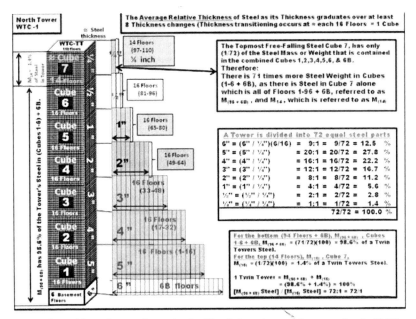

Tower lasted less than an hour, in the North less than an hour-and-a-half. The fires burned neither long enough nor hot enough to affect the steel. It was physically impossible for them to collapse.

As Jesse Ventura has observed, propane burns hotter than kerosene (the constituent of "jet fuel"), yet his camping stove, which is made of steel, does not melt when he uses it on a camping trip. Far from collapsing, both buildings are being blown apart in every direction by enormous sources of energy, where they are being converted into millions of cubic yards of very fine dust and, when destruction is complete, there is no massive pile of debris in their footprint, which is a classic sign of a building's collapse. Unlike WTC-7, the Twin Towers did not collapse, which means that the official account characterizing them as having "collapsed" is another blatant fabrication and deliberate deception.

(10) The controlled demolition

Unlike the Twin Towers, WTC-7 came down in a classic "controlled demolition" at 5:20 PM that day, about seven hours after the destruction of WTC-1 and WTC-2, which I prefer to refer to as "demolitions under control", since they were clearly not classic controlled demolitions. You can see the penthouse kink, where all the floors fall at the same time and, after about 6.5 seconds, there is a stack of debris (mostly floors) equal to about 12% of the height of the original.

By contrast, the floors of the Twin Towers remain stationary, waiting their turn to be "blown to kingdom come" (in the memorable phrase of Morgan Reynolds).

Almost everyone knows that Larry Silverstein acknowledge authorizing the building to be "pulled", which is a term for taking it down by controlled demolition. Far fewer are aware that Barry Jennings (from the New York City Emergency Management Division) was in WTC-7 that morning, where he went to the Command and Control Center, which had its own air and water supply, and found half-eaten sandwiches and still-steaming cups of coffee.

A fireman found him and escorted him out of the building, while explosions were going off and a stairway was blown out from under him. At one point, he felt himself stepping over dead bodies, which he could feel but because of the darkness, he could not see:

Richard Gage and A&E911 focus on WTC-7, where Barry Jennings was inside the building that day.

His story is very compelling and makes the case that this was not a consequence of the destruction of the Twin Towers but an entirely separate event involving the use of explosives.

It would have made for compelling television on C-SPAN when Gage made his recent appearance, but the best he could do was talking about nanothermite for the umpteenth time.

I am sorry, but Barry Jenning's story would have made an impact on the public, especially by observing that he died a few days before NIST would release its report on WTC-7, which he was in the position to contradict on the basis of his own personal experience. Consider the options that we have enumerated here and ask, "Why didn't he talk about them?"

Concluding reflections

The principle that fraud vitiates everything devastates the official account of 9/11, which, by virtue of appealing to 19 alleged collaborators (plus a guy in a cave in Afghanistan), itself qualifies as a "conspiracy theory", which is the most outrageous and easily disproven.

Nothing we have been told by the government can be trusted once we realize they are no longer acting in good faith but are instead perpetrating "reality fraud" upon us, the people.

The challenge then becomes to do our best to get things right.

We should be tolerant of reasonable differences but not of cover-ups or limited hang-outs. Even the three of us are not of the same mind about the image seen in the Pentagon frame, where Mike believes it more closely resembles an A-3 Skywarrior (as I myself have argued in the past), which may have been painted to resemble an American Airlines plane, because the high vertical fin looks more like that of an A-3D, whose length at 76' is about half that of a Boeing 757, where future research should enable us to reduce our differences even further:

If 19 Islamic fundamentalists had hijacked airliners and committed these atrocities, there would have been no reason to plant and fake evidence, which demonstrates guilty demeanor and makes the government complicit before and accessory after the fact. 9/11 was a blatant "False Flag Attack", which puts the ball in the American public's court to create a grand jury to indict members of the Bush/Cheney administration and make them talk, where a good place to start would be the cell-phone faker, former Solicitor General, Ted Olson.

Because until the American people reclaim reality by actual investigation/ verification, we will continue to be mislead and manipulated by one administration after another, as we have been discovering with Biden and Obama.

Source note: This chapter originally appeared as "Top Ten 9/11 Cons: Fraud Vitiates Everything", *veteranstoday.com* (21 August 2014).

8

9/11:
A Photographic Portfolio
of Death and Devastation

by Jack White

The most surreal scene in history was witnessed by millions of people worldwide on television as it happened. Yet the plumes of smoke and the incredible dust clouds from the the pulverization of two of the world's tallest buildings within minutes of each other could not adequately portray the horror of thousands of people dying and the total destruction of many buildings. This photo shows Building 7 amid the dust clouds, serenely waiting its turn to fall about seven hours later for no apparent reason. Two five-hundred-thousand-ton buildings were converted to dust in approxiately ten seconds each. According to *The 9/11 Commission Report* (2004), the buildings were destroyed by the combination of jetplane impacts and jet-fuel-based fires which caused the steel to weaken and bring about a "pancake collapse." The photographic record makes that very difficult to believe.

Left to right, see next page, top to bottom: Demolition starts badly; the top 300 feet of WTC-2 tilted as much as 23 degrees before being "blown to Kingdom come." No one had ever attempted to demolish a building the size of a twin tower, and the dust cloud from WTC-1 helped to distract and cover up problems in destroying WTC-2. As the buildings disintegrated, huge steel columns many feet long were scattered like matchsticks for hundreds of feet. The tower peeled downward as dark explosions shot up, while white ones exploded outward. Above the white explosions, the tower is turning to dust as the lower part awaits its fate. At lower right, as explosions destroy WTC-2, huge sections of disintegrating steel "wheatchex" showered down on WTC-3, the Marriott Hotel. According to the "official account," fires that caused a collapse due to gravity brought down these buildings.

Along Vesey Street were WTC buildings 5, 6, and 7. Lower photo shows two huge cavities in eight-story WTC-6 at center and a smaller but striking gash on the side of Building 5 just above. Neither building was struck by significant debris from either of the Twin Towers, right. Across Vesey Street, at left, is a neat pile that was the 47-story Building 7, which imploded and fell at the speed of gravity into its own footprint. Top photo shows a gash on the side of Building 3, with walls of WTC-1 reeling oddly nearby. Other photos of the hole in Building 6 show little debris of any kind within, which is very difficult, even impossible, for the government to explain. How could a collapse of the towers possibly account for this?

WTC-7, above right, during the attack on the Twin Towers, appears undamaged except for a modest fire at street level. Below right, WTC-7 (on the right) still appears in no distress long after both towers had fallen. Frames (above) from video of the collapse of WTC Building 7 shows a perfectly controlled demolition of WTC-7, which was two blocks away from WTC-1 and 2 and only superficially hit by debris from 1 and 2. At 5:20 PM, over six hours after WTC-1 and WTC-2 fell, WTC-7 came down in free fall into its own footprint, a sure sign of controlled demolition, which causes a "kink" in the center of the building. The official story claims that diesel fuel reservoirs in the building exploded, resulting in fires that brought the building down, even though there is no recorded case of the fire-induced collapse of a large steel-protected building; and only very small fires were burning when WTC-7 "collapsed." Diesel fuel does not explode, and it burns at low temperatures.

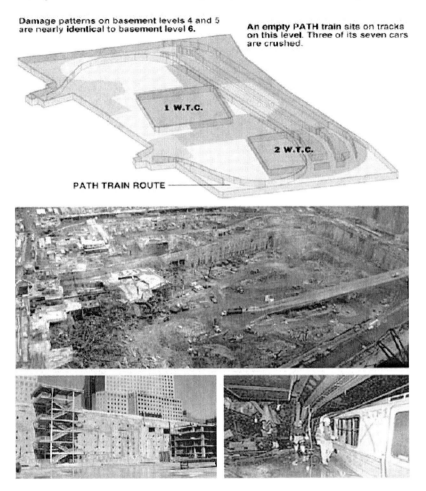

Damage patterns on basement levels 4 and 5 are nearly identical to basement level 6.

An empty PATH train sits on tracks on this level. Three of its seven cars are crushed.

1 W.T.C.

2 W.T.C.

PATH TRAIN ROUTE

The World Trade Center was built on bedrock, protected by an underground "bathtub" or foundation ring (top, left, and diagram) down seven stories below the surface of lower Manhattan to prevent flooding by the Hudson River, only a block away. On September 11 the bathtub mysteriously remained without significant damage despite two huge towers collapsing on it. It was not built to withstand such colossal impact. No foundation structure could remain unscathed after a mountain of quarter-mile high material was dropped on it twice. The intact bathtub appears to contradict the official theory of gravity-driven collapse in which virtually the entire weight of the Twin Towers would crash into the bathtub. Even subway cars within the bathtub were not crushed, lower right.

At bottom, a mysterious explosion shot by an "unknown" photographer before any fire trucks arrived purports to show the explosion of Flight 77 within the building. Researchers wonder how a photographer happened to be directly under the incoming flight with a camera and capture such a remarkable image; some suspect the image was faked and others that it was a later occurrence.

At top are official "before and after" photos of the alleged impact point; upper right shows where the wall collapsed directly over the "impact point" but upper left shows the same area before the wall collapsed, and unbroken windows and undamaged wall are seen at the "impact point" of the "plane," which was 125 feet wide and 44 feet tall. Hard to believe.

At top on next page, fire trucks from National Airport arrived at the Pentagon within ten minutes and had all fires out within seven minutes. They saw no aircraft wreckage or damage to the lawn. They did not know there had

been a "plane crash" because the main fire they found was a burning trailer. The stream of water at left had been a "plane crash" because the main fire they found was a burning trailer. The stream of water at left is being sprayed at the alleged impact point, yet the wall is not visibly breeched. At bottom, a Pentagon security camera captures an image said to be an "incoming plane" (red rectangle), yet it is much too small to be a Boeing 757 (inset) like American Airlines Flight 77, plus it is emitting a trail of smoke like a missile.

United Airlines Flight 93, a huge Boeing 767, allegedly crashed at high speed into a field near Shanksville, Pennsylvania, leaving virtually no crash debris and little damage to grass or trees, see next page. Witnesses described and photos confirm only a small trench in the grassy field. The official story says the soft ground "swallowed" the entire plane and its occupants. A lady named Val McClatchy allegedly took the photo at top of a small puff of smoke claimed to be the plane exploding near her home, yet pieces of the plane were found up to eight miles away.

A coroner called to the scene saw not a single body, but the official story said DNA identified all victims.

Source note: This chapter originally appeared as "9/11: A Photographic Portfolio of Death and Devastation", *jamesfetzer.blogspot.com* (26 January 2010).

9

9/11 Illusions, Special Effects and Other Magic Tricks

by Jack White

Jack White was a legendary photo and film analyst who made magnificent and enduring contributions to the study of JFK, which I archived in three books with color-photo sections by him, namely: *Assassination Science* (1998), *Murder in Dealey Plaza* (2000), and *The Great Zapruder Film Hoax* (2003). He was my dear friend.

He also contributed a color-photo section to *The 9/11 Conspiracy* (2007), where our last collaboration was on this series of studies for a new book on 9/11 that I was editing, which has not yet found a publisher.

Here I want to publish his color-photo section and integrate it with the biographical sketch for "Jack White" from the Spartacus Educational site.

Jack D. White was born on January 17, 1927, in San Angelo, Texas. His parents, John Nathan White and Billie Lorena Dumas White, moved the family to Fort Worth shortly after his birth and he was raised and educated there. After graduation from Amon Carter Riverside High School in 1944, White worked briefly for the Fort Worth Press as a sports writer covering high school sports under legendary sports editor H. H. "Pop" Boone.

During the Second World War White enlisted in the U.S. Navy. After his discharge in 1946, White returned to Fort Worth to pursue his interest in journalism, art, and history. He graduated from Texas Christian University in 1949, with a B.A. in journalism and began an advertising career as copywriter and art director at Yates Advertising Agency in Fort Worth. In 1954, he joined the Witherspoon and Ridings Public Relations Agency in Fort Worth, which later became Witherspoon and Associates, at the time the largest advertising agency in town. White began as the firm's first art director and during his twenty-seven years with the agency rose to vice-president, executive art director, personnel manager, and part owner.

He specialized in design, type management, and photography and developed their in-house facilities for darkroom work, studio photography, and slide show presentations.

Although White had photographed the city since the 1950s, he only began collecting Fort Worth photographs seriously in 1972, when Witherspoon was planning the 100th anniversary of one of its clients, the Fort Worth National Bank. He was in charge of acquiring copies of historical prints of Fort Worth for the bank's annual report, a historical booklet, and an exhibit for the bank lobby. After the anniversary event, he took care to preserve all the exhibit materials. During the next twenty years White reproduced other clients' historical photographs and took hundreds of pictures to add to the collection.

Another of White's areas of expertise and collecting interests is the assassination of President John F. Kennedy in Dallas, Texas, in 1963. He is nationally known as an expert on the assassination and served as a photographic consultant to the House Select Committee on Assassinations during the hearings. He was also a consultant on the Oliver Stone film, *JFK*.

As a result of his interest in the Kennedy assassination, White published two videotapes on his photographic studies of the assassination. He has developed a slide lecture, which he presents to classes and symposia on the JFK assassination and also contributes his research to professional journals.

Massive steel box columns up to 4" thick remained standing after the North Tower collapsed, standing taller than the 47-story WTC7 (left and right) for moments...then suddenly (video frames at top) turned to DUST...a trick worthy of the great David Copperfield.

White, along with David Mantik, Charles Crenshaw, Robert Livingston and Ronald F. White, contributed to *Assassination Science* (edited by James H. Fetzer). He also contributed several articles for *Murder in Dealey Plaza* (2000) and *The Great Zapruder Film Hoax* (2003).

White retired from Witherspoon and Associates in 1981, and formed his own company, Jack White Enterprises, which specialized in free-lance art and photography. In 1984, as business increased, he took on partners. The firm's name changed to VJS Companies, and the company added new services, including typography and photostats. The firm closed for a brief period in 1991, following several setbacks, but reopened later in the year as Jack White Graphic Arts.

Following his retirement, White lived in the White Lake Hills addition in east Fort Worth with his wife the former Sue Benningfield. Their home,

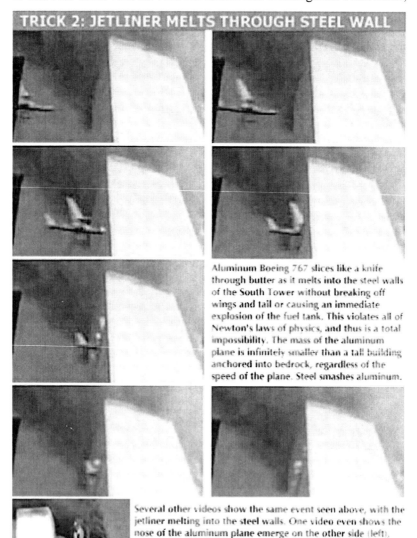

TRICK 2: JETLINER MELTS THROUGH STEEL WALL

Aluminum Boeing 767 slices like a knife through butter as it melts into the steel walls of the South Tower without breaking off wings and tail or causing an immediate explosion of the fuel tank. This violates all of Newton's laws of physics, and thus is a total impossibility. The mass of the aluminum plane is infinitely smaller than a tall building anchored into bedrock, regardless of the speed of the plane. Steel smashes aluminum.

Several other videos show the same event seen above, with the jetliner melting into the steel walls. One video even shows the nose of the aluminum plane emerge on the other side (left), unscathed after plunging through two steel walls and the building's interior core. An aluminum plane cannot penetrate a steel building undamaged. Unless you're a magician.

built in 1970, was designed to focus on a view of the downtown Fort Worth skyline. Jack D. White died, aged 85, on 18th June, 2012.

Jack White's photo studies of the JFK assassination, the 9/11 atrocities, and the Apollo moon landing hoax may be found at *JFK Studies: Jack White's JFK Assassination Photo Research.*

TRICK 3: EXPLOSIONS "JUST LIKE THE MOVIES"

The gas tanks of these jets, if made into a cube, would be 9'x9'x9'...smaller than an average home swimming pool...not much fuel at all compared to the volume of the twin towers. Since most of the jet fuel passed through the South Tower and burned up in a spectacular fireball outside the building, the official explanation that the South Tower collapsed because of an inferno produced by jet fuel burning within the building has to be false. It was nothing more than a "shock and awe" special pyrotechnic effect...just a grand Hollywood illusion.

A Pennsylvania housewife claims she took the photo at left of the crash of Flight 93, within five seconds of hearing the explosion. Nice photo and nice story; are they true? Mathematicians, using satellite photos of the area in the photo, have determined that the distance from the crash site to the porch where the photo was taken from is 1.6 miles. Plotting lines on the satellite photo and measuring them, they determined the black cloud shown would have to be 2200 feet wide! Another impossible magic trick.

TRICK 4: BLOWING ROUND HOLES IN BUILDINGS

Magicians use misdirection to fool their audience. While all eyes were on the Twin Towers on 911, a mysterious force punched holes into two 8-story buildings, WTC5 and WTC6, **above**. Minimal tower debris struck the two buildings. Falling debris does not make round holes. DEW microwave rays do.

At left, Department of Defense art showing plane using DEW weapon, only known device able to do such destruction, using powerful microwave energy blasts. Below the plane note the tall pyroclastic cloud in the distance, magically similar to 911 WTC events.

TRICK 5: MELTING CARS BUT NOT BURNING PAPER

In the blocks around the WTC complex, more than 1400 vehicles of all kinds melted into lumpy singed masses. Buses, fire trucks, cars, and mail trucks blocks away from WTC were destroyed, unhit by falling debris. Many burst into flames, while paper which littered the streets did not ignite. Now that's a good trick....melting and burning metal without burning the paper. Wait a minute....your kitchen microwave will burn metal and not paper (but don't try it). The Pentagon has operational microwave weapons (DEW) seen at lower right.

TRICK 6: 3 STEEL TOWERS DEFY PHYSICS SAME DAY

NEVER IN THE HISTORY OF THE WORLD have steel framed skyscrapers fallen in the same day. NEVER has even one fallen due to fire. On 9-11, three times! The South Tower fell, followed minutes later by the North Tower. By the end of the day WTC 7 came down. All fell at the free-fall speed of gravity, neatly into their own footprints (below, WTC 7) in small piles with almost no damage to adjacent buildings. It takes real magic to defy the law of gravity. And in an amazing stroke of magic, ONLY the seven buildings (right) of the WTC were totally destroyed. And in another lucky deal, the NY Port Athority, which owned all seven buildings, had just leased them to a person who promptly insured them all for billions...against terrorist attacks.

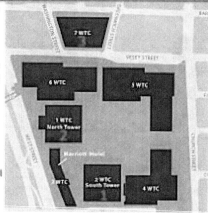

TRICK 7: PLANE WRECKAGE, THERE OR NOT THERE?

If on 9-11-2001 NO jetliners hit the WTC, the Pentagon or a Pennsylvania field as many researchers have concluded, ergo NO AIRCRAFT WRECKAGE CAN EXIST AT ANY OF THE SITES. No planes = no wreckage. Logically, then, any aircraft debris shown is necessarily planted by someone wanting to prove plane crashes happened. No magic; just slight of hand.

First firemen at the Pentagon found no major fire and NO EVIDENCE OF A PLANE CRASH!

Long after the event, FBI agents started "collecting wreckage"; every piece of significant size conveniently was painted with a red American Airlines logo (4 above). None of the wreckage showed any evidence of explosion or fire. But investigators refused to supply part numbers.

Manhattan trick: At Church Street and Murray a large engine part appeared underneath a construction scaffold. An abandoned dolly was nearby (left). Video caught FBI men using a dolly to unload a large object. Some trick!

Source note: This chapter originally appeared as "9/11 Illusions, Special Effects and Other Magic Tricks", *veteranstoday.com* (13 October 2012).

Part IV

New York was Nuked on 9/11

10

Mystery Solved:
The WTC was Nuked on 9/11
by Don Fox, Ed Ward, M.D., and Jeff Prager

A debate has raged for more than a decade about what caused the Twin Towers to "collapse" in approximately 10 seconds each — 9 seconds for the South Tower, 11 for the North. A large and growing percentage of the public has become skeptical of the conclusion of the government's official NCSTAR 1 report, according to which, "NIST found no corroborating evidence for alternative hypotheses suggesting that WTC towers were brought down by controlled demolition using explosives planted prior to 9/11."

Skepticism of NIST's conclusions is well founded. There is eyewitness testimony as well as abundant video and audio evidence of explosions at the WTC on 9/11. There is also seismic data that demonstrates that high powered explosives were used to demolish the Twin Towers. The gross observable video evidence — if you are willing to believe your own eyes — shows that the Twin Towers were destroyed from the top down and the inside out.

We believe that only mini-nukes — which were probably neutron bombs — planted in the center columns of the buildings, detonated from top to bottom and configured to explode upward, can explain what is observed. If they were used to blow apart one ten-floor cube per second, for example, then, since the North Tower stood at 110 floors, that would have taken 11 seconds, while, since the top three cubes of the South Tower tilted over and were blown as one, in that case, it would have taken only 9, which coincides with NIST's own times.

This is a controversial contention. Judy Wood, Ph.D., has proclaimed that a Tesla-inspired directed energy weapon (DEW) was responsible for the destruction of the WTC buildings and has vehemently denied nuclear bombs were used. Steve Jones, Ph.D., and his followers promote the theory that an incendiary (nanothermite) was the cause of the destruction of the WTC buildings, while they also deny that nukes were used. So these seemingly opposed camps agree on one thing: nukes were not used on 9/11!

The nanothermite hypothesis has been discredited on multiple occasions in articles by T. Mark Hightower and Jim Fetzer, including "Has nanothermite been oversold to the 9/11 community?", "Is '9/11 truth' based upon a false theory?", and "Nanothermite: If it doesn't fit, you must acquit". Since it is a principle (law) of materials science that an explosive can destroy a material only if it has a detonation velocity equal to or greater than the speed of sound in that material, where the speed of sound in concrete is 3,200 m/s and in steel 6,100 m/s, while the highest detonation velocity that has been attributed to nanothermite is 895 m/s, it should be obvious: You can't get there from there!

The DEW hypothesis turns out to be difficult to test, since Judy Wood defines DEWs as sources of energy that are greater than conventional and can be directed, which even encompasses micro and mini nukes within its scope. As earlier articles have explained, including "9/11 Truth will out: The Vancouver Hearings II" and "Mini Neutron Bombs: A Major Piece of the 9/11 Puzzle", there are multiple grounds for preferring the mini or micro nuke hypothesis over the DEW alternative, which emerge with particular clarity from a study of the dust samples collected by the US Geological Survey. It is ironic that, while the "thermite sniffers" also focus on dust samples, they seem to have missed what we have to learn from them.

Indeed, the nuclear component of the decimation of World Trade Center buildings 1, 2, and 6–where WTC-7 appears to be a separate case–is the darkest and most closely guarded secret of 9/11. With so many folks claiming different theories it is difficult for average people to know what to believe.

Fortunately, we have scientific proof of what happened at Ground Zero. The dust and water samples reveal the true story of what happened on 9/11. This article thus provides more of the scientific evidence–especially from the USGS dust samples–that settles the debate in favor of the demolition of the WTC buildings as having been a nuclear event.

Debris Ejected over 600 feet

The explosives that demolished the Twin Towers were so powerful that North Tower debris was ejected up at a 45° angle and out over 600 feet into the Winter Garden. This feat alone puts an end to the notion that the buildings were "dustified" where they stood or that an incendiary such as nanothermite was the responsible for the destruction of two 500,000 ton 110 story skyscrapers or that the buildings collapsed due to fire. Consider these photos and graphs:

Debris was ejected at a 45* angle for over 600 feet and impacted with the Winter Garden. Engineers estimate that 1/3 of the buildings were completely vaporized. And as Judy Wood likes to point out, no toilets were found in the rubble. 90% of the debris from the Twin Towers destruction landed outside the building's footprints. What type of explosives could cause this sort of damage? The only thing known to man that can explain this is nuclear bombs.

Proof of Fusion

The Department of Energy (DOE) collected water samples from the basement of Building 6 eleven days after 9/11 that showed tritium levels 55 times greater than background. How does this prove fusion?

Let's start by defining "tritium": *Tritium is an isotope of hydrogen containing one proton and two neutrons. Tritium is radioactive with a half-life of 12.32 years. Also Known As: hydrogen-3, 3H (Helmenstine)* The Canadian Nuclear Safety Commission provides us some excellent background information on hydrogen:

Hydrogen is the most abundant element in the universe, comprising approximately 90% of the luminous universe by weight. Ordinary hydrogen (1H) accounts for greater than 99.985% of all naturally-occurring hydrogen, whereas deuterium (2H) comprises approximately 0.015%. By comparison, tritium (3H) represents only approximately 10 to the -16 exponent percent of hydrogen naturally occurring. Tritium is a rare but natural isotope of hydrogen (H), and is the only natural hydrogen isotope that is radioactive.

The tritium atom is sometimes designated T to distinguish it from the common lighter isotope. Notwithstanding the difference in mass, tritium can be found in the same chemical forms as hydrogen. The most important forms, from the perspective of atmospheric behavior of tritium, are tritiated hydrogen gas (HT) and tritiated water (HTO). These tritiated forms behave chemically like hydrogen gas (H2) and water (H2O).

Natural Sources

Tritium is generated by both natural and artificial processes. Tritium is naturally produced primarily through the interaction of cosmic radiation protons and neutrons with gases (including nitrogen, oxygen and argon) in the upper atmosphere.

Anthropogenic Sources

In addition to its natural sources, tritium also has a number of anthropogenic sources which account for the dominant proportion of the global tritium inventory. Anthropogenic tritium sources include fallout from nuclear weapons testing, nuclear reactors, future fusion reactors, fuel reprocessing plants, heavy water production facilities and commercial production for medical diagnostics, radiopharmaceuticals, luminous paints, sign illumination, self-luminous aircraft, airport runway lights, luminous dials, gauges and wrist watches, and others.

Commercial uses of tritium account for only a small fraction of the tritium used worldwide. Instead, the primary use of tritium has been to boost the yield of both fission and thermonuclear (or fusion) weapons, increasing the efficiency with which the nuclear explosive materials are used.

Thermonuclear Detonation during Nuclear Weapons Testing

Nuclear tests have been conducted in the atmosphere since 1945, producing tritium in amounts that greatly exceed the global natural activity, particularly during 1954 to 1958 and 1961 to 1962 when a number of large-yield test series were undertaken. The tritium activity arising from atmospheric nuclear tests can be estimated from the fission and fusion yields of the weapons tests or from environmental measurements.

For example, the tritium activity produced per unit yield is dependent upon the attributes of the device, as well as on the characteristics of the detonation site, and tritium generation from fusion reactions is much higher than from fission.

The tritium that is produced by a nuclear explosion is almost completely converted to tritiated water (HTO), which then mixes with environmental water. ("Investigation of the," 2009)

What about WTC-6?

Damage to WTC-6 and smoke rising from it
BEFORE the North Tower's "collapse"

We have established that tritium is a rare hydrogen isotope, the vast majority of tritium that is produced is used in nuclear weapons and that the tritium produced by a thermonuclear explosion is converted into tritiated water (HTO). Tritiated water WAS found in the basement of Building 6 at concentrations 55 times background levels. Here is Ed Ward's breakdown of the DOE's water sample data:

1. Trace definition as it applies to quantity: Occurring in extremely small amounts or in quantities less than a standard limit (In the case of tritium, this standard level would be 20 TUs – the high of quoted standard background levels.) http://www.thefreedictionary.com/trace

2. The stated values of tritium from the DOE report "Study of Traces of Tritium at the World Trade Center". "A water sample from the WTC sewer, collected on 9/13/01, contained 0.164±0.074 (2ó) nCi/L (164 pCi/L +/- 74 pCi/L – takes 1,000 trillionths to = 1 billionth) of HTO. A split water sample, collected on 9/21/01 from the basement of WTC Building 6, contained 3. 53±0.17 and 2.83±0.15 nCi/L (3,530.0 pCi/L +/- 170 pCi/L and 2,830 pCi/L +/- 150 pCi/L), respectively. https://e-reportsext.llnl.gov/ pdf/241096.pdf Pico to Nano converter – http://www.unitconversion.org/ prefixes/picos-to-nanos-conversion.html Nano to Pico converter – http:// www.unit-conversion.info/metric.html

3. 1 TU = 3.231 pCi/L (trillionths per liter) or 0.003231 nCi/L (billionths per liter) – http://www.hps.org/publicinformation/ate/q2282.html – (My original TU calculations came out to 3.19 pCi/L, but I will gladly accept these referenced minimally higher values.http://www.clayandiron.com/ news.jhtml?method=view&news.id=1022)

4. In 2001 normal background levels of Tritium are supposedly around 20 TUs (prior to nuclear testing in the 60's, normal background tritium water levels were 5 to 10 TUs – http://www.hps.org/publicinformation/ate/q2282.html).

However, groundwater studies show a significantly less water concentration: Groundwater age estimation using tritium only provides semi-quantitative, "ball park" values: · <0.8 TU indicates sub modern water (prior to 1950s) · 0.8 to 4 TU indicates a mix of sub modern and modern water · 5 to 15 TU indicates modern water (< 5 to 10 years) · 15 to 30 TU indicates some bomb tritium http://www.grac. org/agedatinggroundwater.pdf. But, instead of "5 to 15 TU" (which would make the increase in background levels even higher), I will use 20 TUs as the 2001 environmental level to give all possible credibility to the lie of "Traces".

5. Let's calculate the proven referenced facts. Tritium level confirmed in the DOE report of traces of tritium = 3,530 pCi/L (+/- 170 pCi/L, but we will use the mean of 3,530 pCi/L). 3,530 pCi/L (the referenced lab value) divided by the background level of 20TUs (20 X 3.231 p (1 TU = 3.21 pCi/L) = 64.62 pCi/L as the high normal background/standard level. 3,530 divided by 64.62 pCi/L = 54.63 TIMES THE NORMAL BACKGROUND LEVEL. 3,530 pCi/L divided by 3.231 pCi/L (1 TU) = 1,092.54 TUs.

6. This is my 'fave' because lies tend to eat their young. Muon physicist Steven Jones calls 1,000 TUs "The graphs below show that hydrogen-bomb testing boosted tritium levels in rain by several orders of magnitude. ("Tritium in precipitation,") (Jones, 2006) Yet, calls the EXACT SAME LEVELS quoted in nCi/L as "Traces" and "These results are well below the levels of concern to human exposure" (Jones, 2006). Interesting isn't it.

7. Thomas M. Semkowa, Ronald S. Hafnerc, Pravin P. Parekha, Gordon J. Wozniakd, Douglas K. Hainesa, Liaquat Husaina, Robert L. Rabune. Philip G. Williams and Steven Jones have all called over 1,000 TUs of Tritium, "Traces". Even at the height of nuclear bomb testing 98% – after thousands of Megatons of nuclear testing – of the rainwater tests were 2,000 TUs or less. https://e-reports-ext.llnl.gov/pdf/241096.pdf.

8. It is also important to note that the tritium present was diluted by at least some portion of 1 million liters of water accounting for BILLIONS of TUs.

An important point that Jones glosses over is the dilution of water in the basement of WTC 6. If not for copious amounts of water sprayed on the WTC site undoubtedly the concentration of tritium would have been higher than the measured 55 times normal background levels.

After WTC-6 has been hit and during the South Tower "collapse"

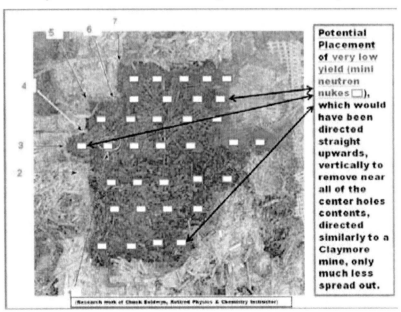

Chuck Boldwyn's suggestion of where they may have been placed and the effects

To sum this up: we see a plume of smoke rising from Building 6, photos that show the building was blackened and bombed out before ANY debris from the Twin Towers hit it, a massive crater in the middle of the building and the DOE found massive quantities of tritium in the basement eleven days after 9/11. Only a thermonuclear explosion explains all of this, which strongly suggests that WTC-6 was nuked. And there is more proof.

An infrared image showing the huge crater in WTC-6 (to the left-foreground)

Proof of Fission

The US Geological Survey collected samples of dusts and airfall debris from more than 35 localities within a 1-km radius of the World Trade Center site on the evenings of September 17 and 18, 2001. The USGS was primarily looking for asbestos in the dust but they found a host of elements in the dust that when analyzed properly proves that nuclear fission took place at Ground Zero.

A quick glance at the chemistry table and immediately the presence of the elements such as cesium, uranium, thorium, barium, strontium, yttrium, rubidium, molybdenum, lanthanum, cerium, chromium and zinc raise suspicions. But deeper analysis shows that these elements correlate with each other according to relationships expected in a nuclear fission event. Jeff Prager has done extensive work with the USGS dust samples and we'll use some of the slides from his Vancouver Power Point presentation to help us analyze the USGS data:

Barium and Strontium

People might argue that strontium and barium could be found in building debris and they would be correct however strontium and barium could never, under any circumstances, be found as building debris constituents in a demolition in these quantities.

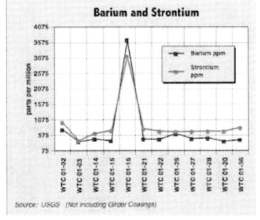

The levels never fall below 400 ppm for Barium and they never drop below 700 ppm for Strontium and they reach over 3000 ppm for both of them at WTC01-16, Broadway and John Streets. Why?

Barium and Strontium are rare Trace elements with limited industrial uses. The enormous peak in Barium and Strontium concentration at WTC01-16 is readily apparent in the chart below. The concentration of the two elements reaches 3130 ppm for Strontium and 3670 ppm for Barium or over 0.3% by weight of the dust. This means that 0.37% of the sample was Barium and 0.31% of the sample was Strontium by weight at that location, WTC01-16, Broadway and John Streets. The Mean concentration for Barium including the very low girder coating samples is 533 ppm and for Strontium it's 727 ppm. These are not Trace amounts. They are highly dangerous and extremely toxic amounts. They are also critical components of nuclear fission and the decay process.

Here we're plotting the concentration of Barium at each location against the Strontium concentration. The correlation between the concentrations of the two elements, Barium and Strontium is extremely high. The Coefficient of Correlation between the concentration of Barium and Strontium at the outdoor and indoor sampling locations is 0.99 to 2 decimal places (0.9897 to 4 decimal places).

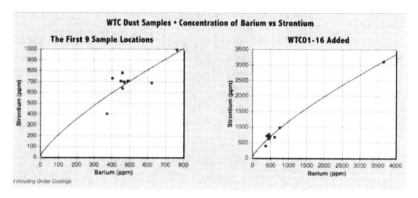

So we have a Correlation Coefficient between the concentration of Barium and the concentration of Strontium of 0.9897, or near perfect. The maximum Correlation Coefficient that is mathematically possible is 1.0 and this would mean we have a perfect match between the two factors we're examining and the data points would lie on a straight line with no variation between them. To obtain a Correlation Coefficient of 0.9897 with this number of measurements (14) around Lower Manhattan is very, very significant indeed.

What this means is that we can say that there's a 99% correlation in the variation in the concentration between these two elements. They vary in lockstep; they vary together. When one element varies so does the other. We can state with absolute mathematical certainty that any change in the concentration of one of these elements, either the Barium or Strontium, is matched by the same change in the concentration of the other. Whatever process gave rise to the presence of either the Barium or the Strontium must have also produced the other as well. Fission is the only process that explains this.

Thorium and Uranium

Next we come to the detection of measurable quantities of Thorium and Uranium in the dust from the World Trade Center, elements which only exist in radioactive form. The graph below plots the concentration of Thorium and Uranium detected at each sampling location. Again, the last two locations, WTC01-08 and WTC01-09, are for the two girder coating samples. The Uranium concentration follows the same pattern as Thorium, although the graph scale does not show this markedly. Uranium follows the dip at WTC01-03 and WTC01-16 but the highest concentration of Uranium also matches Thorium in the second girder coating, WTC01-09, at 7.57ppm. 7.57 greatly exceeds normal Trace element levels. This equals 93 Becquerels per kilogram.

Normal background radiation is approximately 12Bq/kg to 40Bq/kg with 40Bq/kg the highest level we would expect to see. This girder contains more than twice the expected level of uranium. The second girder contained 30.7 ppm of Thorium, 6 times as high as the lowest level of that element detected. Thorium is a radioactive element formed from Uranium by decay. It's very rare and should not be present in building rubble, ever. So we have verifiable evidence that a nuclear fission event has taken place. As we said earlier, Thorium is formed from Uranium be alpha decay. An alpha particle is the same as a Helium nucleus, so this means we have one of the favored fission pathways: Uranium fissioning into a Noble Gas and the balancing elements, in this case Helium and Thorium.

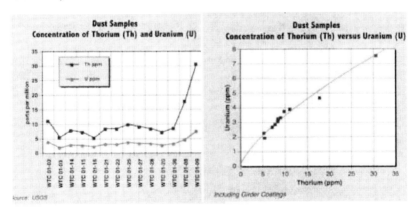

The graph of Thorium versus Lithium including the Girder Coatings has exactly the same form as the graph showing Thorium versus Uranium, also including the Girder Coatings. Without the two Girder Coatings the correlation of Thorium to Lithium in the dust is completely linear. We therefore have compelling evidence that this fission pathway of Uranium to Thorium and Helium, with subsequent decay of the Helium into Lithium, has indeed taken place.

It is out of the question that all of these correlations which are the signature of a nuclear explosion could have occurred by chance. This is impossible. The presence of rare Trace elements such as Cerium, Yttrium and

Lanthanum is enough to raise eyebrows in themselves, let alone in quantities of 50 ppm to well over 100 ppm. When the quantities then vary widely from place to place but still correlate with each other according to the relationships expected from nuclear fission, it is beyond ALL doubt that the variations in concentration are due to that same common process of nuclear fission.

When we also find Barium and Strontium present, in absolutely astronomical concentrations of over 400 ppm to over 3000 ppm, varying from place to place but varying in lockstep and according to known nuclear relationships, the implications are of the utmost seriousness. Fission occurred in NYC on 911. This graph shows that (apart from the very high peak in Sodium levels for one of the indoor dust samples) the Sodium and Potassium concentrations both display this now characteristic peak at location WTC01-16, the corner of Broadway and John Street. Sodium has the same peak as Zinc at WTC01-22, the corner of Warren and West, and like Zinc, falls to a minimum in the girder coatings – far below the concentrations found in the dust. Potassium is very similar except its concentration was not a peak at WTC01-02, Water and New York Streets, but somewhat lower than the next location, WTC01-03, State and Pearl Streets.

Zinc, Sodium and Potassium

There are clear correlations and relationships here which show that the Potassium and Sodium concentrations did not arise at random. They are products of radioactive decay. Remember that Strontium is produced by a fission pathway that proceeds through the Noble Gas Krypton and then the Alkali Metal Rubidium. Similarly, Barium is produced through Xenon and the Alkali Metal Cesium.

We know that Uranium fission favors these pathways through the Noble Gases. Just as radioactive isotopes of Krypton and Xenon decay by beta particle emission to produce Rubidium and Cesium, radioactive isotopes of Neon and Argon also decay by beta emission to produce Sodium and Potassium. We would indeed expect to find anomalous levels of

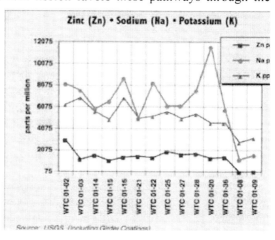

these elements present – what was found is again consistent with the occurrence of nuclear fission.

We know beyond doubt that the only process that can cause Barium and Strontium to be present in related or correlated quantities and any process that can also cause Barium and Strontium to have such strong relational concentrations across different samples, is nuclear fission. We know that if nuclear fission had occurred that Barium and Strontium would be present and a strong statistical correlation between the quantities of each would be found, and we have that, in spades.

What else do we have? Quite a lot. About 400 ppm of Barium and Strontium were measured in two samples of insulation girder coatings (WTC01-08 and 01-09). The concentration of Strontium actually falls somewhat below that of Barium in the second girder sample, WTC01-09, as at WTC01-16, whereas in every othesample the level of Strontium discovered was higher than Barium.

Given the elevated levels of Barium daughter products found in the second girder and even the highest level of Uranium found (7.57ppm just West of and behind Tower One) this shows that active fission was still ongoing in the second girder coating, in the very same way as at WTC01-16 and therefore more Barium was found then Strontium. In other samples where the rate of fission had slowed down to give way to decay, the concentrations of Barium and Strontium reverse, due to the different half-lives. Barium isotopes have a shorter half-life then Strontium isotopes so they decay more quickly and after a period of time when no new Barium or Strontium has been deposited, Strontium will exceed Barium.

The fact that more Barium then Strontium was still found at WTC01-16 and WTC01-09 shows that the overall nuclear processes taking place were somewhat favoring Barium over Strontium and hence Zinc as well. The tighter cluster of Barium (400-500 ppm) and Strontium (700-800 ppm) concentrations across widely separated sampling locations in Lower Manhattan is cast iron proof that Nuclear Fission occurred.

We know that Barium and Strontium are the characteristic signature of fission; they are formed by two of the most common Uranium fission pathways. The fact that their concentrations are so tightly coupled means that their source was at the very epicenter of the event which created the dust cloud that enveloped Manhattan. This was not a localized preexisting chemical source which would only have contaminated a few closely spaced samples and left the remaining samples untouched. The very high concentrations of Barium and Strontium at location WTC01-16 shows that active nuclear fission was still ongoing at that spot; the dust was still "hot" and new Barium and new Strontium were being actively generated, actively created by transmutation from their parent nuclei.

The presence of Thorium and Uranium correlated to each other by a clear mathematical power relationship – and to the other radionuclide daughter products such as sodium, potassium, zinc, lithium, strontium and barium – leaves nothing more to be said. This type of data has probably never been available to the public before and it's an unprecedented insight into the action of a nuclear device. September 11th, 2001, was the first nuclear event within a major United States city that we have incontrovertible proof for and this is without question the most closely held secret surrounding the events of September 11th, 2001.

Anyone seriously interested in 911 truth will naturally be compelled to fully and thoroughly investigate the serious implications raised by this report personally, and I strongly encourage this. The material is complex yet if I can understand it anyone can. No one promised us that the answers to 911 would come easily.

More compelling evidence

There's more compelling and incontrovertible evidence we would like to cover now; in particular, we will discuss the elements:

Lanthanum
Vanadium
Yttrium
Chromium
Nickel
Copper
Lead
Zinc

In this graph Zinc has been divided by a factor of 10 to avoid losing all the detail in the scaling if the 'Y' axis instead went up to 3000 ppm. The variation in Lead is matched by the variation in Zinc almost perfectly across all sampling locations, including the Indoor and Girder Coating samples.

Copper and Zinc

The concentration of Copper follows that of Zinc with one distinct exception at WTC01-15, Trinity and Cortlandt Streets, just several hundred feet East of Building Four. There seem to be two Copper-Zinc relationships. If some of the Zinc was being formed by beta decay of Copper, then the high Copper at WTC01-15 could reduce Zinc, since formation of Zinc by that decay pathway would be retarded by material being held up at the Copper stage, before decaying on to Zinc.

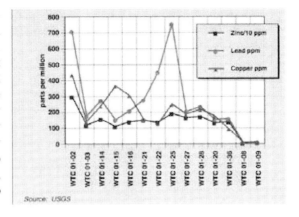

Source: USGS

Therefore this graph does confirm that some of the Zinc was indeed being formed by beta decay of Copper. This would at least be a very small mercy for the civilian population exposed in this event since the Zinc isotopes formed from Copper are stable, i.e. they are not radioactive.

The copper found in the Ground Zero dust is indicative of nuclear fission. If we plot the concentration of Copper against Zinc and Nickel, we obtain the graphs pictured here. The concentration of Nickel was almost the same everywhere, except for the peak of 88 ppm matched by the Copper peak of 450 ppm.

The Copper – Zinc relationship is very interesting, showing in fact two distinct relationships again depending on isotopic composition. There are two radioactive isotopes of Copper (Cu 64 and Cu 67) with short half-lives of 12.7 hours and 2.58 days respectively which decay into Zinc isotopes.

The other two isotopes (Cu 60 and Cu 61) decay the other way by positron emission into Nickel and in fact Cu 64 goes both ways, into both Nickel and Zinc. This would explain why there strongly appear to be two Copper – Zinc relationships.

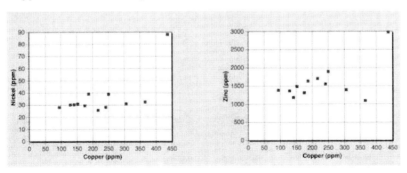

The decay of radioactive Copper by beta particle emission into Zinc would have been another source for the extraordinarily high concentrations of Zinc found in the World Trade Center Dust.

Lanthanum

Lanthanum is the next element in the disintegration pathway of Barium, situated between Barium and Cerium. The concentration of Barium versus Lanthanum is plotted in the graph below. This graph is almost identical in form to the relationship between Barium and Cerium. A similar inverse exponential (cubic) relationship is clearly visible. In this case, Lanthanum is approximately equal to 5 times the cube root of Barium.

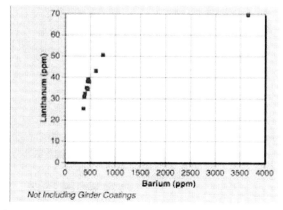

Not Including Girder Coatings

Lanthanum has a much shorter half-life then Cerium; most of its isotopes have a half-life of only a few hours whereas beta decay by Cerium is measured in half-life periods of a month to 10 months. Cerium's beta decay going back to Lanthanum occurs more quickly but Lanthanum's beta decay going back to Barium occurs in a similar time-scale to that – a few hours, so we are left with the net effect of Lanthanum's beta decay being much quicker than that of Cerium, so the concentration of Cerium remaining was higher than that of Lanthanum.

Yttrium

Yttrium is also a very rare element and should not be present in dust from a collapsed office building. Yttrium is the next decay element after Strontium. If we plot concentration

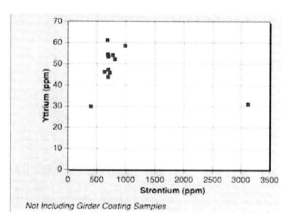

Not Including Girder Coating Samples

of Strontium against Yttrium, we see what happens in the graph above. Strontium 90 has a much longer half-life (28.78 years) than most Barium isotopes so we would not expect to see as high a concentration of Strontium's daughter products as those that are produced from Barium.

This is in fact what we see – the concentration of Cerium (next daughter product to Barium) is higher than Yttrium, the next daughter product to Strontium.

Chromium

The presence of Chromium is also a telltale signature of a nuclear detonation. Its concentration is shown plotted against Zinc and Vanadium in the graphs below. There is a strong correlation between the Zinc and the Chromium concentration. The Coefficient of Correlation is high, 0.89.

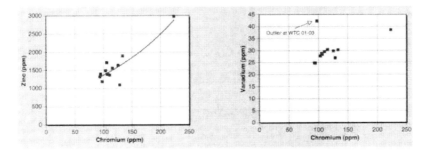

There is also an indication of strong correlation between Chromium and Vanadium within 6 points of lying on an almost perfect exponential curve, with one outlier, WTC01-03, the corner of State and Pearl Streets, of 42.5ppm where the Vanadium concentration reached its highest level.

Looking at the data for Zinc we see that the Zinc concentration for WTC01-02, Water Street at the intersection of New York, is 2990 ppm and this immediately stands out.

In fact, for the outdoor samples, Zinc is the most common Trace element at all sampling locations, with generally between 1000 ppm and 2000 ppm except for this spike of nearly 3000 ppm at WTC01- 02.

This equates to an enormous concentration of Zinc. 0.1% to 0.2% of Zinc in the dust overall and at WTC01-02, 0.299% of the dust was Zinc. This exceeds the concentration of the supposed "non-Trace" element Manganese and Phosphorous and almost equals the elevated Titanium concentration of 0.39% at that same location.

What process produced the zinc?

If we include the data for WTC01-16, the Correlation Coefficient between the Zinc and Barium concentration is 0.007 to 3 decimal places, from which we can conclude that there is absolutely no correlation at all. But if we exclude that one sampling location, where Barium and Strontium concentrations peaked, the correlation coefficient between Zinc and Barium is 0.96 to two decimal places and between Zinc and Strontium, 0.66 to two decimal places. So what happened?

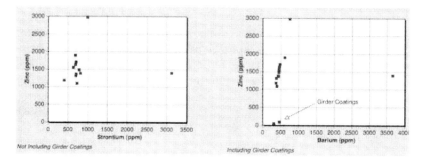

This shows that the Zinc and Barium concentrations are closely related and if we exclude what must have been an extraordinary event at WTC01-16 as an outlier, the correlation is very good. The Product Moment Correlation Coefficient is 0.96. The concentration of Zinc is now 3 times the concentration of Barium but the correlation between Zinc and Strontium is not so clear, showing that the relationship must be more indirect. This is to be expected since Barium and Strontium are produced by different nuclear fission pathways.

In spent nuclear fuel, Strontium is found as Strontium Oxide (SrO) – the Strontium produced by the nuclear fission explosion under the Twin Towers will certainly have been oxidized to SrO by the heat. SrO is extremely soluble in water, so some of the Strontium concentration results obtained may have been distorted by the rain water which fell on New York a few days after the towers were destroyed. There is a very strong linear relationship between Barium and Zinc found at the World Trade Center. This may indicate that a closely related nuclear sub-process gave rise to them, which produced three times as much Zinc as Barium by weight. If so, that would be a very unusual nuclear event.

Ternary Fission

There is a lesser known nuclear process that accounts for this, which would be indicative of very high energies indeed. This process is known as

Ternary Fission. What is ternary fission? From Wikipedia:

Ternary Fission *is a comparatively rare (0.2 to 0.4% of events) type of nuclear fission in which three charged products are produced rather than two. As in other nuclear fission processes, other uncharged particles such as multiple neutrons and gamma rays are produced in ternary fission.*

Ternary fission may happen during neutron-induced fission or in spontaneous fission (the type of radioactive decay). About 25% more ternary fission happens in spontaneous fission compared to the same fissioning system formed after thermal neutron capture, illustrating that these processes remain physically slightly different, even after the absorption of the neutron, possibly because of the extra energy present in the nuclear reaction system of thermal neutron-induced fission.

True Ternary Fission: *A very rare type of ternary fission process is sometimes called "true ternary fission." It produces three nearly equal-sized charged fragments (Z ~ 30) but only happens in about 1 in 100 million fission events. In this type of fission, the product nuclei split the fission energy in three nearly equal parts and have kinetic energies of ~ 60 MeV (Wikipedia contributors, 2013)*

Mini-Neutron Bombs

We have evidence of nuclear fission and fusion taking place at Ground Zero. Fission triggered fusion bombs fit the evidence. These bombs had limited but powerful blast effects, a burst of neutron radiation as well as EMP effects. Mini-neutron bombs appear to be what was used.

What is a neutron bomb? *A **neutron bomb**, also called an enhanced radiation bomb, is a type of thermonuclear weapon. An enhanced radiation bomb is any weapon which uses fusion to enhance the production of radiation beyond that which is normal for an atomic device. In a neutron bomb, the burst of neutrons generated by the fusion reaction is intentionally allowed to escape using X-ray mirrors and an atomically inert shell casing, such as chromium or nickel. The energy yield for a neutron bomb may be as little as half that of a conventional device, though radiation output is only slightly less. Although considered to be 'small' bombs, a neutron bomb still has a yield in the tens or hundreds of kilotons range. Neutron bombs are expensive to make and maintain because they require considerable amounts of tritium, which has a relatively short half-life (12.32 years). Manufacture of the weapons requires that a constant supply of tritium be available. Neutron bombs have a relatively short shelf-life. (Helmenstine)*

Per Sam Cohen, *"In a broad sense, the neutron bomb is an explosive version of the sun; that is, the relevant energy it emits comes from thermonuclear, or fusion, reactions involving the very lightest elements. To be specific, its fuel consists of the two heavier nuclei of hydrogen, named deuterium and tritium. By means of a fission trigger, a mixture of these two nuclei is compressed and heated, as happens in a hydrogen bomb, to cause nuclear reactions whose principle output is in the form of very high energy neutrons.*

Also produced will be blast and heat, but so predominant are the neutron effects against human beings, who are a hundred to a thousand times more vulnerable to radiation than blast and heat, that by bursting the weapon high enough off the ground the only significant effects at the surface will come from radiation. In so doing, the blast and heat effects will not be strong enough to cause significant damage to most structures. Hence, a bomb which, accurately but misleadingly, has been described as a weapon that kills people but spares buildings." (Cohen, 2006)

Neutron Radiation and EMP Effects

Neutron radiation and EMP appears to be responsible for the "toasted cars" found near Ground Zero. What is **neutron radiation**? From the Shots Across the Bow Blog:

*To understand **neutron radiation**, imagine a pool table set for the start of a game. 15 balls are in the middle of the table, with the cue ball set for the break. The cue ball is a free neutron. When the neutron hits the nucleus, one of three things might happen. First, if the cue ball doesn't have enough energy, or hits at the wrong angle, it caroms off, barely disturbing the pack of balls. Second, if the ball has too much energy, it slams through the pack, breaking it up. This is fission, and results in fission products, more free neutrons, and energy. Third, if the ball has just the right amount of energy, it just makes it to the pack and joins in, becoming another neutron in the nucleus. Here is where our analogy breaks down, because many times, when a nucleus gets another neutron, it becomes unstable, and begins to decay, emitting alphas, betas, or gammas. This is called "activation" and is one of the trickier problems with neutron irradiation and the physical properties of the irradiated matter can be quite different from the original. ("A nuclear power,")*

A large quantity of high energy neutrons bombarding an object will cause the atoms in the material to move i.e. heat up. This is why so few bodies were found at Ground Zero – most of the people that were near the Towers were vaporized either by the blast and heat effects of the bombs or the neutron radiation that was released.

The "Toasted" Cars

Ted Twietmeyer has a post on Rense's website that goes a long way towards explaining the toasted cars found near Ground Zero. Twietmeyer attributes the damage to aluminum vehicle parts such as engine blocks and mirrors to strong EMP eddy currents produced by nuclear detonations at Ground Zero: *"and what else do eddy currents create? HEAT if the currents are strong enough. The stronger the eddy currents, the more heat which will be generated. Although magnetic fields are being created, they are temporary in aluminum because it is not magnetic, but paramagnetic. This means aluminum will be affected by magnetism, but it cannot be magnetized.*

A vector is simply a line that shows direction and usually has an arrow. Arrows are not shown above, in an attempt to simplify the image. The direction of force is from upper left to lower right. The notated image above provides a possible explanation for the location of the source of the magnetic pulse, and why some vehicles were damaged and others were not. This parking lot may be the best evidence in support of my theory.

"Sacrificial vehicles" shielding others showing pulse vectors

Yellow lines indicate the pulse(s) blocked by the rear row of vehicles. It appears the entire outside of all rear vehicles were destroyed. Note how several hoods on the rear row of vehicles have white dust or ash, indicating an intense heat originating from under the hood. This is probably caused by the engine block vaporizing, and the white dust may be aluminum oxide.

If the vehicles are still around somewhere in a junk yard, some simple lab tests will confirm this.

White lines show the pulses that reached the vehicles in the foreground. Orange shapes around each car show the damage threshold line. The cars are basically undamaged below these lines and some might be repairable. If it wasn't for "sacrificial" vehicles at the rear, those in the foreground would have been completely burned.

Note that white and yellow lines are not meant to be a literal interpretation to show size of the pulse, how many lines of force hit each vehicle, etc... Each line is intended to show only the direction the pulse(s) came from. Regardless of whether this parking lot is close to the WTC or not, it clearly shows that the nuclear device (or pulse source) was high above the ground. If the pulse source were close to the Earth, then vehicles in the foreground would have been completely shielded from the pulse." (Twietmeyer, 2007)

Ed Ward's take: I believe some of what he attributes to EMP was done by neutrons – in particular his linear evaluations (angle computations) would seem more neutron than EMP. EMP should tend to flow around – seems to be a correlation of dust cloud carrying EMP. So the linear blockage of cars protecting other cars would seem to be more appropriate for neutrons. Other than that seems on the money, IMO.

The Temperature of the Pile

Temperatures at Ground Zero were 600 to 1,500 °F or even higher for 6 months after 9/11. Firemen were fighting fires at Ground Zero for 99 days after 9/11. AVRIS data showed that temperature in one spot was 1,341 °F on 9/16/01. These high temperatures could be attributed to neutron bombs that were detonated underground in order to destroy the foundations of the Twin Towers. Some of the hotspots may have been unexploded nuclear fissile material reacting underground. The workers at Ground Zero experienced hellish working conditions. One Ground Zero worker, Charlie Vitchers, describes the nightmare:

"The fires were very intense on the pile, the heat was very intense. In some places you couldn't even get onto it. In some areas where you could walk, you'd travel another five feet and then you could just feel the heat coming up and you would have to just back off. You'd say to yourself, "I can't see a fire, but I can feel the heat, so something's wrong here," and you'd back off.

That was one of the concerns we had about putting equipment on the pile, because the operators were sitting eight or ten feet up above the debris pile in their cabs and couldn't feel the heat. But they're carrying a hundred gallons of diesel fuel, hydraulic hoses, and other flammables, and there was nothing to stop the heat from wrecking the machine. If they got stuck in a place where the heat was so intense that it set his machine on fire, that operator wasn't going to make it out.

We were so lucky. We didn't lose anyone. We lost a lot of equipment, mostly due to collapses, but didn't have any piece of equipment catch on fire or anything like that. But hoses melted, and there was a lot of damage to tires- some of them melted just from being too close. I mean, the bottom of your shoes would melt on some of the steel. Some of that was so hot you could feel the hair on the back of your neck start to burn when you walked by. There were cherry-red pieces of steel sticking out of the ground. It was almost like being in a steel-manufacturing plant. You just couldn't physically go near that stuff.

Every time a grappler grabbed a piece of steel and shook it out, it would just fan the fire, like a fan in the fireplace. All of a sudden there'd be smoke billowing out. The Army Corps of Engineers eventually supplied us with infrared aerial shots of where the heat was. It was like looking at the blob. The fire was moving under the pile. One day it would be here, it would be 1,400 degrees, the next day it would be 2,000 degrees, then five days later it wouldn't register over 600 degrees." (Stout, Vitchers & Gray, 2006)

We are not so naive as to suppose that Steve Jones or that Judy Wood would be converted by the evidence we have presented, where Judy and her followers, in particular, have proven to be completely hostile to even very modest criticism of her work.

But we believe that the evidence derived from the dust samples collected by the USGS–which, after all, is a government agency–provides overwhelming proof that contradicts the government's own "official account" and establishes beyond a reasonable doubt that the destruction of the WTC was a nuclear event.

Conclusions of this Study

Evidence for fission and fusion abounds at Ground Zero. Tritiated water in any significant quantity is a telltale sign of a thermonuclear explosion. A 170 meter high plume of smoke was observed rising from Building 6, and massive amounts of tritiated water were found in the basement. It appears to be beyond reasonable doubt that this building was nuked, because no alternative explanation is reasonable.

The Twin Towers were 500,000 tons each and destroyed in 9 and 11 seconds respectively with debris ejected hundreds of feet out. There can be no doubt that the Twins Towers were nuked as well.

The USGS dust samples prove beyond all doubt that nuclear fission took place at Ground Zero. Fission triggered fusion bombs such as mini or micro neutron bombs explain the dust and water sample evidence perfectly.

The destruction of the Twin Towers was an unprecedented use of nuclear bomb technology. The public had never before witnessed anything like it. While Steve Jones and Judy Wood, among others, have added to uncertainty over what happened to the WTC buildings on 9/11, the mystery has finally been solved. The World Trade Center was nuked on 9/11.

Source note: This chapter originally appeared as "Mystery Solved: The WTC was Nuked on 9/11", *veteranstoday.com* (1 May 2013).

References

A Nuclear Power Primer: Part 3: How Does Radiation Hurt Us and How Much Does it Take? (n.d.). Retrieved from *http://www.shotsacrossthebow. com/index.php/site/comments/a_nuclear_power_primer_art_3_how_does_ radiation_hurt_us_and_how_much_does_/*

Clark, R., Green, R., Swayze, G., Meeker, G., Sutley, S., Hoefen, T., Livo, K., Plumlee, G., Pavri, B., Sarture, C., Wilson, S., Hageman, P., Lamothe, P., Vance, J., Boardman, J., Brownfield, I., Gent, C., Morath, L., Taggart, J., Theodorakos, P., & Adams, M. USGS Spectroscopy Lab, (2001). Environmental Studies of the World Trade Center Area After the September 11, 2001 Attack (Open-File Report 01-0429). Retrieved from the U.S. Geological Survey (USGS) website: *http://pubs.usgs.gov/of/2001/ ofr-01-0429/*

Cohen, S. (2006). F*** you! Mr. President: Confessions of the Father of the Neutron Bomb. (3rd ed., pp. 123-124). Retrieved from *http://www.AthenaLab. com/Confessions_Sam_Cohen_2006_Third_Edition.pdf* (Cohen, 2006)

Helmenstine, A. M. What is a Neutron Bomb? Retrieved from *http:// chemistry.about.com/od/chemistryfaqs/f/neutronbomb.htm* (Helmenstine)

Jones, S. (2006, September 28). Hard Evidence Repudiates the Hypothesis That Mini-Nukes Were Used on the WTC Towers. Retrieved from *http:// www.journalof911studies.com/letters/a/Hard-Evidence-Rebudiates-the- Hypothesis-that-Mini-Nukes-were-used-on-the-wtc-towers-by-steven-jones. pdf*

Minister of Public Works and Government Services Canada, (2009). Investigation of the Environmental Fate of Tritium in the Atmosphere (INFO-0792). Ottawa: Canadian Nuclear Safety Commission (CNSC). *http://nuclearsafety.gc.ca/pubs_catalogue/uploads/Investigation_ of_Environmental_Fate_of_Tritium_in_the_Atmosphere_INFO-0792_e. pdf* ("Investigation of the," 2009)

Semkow, T., Hafner, R., Parekh, P., Wozniak, G., Haines, D., Husain, L., Rabun, R., & Williams, P. U.S. Department of Energy, Lawrence Livermore National Laboratory (2002). Study of Traces of Tritium at the World Trade Center (UCRL-JC-150445). Retrieved from llnl.gov website: *https://e reports-ext.llnl.gov/pdf/241096.pdf*

Stout, G., Vitchers, C., & Gray, R. (2006). Nine Months at Ground Zero: The Story of the Brotherhood of Workers Who Took on a Job Like No Other.

(Google eBook ed., pp. 64-65). Simon and Schuster. Retrieved from *http://books.google.com/books?id=4VD–5- T5IcC&lpg=PA62&ots=I8PEz77Z PT&dq=ground zero grappler&pg=PA64* (Stout, Vitchers & Gray, 2006)

Ternary fission. (2013, March 22). In Wikipedia, The Free Encyclopedia. Retrieved April 19, 2013, from *http://en.wikipedia.org/w/index. php?title=Ternary_fission&oldid=546177060*

Tritium in Precipitation. (n.d.). Retrieved from *http://www.science.uottawa. ca/eih/ch7/7tritium.htm*

Twietmeyer, T. (2007, March 24). What May Have Melted the WTC Vehicles. Retrieved from *http://rense.com/general75/melt2.htm* (Twietmeyer, 2007)

Source note: This chapter originally appeared as "Mystery Solved: The WTC was Nuked on 9/11", *veteranstoday.com* (1 May 2013).

11

2+2 = Israel Nuked the WTC on 9/11

by Don Fox

"[I]f New York was outsourced to the Mossad and if the Twin Towers were nuked, then the nukes that were used must have been Israeli....[N]o alternative explanation is reasonable."– Jim Fetzer

How many wars is the US supposed to fight for Israel? How many of our sons and daughters must die? How much of our national treasury and moral standing must be squandered to insure Israeli domination of the Middle East?

Does any serious analyst actually believe that the Syrian government–which has been routing the rebels for the past several months–would jeopardize its standing in the eyes of the world by launching a gas attack when it has no reason to do so?

Does anyone believe that doing so on the eve of the arrival of a UN inspection team would be rational? Are the American people so stupid and gullible that we are going to fall for the same "song and dance" from the nation's leaders who so completely misled us about the massive surveillance being conducted by the NSA?

They lied to us about Iraq. They lied to us about Libya. They lied to us about Iran. And what could be more obvious than that they are lying to us again about Syria? The US is wreaking havoc in the Middle East for Israel. We have become Israeli liars, enforcers, stooges and dupes!

The absurdity of the American position by claiming that it needs to punish Bashar Assad for the violation of international law was apparent today when Charles Heyman, a former British officer who edits The Armed Forces of the UK, *observed that attacking Syria without a mandate from the UN Security Council would itself be a gross violation of international law, rather like the claims made during the Vietnam war that "they had to destroy the village in order to save it"! Under Barack Obama, the US has become an international joke.*

Some historical background

We know that 9/11 involved close collusion between the Neocons in the Department of Defense and the Mossad to create a pretext for the US to invade the Middle East and deconstruct the modern Arab states by converting them into statelets to promote the domination of the Middle East by Israel.

We know that New York City appears to have been outsourced to Israel and that the destruction of the Twin Towers, unlike WTC-7, can only be explained on the basis of sophisticated arrangements of mini or micro nukes. We have proven this again and again and again. It is beyond reasonable doubt.

The most powerful proof, ironically, comes from dust samples collected by the USGS, which substantiate the presence of elements that would not be present in this form had the destruction of the Twin Towers not been a nuclear event. Those include:

Barium and Strontium: Neither of these elements should ever appear in building debris in these quantities. The levels never fall below 400ppm for Barium and they never drop below 700ppm for Strontium and reach over 3000ppm for both in the dust sample taken at Broadway and John Streets.

Thorium and Uranium: These elements only exist in radioactive form. Thorium is a radioactive element formed from Uranium by decay. It's very rare and should not be present in building rubble, ever. So once again we have verifiable evidence that a nuclear fission event has taken place.

Lithium: With the presence of lithium we have compelling evidence that this fission pathway of Uranium to Thorium and Helium, with subsequent decay of the Helium into Lithium has taken place.

Lanthanum: Lanthanum is the next element in the disintegration pathway of the element Barium.

Yttrium: The next decay element after Strontium, which further confirms the presence of Barium.

Chromium: The presence of Chromium is one more "tell tale" signature of a nuclear detonation.

Tritium: A very rare element and should not be found at concentrations 55 times normal in the basement of WTC-6 only eleven days after 9/11, which is another "tell tale" sign of nukes.

But the proof also includes the dramatic incidence of cancers associated with nuclear events, where, as Jeff Prager has observed, (a) Multiple Myeloma in the general population at a rate of 3-9 incidents per 100,000 people, but the rate was 18 per 100,000 among first responders; (b) that other cancers relatively unusual cancers have appeared among the responders, including non-Hodgkins lymphoma, leukemia, thyroid, pancreatic, brain, prostate, esophageal and blood and plasma cancers; and (c) that, as of March 2011 no less than 1,003 first responders died from various cancers. Those familiar with the available evidence who continue to deny that 9/11 was a nuclear event would appear to be either cognitively impaired or deliberately deceptive.

How it was done

WTC-7 was destroyed by a classic controlled demolition, where all the floors fell at the same time, none of its floors were blown apart, and there was a stack of debris equal to 12% of the original height of the 47-story building (about 5.5 floors of debris). The Twin Towers, by contrast, were blow apart sequentially from the top down; they were converted into millions of cubic yards of very fine dust; each floor remained stationary until its turn came; and, when it was over, the buildings had been destroyed below ground level: there was no stack debris (which should have been around 12 floors high). They did not collapse. They were

blown apart using mini or micro nukes, which too many have continued to deny for too long.

Indeed, if we assume that it was done by blowing one ten-floor cube per second, then the time for the destruction of the 110-floor North Tower would have been approximately 11 seconds, which is the time estimate of NIST.

And when we note that the top three floors of the South Tower had begun to tilt and were blown as one, then the time for its destruction would have been approximately 9 seconds, which is also in agreement withe the time estimate of NIST. This appears to have been roughly how it was done, where we will continue to fine-tune the sequence as we continue.

But what is most striking is that we know the Twin Towers were nuked and we know that New York appears to have been outsourced to the Mossad. What we have now realized–it is like adding "2" and "2"–is that, if New York was outsourced to the Mossad and if the Twin Towers were nuked, then the nukes that were used must have been Israeli. *And that by itself may explain why New York was outsourced to the Mossad. Israel has refused to sign the Nuclear Non-Proliferation Treaty.*

Israel does not allow inspectors. Unlike the US, whose nuclear arsenal is tightly controlled, Israel could use its nukes–as it appears to have recently done in Syria–without having to answer to anyone and without any risk of detection. Indeed, we have now proven this beyond a reasonable doubt, because no alternative explanation is reasonable.

Did Israel Nuke the WTC on 9/11?
By Don Fox

There are voices in the 9/11 Truth Community who believe that determining the exact cause of the World Trade Center building's destruction is unnecessary and perhaps even a waste of time. One often hears comments that the official government account is blatantly false and that should be sufficient to get a real investigation launched into the events of 9/11. However the track record of government investigations into government crimes is rather poor (see the Warren Commission and the House Select Committee on Assassinations). Since an honest official investigation into 9/11 with subpoena powers is not likely to happen the task has fallen to private citizen researchers to determine what really happened that awful day.

Before you can determine WHO committed a crime you first must determine HOW it was done. No doubt that the events of 9/11 were some of the most outrageous crimes ever committed so the effort to determine HOW it was done is certainly justified. 9/11 has radically changed the world and certainly not for the better. In order to understand how the post 9/11 world actually works, determining WHO and HOW it was done is are vital questions. Merely stating that "9/11 was an inside job" is not good enough.

The major alternative theories of the destruction of the World Trade Center buildings include the directed energy weapon (DEW) (non) theory (associated with Judy Wood and Andrew Johnson), the nanothermite theory (associated with Steve Jones, Kevin Ryan and Richard Gage), the big nuke theory of Dimitri Khalezov (150 kt subbasement nukes) and the mini-nuke theory (associated with Dr. Ed Ward MD, the Anonymous Physicist, Dr. Bill Deagle, Jeff Prager and myself). We have determined that the mini/micro nuke hypothesis best fits the evidence. See the Mystery Solved and the Mini-Neutron Bombarticles for a full break down of the WTC Mini-Nuke Theory.

Nuclear Bombs Narrows the List of Suspects

Very few groups have access to nuclear bombs. Officially there are five countries designated as Nuclear Weapons States: China, France, Russia, United Kingdom and the United States. Three more countries have conducted nuclear weapons tests: India, Pakistan and North Korea. There is another country who refuses to confirm or deny that it has nuclear weapons: Israel. Though it is believed that Israel has produced enough weapons-grade plutonium for 100-200 nuclear warheads. Former President Jimmy Carter has stated that Israel has more than 150 nuclear weapons.

Of these Nuclear Weapons States which ones would have had the motive, means and opportunity to detonate nuclear bombs in downtown Manhattan? The Twin Towers were destroyed by a very sophisticated arrangement of mini-nukes that were placed in the core columns of the buildings, detonated sequentially from top to bottom and configured to explode upward. This arrangement allowed the nukes in the upper floors of the buildings to explode without destroying the bombs beneath simulating a free fall collapse. This was the epitome of an Inside Job!

I think we can safely rule out China, France, Russia, the UK, India, Pakistan and North Korea. None of these countries would have had access to the core columns of these giant skyscrapers required to pull of this feat. Had the Towers been destroyed by an ICBM or a sub-based missile then some of these other Nuclear States may be suspects.

Certainly the United States military and intelligence community had the ability to pull off 9/11. The United States is the world's leading nuclear superpower with the most advanced nuclear weapons arsenal. However the United States is a signatory to the Nuclear Non-Proliferation Treaty (NPT) and several treaties (SALT, START I, START II, START III and New START) with the former Soviet Union/Russia.

The Treaty on the Non-Proliferation of Nuclear Weapons, also referred to as the Nuclear Non-Proliferation Treaty (NNPT), obligates the 5 acknowledged nuclear-weapon states (the United States, Russian Federation, United Kingdom, France, and China) not to transfer nuclear weapons, other nuclear explosive devices, or their technology to any non-nuclear-weapon state. Nuclear weapon States Parties are also obligated, under Article VI, to "pursue negotiations in good faith on effective measures relating to cessation of the nuclear arms race at an early date and to nuclear disarmament, and on a treaty on general and complete disarmament under strict and effective international control."

Non-nuclear-weapon States Parties undertake not to acquire or produce nuclear weapons or nuclear explosive devices. They are required also to accept safeguards to detect diversions of nuclear materials from peaceful activities, such as power generation, to the production of nuclear weapons or other nuclear explosive devices.

This must be done in accordance with an individual safeguards agreement, concluded between each non-nuclear-weapon State Party and the International Atomic Energy Agency (IAEA). Under these agreements, all nuclear materials in peaceful civil facilities under the jurisdiction of the state must be declared to the IAEA, whose inspectors have routine access to the facilities for periodic monitoring and inspections. If information from routine inspections is not sufficient to fulfill its responsibilities, the IAEA may consult with the state regarding special inspections within or outside declared facilities.

The United States nuclear arsenal is subject to inspections. Is it possible that some "loose nukes" made their way from the US stockpile to Ground Zero? It is possible but not a slam dunk by any stretch of the imagination. It appears more likely that nukes from an uninspected, rogue facility like Dimona would be used in an operation such as 9/11.

All Roads Lead to Dimona

As NTI.org has observed, "Israel has not joined the Treaty on the Non-Proliferation of Nuclear Weapons (NPT) and is widely viewed as the first and only country in the Middle East to possess nuclear weapons. Believing a nuclear weapons deterrent to be essential vis-à-vis Israel's Arab adversaries, Prime Minister David Ben Gurion instituted a nuclear weapons program in the mid-1950s as part of his "activist defense policy." Consistent with Prime Minister Levi Eshkol's declaration that "Israel will not be the first nation to introduce nuclear weapons to the Middle East," Israel maintains a policy of "nuclear ambiguity," or "nuclear opacity," refraining from overt admissions that it possesses nuclear weapons, nuclear tests, or threats to its adversaries that explicitly involve nuclear weapons.

Israel has also made extensive efforts to deny other regional actors the ability to acquire nuclear weapons, most prominently in the air strikes against Iraq's Osiraq Reactor in 1981 and Syria's suspected reactor near Al-Kibar in 2007."

President John F. Kennedy was deeply concerned about Israel using the Dimona nuclear plant to produce nuclear weapons. He wrote a letter concerning Dimona to Prime Minister Levi Eshkol on July 4th, 1963:

Dear Mr. Prime Minister:

It gives me great personal pleasure to extend congratulations as you assume your responsibilities as Prime Minister of Israel. You have our friendship and best wishes in your new tasks. It is on one of these that I am writing you at this time.

You are aware, I am sure, of the exchanges which I had with Prime Minister Ben-Gurion concerning American visits to Israel's nuclear facility at Dimona. Most recently, the Prime Minister wrote to me on May 27. His words reflected a most intense personal consideration of a problem that I know is not easy for your Government, as it is not for mine. We welcomed the former Prime Minister's strong reaffirmation that Dimona will be devoted exclusively to peaceful purposes and the reaffirmation also of Israel's willingness to permit periodic visits to Dimona.

I regret having to add to your burdens so soon after your assumption of office, but I feel the crucial importance of this problem necessitates my taking up with you at this early date certain further considerations, arising out of Mr. Ben-Gurion's May 27 letter, as to the nature and scheduling of such visits.

I am sure you will agree that these visits should be as nearly as possible in accord with international standards, thereby resolving all doubts as to the peaceful intent of the Dimona project. [3-1/2 lines of source text not declassified]

Therefore, I asked our scientists to review the alternative schedules of visits we and you had proposed. If Israel's purposes are to be clear beyond reasonable doubt, I believe that the schedule which would best serve our common purposes would be a visit early this summer, another visit in June 1964, and thereafter at intervals of six months. I am sure that such a schedule should not cause you any more difficulty than that which Mr. Ben-Gurion proposed in his May 27 letter. It would be essential, and I understand that Mr. Ben-Gurion's letter was in accord with this, that our scientists have access to all areas of the Dimona site and to any related part of the complex, such as fuel fabrication facilities or plutonium separation plant, and that sufficient time be allotted for a thorough examination.

Knowing that you fully appreciate the truly vital significance of this matter to the future well-being of Israel, to the United States, and internationally, I am sure our carefully considered request will have your most sympathetic attention.

Sincerely, John F. Kennedy

US inspectors DID go to Dimona; however, they were not allowed to tour the entire facility:

Under pressure from the newly elected American president, Israel reluctantly agreed in 1961 to U.S.-Israeli bilateral inspections of the Dimona nuclear facility. The inspections at Dimona were tightly controlled by the Israelis, and restricted to the first floor of the facility. U.S. inspectors were not allowed to bring their own technical instruments, take measurements, or see the control room, instead being shown a mock-up.

It was later learned that the Israelis went so far as to wall-up elevator banks down to the underground reprocessing facility in order to evade discovery. When inspections ended in 1969, the visits had never produced any evidence of weapons-related activity or a plutonium-reprocessing facility, but inspectors often were left highly suspicious of illicit activities.

The Nixonian Compromise

The sham of US "inspections" continued until Nixon struck a deal with Golda Meir whereby Israel would not openly declare or test its nuclear capability and the US would cease inspections and stop pressuring Israel to sign the NPT.

Production model of nulcear weapons core

The gap between JFK and Nixon in regards to the Israeli nuclear program was enormous. Kennedy was not going to let Israel dictate terms to him. JFK was determined to stop Israel from producing nuclear weapons. If it turns out that Israel DID nuke the WTC buildings then there is a direct historical path from JFK's assassination to 9/11. Had JFK lived to serve

Dimona's plutonium separation control room

179

a second term Israel's nuclear program may have been dismantled before they could have nuked anybody.

Mordechai Vanunu worked at the Dimona plant and took photographs inside the facility in 1985. Vanunu revealed that indeed Dimona was producing nuclear bombs. Vanunu's whistleblowing got him 18 years in the hoosegow; the first 11 ½ were in solitary confinement.

By the late 1970s Israel was believed to have produced thermonuclear weapons, mini-nukes in the 1980s and neutron bombs by 1995. While Israel's nuclear arsenal was no match for the United States or Russia, Israel was certainly capable of pulling off the nuclear destruction of the World Trade Center buildings.

Why Were Israelis Dancing on 9/11?

Mike Rivero has an excellent post about the Dancing Israelis:

The New York Times reported Thursday that a group of five men had set up video cameras aimed at the Twin Towers prior to the attack on Tuesday, and were seen congratulating one another afterwards. Police received several calls from angry New Jersey residents claiming "middle-eastern" men with a white van were videotaping the disaster with shouts of joy and mockery. They were seen by New Jersey residents on Sept. 11 making fun of the World Trade Center ruins and going to extreme lengths to photograph themselves in front of the wreckage. Witnesses saw them jumping for joy in Liberty State Park after the initial impact. Later on, other witnesses saw them celebrating on a roof in Weehawken, and still more witnesses later saw them celebrating with high fives in a Jersey City parking lot.

According to ABC's 20/20, when the van belonging to the cheering

Later the Dancing Israelis appeared on an Israeli talk show

Israelis was stopped by the police, the driver of the van, Sivan Kurzberg, told the officers: "We are Israelis. We are not your problem. Your problems are our problems. The Palestinians are your problem."

One of them declared that he was there to "document the event." Who knew there was going to be an event to document? The actions of the Dancing Israelis lead a reasonable person to conclude that they were Mossad agents. It certainly appears that the Dancing Israelis knew the buildings were going to be nuked. They were cheering and high-fiving after the extremely sophisticated nuclear demolition sequence was pulled off to near perfection.

Are Shills Covering Up Israeli Nukes at the WTC?

The hysterics of the Wood Cult and the other nuke-denying shills makes a lot more sense if indeed they are covering for Israel's rogue nuclear program. The shills will throw ANYTHING out there to divert people from looking at nukes: hurricanes, directed energy weapons, John Hutchison's lab and nanothermite – anything to keep your eye off the ball. If you disagree with Judy Wood, Pete Santilli, Andrew Johnson, Emmanuel Goldstein, Thomas Potter or any other members of The Cult you will be subjected to attacks, intimidation and even death threats!

Richard Gage does not allow discussion of any explosives except nanothermite. But of course nanothermite is not an explosive! This has been demonstrated again and again by T. Mark Hightower, who is a chemical engineer, and Jim Fetzer, who have published three articles about it, namely: "Has nanothermite been oversold to the 9/11 Truth community?", "Is '9/11 Truth' based upon a false theory?", and "Nanothermite: If it doesn't fit, you must acquit".

These have been out for years and demonstrate conclusively that nanothermite cannot possibly have been responsible for blowing the Twin Towers apart. Yet Richard Gage and A&E911 continue to promote the theory that it was done by nanothermite:

Some Sobering Thoughts

9/11 was the most historically significant event since the Kennedy assassination. Understanding current events is impossible if you do not understand 9/11. The 9/11 scam was used to justify foreign wars of aggression in Iraq and Afghanistan, the TSA assault on travelers and the loss of civil rights for American citizens. The biggest question is who was really behind the events of 9/11?

The destruction of the WTC buildings was a nuclear event. Only a handful of countries are considered Nuclear Weapons States. Of those countries only the United States and Israel would have had the necessary access to the buildings to plant the bombs. However the United States nuclear arsenal is subject to inspection by international organizations so the odds of the bombs coming from the US stockpile are much lower than the rogue Nuclear Weapons State Israel.

Israel neither confirms nor denies that they have nuclear weapons but it's an open secret that they have several hundred nuclear devices. Israel does not allow inspectors into the Dimona facility. When the US inspectors showed up in the 1960s, the Israelis cemented the elevator banks shut so that they could inspect only the first floor. These are not the actions of a Nuclear Weapons State with nothing to hide. The 9/11 wars have primarily benefited Israel. Who had the motive, means and opportunity to nuke the World Trade Center Buildings? The answer is as obvious as "2" plus "2".

Source note: This chapter originally appeared as "2 + 2 = Israel Nuked the WTC on 9/11", *veteranstoday.com* (1 May 2013).

12

9/11: A World Swirling in a Volcano of Lies

by Dennis Cimino with Jim Fetzer

The contentious debate over how the Twin Towers were destroyed has pitted those favoring large ("basement") nukes against those identifying small nukes distributed in the elevator shafts throughout the buildings against those promoting thermite (or "nanothermite").

Some of the most interesting and important research on the mode of destruction of the World Trade Center (WTC) on 9/11 has come from "the Anonymous Physicist", *who has endorsed the use of mini or micro nukes but has also suggested that a mix of devices was employed.*

Having devoted several articles to the destruction of *the Twin Towers and perhaps also of WTC-7 ("Building 7") using mini or micro nukes,* I regard it as of scientific value to review the bidding from time to time, in case something significant may have been overlooked.

The Anonymous Physicist has drawn a parallel between the efforts that have been made to obfuscate and confound the public about the death of JFK, which has been comparable to what has been done in relation to 9/11. As he observes,

> *With the analogous JFK assassination, when enough people saw that the patsy Oswald (himself CIA/ONI) could not be the culprit shooting from behind, as the fatal shot was from the front; the PTB put out a "Babel" of CONTROLLED alternatives: Mafia, LBJ, Cubans, Grassy Knoll, rogue elements, etc (some of which were involved). All of that was to hide the horrifying, ultimate truth that the alleged government protector did it—as has been discussed by Spooked previously.*

> *With 9/11, the Babel of planes/fuel/gravity, thermite/thermate, DEW, car bombs in the basement, and surely more to come, was waiting when a critical mass of people rejected the (always) ludicrous, official, "investigation" conclusion. The massive, rapid outward—as well as downward and upward—explosions of the two towers, the toasted cars (but not paper), and popping ceiling lights (Ondrovic—see below), the micron-sized dustification of tower contents, the levels of tritium and heavy metals, the underground molten steel and high temperatures weeks and months later, **all can only be accounted for by nuclear devices and their EMPs.***

He agrees with the Finnish expert that fission-free fusion devices were likely used, where the Finnish expert states that a 1 kiloton (TNT equivalent) basement fusion device was used on each tower. However, the Anonymous Physicist:

> *(a) believes that a total of 1/10th of that amount was more than sufficient, including the power needed for vaporization/dustification of each tower's contents.*

> *(b) believes this 1/10th kt total-energy-per-tower occurred in several blasts (per tower), and in just one per other WTC buildings (possibly 3, 4, 5, 6); and,*

> *(c) believes that WTC-7 did not have a nuclear device used during "collapse" but could have had one just afterwards to vaporize evidence as all the federal alphabet agencies were in that building,–and it would have been the likely planning/command center for 9/11 with a lot of evidence to be definitively "lost."*

In this article, Dennis Cimino, who has made multiple contributions to the study of 9/11, Sandy Hook and other staged events, reconsiders the views of Dimitri Khazelov, which he suspects may hold new significance for at least one aspect of 9/11, even while continuing to endorse the pivotal role of micro or mini nukes:

A World Swirling in a Volcano of Lies

On the morning of 11 September 2001, we were all treated to a mind numbing Max Headroom 'stutter' of video rubbish that forever indelibly imprinted the ostensibly 'fake' story that was MSM fabricated and repeatedly foisted upon our ill-prepared and unsuspecting minds that morning. Much of it clearly had to have been created at the very least, days before 9/11, by virtue of the fact you just don't crank out CGI generated aircraft whacking a building with any modicum of realism of any kind in ten or fifteen minutes time without at the very least really wishing you hadn't aired it.

That was the case with the two different trajectories of UA-175, one shown in Europe which was pretty much a 25 or more degree 'nose down' dive into the South Tower, and the U.S. 'enthralled and transfixed' in horror morons got to see a plane appear just popping into the frame without proper entry, flying a very flat and straight and level trajectory, and nary an image of the other tower hi–even with the Naudet brothers on the ground with camera lenses pointed skyward to catch it all.

The nose-out phenomenon

Needless to say, CNN did screw up on the air at least once that morning, the forward nose of UA-175 barreling out of the other side, more or less unscathed and not blunted, and then the 75 or so feet of forward nose and fuselage then just magically 'vaporize' and went nowhere else.

The next airing of that same sequence is with a black bar that prohibits you from seeing this obvious goofy screwup that a sequence editor clearly missed before he vetted the thing for prime time foisting on the sheeple that Day of Infamy.

It took some of us years to go back and re-examine this stuff with a very critical eye, and indeed many like me were hard to sell the 'no planes' theory because we had all seen it on our television sets that morning over and over and over and over again. So, ten years later, some of us took a much closer and very hard look at the physics and the impossible airspeed, which such wide bodied jets could never achieve (512 knots, indicated air speed) at more or less 700 feet above ground in very cold dense air that morning.

The impossible entry

A few experts, like John Lear, made exceptional notes of it even before he knew the preposterous speeds they reported that radar track had been recorded in RADES 84 data moving at on it's way to impact.

Things like 'no shadows' and when you slow that video down frame by frame then pieces of the plane 'disappear' and then magically 'reappear' before impact with a very very hard building with a static mass many thousands of times greater than even a 512 knot, 110 ton aircraft with inertia built up behind it.

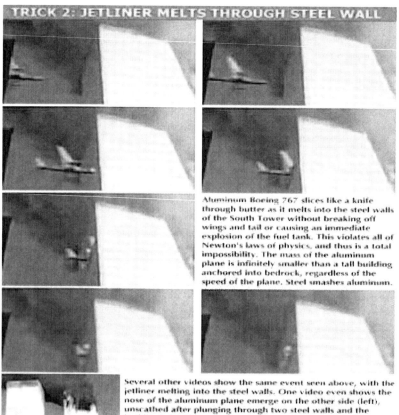

TRICK 2: JETLINER MELTS THROUGH STEEL WALL

Aluminum Boeing 767 slices like a knife through butter as it melts into the steel walls of the South Tower without breaking off wings and tail or causing an immediate explosion of the fuel tank. This violates all of Newton's laws of physics, and thus is a total impossibility. The mass of the aluminum plane is infinitely smaller than a tall building anchored into bedrock, regardless of the speed of the plane. Steel smashes aluminum.

Several other videos show the same event seen above, with the jetliner melting into the steel walls. One video even shows the nose of the aluminum plane emerge on the other side (left), unscathed after plunging through two steel walls and the building's interior core. An aluminum plane cannot penetrate a steel building undamaged. Unless you're a magician.

Lear's US District Court affidavit is perhaps the most lucid and logical assessment ever advanced about this matter (one minor error notwithstanding). He hits the nail on the head. It's nonsense to expect the plane (Flight 175) to not have done an "accordion" upon impact with the South Tower, had a real plane actually hit the building. Moreover, the structure would have swayed from the transfer of energy, which did not happen–for the obvious reason that no transfer of energy occurred (it was not a real plane).

He noted that nothing came off the parts impacting the exoskeleton of the building, and this was STEEL and not aluminum, so it was pretty substantial even at that level of the building. No luggage, bodies, or internal components bounced off the rather substantial and at rest mass of the South Tower.

Amazingly, no deceleration could be discerned as the plane effortlessly slid into a steel structure without even deforming. No strobes, no reflections off the plane's shiny skin coming from the light of the day on the building just immediately before impact and, much to my chagrin when I looked, no signs of 'wingtip vortices', which would have been substantially powerful vortices at that speed and which would have no choice but to impact the building post-crash and cause swirl patterns in the smoke which were not evident at all. Meaning: no lift was being generated by those wings on UA-175, which is aerodynamically impossible.

The gullible public

To the layperson, that is not a problem, because most have no clue that the wing generates these vortices once it's at least ½ wingspan above the ground in height generating flight. In any case, the clues of CGI fakery were multitudinous and quite obvious once you looked, especially if you ever bothered to watch the late Gerard Holmgren's presentations about the fakery. He laid it out so well that not even a layperson could come away without substantial 'doubts' about what they thought they had seen. Gerard's work was a lasting gift to our sanity, but many know not of it.

My reason for bringing up that CGI fakery is because we saw many things that day in mind numbing repetition, which we bought without reservation, but upon maybe even the closest look or glancing blow of application of logic, the information jammed into our optic nerves was *anything but* reality based. Colossal fireballs, black smoke billowing, an engine hurtling out through the side of the South Tower that later would be proven to have forced the 'planting' of the WRONG ENGINE TYPE on a sidewalk UNDER A SCAFFOLD while onlookers watched guys unload it with a hand truck from a white van and then depart. But they dropped off a JT-9 engine, which United did not use on its B-767s.

Pickup or delivery?

Newsworthy things were happening on 9-11 at Church and Murray, so Fox News was there. An FBI van is parked on Murray at the Church intersection, door open. An FBI agent stands guard over something not seen in other photos at this location. Blue-clad FBI agents appear beside the van and seem to struggle with something heavy. There appear to be six FBI agents and a photographer in the video frames. Another image taken at the deserted corner, right, shows a dolly used for moving something. What does the complete video show...a pickup or delivery?

They also left a Dave Clark aviation headset with helicopter interface cord,next to this 'wrong power plant' they stood on end, and–get this–*they left the hand-truck behind, too!* You cannot make this stuff up, really. The WRONG engine was planted by people we presumed to be F.B.I., but who they really were remains a mystery. Clearly to grab the 'wrong' engine and drop it off shows a lot of haste and lack of preparation, but maybe that was done on purpose. Maybe these obvious screw ups have been like recent hoaxes where they leave clear red herring clues that are in reality, non-sequiturs like Dorner's twice found wallet had been in that hoax. That's a bit beyond incompetent, isn't it?

Doubting my lying eyes

Anyway, like many others, I began to doubt what my lying eyes had told me. Sure we saw that plane impact over and over again. But we also never here in the U.S. saw the same sequence of the same exact alleged plane coming down at a very steep angle to impact. How can it be both ways? In the U.S. version, the plane is straight and level. Not so in Europe. And yeah, in the U.S. version the plane doesn't come into the frame from the right side of the screen, it just materializes there and continues as if it beamed there from an alternate reality somewhere.

Notwithstanding the things noted about the obviously CGI generated plane that never breaks a sweat entering a moderately resisting steel structure, the plane at least in one view by CNN comes out the other side unscathed and not deformed or blunted after hurtling through thick steel columns that it couldn't possibly have missed all of them on the way through at that angle. So what gives? Very good question.

We bought so much fakery that in two months we were so brainwashed and numb we could barely stand to look at a TV screen for fear we wouldn't see that same plane barrel into the tower and enter it totally without a counter reaction upon impact with it. Yes there was a fireball and yes there was a slotted entry, but here again, 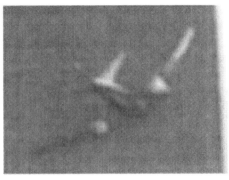 even the slot dihedral angle of the B-767 wing doesn't match up.

Sure the airfoil would be somewhat distorted maybe in a dive maneuver and then pull out before impact but as we saw in the U.S. there was no dive. So, why the wing dihedral change? Dihedral is the angle of incidence with the fuselage that is engineered into the aircraft to create ROLL STABILITY and enhance that characteristic in the flight performance of the machine.

Flight 175 still in the air

So, we know the wing had a set dihedral and more or less would not have a reason to be different on impact with a building given the fact that no apparent resistance of any kind was seen in video analysis by virtue of no deceleration occurring post impact. John Lear called it right, and many of us experienced pilots also did. Some of us knew that even a modified

ACARS CONFIRMED - 9/11 AIRCRAFT AIRBORNE LONG AFTER CRASH
UNITED 175 IN THE VICINITY OF HARRISBURG AND PITTSBURGH, PA

(PilotsFor911Truth.org) - Aircraft Communications Addressing and Reporting System (ACARS) is a device used to send messages to and from an aircraft. Very similar to text messages and email we use today, Air Traffic Control, the airline itself, and other airplanes can communicate with each other via this "texting" system. ACARS was developed in 1978 and is still used today. Similar to cell phone networks, the ACARS network has remote ground stations installed around the world to route messages from ATC, the airline, etc, to the aircraft depending on it's location and vice versa. ACARS Messages have been provided through the Freedom Of Information Act (FOIA) which demonstrate that the aircraft received messages through ground stations located in Harrisburg, PA, and then later routed through a ground station in Pittsburgh, 20 minutes after the aircraft allegedly impacted the South Tower in New York. How can messages be routed through such remote locations if the aircraft was in NY, not to mention how can messages be routed to an aircraft which allegedly crashed 20 minutes earlier? Pilots For 9/11 Truth have briefly touched on this subject in 9/11: Intercepted through the excellent research of "Woody Box", who initially discovered such alarming information in the released FOIA documents(1). We now have further information which confirms the aircraft was not in the vicinity of New York City when the attacks occurred. read more...

B-767 couldn't get to '512' knots at 700 AGL (above ground level) under any conditions, due to the drag coefficient going up by the CUBED as speed increases in dense air.

So, nobody in the general population batted an eye when the government released the speed data from the radar track of UA-175, which, by the way, was still in the air over a place far far far away, post impact, by virtue of it's ACARS DATA LINK transmissions which UA dispatch person Ballinger had good solid notes about, which he presented to the 9/11 ConMission people, no doubt keeping his original printouts in an undisclosed location. Today that data is in NARA archives under TOP SECRET classification, for only one good reason. They want that cat in the bag.

In two places at the same time

So we have aircraft doing impossible things, going too fast, coming out the other side, and their data links operating for hundreds of miles after the planes were allegedly fully destroyed. How can this be? How can anyone believe the real UA-175 and real UA-93 could have been destroyed when ACARS data shows this not to be true? How?

United 93 Still Airborne After Alleged Crash - According To ATC/Radar

04/28/09 (PilotsFor911Truth.org) - Recently it has been brought to our attention that Air Traffic Control (ATC) transcripts reveal United 93 as being airborne after it's alleged crash. Similar scenarios have been offered with regard to American 77 and American 11 showing an aircraft target continuing past its alleged crash point in the case of American 11, or past the turn-around point in the case of American 77. However, both these issues can be easily explained by "Coast Mode" radar tracking. This is not the case with United 93.

Radar Coast Mode activates when a transponder is inoperative (or turned off) and primary radar tracking is lost, which enables ATC to have some sort of reference of the flight after losing radar coverage of the physical aircraft. When an aircraft target enters "Coast Mode", ATC is alerted in the form of a blue tag on the target as well as the tag letters switching to CST. ATC will readily recognize when an aircraft enters "Coast Mode".

According to National Transportation Safety Board (NTSB) Flight Path Study, United 93 allegedly impacted the ground at 10:03am, September 11, 2001. The following transcript excerpts are provided by the Federal Aviation Administration. It is a conversation between Air Traffic Control System Command Center - East, Management Officers (ntmo-e) and other various facilities. The conversation is as follows in real time:

My point is that in eleven now going on twelve years, we have had a lot of time to look at still shots and videos of the day. Ostensibly these little clues all lead at least in my mind, to a glaring fact. That fact is that the planes allegedly that had struck these buildings and crashed into a field in Pennsylvania no way could be 'destroyed' and in fact they remained in the F.A.A. aircraft registry for more than 4 full years after they were allegedly irrevocably totally utterly in pieces. Make any sense? Not on your life. The aircraft we knew as American 11, and its sister ship, American 77, were not even scheduled to fly on 9/11, according to Bureau of Transportation Statistics records.

Pentagon Implausibilities

We have no real evidence to support UA 11's impact with the North Tower other than the video fakery. As for FLT-77, anyone looking at the Pentagon lawn 9 minutes later in photos saw virtually NO WRECKAGE until a C-130 piloted by Cdr. O'Brien of the Air National Guard, began to seed wreckage from a BUGA COLOMBIA crash that took place in December of 1995.

One piece even had jungle vine still wrapped on it after it landed on the previously post crash PRISTINE lawn. People like Mike Rivero swear on a stack of bibles we are 'pod people' for asking where 100 tons of airplane went because there are no wing slots nor are there engine penetrations of the façade.

And, not one drop of JET A fuel on the lawn after the alleged nearly full airplane struck '6' poles on it's approach at 465 knots, again, an impossible speed due to phenomenal drag resistance at such low altitudes in cold dense air.

Impossible speed at low altitude

Top speed down there not much better than 365 knots max, per BOEING's assertions during a phone call with one of their test pilots. Those of us who ask; "where is the 100 tons of wreckage at" get; "Oh, you're pod people" by Rivero and other shills. Clearly they cannot think us to be that stupid.

NASA Flight Director Confirms 9/11 Aircraft Speed As The "Elephant In The Room"

06/22/2010 - (PilotsFor911Truth.org) Recently Pilots For 9/11 Truth have analyzed the speeds reported for the aircraft utilized on 9/11. Numerous aviation experts have voiced their concerns regarding the extremely excessive speeds reported above Maximum Operating for the 757 and 767, particularly, United and American Airlines 757/767 Captains who have actual flight time in all 4 aircraft reportedly used on 9/11. These experts state the speeds are impossible to achieve near sea level in thick air if the aircraft were a standard 757/767 as reported. Combined with the fact the airplane which was reported to strike the south tower of the World Trade Center was also producing high G Loading while turning and pulling out from a dive, the whole issue becomes incomprehensible to fathom a standard 767 can perform such maneuvers at such intense speeds exceeding Maximum Operating limits of the aircraft. Especially for those who research the topic thoroughly and have expertise in aviation. read more...

So, my point is that the things we thought we knew were not necessarily based in hard reality. You cannot have so many departures from laws of physics and aeronautical science to then come to believe what you thought you saw was remotely valid. Planes that are destroyed cannot have operational data links over which the pilots have no control–and for hundreds of miles after they have crashed. So what gives? How can this be?

We have seen for decades how HowLieWood has in move after movie after movie shown us space wars, building being blown up that never were harmed, and impossible feats in fantasmagorical fashion in many many movies and for that matter, television series shown us since the mid to late 1960's.

Then in, oh, about 1968 or so, COLOR came around and gave us much more realism with studio effects that for the most part till computer technology became widely used, was not so badly done using simpler tools that required skill but no computers to create these fake realities in movies.

Other examples of fakery

For decades we had been pre programmed with this nonsense till we blindly began to extrapolate that kind of stuff into everyday life. I've seen a real building in Los Angeles blow up, I have witnessed plane crashes, and seen automobiles crash in real life. Seldom do these things happen with the dramatic visual effects that you see in movie theaters.

THERE'D BE BLASTED ON LUNAR DUST ON THE EXTENDED LANDERS FEET FROM THE MAIN ENGINE TOO

no sign of a blasted out rocket motor exhaust crater the main engine would have made as the LEM descended onto the moon

In any case, I want to bring up a very powerful example. In 1969, we were shown a lunar landing that by any sane person's estimation, could not have occurred with visual cues that show STUDIO LIGHTING and LUNAR WINDS (blowing a flag around in a vacuum) and yes, shadows being cast in differing directions on the lunar surface when only ONE light source bright enough to cast them, was the SUN and it wasn't hop scotching around in space far as I know, so shadows showing multiple incident light from more than one source on the moon were not possible. Yet they happened.

Back in that very, very, sad Stanley-Kubrick-created fakery, we saw a 10 thousand pound thrust main engine not blow a large crater under the LEM, and we didn't see any dust blown into the landing pads on the end of the main landing gear struts. In 1/6th gravitational field that is not possible. Nor is it possible that when an astronaut falls forward that his ass is lifted when the guy helping him is in front of him, clearly by a wire from above. Yet it took place. On Apollo 11. What also happened is an Astronaut named Neil Armstrong stepped off the LEM into inches of very fine dust that the main engine would have blown away all the way to bedrock as the LEM landed that day.

So many signs of fakery, including faces not being allowed to be seen in what would appear to have been mirrored helmet visors when in fact even the reflections on those don't work, AND we see flags waving in a breeze that cannot possibly be there, and we even have camera crosshair placement that cannot be and clearly doesn't work. So many clues of fakery we missed then, too, including that the landing pads would have left marks showing how they slid in the soft dust on touchdown, because of the cantilever shock-absorbing action of the struts. That no such sliding took place indicates that the LEM was put in place by being lowered using an overhead crane. For decades we missed indications like these.

Signs of foreknowledge of 9/11

We had so many chances to see through the obvious rubbish and ruses but today, I would bet that in light of calling out these insidiously simple facts, people will decry I am a 'moon bat' for inferring that our astronauts defied the VAN ALLEN RADIATION region around the earth which would have FRIED THEM on the way to the moon, and pointing out these facts seen with a wind whipped by fans flag in a LUNAR STUDIO SET and an impossibly crane placed LUNAR LEM lander that looks like it was set there and nary disturbed a single pebble or blew dust into the lander's pads as it touched down. C'mon folks. Really.

Series 9/Episode 1, 21 September 1997, opens with "New York 9/11", focuses on the Twin Towers, and ends with a lavish animation of the Washington Bridge, which was also a target. It wouldn't be so bad if they didn't just also rub our noses in our ignorance and blind acceptance of stuff that wouldn't cut it in a bad B  GRADE MOVIE. Yet we bought it all, and ignored the nose rubbing in the poo like the SIMPSONS hint above that took place long before 9/11 was a dream in the Israeli PM's nut sack. We get played. They toss up hints before the ruses are even pulled off, and in a way, it subliminally preps you for just rote acceptance of what rational people could never possibly accept.

In any case, I went long in this pass here but the reason is, the situation we have is that per these observations, we all have been asleep at the proverbial reality wheel for a long time here. They pull these things off, and we just buy them. Our brains having been pre-conditioned for years to go in the direction of, "Oh hell, if it looks even remotely possible, I will buy it even with a nonsensical explanation" and that, when our brains say to us, "That does not compute." Most are incapable of even thinking, much less computing anything.

Volcanoes of vermiculite

So, back on to the picture featured here. Clearly, that is hundreds of tons of pulverized VERMICULITE used in the floor slabs of the WTC towers. According to NIST the steel weakened and the buildings, floor by floor, pancaked and crushed everything. Well, in a movie studio that might happen, but not in real life. In real life, things just don't instantly pulverize without a massive application of a lot of force. Granted, the asbestos-laden VERMICULITE is not concrete.

It's significantly more like gypsum or DRYWALL and as many of us have seen in our own homes, a pissed off kid or spouse can drive a fist through that without going to the hospital for treatment. Surely though, this asbestos and less hardened fire retardant floor material used could not be so pulverized in totality more or less in the same instant without a huge amount of force being brought to bear on it.

So how did that force come into existence and how did it get applied to make almost all of the vermiculite material completely fall apart and become dust not floor by floor but before the structure had even fully gotten to the half way implosion point. How could it happen? How could the aggregate totality of every pound of  the floor slab material all in an instant be pulverized?

Vermiculite is fibrous and therefore by the very nature of that mixture, tends to much more evenly disperse force in multiple off impact vectors so that you might drive your fist through a wall but the rest of the wall remains solid and relatively not turned to dust. Much more rigid concrete on the other hand, shatters and because it doesn't yield easily, tends to fracture and break up in larger chunks long before it turns to a powder state.

What was real, what was not

I pondered that for a long time and drew some amazing conclusions that until further notice need to be examined better to fully get a handle on what was 'real' that day and what could not be real. I began to really question the validity of much of the stuff we saw presented to us that day. Over and over and over again, we saw planes that simply did not get destroyed, allegedly slam into a building effortlessly and then blow up once inside of the building, in that case, the South WTC tower. On it's face we have over decades been pre-programmed by not only MSM with rubbish, but by HowLieWood fakery that entertained us for all those years. The end result is a population that is best characterized by a movie called, "Idiocracy".

My main intent here wasn't to spend the whole column pointing at the fakery, but it was important to preface the main course of this too long meal with some rationale about how and why we got so easily rooked. Some of us are a bit brighter, have the physics backgrounds, the common sense, and the ability to think. Yet, in ten years how many would dare talk about 'no planes' involved in the 9/11 hoaxing? That group is growing by the way, but it's still in it's infancy. After 12 years now and then some, you'd expect more people to be questioning ALL OF IT. Not happening that way quite as fast as it should. Meaning, the social programming of nonsensical muck on the tube has brought us to a place where ridiculously bad crap gets eaten up and incorporated into people's psyche's and then spit out again in echo-chamber repetition of rote memorized excuses and epithets hurled to demean and demoralize those of us who see the fakery.

What I meant to get into right off the bat is that the video, the still photos, and much of the narrative pre-programmed us to accept muck we otherwise would not have. Very few of us saw that top photo and understood the totality of that shot. Many would go, "So what?", and not think twice. But to any person with any background in testing of materials and matter in a real

world, you cannot see that without understanding that if it is real, that virtually all of the flooring in the buildings was rendered unto dust not floor by floor, but almost in one instant. And that is very, very telling.

Khazelov's theory of 150kt nukes

We have had people like Khazelov come forward and tell us about nuclear weapons being used at WTC in NYC that day. His main theory is that 150kt weapons were used in all '3' out of a total of '4' utterly destroyed and demolished, in one case, cratered as was WTC-6, buildings. That is like using the same size hammer to drive railroad spikes and thumb tacks. May be a bad example but excessive force in that range would have probably destroyed much of lower Manhattan that morning not just from blast damage but by radiation. Some of us had asserted, unlike Khazelov, that 'mini' or 'micro nukes' had been used, but they could not so instantly and totally render ALL of the vermiculite material in the floor slabs unto dust in an instant as apparently was the case here.

Yes, we can also say, "Oh, it wasn't an instant–it took seconds", which is also true, but the total collapse sequence took almost 10 seconds per tower and same goes for WTC-7 which went down a bit later than BBC planned by their script because they reported it down on a broadcast a full half an hour or so before it actually IMPLODED by controlled demolition squibs and charges.  We know that from the morning till 5:20 PM that insufficient time elapsed to put charges in as Silverstein asserted because he had admitted the building was damaged and had to be 'pulled' and so it was. But clearly that sequence had started before Barry Jennings got evacuated because the lower lobby was more or less destroyed with dead bodies in the lobby long before he got taken out by fire-fighters who came to get him out.

All total, we had '4' buildings completely utterly destroyed. Allegedly '2' planes were involved. Then magically the week or more long work to put in charges in WTC-7 got done in a few short hours. Really?

In my final analysis here, I had cited to others that the neutron radiation from even small devices would have caused a huge amount of X-radiation to occur, by a phenomenon called "Bremsstrahlung" emission of X-radiation. If Khazelov was right, the steel in the WTC towers would have created enough of that to really 'fry' people just like the Van Allen radiation would have fried the Apollo 11 crew on their way to the Moon in 1969. And we do have reports of persons being "vaporized" in the vicinity on the otherwise pretty evacuated streets that day, which further confirms the use of nukes to take them down. And as many as 1000 may have been turned to toast in the building itself, where Don Fox has an excellent article discussing this issue, including a segment of an interview with Fr. Frank Morales, a first responder, on "The Real Deal".

We can count out the 4000 recipients of the ODIGO messages that warned Jewish people not to come, but that still doesn't explain the dearth of people in that area that morning at a time when it's normally teeming with workers. In a very real sense, this effect cited above would have irradiated so many people on the streets and in adjacent buildings who were watching.

And, this effect would have probably done considerable damage to solid state electronics nearby for at least a good 1/8th of a mile in all directions, perhaps not uniformly so but still it would have been a major problem in the aftermath. Radios still worked locally. Even a helicopter flying close enough and would have been adversely impacted and possibly brought down, wasn't even fazed. So nuclear artifacts you'd expect were notably not there. Only question here is what kind of nuclear device deviates so grossly from what we know about them from their uses across the globe in test after test after test?

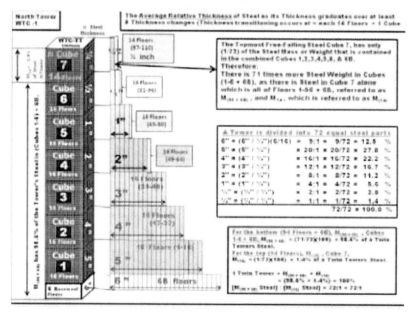

In any case, the look at the evidence that this piece is intended to hopefully trigger, isn't intended to cause rancor and general bickering amongst co-workers and others who get into discussions about the fakery, but what the intent is here is to get people to ask again, maybe for the first time; "what the hell happened that day?" and not let others tell you by 'consensus' that this is the ONLY way to the truth. That word equates to 'group think' in reality. No TRUTH can come from that. No way.

So, Khazelov may not have had it right but he was on the right path, because the total pulverization of the floor slabs of VERMICULITE fibrous material of gypsum and drywall and other components of concrete, made it impossible for floor by floor, NIST pulverization to happen without adding a whole lot of time to the collapse and hence really prolonged the near free fall speeds we saw that day.

Nuking the Twin Towers on 9/11

Guys like Don Fox, and Jeff Prager, and many of us contended that something unusual and well beyond just thermite was employed to do this to these buildings, especially WTC towers 1 and 2. For what it's worth, WTC-7 more or less has all the earmarks of classical, very, very, very tried and true Controlled Demolition using thermite charges to cut the core out first. We saw the squibs firing, heard the pops. Down it came, about half hour after the BBC script said it did.

And, what happened to WTC-6 that hollowed it out like a spoon in soft ice cream that day? Chuck Boldwyn's presentation proved that the undamaged mass of the WTC towers could not have been brought down by a small percentage of the buildings being asymmetrically damaged by alleged plane impacts.

In any case my assertion is two-fold:

One: Much of what we thought we saw clearly was not reality. Unfortunately, it's too late to erase our brains of it. It's in there, indelibly imprinted on our psyche's forever till we die.

Two: We need to cull out the stuff that the government has strewn into the mix that lessens the degree of certainty to the point of dissuading sane and thoughtful people from even bothering to question the official nonsense and fantastic story that 19 guys with box cutters who were mostly proven to be still alive days later, overcame NORAD defenses and flew planes beyond their capability and experience in ways only professional seasoned pilots might do or achieve.

But what we can do is ask how the X-radiation issue got dodged and didn't occur if as we believe, nuclear devices of a 'small' size were used. Clearly even controlled demolition could NOT have almost simultaneously end-to-end, pulverize every cubic meter of vermiculite used in the WTC tower flooring. But something did that on 9/11.

So, what did it? RDX didn't do it. It's a powerful and moderately heavy type of highly energetic explosive that is used to blow things to smithereens.

If one were to sit down and try to force transfer the amount of that to pulverization of all of the vermiculite at once more or less and then we have a problem. I don't think they could have installed so much RDX in the towers even given a lot of time, without causing the threat of an accidental detonation of it by things you cannot control that act as 'initiators' of the explosions.

The proponents of 'Oh, they put these in during construction' have no clue what EMI (electromagnetic interference) and or HIRF. Joe Kennedy, Jr., knew for a brief instant as his bomber got vaporized by that, while fully loaded with ordnance.

Concluding mixed reflections

It's pretty clear that Khazelov may have been partially correct, albeit he used a broad brush to paint both slats and toothpicks. And, he got the yields wrong for the type of damage done. But, it is beginning to look like he was right insofar as high yield devices were employed from the bottom up.

These devices were so powerful that pulverizing the vermiculite was not a big problem when the charge was detonated in a fashion that vectors the force almost entirely into the targeted material. From the basement, that means 'up', for sure.

The buildings were being destroyed from the bottom up in close proximity to being blow apart from the top down using micro or mini nukes inside the elevator shafts, where the falling debris masked the more powerful explosions necessary to destroy the lower, thicker portions of the towers.

The suppression of the blast shockwave and the noted X-radiation and even neutron problem might have been aided by the instant pulverization of a material that by it's very nature would have interfered with the effect that is known as "Bremsstrahlung" by suppressing the direct electron interaction during the detonation, in much the same way that boron interferes with neutrons.

Needless to say, sound waves are diffused by clouds of heavy rain, and dust, and in this case, finely particulate suspended in air matter, effectively attenuating or rolling off the sharp impulse 'bang' that would have been heard but was not heard. Sure firemen heard in the buildings; "bang bang bang bang bang bang", over and over, again in squib firing precision sequencing. We know that, in addition to heavier than normal demolition charges, that cutter charges were instrumental in destroying the Twin Towers.

It was an unprecedented and risky gamble that, while the top 30 floors of the South Tower tilted to the side, they were able to blow it before it could could come crashing to the ground. And thermite charges were used as core column cutters because the angular cuts are evident IMMEDIATELY in the rubble not done days later as some would irresponsibly assert in the blogs.

So, in a way, those who have pointed the finger at thermite are in their own way, partially correct. It was employed but not the principal cause of the buildings' demolition.

Twelve plus years has elapsed and we are close but no cigar yet. We know more, but we also know 'less' in that so much obfuscation and rubbish has emerged that five years ago we were probably in some ways better off not having heard some of that.

But we are getting closer. From the perspective of psychology, the public has had an extremely difficult time accepting the idea that the security companies that were supposed to be protecting the buildings were engaged in preparing them for destruction and that the government on which we depend for our own nation's security would so grossly violate it to promote a political agenda.

Source note: This chapter originally appeared as "9/11: A World Swirling in a Volcano of Lies", *veteranstoday.com* (14 February 2014).

Part V

The Pentagon:
What didn't Happen

13

The "Official Account" of the Pentagon is a Fantasy

by Jim Fetzer

Among the most fascinating aspects of 9/11 research has been the on-going controversy over whether the absence of evidence that a Boeing 757 hit the Pentagon should or should not be publicized within the  movement, especially by Jim Hoffman, who has published several articles maintaining that the physical evidence as well as the witness reports supports a Boeing 757 having hit the building.

One of the more bizarre aspects of his defense of the "official account" of the Pentagon attack is to cite the Sandia test, in which an F-4 was strapped onto a rail car frame and run at around 500 mph into a nuclear-resistant concrete barrier.

The plane blew apart into millions of tiny pieces, implying that that was what ought to have been expected of the Boeing 757 at the Pentagon. The building consists of 12 inches of concrete, 8 inches of brick, and a facade of 4 inches of limestone, which is a very porous stone. Even Major Gen. Albert Stubblebine, USAF (ret.), concluded that no Boeing 757 had hit the Pentagon for the obvious reason that he could discern no imprint of the wings on the building.

Stubblebine, of course, was the NSA's signals intelligence image analyst, but that has not deterred Jim Hoffman, who has also argued that discussing the Pentagon "might be a trap", since the Pentagon might release some of the more than 80 videos it possesses that would show "what really happened" as opposed to the five frames it has released, one of which shows the image of a small plane that is about half the size of a Boeing 757.

Why anyone should take Hoffman seriously about any of this is beyond me, because, based upon my personal experience, he has gone out of his way to manipulate the 9/11 Truth community, even to the extent of creating an elaborate pretext to excuse Larry Silverstein from having made an obvious concession to the controlled demolition of WTC-7 with his "pull it" remark during an interview with PBS. He has had some effect, it would appear, since even David Ray Griffin, perhaps the leading expert on 9/11 in the world today, has avoided pushing the Pentagon front-and-center, where it properly belongs. As Dennis Cimino explains, the "official account" is a fantasy, where the American public would benefit from knowing that even the Pentagon attack was a fabrication and a fraud.

The Pentagon attack is a fantasy
by Dennis Cimino

On September 11, 2001, we were told by the U.S. government that at 9:38 a.m. on that day, a Boeing 757 jetliner impacted the building at a speed of approximately 465 knots after executing a 330 degree turn for no apparent reason any sane person can think of, as the building is highly distinguishable from virtually any altitude above 2000 feet for several miles. The official story has the flight path just to the side of the west wing of the White House, which in any person's estimation is a significantly more important target than is the building that houses the military managers who run the Military Industrial Complex.

We were also told that nobody could have foreseen this type of attack, even though just a year earlier, a drill was held, and a nearly identical B-757 American Airlines plane was flown by Chuck Burlingame himself, as the Pentagon ran a preparedness drill to simulate such an attack.

Unfortunately, many people in America are unaware that the Washington, D.C. area has Raytheon "Basic Point Defense" missile battery armament embedded on several building rooftops there, using Sea Sparrow air defense missiles, much in the same fashion that Moscow has a system that NATO code named 'Yo Yo' that maintains radar surveillance and provides protection to the Kremlin and other high value targets from military incursions.

Pentagon Mass Casualty Exercise, 24-26 October 2000

In other words, the Pentagon was protected not only by these missile batteries, but also had in place a number of adjacent fighter bases which provided a fairly high level of protection given the fact that the plane inbound to the Pentagon from the east was not supersonic as are the adjacent fighter jets based in the area, and therefore easily could have been intercepted and at the very least, temporarily deflected off course if not shot down, if need be, long before it reached the target on the building, known as 'The Catchers Mit' due to recent renovations which added several inches of KEVLAR armor to that face of the building to protect the occupants.

For those of you who are not familiar with Kevlar armor and how it works, the only much more vastly superior but significantly more expensive armor is ceramic in nature and is often used jointly with Kevlar to protect personnel from high energy armor piercing rounds fired by tanks and other anti armor weapons such as are mounted on most military attack helicopters, for instance, such as the 30mm cannon and the infamous Obama well used 'hellfire' anti tank missile system.

In addition, there is a system, known as "Identification Friend or Foe" aka I.F.F., which uses a special MODE 4A feature that only military aircraft use, whereupon special encryption. Additionally, a mission specific MODEX aka SEDSCAF number for each plane is assigned and if it does not meet the PLAN OF THE DAY for the area, IT STILL IS NOT GOING TO PASS MODE 4A MUSTER. It would be shot down. No "ifs", no "ands" and no "buts"!

The proper MODEX / SEDSCAF NUMBER is what enables an aircraft them to penetrate prohibited or military restricted airspace such as that which surrounds both the White House and the Pentagon, as well as a number of military installations around the globe. This feature is necessary to prevent the possible mis-identification of a civilian aircraft by military air defense personnel who man radar scopes in the Washington, D.C. area, 24/7, watching for unauthorized aircraft who do not have the proper MODE 4A response capability or code in use with their "on board" transponders. Only military aircraft have this Mode 4A capability, or what is often referred to as 'crypto Beacon Video' military ATC specialists.

The "hit point" on the ground floor

In any case, the reason I mention this is that there are several echelons of protection which allegedly all summarily 'failed' us on Sept. 11th., 2001, and allowed an unidentified plane hurtling towards Washington, D.C.'s protected airspace, long after the First targets in New York had already been seriously damaged. To be honest, it is simply not possible for virtually every one of these systems to have been overcome by 19 guys wielding no more than box cutters. It took a lot of sabotage or unplugging on the ground to do that.

In any case, there was plenty of warning that an 'unknown' and presumed 'hostile' target was inbound to the Washington, D.C. area from the area around West Virginia to the east, and more than sufficient time existed to scramble fighters and or light off the Basic Point Missile Defense or BPDMS radar systems (AKA as N.S.S.M.S.) and missile defenses that are installed in rooftops there in the Washington, D.C. area since the mid 1980's. Basic Point Defense uses a CW target illuminator radar to allow the semi-actively guided Sea Sparrow missile to radar home on reflected energy coming back from the target aircraft after the radar has locked onto the target.

Though these are short range, they are so effective many high value targets in the Navy use this system, with its infamous MK-112 Fire Control radar system. It's known that NATO's Sea Sparrow was in place in the mid 1980's in Washington, D.C. as point defense against air attack. It's not unreasonable to assume that an updated version of N.S.S.M.S. / Mk 112/MK-115 would be there in September, 2001., by any stretch of the imagination. In all likelihood, it would be a version of the PAC-3 'Patriot' Missile system, another Raytheon toy.

One more point would like to make is that the White House, which this aircraft would breeze right past, had agents on the roof with shoulder-fired

STINGER MISSILES, and on this particular day, you can rest assured that with the unknown target hurtling toward Washington, D.C., those agents were on that roof with those STINGER MISSILES out of their cases and on their shoulders as they scanned the clear morning sky for the coming intruder plane. Why did they not fire at it?

So, on September 11, 2001, what took place was a plane that was not a scheduled air carrier flight, per the Bureau of Transportation Statistics or BTS database, departed Dulles International from a departure gate that does not match the coordinates transmitted by FDR data stored in the CPM provided by the N.T.S.B., flight data recorder records, on that non-scheduled American Airlines flight, aka 'FLT 77' per the government's submission, where this flight allegedly left Dulles with a hijacker on board who was capable of flying a very sophisticated and complex airplane that even the average pilot in the F.A.A. pilot registry could probably not really fly with such precision.

This plane took off, climbed to it's cruise altitude, and then over West Virginia, was hijacked in 3 minutes time, and then executed a 'standard rate' turn which no hijacker would have performed with such precision, and immediately turned inbound to the perfect heading that would take it directly to the Pentagon, even though for hijackers to do this, would have meant they would have had to know exactly where the aircraft was immediately -- and I do mean, IMMEDIATELY -- and then have the requisite knowledge of how to re-program the complicated FMS computers in the aircraft to display target area data to them, because as you might have guessed, they did not bring their own GPS system with them on the planes that would have given them immediate positional information as well as a much more immediate way of turning the plane onto a magnetic heading that would take it to Washington, D.C. from that nice precise standard rate turnaround in the skies over West Virginia.

Impressed? I sure am, as would be many B-757 line captains who fly this airplane every day, especially with the level of complexity the FMS or Flight Management System on that airplane has, that has on at least one occasion, led to the crash and destruction of a similarly equipped American Airlines B-757 in the mountains just outside of Cali, Colombia just a few years before this.

What was more alarming that day is that during the '3' minute hijacking interval, neither the cockpit door opened (reported via the Digital Flight Data Acquisition Unit or DFDAU as it is known) and the autopilot did not disengage. Now imagine yourself being Captain Chuck Burlingame and his copilot, sitting in their seats, when these hijackers slid under the door crack on the floor and re-constituted themselves as full fledged box-cutter wielding terrorists, who then proceeded to cut the heads off these two airmen

Newly discovered photo shows that no 757 struck the Pentagon at point of impact!

A newly discovered photo (above) taken within the first 30 minutes before the wall collapse, above, is the first photo clearly showing the OFFICIAL IMPACT POINT (yellow arrow) BEFORE the collapse, without being obscured by smoke. Note the two cars and the two second floor windows (A) as reference points, it is IMPOSSIBLE that a giant 757 airliner struck the impact point WITHOUT BREAKING THE WINDOWS (black arrow) OR LEAVING ANY MARKS OR OTHER SIGNS OF IMPACT OF THE FUSELAGE, TAIL, OR WINGS! Obviously, if such a plane hit the impact point at GROUND LEVEL, as the photo above shows, its 125' wingspan would have struck the two cars before striking the wall. The photo also shows NO BREACH OF THE WALL at point of impact where plane wreckage could have entered the Pentagon building. If the plane wreckage could not enter the building, where did it disappear to? Where is the plane debris? Where are the bodies? What is the truth?

whose job is to protect their aircraft and it's passengers at all costs. Neither of these guys were 98-pound weaklings, yet in three minutes they had been incapacitated and were out of their seats without touching either the yokes or the rudders, which would have immediately DISENGAGED the aircraft's autopilot system which was flying the machine at that time.

The plane did not yaw, roll, pitch or otherwise change any flight parameter but remained perfectly on course, and for some reason, two minutes later the hijackers finally decided to turn OFF the transponder to make it a bit harder for ATC to be positively sure this plane was the same one they were watching before the hijacking took place. Now, one more thing you need to know is that for either of the flight crew to either push the talk button on the yokes or to change the transponder code to one that tells the ATC personnel monitoring the flight that they were in a 'hijack' situation, would have taken mere seconds to do. Yet, this was not done.

And the autopilot did not disengage though it is presumed the two pilots would have resisted and fought for their very lives and at least kicked the rudder pedals and or moved the yokes. Yet they did not do any of these things. Merely holding the push to talk button and screaming whilst having one's head cut off would have gotten someone's attention, I do think. Too many ways the crew could send a duress message to the ATC en route centers, and not once was this attempted. Why? The best and most reasonable reason is that these were not hijacked planes at all, but planes flown by military personnel or crews who thought they were innocently participating in the drills.

And as such, these would NOT have been passenger flights, as it is illegal to use passengers in military exercises under any circumstances, due to the risk involved. This is another clue that points to the fact that no hijacking took place in this aircraft at all, because had that been the case, they had plenty of time to use a duress system to alert ATC that they were under attack in that cockpit.

In any case, the precision turn executed and the immediate orientation onto the course to the Pentagon is kind of indicative of a professional pilot and not a hijacker being at the controls, because the crew who flew that plane knew precisely where the plane was when they turned directly onto a course which would then take them directly into the target, which that morning was the Pentagon. Given the fact that it is quite impossible for these freshly in the cockpit hijackers to know where the plane was when they took it over, and furthermore, to know the exact on course heading back to the Washington, D.C. area to attack the Pentagon, is again quite telling of who really was still at the controls of this plane.

It surely was not a hijacker who just got into the cockpit a couple minutes ago, based on this immediate orientation and turn onto course to the target. This process would have taken several minutes. It did not take several minutes. It was immediate. Mighty clairvoyant airmen these guys were, and powerful too, to overcome the crew in three minutes time while ensuring the autopilot never disengaged even for a split second, nor had the cockpit door opened to let them in. (See cockpit door diagram below)

Then, later as they got closer in, they did something puzzling for a crew of neophyte hijackers. On their way down thru Flight Level 180, or 18 thousand feet, they magically, without having listened to the ATIS or automated terminal information service, broadcast from Dulles International Airport that morning, these guys somehow

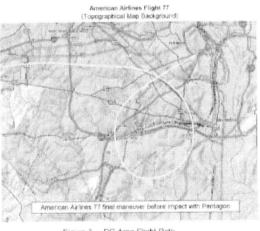

Figure 3. – DC Area Flight Path

knew the barometric pressure reported on that automated broadcast though no controller passed that information to them, and they set that in the Kollsman window on BOTH of the cockpit altimeters simultaneously.

That's not only clairvoyant, that's SYNCHRONIZED knob twisting going on there, by any pilot's standards. Machine precision out of hijackers turning two knobs at the same time in perfect, instantaneous fashion, is extremely unlikely for these guys, yet that was exactly what took place when both the hijacker and his co-hijacker buddy, who must have gotten VERY lucky to pick those barometric pressure numbers for DCA that morning out of their asses, because they had no way of knowing them otherwise…as no radio in the cockpit was tuned to the ATIS frequency, as that is recorded in the FDR data and not reflected in the data the N.T.S.B. released from that plane's Flight Data Recorder.

Not withstanding the absurdity of this kind of coordinated crew work, it really ranks as one of the most glaring issues of the morning because the crew could not have known those numbers they put into both altimeters via the Kollsman setting knobs that morning on their descent. They could NOT know them nor could they have so precisely guessed them.

And then they did something quite unusual. They were able to penetrate that highly protected airspace without the proper MODE 4A military I.F.F. response, and no communications with ATC of any kind, no clearance issued of any kind, and they flew a nice leisurely 330-degree turn after passing right past the White House, the more desirable high value target, than their intended Pentagon target could ever dream to be. After they completed the turn, they managed to accelerate the aircraft well beyond 150 knots faster than it could ever possibly fly at that altitude, even full throttle. They did this without touching the rudder pedals for even one moment after their hijacking of the plane several minutes earlier, too!

Needless to say, to perform a coordinated turn as the N.T.S.B. flight data recorder data shows, they would have had to use rudder inputs, but they never touched the aircraft rudders once during their entire time in the cockpit after they slid under the crack below the cockpit door to gain entry. Was this because neither of them had legs? They walked onto the plane and did not require wheelchairs, so is it not a little strange or odd they never ever once touched the rudder pedals in that plane?

After careful analysis of the flight data recorder stuff provided to us by the N.T.S.B., in their recreation, we see the fact the rudders and the yoke were not moved nor did the autopilot disengage while the crew fought for their very lives in that cockpit. And, at no other time did the rudders ever get so

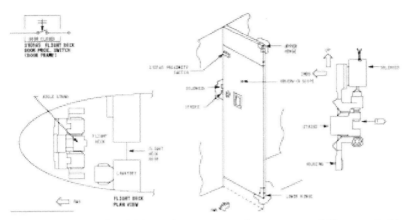

much as a passing foot kick. At the very least, these guys would have probably inadvertently tested them a bit with their feet, yet they never touched them.

And to do the nice 330 degree turn into the building, they would have absolutely NEEDED TO USE THE RUDDER to carry this out in what is called COORDINATED FLIGHT without slipping or skidding the plane in three dimensional space that morning. We know they flew a perfectly coordinated turn because the data the N.T.S.B. released to us shows us that. To do this, the rudders would have absolutely, beyond all reasonable doubt, been needed to accomplish this. No accomplished pilot could do that 'flat footed' with his or her feet not on the rudders. Impressive performance here, execution of coordinated high G turns without rudders used at all by the hijackers.

The government maintains that the radar track for this aircraft was 'lost' over a 'radar hole' that exists in the radar coverage map over West Virginia, and that as they neither had radio contact with the crew, nor a valid Radar Beacon or IFF code sqwawk coming from the aircraft's transponders when the track was lost going west, one has to ask how the track was lost and why it was impossible for the continuous tracking by at the very least, PRIMARY RADAR did not happen that morning.

Directly under this airplane's wonderful fantasmagorical RADAR HOLE the track was lost over, was a long range, height finding military radar system known as FPS-117. This radar, mounted right on top of a ridge, was virtually directly underneath FLT-77 when the radar track was lost. This radar has a nominal range of 200 miles, and has the capability to be in 'redcap' or reduced capability mode without full power output of its transmitter, and still offer short range primary or skin paint track of aircraft flying within 80 nautical miles of it.

This radar station was in operation on Sept. 11, 2001, and was not called out in any documentary evidence as being out of commission or off-line that morning, yet the government asserts that a 'radar hole' existed in its tracking or service volume area that morning, and nobody reported this long range height finder radar as either in low power final driver or 'down' for maintenance.

How can this be? How can we have lost track of this target over West Virginia that morning with a very powerful, very capable long range height finding air search radar below that did not need MODE C to get a rudimentary and somewhat less precise altitude resolution from its multi beam array scanning the skies there that morning? Very very good question.

In any case, as nobody really had ascertained that this plane was, in fact truly the same one that was tracked outbound into the approximate vicinity of this FPS-117 radar site, it is astonishing that virtually everyone in official channels automatically assumed this unidentified airplane which had no transponder replies, and had no communications  with ATC of any kind, was still the one and the same airplane seen on radar going the other way.

Based on this assumption, a whole lot of ATC specialists have been wrongly trained because their protocols prohibit making an assumption like this without specific NORDO or NO RADIO procedures that tell ATC that the crew has heard transmissions from the ground and has followed instructions issued so ATC can now state that this plane is in fact the one they lost radar track on and had lost communications with.

Those protocols for identification of unknown air targets have been in place and used very successfully for many decades and yet they were ignored and this unknown track was decried as 'FLT 77' by everyone on the ground. Mighty convenient that a radar hole that should not have been there allowed this window of uncertainty to be there, and then a nonsensical non-standard supposition as to who the target indeed was, superseded tried and true protocols for target identification in lieu of two-way radio contact or transponder replies from the target.

This is mighty smelly stuff here, regarding the radar hole and the assumption that this was still FLT-77 with no empirical evidence to support that assertion of any kind. In other words, NO air traffic control person has the right to make that assumption under any circumstances, but this was instantly done on Sept. 11, 2001 for some unknown or heretofore unknown reason that morning. Why?

An ATC specialist named Danielle O'Brien was watching this radar target track inbound at a high speed, and in her official statement about it, she cited not only the drastically higher speed inbound but an unusual degree of target maneuverability, more or less telling her colleague, another controller, that to her it looked too fast and maneuvered to abruptly to be a commercial airliner. In light of this, designating this plane as the one and the same which was NORDO and lost track on the outbound leg just before the infamous radar hole over West Virginia, becomes even more questionably nonsensical to two experienced ATC personnel watching it fly into the Washington, D.C. class bravo restricted airspace that morning. In any case, this observation by Ms. O'Brien and her co-worker seems to at least on its face indicate that whatever aircraft that was on the inbound track certainly was much more maneuverable and significantly faster than a B-757, even as the official RADES 84 data contradicts her and her colleague.

How can this be? Is it that the controllers were in fact 'wrong' and the later produced RADES 84 radar track data much more correct? Both of them cannot be correct. One is blatantly incorrect and intentional disinformation. But which one is telling us the truth? The same people who told us the radar hole existed over West Virginia, on top of an operational long range 3-D height finding radar system?

In any case, the plane continues inbound, without interception. And by all indications, the manner in which the aircraft is being controlled tends to reflect skilled airmen at the controls and not neophytes who had difficulty controlling a Cessna 172 Skyhawk and were denied rental of one due to their inability to pass a pre-rental checkout for that. Is anyone seeing the big picture here yet? They took over the plane in a scant 3 minutes, without disturbing the asleep crew and pulled their slumbering inert bodies out of the seats and did not touch either the yokes or the rudders during the time they removed these snoozing crewmen who were so asleep at the wheel they didn't even use any of the simple and very tried and true duress procedures to alert ATC they were being interfered with. Somehow I don't think so.

In any case, the hijackers then descended, and flew right by the White House and a contingency of secret service agents who had to at that point been standing on the roof with the over the shoulder STINGER missiles at the ready, waiting for them to come into firing range. FLT 77 was indeed well inside STINGER firing range as it whipped past the White House on the way into the Pentagon that morning. Were those agents taking a nap? Or had they simply been told not to fire on this plane? I know that in 1987, the secret service crew

Airline On-Time Statistics

Detailed Statistics > Departure Statistics

Airport: Washington, DC - Washington Dulles International (IAD)

ORIGINAL Bureau of Transportation Statistics Chart Showing No American A Flight 77 Scheduled to Depart Washington Dulles Airport on 9-11-2001

who guards that building were armed with STINGER MISSILES because an ATC specialist warned me to not fly lower than 1,000 feet over that building on my way further north that evening or risk getting one up my, uh, tailpipe. So we know someone dropped that ball that morning, or did they get told to hold their fire?

And then the hijackers fly the oh-so-notoriously-ridiculous-330-degree descending turn, which not only puts them at more risk for a shoot down, but makes no sense because their job was to fly that plane into the building. Why the turn? They couldn't possibly not seen it as they whipped past the White House that morning. The skies were clear. There was no fog or cloud cover. Did someone get lost suddenly?

What we know from the FDR recreation the N.T.S.B. provided to us, is that this plane executed a very high speed descent at a vertical descent rate that was at the very least, 4,400 feet per minute, easily 3,000 feet per minute faster in the dive than normal landing aircraft typical do on their final approaches to a runway. This equated to a terminal velocity in the end of more than 150 knots beyond the never exceed speed for this aircraft at this altitude. Oh, I know, I have seen in the blogosphere the 'hogwash, these planes fly at 585 miles an hour all day long' said over and over again, so therefore this speed limit we cite clearly must be 'wrong' and not correct. Is it?

The sad reality for those same people who cite this 585 miles an hour speed, is that this speed can only be achieved and maintained in less dense air, at very high altitudes. Down low, in very dense air with significantly higher drag coefficients applicable to the plane down so low, the plane's cannot achieve these speeds. And the only limit is not just the drag limitation, but the fact that with the increase in speed in a banked turn, comes the increased force of gravity or 'G' forces. On September 11th., this aircraft pulled '6' G's on its turn into the building that day, at a speed more than 150 knots beyond its design limits at this altitude.

We know this because we called Boeing and asked them if these impossible speeds were even possible at these altitudes. Their answer, was a laughable; "Uh, no!" by their spokesperson. But to get back to the turn and the necessity of one when the building was clearly right in front of the hijackers faces as they descended, is anyone's guess. But some of us surmise the turn was necessary because the imperative was not just to whack the building just anywhere, but to strike it in a particular location. That location, is known as the recently heavily reinforced and renovated 'Catchers Mit', and the portion of the building that was hit was filled with Navy comptroller's office personnel who were tracking the missing 2.3 trillion dollars cited during hearings on Capitol Hill on the prior morning, held by Congresswoman Cynthia McKinney.

We can only wonder at this point what the rationale was for circling and exposing this plane to shoot down, hence preventing it hitting its target. Nevertheless, the hijackers circled. But they did so in a fashion that absolutely flies in the fact that extremely unskilled and untrained pilots were at the controls. They executed this high speed turn and somehow managed not to lose control of this plane in a region of its control capabilities that would absolutely mandate that the pilot have exceptional flying skill to do this maneuver without losing control of this aircraft.

Do you still believe that Hani Hanjour was in the cockpit flying this plane now? That is a stretch, in any reasonable person's estimation to still believe that, if we can trust ANY of the data the N.T.S.B. released to us from the FDR on that aircraft. But this was not the end of the superb airmanship exhibited by Hani that morning. He got better at it!

What is so much more impressive is that Hani flew the plane so low that he clipped six light poles on the approach to the building at 460 plus knots, but when he did this, the leading edges of the wings did not shed a single piece, nor were the fuel tanks ruptured, which at that time were more or less full of highly flammable JET A fuel. We know five of the six poles were sheared, yet no huge fireball explosions as wings were impacting the poles, and nary one piece of leading edge components such as the leading edge slats, were even damaged or left the plane. Now that is mighty impressive flying! That Florida instructor pilot who declared him to be incompetent and quite incapable of safely renting a Cessna 172 Skyhawk, surely had him pegged wrong, didn't he? Didn't he?

Anyway, what is even more phenomenal, is this aircraft was flown down in a region less than ½ wingspan from the ground, known to any experienced pilot as 'ground effect' region or zone. The importance of knowing this, is that no airplane at full throttle flown in ground effect, would want to continue to descend further.

Matter of fact, at 465 knots, the plane would have, without full nose down pitch (which the flight data recorder shows was not the case) would have been required to overcome the 'ground effect' cushion and lift coefficient going on, and the plane would have had no choice but to climb. To force it into the building more or less at the base of the wall where it hit, on the ground floor level, the hijackers would have had to be using FULL NOSE DOWN PITCH to do this.

Not true, says the FDR data given to us by the N.T.S.B. No aircraft in GROUND EFFECT wants to descend further into it at high speed. They all want to climb and even with 10 or more degrees of commanded nose down pitch, a plane of that class would still want to climb out of ground effect due to a huge surplus of lift it was generating. Any pilot wants to challenge this, be my guest. Simply is not disputable here. It cannot be done. This particular aerodynamic fact is irrefutably the most damning road block to the whole cockamamie story about the final portion of this outrageous flight.

Interestingly, the N.T.S.B. gave us two sets of data. One set shows that the FL-180 reset took place per their recreation (and I will get to that again here in a second) and furthermore, the derivative data they provide to us shows that this reset did not take place at all, per the FDR data.

How can this be? According to the N.T.S.B., the .csv or comma separated variable data was a derivative of the Crash Protected Memory file in the L-3

Model 2100 Flight Data Recorder on this airplane. Yet, this clearly is not the case at all.

The last data record the N.T.S.B. has from this recorder places the aircraft INSIDE THE OUTER WALL at a height of 380 feet above ground level. This is extremely problematic for the official story, because we know that per their version, the plane did not nose dive the building from on top of it, but impacted the outer wall after hitting '6' poles on the approach that did not fold over or shear because they were made out of balsa wood that morning. The poles were not made of balsa wood. They were heavy aluminum. They are a trajectory record. A record that belies the fact that a B-757 could not fly the profile the FDR data set says it did, and still strike those poles at those heights.

The plane was simply TOO HIGH to strike those poles if we are to trust the FDR data even a little bit. So what gives with the poles? If they were planted as some assert, then why plant something that destroys your FDR premise totally? Very good question here, at the very least, it infers someone snuck the pole through the window of the taxi cab that the one pole narrowly missed pegging the driver of that morning as it flew off the ground after it was hit by 'something' and then driven through the windshield of that taxi. People like to cite the fact these poles have blowtorch marks on the bases of them and were planted. Were they planted. Know anyone who can javelin throw one of these poles through the windshield of a taxi cab? I don't.

Now one thing I had not mentioned so far is that there is one problem with this altimeter setting that took place, well beyond the fact the hijackers had no constructive way of knowing the proper number to put into the Kollsman window. Remember how I told you that after the hijacking they had waited a number of minutes to turn to 'off' the aircraft's transponder?

Well, when they did that, they just negated the main reason for any aircrew doing the altimeter reset to the local barometric pressure setting the crew had no way of knowing what it was because as I stated, they neither tuned in the ATIS frequency for Dulles airport, nor had they gotten this from ATC that morning, and to my knowledge, ATC had not broadcast this to anyone on that frequency the plane's radio was set on. So first, I have two questions.

How did these clueless hijackers so very perfectly twist both Kollsman window knobs on both altimeters and set them to the heretofore unknown DULLES barometric pressure without knowing what that number was, and second, why would they bother with the primary reason they'd do that, turned to the 'off' position way back long ago over Pennsylvania? They were not going to execute a landing at Dulles, so precision on the altimeters was neither necessary, nor was it done to allow the plane's MODE C or altitude reporting via the transponder, to allow ATC to warn other traffic about the American B-757's altitude as it descended through very congested airspace.

Needless to say, only an experienced line crew would have done this step, and certainly not after turning OFF the transponder, which was the last way ATC had of knowing the altitude of this plane as it barreled into the Pentagon at an impossible 465 knots, well beyond its capability. How did the hijackers know this number to set, and how did they both set both altimeters exactly at the same moment in time, per the FDR record? On the climb through FL-180, that's easy to do, it's a mere button push to put in the baro reference of 29.92 for everyone at high altitude to be *using the same reference*. Not so on the descent. This required precision well beyond the capability of these neophyte and highly inexperienced, incapable airmen.

Well, from an experienced pilot's standpoint, going back to West Virginia where they executed the standard rate turn that no hijacker would have bothered with in the first place, that was one of the first clues beyond the impossibility of entering  the cockpit without opening the door, or hijacking the plane without the crew either changing the transponder code to 'hijack' and broadcasting it on the radio. Second, the no disengage of the autopilot doesn't work for me, as the crew would have kicked the rudders and the yokes and the autopilot would have disengaged during any *struggle* to take the plane over.

And for the rudders to be static and non moving for the rest of the flight, except for small deflections attributable to 'air loads' or deflection by the relative air movement against them, the rudders were for all practical purposes, 'dead' meaning the hijackers legs were not working, or both hijackers exercised extreme body control and kept their feet off of those pedals. And they executed a 330 degree coordinated turn without slipping or skidding the plane, at an impossible 465 knots airspeed, when an accelerated stall most assuredly would have been the likely result of such a course of action on their part.

We know the rudders worked on the climbout as Burlingame used them to compensate for thrust related yaw on takeoff, and that's reflected in the FDR data record. After the hijackers took over, the rudders might just as well have been dead weights down there under their feet, because they simply were never again used. Why? Or more appropriately is 'How?' with regard to the total lack of rudders by the hijackers, while maintaining COORDINATED FLIGHT?

When the last known FDR records show the plane 380 feet above the ground, well inside the wall of the building, position wise, and I might add, at a height that would have precluded nailing those six poles on the way in without shedding leading edge parts or causing massive fuel tank ruptures and fireballs, I have to say; "uh no" to all of this foolery here. The initial claim by the government as to 'why' the FDR record ends too high and inside the building's perimeter is that the recorder failed six seconds before impact. Oh really? By the very standards the recorder must meet, it could not be so

far behind recording the data as this, as it would by those same standards probably still be recording for at the very least, 500 milliseconds after building impact, even if the sensors feeding the DFDAU had ceased to exist due to impact destruction with the outer wall.

For the government to claim that the recorder was simply 'not caught up' as they asserted, or had suddenly without explanation, failed, without the plane having hit anything yet, as it clearly was too high, is both absurd and ridiculous. Time after time the excuse is the FDR just couldn't keep up with the data being pushed into it from the DFDAU. In reality the FDR is in fact capable of keeping up. It has to faithfully and accurately store data in a fashion that allows accident investigators to determine what happened to the plane in its final moments of flight, hence it cannot be hobbled in a way that makes it a 'historical' artifact collector of the plane's better moments before impact.

Its job is to tell investigators right up to the moment of aircraft breakup, what the plane was doing. In this case, for at least 400 to 500 milliseconds (half a second) after building impact or total airframe disintegration and power loss. That's per its mandatory specification it must meet to be certified for use on Part 23 category aircraft.

Many discrepancies existed with that Flight Data Recorder record and the N.T.S.B. recreation. First, the final flight path of the plane the government says was flown, *does not match* this record. This is not an assertion. This is a fact.

Second, the FDR itself was found 'twice' at the Pentagon. Now for those of you who are unfamiliar with the actual location of the unit on the American Boeing 757 aircraft, it is in the tail of the plane to preserve it for as long as possible as most planes do not crash 'tail first' into anything even if the government claims the box can quit without provocation or reason, six seconds before impact with anything. The unit was found both at the entry hole, and deep in the building, underneath more or less 'intact' pilot seats. This is a bit problematic in the sense that the box itself has insufficient mass to penetrate the building on its own without help after the severe deceleration of the plane as it struck the heavily reinforced 'Catcher's Mitt' outer wall with the Kevlar jacketing and, furthermore, how did it get found 'twice' when only ONE flight data recorder exists on this plane?

What is even a better question, is how did the data in the crash protected memory module get downloaded from the crash protected solid state memory a full DAY before the discovery of the unit on the premises? That's right from the time stamp on the data given to us by the N.T.S.B. Now I know that you're thinking; "oh, someone forgot to set the time on the system that downloaded the data then, obviously."

Well, unfortunately there is a very precise process for setting the derivation bench system to take that data from a crash system and download it, and part of that process means you cross check the time the system says it is at. And most assuredly, there are many many other safeguards that are done to ensure that the data is not written to. Unfortunately for this data record set, it was written to. And that was not accidental.

The reason we know this, is that the only way data in the file header or preamble could be erased or reset to 'zeroes' is that the requisite jumper wire required on the bench setup that would be used to dump the CPM or crash protected memory data from the recovered CPM module, had to be in place when it would have been both not normally there at all and an intentional 'addition' by someone, and second, the bench unit used to talk to or communicate with the CPM module would not have any Aircrat ID or Fleet ID data loaded into it as a NOT FOR FLIGHT unit., and upon connection with the never ever ever in place jumper wire EXCEPT FOR INTENT

TO WRITE operations which would be prohibited by any reasonable data extraction protocols for a crash unit, the jumper had to be there to ERASE these two critical links to the plane itself that would not otherwise be blank. On this unit's FDR data, both fields are inexplicably 'blank' or zero'd out.

On bootstrap, the FDR does a BIT TEST or built in test function. Part of this BIT test is to validate the header / preamble data in the front of the file in the non-compressed portion of the CPM memory data, against the FDR UNIT's own ROM values for AC ID and FLEET ID. In the case these do not match on bootstrap, the FDR sends a 'FDR FAIL' or command priority message to both EICAS flight displays in the cockpit.

Furthermore, the pre-download checklist used by ANY agency downloading CPM memory module data stipulates that the requisite PIN JUMPERS to enable a CPM module write operation be verified ABSENT or NOT IN PLACE to prevent accidental record modification or data erasure. The only way the AC ID and FLEET ID data could be zero'd out on this box is that the jumper on the bench unit used to extract the data, was, in fact, there. That was the LAST linkage of that file to the airplane known as N644AA, other than serial numbers the F.B.I. and N.T.S.B. repeatedly refuse to provide to us under very specially and properly written F.O.I.A. requests. In any case, if this data was somehow erased or zero'd out by some technician before that aircraft took off, the unit would have failed BIT on power up on the airplane's essential bus, and that is a 'no go' situation.

Only a not for flight unit would write 'zero's to that header and preamble data, and only a NOT FOR FLIGHT unit would ignore the BIT failure due to masking in the BIT ERROR MAP of the unit. In all likelihood, on this particular airplane, the FDR would have been a Sunstrand model 700 FDR, versus the L-3 Model 2100 unit, based on data from other aircraft in the production string. Are we to believe that this machine got the L-3 unit and the sister ships produced on the line got the others by accident? I don't think that's too very realistic, although it is possible. An FDR FAIL message is a "no push-back" for any Part 23 airplane, prohibiting flight.

We have covered the flight to the building pretty well, but notwithstanding these issues I have mentioned, we now have a big problem. The dearth of airplane wreckage, and for that matter, copious amounts of unburnt fuel that would have been splashed all over the lawn after the light pole hits,which would have deeply embedded those poles into the wings at the very least to the fuel tanks. A 465 knot airliner full of JET A hits light poles full of fuel and the wings don't rupture and explode on impact with these poles? Only in a roadrunner cartoon could this be like this, folks. This is NOT reality.

In addition, the hole in the building was a single hole. No engine penetration holes, no wing entry slots, and no fuel anywhere. Where did the wings and significant parts of the horizontal and vertical stabilizers go? Where did 5,300 gallons of JET A fuel go? Where were the bodies, the luggage, the parts of the plane that COULD NOT HAVE PENETRATED THE BUILDING go to?

How did two Rolls Royce, seven ton hurtling engines with the equivalent mass of a locomotive engine at that speed, not punch holes in the building and yet only *one* engine is found in the building, after presumably taking a back door in because it surely didn't go through the front wall with no entry hole, for sure!

The entry hole was 16 feet across. Vertical and Horizontal structural members were visible right after impact. The fuselage of a B-757 is significantly wider than this. The two, nearly 7 ton, RB-211, Rolls Royce engines on this plane were an ever so solidly predictable 48 feet apart, meaning we could easily know where they'd penetrate the building given this fact. There are no holes at those locations. The floor slab there at the place an 80-ton plane moving at 465 knots final speed has impacted, is not chipped, cracked or damaged in any way. How can this be?

Well, to any reasonable person, this cannot be. It is not reasonable to state that the lion's share of an 80-ton aircraft could totally disintegrate. Fire could not consume it all, as the fire post impact was not really that intense because  computer monitors and open books were neither melted nor singed post fire. Matter of fact, until the building collapsed, the minimal damage at the Pentagon was almost laughably NOT possibly from any airplane impact. A Toyota Tercel with 50 gallons of jet fuel in it would have created more damage, in all likelihood. An 80-ton airplane with more than 5,300 gallons or nearly 20 tons of fuel hits the building and no fuel is there all over the premises, no wings, no fuselage, no body pieces?

In the trial of Zacarias Moussaoui, the alleged 20th hijacker, the government presented photographs of the dead occupants of FLT 77, the non-scheduled, per the BTS flight that allegedly hit the building that day. None of the bodies were really dismembered in any photos they presented, nor were they burnt. They were for the most part, fully UNBURNT and INTACT human beings. These people hit a heavily reinforced building in an aluminum airplane at 465 knots, and maintained their body integrity? I don't think so. I truly don't think so.

Years later, N644AA was stricken from the F.A.A. registry, after remaining, just like the other third aircraft, as viable registrations in the F.A.A. database, until 2005. To date, there has been not one single component per the requisite aircraft production 'trailing documents' Boeing requires to build airplanes and certify them, positively identified from any of the wreckage recovered, far less than a ton, by the way, from an 80 ton airplane. What is interesting about the 'wreckage' the government touts is from N644AA or the non-scheduled flight 77 from the Dulles Airport that day, is that one piece (shown below) being handled by presumably F.B.I. agents (with badges in their pockets, by the way!) at the site that morning, has corrosion streaming from rivet holes that had rivets in them moments earlier.

Another larger piece has jungle vines still wrapped around it. A pilot who's flown this particular American Airlines plane identified the one part on the lawn as having come from a much earlier version model B-757-200, same genus as the one that crashed near Buga, Colombia in 1995. Hmmmm?

In the end of December 1995, an American Airlines B-757, on a night approach into Colombia, got lost on the approach due to improperly programming the same FMS system the hijackers so adroitly reprogrammed on Sept. 11, 2001 and turned onto course using, and the plane's crew failed to retract spoilers on the missed approach and slammed into the mountain there in what is called Controlled Flight Into Terrain. All but one soul were lost on that plane's crash. There was very little post crash fire, and the wreckage sat in the Buga, Colombia jungle for months before it was fully recovered and shipped to the U.S.

More than one person has asked the F.A.A. and N.T.S.B. to show us the wreckage of both aircraft, but the U.S. government cannot tell you where the wreckage is from the Buga, Colombia crash. Certainly it didn't dissolve. Or walk off. Or get lost on its own. The government asserts that they have the wreckage safe in Iron Mountain, locked up. If so, why not show us both sets then. We'd love to see them, and the Boeing production trailing documentation that shows every single serial number of these components, With so many clues that exist that point to out and out 'fraud' and 'lying' by the U.S. government about the nature of what happened at the Pentagon that day, they failed to tell the American public that depleted uranium was detected and decontamination procedures for D.U. as it is called, were taken at the Pentagon that morning. Why?

First, the renovation to 'The Catchers Mitt' did not incorporate D.U. for obvious reasons. Second, for it to be there, it means a form of 'munitions' was used in the Pentagon attack or it would not be there. Oh, I know, Boeing used it in the construction of N644AA when they built her, so that explains it. No. The only known use of D.U. in any civil Part 23 or transport category airplane in U.S. registry is on the McDonnell / Douglas DC-10/MD-11 aircraft. It is used as anti-flutter ballast in the horizontal stabilizes of that aircraft type. Not used in B-757, or any other commercial airplane other than the DC-10 / MD-11 genus aircraft. Post cleanup of the Pentagon / Department of Defense poured as much as 24 inches of gravel and aggregate in the approach area where the blow-back from the impact with that wall was known to contain D.U. contamination. How the D.U. got there is a big mystery.

One of the more peculiar things about the well photographed 'C' ring 'hole' is that we have a nice symmetrical, even, cookie cutter 'hole' in the brick wall, several wall layers deep in the building. Now we know that the airplane the government says did this was a standard, run of the mill, right-off-the-production-floor without enhancements, B-757-200 series jetliner. It wasn't a Titan ICBM, and it surely wasn't a tunnel borer with wings, either. Logic would dictate that the very frangible and flexible fuselage of N644AA, the alleged airplane that punched this hole, would have long before the 'C' ring, accordioned like the frangible metal tube that it is and

at the worst, had it truly been able to pentrate that deep, made a very ragged and quite uneven hole at this location. And surely the words, "PUNCH OUT", would not have been pre-painted there in that location before aircraft impact by any Pentagon employees.

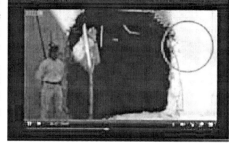

It's a bit of a stretch to surmise that this airplane was so very rigid and sturdy as to make such a nearly perfect hole in the wall, after being torn asunder by the 'E' and then the 'D' rings, respectively, as it faced incredible mechanical resistance, post impact with the KEVLAR jacketing in place on this section of the building. Furthermore, post crash, there'd be no need to "Punch Out" anything there, except maybe the idiot who photographed the neat cookie cutter hole for release to the press, with "PUNCH OUT" painted adjacent to it. It does really fly in the face of probability here, does it not? This is more than hypothetical guesswork. It wouldn't happen that way.

I don't think I need to tell you what conclusions to draw here, but from a number of very valid standpoints, the entire government story about the Pentagon attack is completely not adding up. It cannot add up. It never did add up. Not for a second. If we are to believe the official story, a number of very very impossible breaches of physics, aerodynamics, airmanship and common sense took place on September 11, 2001. Interceptors were not launched and directed to this flight as it came in over West Virginia--and hurtled toward the building. No possible way the plane could possibly have the proper MODE 4A reply to the military radars scanning the skies over Arlington that day.

The issues cited about the flight itself are both nonsensical and unreal to any trained and experienced pilot. And to be certain, it's laughable and sad that people can see the pristine, no parts from the pole strikes, no jet fuel from tank ruptures, lawn, and the total bulk of an 80 ton airliner not present when it could not have possibly flown through the hole and left the vertical and horizontal structures still in that entry hole, with no engine or wing penetrations or vertical or horizontal stabilizer structures, body parts, luggage and other components all over the lawn there. After the initial explosion, there was very little visible wreckage there. A fighter pilot dispatched to overfly the scene reported back that there was no evidence of any aircraft impact there of any kind. Not until a 'spook' U.S. Navy C-130 Hercules overflew the place.

Later this pilot stated he never got within 4 nautical miles, when in fact eyewitnesses saw him directly overhead. Why did he lie? What was his real purpose for being in the air that morning? You don't just jump into a C-130 and fire it up in a minute and launch. Just the pre-flight would have taken several minutes to perform. In other words, it had its orders long before it launched that day because it was not a fighter with a crew sitting in it ready to intercept someone intruding in that airspace. This was a specially equipped 'spook' bird, an intelligence asset bird, and like the orbiting E-4B which was in the sky before it all went down that morning as a part of 'Amalgam VIRGO' and other Richard Cheney exercises, this plane too was also an exercise asset. But for what purpose? For what purpose?

April Gallup, a Pentagon worker who carried her son through the hole the plane allegedly disappeared through, saw not one body part, not one plane component, and smelled zero jet fuel when carrying her son on her shoulders out to safety that morning, just moments after the plane hit. At the very least, April would have been wading through  pools of unburnt jet fuel, blood, and viscera, and working her way through miles of wiring from the plane. As it worked out, she saw no evidence of any aircraft, body parts, other signs that N644AA had just flown in there and disintegrated into small pieces as the government asserts.

Of the more than 80 video cameras that would have let us see N644AA's final flight to the Pentagon that day, the F.B.I. has chosen to show us five frames of video that do not show a B-757 just prior to building impact. And interestingly, eyewitnesses who worked at the Arlington National Cemetery and who were interviewed extensively after the event, substantiate a de-facto 'flyover' of the building by a very large transport category aircraft, one eyewitness, identified as 'NEIT-428', describes a scene where he could see the face of the pilot just after the explosion from whatever struck the building, banking away and flying towards Washington, D.C., and his testimony is NOT the only testimony that supports the flyover.

The very data the N.T.S.B. provided to us proves that the airplane or aircraft the data may have come from absolutely was over the roof of the building at a height well above it before the data record ended for no apparent reason, because the plane simply had at that point impacted NOTHING YET and was too high for an impact with the Pentagon. Why?

When NEIT-428 was questioned about 'why' the government seemed to be unconcerned about his steadfast unchanging testimony about the flyover he witnessed that day, he simply stated; "they must not think me to be important enough..."

Of all of the eyes that were there that day, his were the most uncolored by technical issues. He simply saw what he saw. He saw the pilot's face as the aircraft flew over the building after the explosion, and banked away towards Washington, D.C.

Even though the interviewer constantly tried to lead him other directions, he steadfastly stuck to his story. He refused to be deflected or convinced to tell something different. The investigator who was sent to interview him repetitively lead him in the questioning and this man steadfastly refused to have words put into his mouth. And he was not alone.

The government cites so many eyewitnesses who swear almost on a stack of bibles that they saw the plane impact the Pentagon that day, but to the last person, these eyewitnesses neither were in position to see the impact, or were otherwise proven to not be able to see that airplane strike the building that day like NEIT-428 and his co-workers were from their exceptional view at the cemetery across the highway. You'd think that based on all of the controversy, the F.B.I. would just release some of those videos to prove NEIT-428 and the hosts of others who saw the flyover, totally in error, wouldn't you? Seems reasonable to me.

And it should seem reasonable to you if you believe that the job of the F.B.I. is to protect something called JUSTICE in this country. Clearly their job is something quite different based on the nice clear pictures of their agents with badges in pockets strewing weathered wreckage from the 1995 Buga Colombia B-757 crash that morning. They most assuredly seemed to have been pre-positioned to grab those videos so fast that morning so we would never ever see them. We got 5 frames out of miles of tape recorded on almost 90 cameras. Why?

Someone has been lying to us about what happened at the Pentagon on September 11, 2001.

Source note: This chapter originally appeared as "The 'Official Account' of the Pentagon is a Fantasy", *jamesfetzer.blogspot.com* (25 June 2012).

14

Reflections on the Pentagon: A 9/11 Photographic Review
by Dennis Cimino with Jim Fetzer

"Frank Legge paid special attention to a prominent piece of fuselage, which had come from a Boeing 757–not one that had hit the Pentagon on 9/11, but one that had crashed in Cali, Columbia, in 1995"–Jim Fetzer

As we explained in "Limited hangouts: Kevin Ryan, A&E911 and the *Journal of 9/11 Studies*", the Pentagon serves as a litmus test for those who profess to be dedicated to exposing falsehoods and revealing truths about 9/11.

By that standard, the *Journal of 9/11 Studies* does not measure up, because articles published there by Dr. Frank Legge, by Legge with Warren Stutt, and by Dr. John D. Wyndham on the Pentagon are intellectually indefensible.

Dennis Cimino

They attempt to demonstrate that a Boeing 757, designed as "Flight 77", hit the building and caused the death of 125 Pentagon personnel as well as its passengers and crew. But no passengers or crew died in a plane that did not crash.

What did and did not happen at the Pentagon has become a source of immense controversy within the 9/11 research community, which I have found difficult to appreciate, since books by Thierry Meysson about the Pentagon, 9/11: The Big Lie (2003) and Pentagate (2003)–were the first serious studies of 9/11 I read and convincing that no plane had hit the building. "What didn't happen at the Pentagon", for example, was published by rense.com in 2009 and then republished in my own blog in 2010. And when Gordon Duff invited me to write for Veterans Today, my first article, "Seven Questions about 9/11", published in 2011, also focused on the Pentagon.

Among the points I made is that the official trajectory–of a Boeing 757 traveling over 500 mph and flying low enough to take out a series of lampposts–is neither aerodynamically nor physically possible. Such an aircraft at that speed could not have come closer than 60' or even 80' of the lawn because of (what is known as) downwash. And had a plane encountered a series of lampposts, the effects on a plane traveling over 500 mph hitting stationary lampposts would be the same as if the plane had been stationary and hit by lampposts traveling over 500 mph: its wings would have broken open, its fuel would have exploded and it would have careened on fire across the lawn. They missed two of my crucial questions:

(4) The lack of debris

Although many Americans are unaware, the hit point on the Pentagon is on the ground floor. There is a hole about 10' high and 16-17' wide, which is surrounded by a chain-link fence, two enormous spools of cable and a pair of cars, where there are unbroken windows beside and above the opening. What we do not see is an enormous pile of aluminum debris, broken wings or the tail, bodies, seats or luggage. Remarkably, not even the engines were recovered from the crash site—although a part of a compressor, which was too small to have come from a 757 and too large for a cruise missile—was later reported to have been found. Even more striking to me, however, is this photo of the civilian lime-green fire-trucks as they extinguish the fires.

Since these fire trucks arrived after the crash and spent fifteen minutes or so putting it out, I have been struck by the clear, green, unblemished Pentagon lawn. It looks so smooth, I expect Tiger to appear with his caddy to practice his game. My question, therefore, is, why is there no debris on the lawn?

When he published, "What Hit the Pentagon? Misinformation and its Effect on the Credibility of 9/11 Truth", Frank Legge paid special attention to a prominent piece of fuselage, which had come from a Boeing 757. Although he did not appear to know it at the time, this was authentic debris from a

Boeing 757–not one that had hit the Pentagon on 9/11, but one that–as James Hanson had already found by 2007–had crashed in Cali (or Buga), Columbia, in 1995, where the keys to its origin include its lack of effects from intense heat or from a violent crash–and a piece of vine.

No doubt there will be some who dismiss this photograph on the grounds that it cannot be proved that the debris came from a 757. Such people have failed to understand the logic of thi paper. The essential point is that there is no proof that the debris is not from a 757.

As I had explained to the BBC when it came to my home near Madison, WI, and interviewed me for eight (8) hours for its first "Conspiracy Files" documentary about 9/11, the most stunning and revealing aspect of alleged crash at the Pentagon was the virtually complete absence of any debris from a Boeing 757, including no wings, no tail, no bodies, no seats and no luggage. They just weren't there. And even the engines, which are virtually indestructible, were not recovered from the site.

But the distinctive piece of debris has to have been dropped on the lawn by a C-130, which was circling the Pentagon: The probability that a Boeing 757 could have hit the Pentagon and not left debris from its wings and tail or even its engines–not to mention bodies, seats, and luggage–is zero.

The probability that the alleged trajectory could have been flown in violation of the laws of aerodynamics is less than zero–since violations of these laws is not even physically possible. The probability that such a crash, had it been possible, could have left a smooth, green, unblemished lawn is

(5) The planted fuselage

Later, of course, debris would start showing up. Since there was none even as the fire trucks were extinguishing the fires, it has to have come from somewhere. It would have been difficult to have had officers and enlisted men carry pieces of debris out onto the lawn without being observed, so it has occurred to me that perhaps it was dropped from a C-130, which was circling the Pentagon that morning. That's my best guess. I am open to other possibilities, but I haven't been able to think of real alternatives. One piece of debris has been used to cement the case for the crash of Flight 77.

One of the oddities about this debris is that it shows no signs of having been exposed to those fireballs and includes a piece of vine. Another student of the Pentagon, James Hanson, a newspaper reporter who earned his law degree from the University of Michigan College of Law, has traced that debris to an American Airlines 757 that crashed in a rain forest above Cali, Columbia in 1995. "It was the kind of slow-speed crash that would have torn off paneling in this fashion, with no fires, leaving them largely intact." My question is, how did this piece of fuselage wind up on the Pentagon lawn?

zero. The probability that debris would have been planted, had this event been authentic, would likewise have been extremely low. That all of these things should have occurred, if the alleged crash had been contrived, however, is precisely the opposite. Indeed, it is difficult to imagine any reasonable alternative, as the photographic record confirms.

On the Pentagon: Whom are we supposed to believe?
by Dennis Cimino

Jim Fetzer asked me to participate in our earlier article, "Limited Hangouts: Kevin Ryan, A&E911 and the *Journal of 9/11 Studies*", from an analytic angle, where I enthusiastically joined in the effort to address the pathetic and sad attempts by the faux truthers–namely, Richard Gage, Kevin Ryan, Mr. Legge, Mr. Stutts, and Mr. Wyndham–to promote indefensible assertions made in the position papers we have addressed. Here I want to elaborate on the photographic proof that no Boeing 757-200 hit the Pentagon.

From the initial sentences of these articles, which are effectively being offered as incontrovertible proof that a B-757-200 struck the Pentagon on 9/11/2001–during what can only be assessed as a very elaborate hoax and ruse played out against the world that day–it is clear they are making the contrary assertion that a very complex aircraft was hijacked and flown with a great deal of precision into an impossible building entry that left no wreckage of the empennage or fuselage, nor wing, tail, or rudder fin (aka vertical stabilizer), when it hit the Pentagon that morning. We are to believe around 80 percent of the "official story" to simplify our understanding.

I wish to call everyone's attention to these three photographs of the "Pentalawn", as we call it in many places. The first was snapped less than 10 minutes after an explosion made the hole on the façade of the building.

Note that there is virtually no wreckage in front of the entry hole. You won't see this photograph in any of the Legge-Stutts-Ryan-Gage-Wyndham fraud, because this photograph by itself tells the "hole story", as I laughingly refer to it as. Notice, too, the difference between the guard rail in the first (which is rusted) and in the second (which is not), which shows that at least some of the photos from the Pentagon were photoshopped:

More photos that simplify matters

And the fact of the matter is that there are many more photos taken early on that demonstrate the absence of the kinds and quantity of debris that would have been present had a Boeing 757-200 actually crashed there. As Jim Fetzer has observed, it is possible to prove a negative, as we do when we visit our living room and find no signs of the presence of an elephant, when those signs should be present if an elephant were there.

We thereby prove that no elephant is in our living room, just as the absence of signs that a plane crashed at the Pentagon prove that no plane crashed at the Pentagon.

The bottom

image on the previous page is one from the Pentagon helipad, showing that no Boeing 757-200 crashed at that location, either:

As you can see, inside the entry hole some structural members of the building are visible. But do you still think an airliner slid in this hole and disappeared?

This is the entry hole. Yes. That is where 80-100 tons of airliner and wings went, according to what they would have us believe. Had an airliner truly struck the building in this location, not only would there be problems with fuselage entry through this hole, but clearly there are no slots present where wings entered the building either. Indeed, not only are those wing slots not there, we also do not have two engine penetration holes 48 feet apart where they, too, would have had to enter to not be seen in the above photograph.

The most powerful proof

Now this photograph is the most powerful indicator to the world that the wreckage that these men advance as "proof positive" could not have been the immediate result of an aircraft impacting the building, because not a single part of the plane is visible on the lawn. So one should ask, "How did any of the purported wreckage arrive there–and why so late?"

Here it is post-collapse and *there is still no real wreckage yet either.* Given this late photo shows virtually no wreckage from an aircraft of the kind and quantity expected–period. End of story.

Here is one more post-collapse shot, which is also consistent with the absence of the expected field of debris:

A jet engine will miraculously appear in the vicinity of this generator; it is not there now but was planted later:

Legge's "Proof of Impact"

In Mr. Legge's astonishingly unsubstantiated "white paper"–a good term for articles published in the *Journal of 9/11 Studies*–he makes the claim that his photo of the main floor offers proof of airliner impact at this location:

As you can see, there are no aircraft components in this area. Per Mr. Legge's statement, this photograph is indisputable evidence of an airliner impact in this location. Really? How did he deduce this? As many people might remember, a reporter named Jamie McIntyre had that morning observed that he saw no proof of an airliner having crashed there. Now we can all maybe in retro have asked McIntyre to go get his eyes checked, but then you would also have to send an F-15 pilot who also overflew the Pentalawn a few minutes later and likewise assessed that he, too, saw no evidence of an airliner impact there.

The Buga, Columbia crash

Unbeknownst to many people globally, a very little known American Airlines accident in Buga, Colombia in the end of 1995, provided the small amount of 757 wreckage that would be photographed on the Pentalawn, which was dropped later that morning from the lowered cargo ramp of a C-130H transport aircraft under call sign, GOFER SIX, flown by Cdr. Steven O'Brien of the Air National Guard.

This is the source of the small amount of plane parts seen on the Pentalawn after the explosion took place. GOFER SIX was the only aircraft allowed to be in the air in the immediate aftermath of this incident and had just enough cargo capacity to air drop these small fragments seen on the Pentalawn after the above photograph with NO WRECKAGE visible was taken by a U.S. Army enlisted woman. That photograph alone proves beyond reasonable doubt that there was no aircraft impact on that building that morning. There was no wreckage 9 minutes later. Notice the arrival of wreckage is evident here, when it was not there in the earlier shots:

The wreckage placement team has decided that the time is right for them to perform their assigned tasks:

Notice that rivet holes have already popped from corrosion on this allegedly fresh piece of 757 wreckage:

241

The series of lamp posts

The official story claims that this aircraft, N644AA, a B-757-200, flown by "Chic" Burlingame, had 5,300 gallons of JET-A on board when it pushed back from the concourse that morning and, notwithstanding a very modest amount consumed enroute, the lion's share of the remainder of the onboard fuel should have been all over the lawn after the plane struck six lamp poles

on its way to the building. Had this actually been the case, the fuel in the wings would have provided some spectacular pyrotechnics on the way to the building, because the wings would have been ruptured all the way to the fuel tanks and the voltage potential between the poles and the plane would have ignited massive fireballs for us to see–not to mention the shredding of wing components as the leading edge slats would have been torn from the wings on the way to the building post-impact with those poles.

If you believe the plane struck the poles on the way to the building, then you cannot with a straight face assert there would be no damage to the aircraft as it struck those poles at that speed. Certainly that no fuel explosions or wing components separated as clearly they did not, apparently. Virtually all of the fuel in this aircraft was in the wings. Yet no fuel was present at the Pentagon lawn, no wing wreckage was found and no signs of the B-757's massive wings or tail anywhere near the entry hole, which was too small for them to have politely neatly folded in, had the plane turned into a barn swallow and tucked the wings before impact. It's not possible these massive wings vaporized. They would be there–mostly intact–and outside, due to the lack of wing entry slots in the façade of the Pentagon. So where did they go?

And, even more importantly, where are the engine entry points? Where? The west portion allegedly hit by this plane had just been reinforced with Kevlar jacketing, making it even more likely to repel the penetration of the wings, which remain invisible in every photograph either inside or out. A key point of the official theory that these wings are not visible outside because they are inside.

In Legge's photo, however, you cannot see a single aircraft component: no wings, no main spar, no spar box, no fuselage components, no seats, no overhead bins, not even a seat cushion. And, remarkably, not one torso or body part.

It's physically impossible that such a plane could effortlessly penetrate the building without being destroyed by the heavy reinforcement of that façade, no matter how fast they assert it was flying, which was in this case beyond its aerodynamic capability.

What does this mean?

I have carefully read the assessments of another researcher about this absurd position that these gentlemen advance, where Mr. Ryan's recommends that we ACCEPT AS TRUE as much as we can of the official story. Our puzzlement about the dearth of wreckage, body parts and other things unpleasant, are somehow buried in the rubble. *So we are supposed believe an American Airlines jet flew at an impossible 465 knots speed into this building, hitting six poles en route, yet the wings didn't rupture or fireball–and the plane did not have enough structural integrity post-crash to remain visible outside the building?*

When Pentagon employee, April Gallop, crawled with her son from the building through the entry hole, she saw no evidence at all to support the assertion that any aircraft had struck the building that morning. Not one body part, not one plane component, not one strand of aircraft wiring, not one seat cushion, nothing from a plane visible to her, and amazingly, no pools of jet fuel which would not have been burnt if they assert the plane made it into the building. Are we to believe April Gallop or those who are lying to our very eyes?

The repetitious *'believe, believe, believe'* and *'accept, accept, accept'* suggestion by Kevin Ryan and indeed his henchmen who would wish us to so believe, is that much of an 80 ton aircraft could crash at the Pentagon and leave such a dearth of wreckage. Mr. Legge asserts that those of us who beg to differ are doing a 'disservice' to the truth community that he would like us to believe he is a valid part of, when neither he, nor Ryan, nor Stutts nor Wyndham has any experience or valid credentials in aviation or aircraft certifications, or aircraft operations; yet they pose as the arbiters of 9/11 Truth? How could anyone, after reviewing these photographs, continue to place faith in any of them–or in the Journal of 9/11 Studies, for that matter?

The proponents of the official story have told us that to not believe them, and to reject the nonsensical 'official story' is doing a massive disservice to the truth that they apparently are the sole arbiters of. Sound familiar? Which is it? Do we live now in a world where persons without ANY recognized credentials in these areas of AVIATION and FLIGHT and AIRCRAFT BUILDING AND CERTIFICATIONS now can suddenly be the very experts that tell us that the OFFICIAL GOVERNMENT STORY is TRUTH and that it's perfectly fine that nearly 80 tons of airplane wreckage simply turned into vapor at the Pentagon? Apparently so. But it's nonsense.

I have examined the documents Mr. Fetzer has cited in this article, written by these men, and have deduced that in spite of their very grandiose and outrageous claims in them, they have totally failed to prove that not 80 percent, not 60 percent, not 10 percent of the official story about the entire day holds any water, let alone that we should now trust  them, without any requisite backgrounds or credentials, to assess for us that we should now believe the official government story that indeed a plane was involved in striking the Pentagon that morning.

From my viewpoint, these men lack the requisite experience, background, credentials and knowledge to asses a dog fight let alone adjudicate this matter in a fashion that would lead anyone to see it for the pathetic psychobabble attempt by them to market a pile of lies that defies the evidence.

A missile or a Global Hawk?

Some have postulated that enough evidence of some form of air vehicle striking the Pentagon exists–and that appears to be the case. We have shards of very fine pieces of fiberglass, all over the area near the helipad and the helo control tower. A truck parked there has been fire damaged, but none of the glass is broken in that truck, which means whatever hit there didn't hit with enough force to create shockwaves that would shatter the glass in the truck. So what created these shards of fiberglass? Could it have been one of these? The Air Force, incidentally, in the months after 9/11, reported that it had "lost" two of these in Afghanistan, which were never recovered.

John Danner, an EMT and commercially rated pilot, who was in the vicinity that morning, reported he observed a Global Hawk approach the building that morning. If this is true–which I believe it may be–then why was it there? What function did it serve?

If there was a B-757-200 involved that day, any one of the Pentagon's camera tapes would have shown that clearly to us en route to the Pentagon. So why withhold that from us? For what good reason? The only logical explanation is that the myriad of recordings clearly do not show a B-757-200 flying and striking the Pentagon as we have been maliciously and fraudulently told.

Clearly the government has not come clean here, in that IT holds the indisputable proof of what did and what did not fly over or fly into the Pentagon. We have the eyewitness testimony from N.E.I.T. 428's Mr. Russell Roy interview by the Army, as you can easily verify for yourself, reporting that he saw a plane overfly so low that he could see the pilot's face that morning as he pitched his plane up and banked away and flew away to the northwest towards Washington, D.C.

This man's testimony is damning 'prima facie' evidence of a 'flyover or flyby' as is the excellent work of C.I.T.'s analysis and interviews of several very close-in eyewitnesses that more or less reinforce the fact that a large aircraft flew a low approach to the building but then swerved over it. And this 'low approach' was not in sync with the external explosion at all, which means someone got his timing off a bit. Russell Roy could clarify this, if he is still alive today. But his interview still stands as proof of an aircraft having been close enough to the Pentagon and then departed, meaning we have ascertained that 'something' did not strike the building but flew over it.

Some in the truth movement believe that John Farmer, aka as Blue Collar Republican, a known 'well poisoner' in the 9/11 research realm, by the way, misused the Russell Roy interview transcripts to obfuscate and or muddy up the water about what really did occur at the Pentagon on 9/11. It is my professional opinion that the once fairly reliable source, Mr. Farmer, was co-opted and 'bought' by someone with a lot of cash to dangle, but I cannot certify the reason he went from once being a good source of information to being a definitive and certain 'well poisoner' for his later work, before he left the 9/11 Truth community in a huff.

What about the E4B?

One question remains in that it was well-photographed that day over Arlington, high above the ground, an 'E4B' 'TROUT' doomsday aircraft was seen in a 'hold' pattern up high and yet this aircraft does not appear in the heavily-doctored RADES 84 data for good reason. Is this the plane people seem to be pinning on Russell Roy's observations that morning? Somehow as relevant as the E4B sighting is to the whole thing, it was up so high above Arlington that connecting it directly to a Pentagon overflight is a bit of a stretch, if not an absolute attempt to obfuscate the tight close-in recollections of Mr. Roy that morning.

He was an Arlington Cemetery worker, in a very good position to see everything but the Pentagon itself from his viewpoint. At the very least we have enough damning information that firmly places O'Brien's C-130H in tight and close to the Pentagon for wreckage seeding operations as I assert, contrary to his own disinformational claims that he was never anywhere within 4 n.m. of the Pentagon.

And today, nobody has really addressed the *clearly 'supervisory' role of the E4B aircraft* in the operation in Arlington to attack the Pentagon using a missile. A solid fuel rocket motor propelled, D.U. penetrator equipped, land attack missile.

My assertion that an AGM-65J 'maverick' missile (below) was used to punch the 'entry' hole seems to fit well in what NEIT-428's testimony states happened that morning, namely, that a large explosion occurred and then the flyover took place a few seconds later.

Additionally, we also know that decontamination procedures for D.U. or 'depleted uranium' were being followed as it had been detected immediately after the explosion, so crews were washing people down to get D.U. off of them.

As I have stated, this indicates a penetrator warhead was used and, although I cannot pin the tail on AGM-65J with certainty, it's inclusion in the Navy weapon's inventory that year makes it the perfect candidate.

In the photograph on the opposite page, you can clearly see the use of 'masking' of the D.U. signature by the military having procured a huge amount of granite aggregate and other cover being laid down in the blowback area. Had an airliner been the whole gig, why would the government need to lay down rock to mask and suppress the radiation from fragments in the soil?

I don't think they were landscaping. In other words, nobody can justify this masking of the underlying fragments of D.U. by the use of enormous quantities of radioactive granite fragments and other aggregate. So this, too, appears to be an attempt by the government to cover up the use of a D.U. penetrator warhead missile of some sort.

Kevin Ryan, Richard Gage and CIT

One of the leading sources of good solid detective work regarding the Pentagon attack is Craige Ranke's Citizen Investigation Team (or C.I.T.), where their work on its own destroys the official story that a B-757-200 flown by inexperienced and incapable hijackers were somehow able to skillfully fly this machine to a pre-designated spot in the 'Catcher's Mitt', which they hit with a great deal of precision and without being challenged or shot down by interception that day.

If one wishes to take the bait and believe Kevin Ryan and Richard Gage and the Legge-Stutts-and-Wyndham Disinformation team and, just for simplicity sake, believe the government because that is less confusing, then one also has to ask these same disinformation peddlers 'how' we are to dispose of all of the damning evidence that suggests that they are in fact shills pushing the official government story, when so much contradictory proof destroys their assertions altogether? Simpler theories, as Jim Fetzer has reminded us many times, are only preferable when they can account for the same body of evidence.

Which is it going to be? Do as Kevin Ryan suggests and believe the official story because it is the easiest path? or follow the more logical and complex one, which implies that, no matter how hard they try, they simply cannot place a B-757-200 crash at the Pentagon, due to the total utter lack of wreckage in the immediate aftermath? The evidence we have reviewed here supports the possibility of a missile strike guided by remote control from the circling E4B 'TROUT' airplane above the area that morning.

But it does not support Flight 77 having crashed there. None of their work even touches O'Brien or the E4B's presence. Why? They weren't there merely by coincidence that morning, folks.

We know the Pentagon had more than 80 video tapes of what happened that morning. "Show us the 80+ tapes", Mr. President! Let us see what really happened at the Pentagon on 9/11." The government will never ever come clean about this ruse, because to do so would de-legitimize it fully and make it painfully clear that we are prisoners in a nation run by criminals and knaves, not a nation ruled by law. This event that took place going on almost 13 years now is the one that is the deal breaker. America was hijacked but those hijackings did not happen to any airliners that day. They happened in the very buildings we trust these frauds to govern from in the Beltway. That is where the hijackings really took place.

Source note: This chapter originally appeared as "Reflections on the Pentagon: A 9/11 Photographic Review", *veteranstoday.com* (16 August 2014).

15

No Boeing 757 hit the Pentagon

by An Aeronautical Engineer with Jim Fetzer

"This article explains why high-speed flight in relatively close proximity to the ground [as for Flight 77] is virtually impossible – in any fixed-wing aircraft" –An Aeronautical Engineer

Among the most important proofs that no Boeing 757 hit the Pentagon is that the official trajectory — barely skimming the ground at over 500 mph and taking out a series of lampposts — is both aerodynamically and physically impossible.

I have argued in the past that it is aerodynamically impossible because ground effect would not allow a 757 flying at that speed to get closer than 60 or even 80 feet to the ground, where 80 feet is higher than the Pentagon at 71 feet is tall.

And it is physically impossible because the effects of a plane flying over 500 mph hitting a series of stationary lampposts would be the same if the plane had been stationary and hit by lampposts flying at over 500 mph: they would have ripped the wings open, where the jet fuel stored in them would have burst into flames and the plane could have cartwheeled across the lawn.

While I regarded my arguments as impeccable, I was faulted on the ground that "ground effect" would not make it impossible for a Boeing 757 to barely skim the ground, which led me to look further into the matter and discover that I had the right concept but the wrong name, where it is better described as "downwash", as the technical study that follows explains in detail.

That was a benefit from participating in the thread on Truth and Shadows, "Gage concedes his entry into 9/11 Pentagon quagmire has been divisive". But some of those who were participating displayed scant familiarity with the evidence, which Dennis Cimino and I have recently surveyed in our study, "Reflections on the Pentagon: A 9/11 Photographic Review".

It also became clear that some students of 9/11 do not know the basics of "No Plane Theory" (or NPT, as it is sometimes called), which maintains that *none of the official 9/11 aircraft–for Flights 11, 77, 93 and 175–actually crashed on 9/11.* It does not mean that no planes at all were involved on 9/11, where the trucker buddy of a friend of mine from JFK research had told

him that he had been in front of the Pentagon and watched as a commercial carrier flew toward it and then swerved over it, as I have explained in many places.

Indeed, the work of CIT and others supports the inference that a plane had flown toward the Pentagon, but that its trajectory took it north of the nearby Citgo station, which became a bone of contention; because it the plane was north of the Citgo station rather than south, it cannot have been Flight 77. The presence of that plane, which CIT has documented, therefore, does not defeat NPT and the following study strengthens it. But there should be no more doubt that the official story of a Boeing 757 hitting the Pentagon is not even possible.

GROUND EFFECT vs INDUCED DRAG
(Or, the difference between Downwash and Wake Turbulence)
by An Aeronautical Engineer

Preface

Many online debates about the "Pentagon 757" continue to confuse an aerodynamic phenomenon known as *Wake Turbulence* (caused mainly by Induced Drag) with *Ground Effect* (caused as a reaction to downwash).

Simulation of alleged Boeing 757 impacting the Pentagon (depicted to scale)

In a nutshell:

Ground Effect is a reaction to the downwash sheet produced by the wing; it is a function of Lift.

Wake Turbulence (i.e., wingtip vortex) is produced by wingtip 'spillage'; it is a function of Induced Drag.

Numerous illustrations of 'tip vortices' have been circulated online for years with intent to "explain" ground effect. Such arguments are based on a misunderstanding of some of the fundamental principles of aerodynamics (I.e., the pure *science* of aerodynamics practiced by degreed engineers, as opposed to the few hours of "Theory of Flight" taught to pilots at flight school).

In discussions on flight in close proximity to the ground, proponents of this argument confuse the effects of tip vortices with those of ground effect. They argue that since tip vortex energy rapidly dissipates during flare, so would "ground effect" be mitigated, thereby permitting an aircraft to be flown at high speed, in straight-and-level flight close to the ground. This assumption is false.

[NB: Ground effect, too, obviously, is greatly diminished (in fact, reduced to zero) during the landing flare, which is performed at or near stall speed. Indeed, it is this reduction in ground effect that allows an aircraft to "land"! This discussion, however, concerns the forces produced by ground effect while the craft is in high-speed flight near to the ground.]

This article explains why *high-speed* flight in relatively close proximity to the ground is virtually impossible – in any fixed-wing aircraft*.

[* An exception would be cruise-type missiles, whose flying surfaces are more akin to horizontal fins than wings, and thus have extremely high wing

loadings (lbs/sf) — much higher even than of ground-attack fighter-bombers. NB: Commonly invoked photos of aircraft in flight close to the ground do not depict flight at anywhere near maximum speed; they are photos taken of craft flying at greatly reduced throttle settings – which is what actually happens during any landing!]

This discussion will delineate why the highly energized ground effect region beneath the wings, whose intensity is directly proportional to the lift generated by the aircraft, would prevent the craft from getting any closer to the ground than approximately one half its wingspan *while flying at high speed.*

In the case of a Boeing 757, given its wingspan of 124 feet, this would equate to roughly 62 feet AGL.

[NB: Sixty-two feet is a theoretical minimum; a practical minimum would actually be considerably higher. In a real-world situation (such as allegedly at the Pentagon), a pilot — especially one as demonstrably inept as Hani Hanjour who could barely fly a trainer — probably could not have got within 100 feet of the ground in a Boeing 757 flying at 400 mph.]

The Fundamentals

In order to gain a clear understanding of what constitutes Ground Effect, one must first gain a grasp of how Lift is generated. Only then can one understand the dynamics of *Downwash*, the main contributor to ground effect, and how this differs from the factors that contribute to wingtip vortices.

In order to properly understand Lift, one must first let go of the common Bernoullian theory we're all taught in school (and flight school), and approach it from a Newtonian viewpoint. As I shall show, the Bernoullian explanation — embraced by students and most pilots alike — is an illustration of convenience that is fundamentally flawed.

While *Circulation Theory* constitutes the most technically accurate method of computing Lift, the Newtonian explanation can also be employed to graphically describe Lift without introducing the misconceptions and errors inherent in the Bernoullian version.

In order to really understand Lift, one needs to abandon explanations based on Bernoulli's theorem, and clearly comprehend the following:

An aircraft's wing, basically, is an AIR DEFLECTOR. As an aircraft moves forward, the wing essentially deflects the resultant airstream downward. This downward deflection of air causes an equal and opposite reaction upward. This upward reaction (equal to the weight of the aircraft when in level flight) is what is termed 'Lift.'

This downward deflection of air, which occurs along the entire span of the wing, is also what constitutes *downwash*. This downwash 'sheet' has a vertical component that is normal (I.e., at a right angles) to the direction of flight.

When an aircraft flies in close proximity to the ground, it is this vertical component of Downwash that causes the 'cushion' of air between the wing and the ground. This "cushion," when sufficiently energized (by an aircraft's high speed), behaves much like a pneumatic "spring," and tends to resist any action against it — such as that caused by a pilot trying to *force* the aircraft down against it.

This is what is known as Ground Effect. To summarize:

Ground Effect:

Is directly proportional to the speed of the aircraft (i.e., faster the speed, stronger the ground effect)

Becomes discernible when an aircraft descends to within approximately ONE wingspan of the ground

Becomes progressively more pronounced as the craft descends further

Reaches its maximum value when the aircraft is at a height of approximately one HALF wingspan, at which point it begins to demonstrate characteristics of incompressibility (i.e., offers resistance, or "pushes back")

This is a Law. This Law applies to ALL fixed wing aircraft.

The faster the airplane flies, the stronger the downwash, more pronounced the ground effect. When speed is reduced, downwash is reduced, ground effect is diminished, and the aircraft is able to get closer to the ground. This is what happens during landing.

Wingtip Vorices/Wake Turbulence

Wingtip vortices, on the other hand, are the principal source of 'induced drag', and the main contributors to wake turbulence.

These tip vortices are a result of the 'spillage' of high-pressure air from beneath the wing to the low-pressure region above it. Obviously, this natural tendency for pressures to equalize can occur only at the tips (it would be impossible elsewhere along the wing since it would be prevented by the intervening wing structure). When this tendency to equalize pressures is satisfied at the tips, it results in powerful counter-rotating conical vortices that are carried rearward by the slipstream.

*[NB: These wingtip vortices, the biggest contributor to what's loosely referred to as "wake turbulence", can, when generated by a large aircraft, present a serious hazard to light aircraft flying in its wake. The effects of wake turbulence are also notoriously problematic at airports with parallel runways, because they tend to traverse the ground **outward** when aircraft approach the ground and flare to land.*

This is the reason parallel runways are designed with ample separation between them.

It also explains why air traffic controllers ensure sufficient separation between aircraft queued to land — especially at airports with minimal runway separation and frequented by "heavies." The energy inherent in these vortices is directly proportional to the weight of the aircraft, its speed, and the wing's angle-of-attack. This 'wake turbulence' decays relatively slowly at altitude, where their energy is greatest due to high cruising speed. This is the reason light aircraft pilots go to great lengths to avoid crossing wakes created by heavies.]

To gain a clearer understanding of the distinction between tip vortices and downwash, let's do a quick thought experiment. Let's imagine an aircraft with inordinately large wingtip "fences," i.e., vertical plates at the tips. This would, in theory, reduce any pressure-induced spillage at the tips to zero, and thereby preclude the formation of vortices.

But this would have virtually no effect on the spanwise downwash sheet! As will be explained further below, a wing's downwash is what *reactively* produces Lift. Wingtip vortices, on the other hand, are the primary contributors to *induced drag*. The fancy Winglets evident on many modern airliners and executive jets represent a design effort to minimize spillage at the tips, thereby reduce induced drag, and as a consequence, improve operational efficiencies (E.g., fuel savings).

To better understand downwash, here's another interesting thought experiment: If one were to place a very long weighing scale — as long as,

say, the wingspan of a Boeing 757 — on the ground, and then fly a 757 just a few feet above it, the scale would momentarily register the total weight of the aircraft! It is the force of the downwash that causes this reading. In the case of a Boeing 757, the scale would fleetingly read over 200,000 lbs — the actual weight of the air deflected downwards (which is equal to the weight of the aircraft).

During straight-and-level flight, the force of the vertical component of the downwash will always be equal to the gross weight of the aircraft (according to Newton's Third Law, as will be discussed later).

The Three Descriptions of Lift

Let's begin by defining three descriptions of lift, only one of which is commonly used in flight schools and pilot training manuals.

1. Circulation Theory

Generally called the 'Mathematical Aerodynamic Description of lift,' it is used principally by aerodynamicists. This description uses complex mathematics and/or computer (CFD) simulations to calculate the lift of a wing. It often uses a mathematical concept called "*Circulation*" to calculate the acceleration of the air over the wing. Circulation is a measure of the *apparent rotation of the air around the wing*.

While useful for calculations of lift, this description is rather abstruse, and does not lend itself to an intuitive understanding of flight, which is why it is rarely used (or known) outside the realm of aerodynamicists.

2. Newtonian Theory

This description (also far more accurate than the Bernoullian explanation, as shall be shown) is presented here in order to provide a clearer understanding of downwash (and therefore, ground effect). We shall call this the *Newtonian* Description of lift. This description of lift is based primarily on Newtonian laws and a phenomenon called the *Coanda Effect*.

It is uniquely useful for understanding the phenomena associated with flight, and useful for an accurate understanding of the relationships in flight, such as how power increases with load, or how stall speed increases with altitude. It is also a useful tool for making rough estimates ("napkin calculations") of lift. The Newtonian Description of lift is also useful to pilots who desire to gain an *intuitive* understanding of how to fly the airplane.

3. Bernoullian Theory

This we shall call the *Popular* Description, which is based on Bernoulli's theorem. This is the explanation we've all been taught in High School. The primary advantage of this description is that it is easy to understand and has been taught for many years. Because of its simplicity, it is used to describe lift even in flight schools and flight training manuals. Its major disadvantage is that it relies on the "principle of equal transit times", or at least on the assumption that because the air must travel farther over the top of the wing it must go faster.

This description focuses on the *shape* of the wing, and prevents one from understanding such important phenomena as inverted flight, power, ground effect, and the dependence of lift on the angle-of-attack of the wing. In the following discussion, in order to keep things as simple as possible, we shall discuss only the latter two concepts: the Newtonian Description, and the Popular Description.

Bernoulli – The Popular Description of Lift

Students are usually taught that an airplane flies as a result of the Bernoulli principle, which says that if air speeds up, the pressure is decreased. (In fact this is not always true. For instance, the air flows fast over the airplane's static port—a little orifice on the side of the fuselage—but it still measures the correct static pressure that the altimeter, and other instruments, use as their reference.)

This theory attempts to show that a wing generates lift because the air flows faster over the top, thereby creating a region of low pressure. This explanation usually satisfies the curious, and few challenge its conclusions.

Some may wonder *why* the air goes faster over the top of the wing — and this is where the 'popular description' begins to fall apart.

In order to explain *why* air travels faster over the top of the wing, many have resorted to the geometric argument that the distance the air must travel is directly related to its speed.

The usual claim is that when the air separates at the leading edge, the part that goes over the top *must* converge at the trailing edge with the part that goes under the bottom. This is the so-called "principle of equal transit times".

It would be reasonable to ask if the numbers calculated by the Popular Description really work. To that end, let's look at a relatively simple example. Take the case of a Cessna 172, a popular, high-winged, four-seat airplane (and the one Hani Hanjour could barely fly). Its wings must lift 2,300 lb at its maximum flying weight (i.e., its Gross Take-Off Weight, or GTOW). Given the particular airfoil shape of the Cessna's wing, the path for the air over the top of the wing is only about 1.5% greater than under the wing. Using the Popular Description of lift, the wing would develop only about 2% of the needed lift at 65 mph, which is about the slowest possible flying speed (pre-stall) for this airplane.

In fact, calculations based on the Popular Description would suggest that the minimum speed for this wing to develop 2,300 lbs of lift is *over 400 mph* — which, of course, is absurd.

If one reverses the problem and asks what the difference in the path of the air would have to be for the Popular Description to account for 2,300 lbs of lift at that same airspeed (65 MPH), the answer would be 50%. I.e., The thickness of the wing would be almost the same as the chord length! *[Chord is the straight-line distance from a wing's leading edge to its trailing edge.]* In other words, the profile of the wing would look much like that of a whale, with a huge bulbous upper surface!

But here's the rub: Who says the air that separates at the leading edge of the wing *must* meet at the trailing edge at the same time?

This is key.

If you conducted an experiment in a simple wind tunnel using smoke streams, you would see that the air that goes over the top of the wing gets to the trailing edge considerably *before* the air that goes under the wing. In fact, the air is accelerated much faster than would be predicted by the "principle of equal transit times". Also, on close inspection one would see that the air going under the wing is slowed down from the "free-stream" velocity of the air.

The principle of equal transit times holds only for a wing with zero lift.

The Popular Description also implies that inverted flight is impossible (the air would then have to travel a greater distance along the *underside*). It certainly does not address aerobatic airplanes, which have symmetrical wings (the top and bottom surfaces have identical camber, I.e., the same 'shape'), or how a wing adjusts for the great changes in load such as when pulling out of a dive or in a steep turn.

So, why has the Popular Description prevailed for so long? One answer is that the Bernoulli principle is easy to understand (remember the classroom example of the bottle of perfume with the squeeze bulb?). There is nothing wrong with the Bernoulli principle, or with the statement that the air goes faster over the top of the wing. But, as the above discussion elucidates, our understanding is not complete with this explanation. The problem is that we are missing a vital piece when we apply Bernoulli's principle.

We can calculate the pressures around the wing if we know the speed of the air over and under the wing, but how do we determine the speed? As we will soon see, the air accelerates over the wing *because* the pressure is lower, not the other way around!

Another fundamental shortcoming of the Popular Description is that it ignores the 'work' that is done. Lift requires power (I.e., work/time). An understanding of power is key to the understanding of many of the interesting phenomena of lift. It would behoove readers who are pilots to pay particular attention.

A Napkin Calculation

Let us do a napkin calculation to see how much air a wing might divert. Again, let's take as an example the Cessna 172, a trainer with which this writer is familiar.

A Cessna 172 weighs about 2,300 lbs. Travelling at a speed of 140 mph, and assuming an effective angle of attack of 5 degrees, we get a vertical velocity for the air of about 11.5 mph right at the wing. If we assume that the *average* vertical velocity of the air diverted is half that value, we calculate from Newton's second law that the amount of air diverted is on the order of **5 tons**.

Thus, a Cessna 172 at cruise is diverting about **five times its own weight in air per second** to produce lift.

Now, imagine how much air is diverted by a ***250-ton*** Boeing 747 on takeoff!

Diverting so much air downwards is a strong argument against lift being just a surface effect as described through the common Bernoulli Effect; in reality, only a small amount of air traveling around the wing actually accounts for the lift. In fact, if we were to attribute sustainable lift to the Bernoulli principle, in order to divert 5 tons/sec the wing of the Cessna 172*must accelerate all of the air within 18 feet above the wing*! One should remember the density of air at sea level is about 2 lb per cubic yard.

So how does a thin wing divert so much air? When the air is 'bent' around the top of the wing, it pulls on the air above it and accelerates that air downward. Otherwise there would be voids in the air above the wing. Air is pulled from above. This pulling causes the pressure to become lower above the wing. It is the acceleration of the air above the wing in the *downward direction* that produces lift. As to *why* the wing bends the air with enough force to generate lift will be discussed in the following section, "Coanda Effect."

Also, as the wing moves along, air is not only diverted down at the rear of the wing, but air is pulled *upwards* at the leading edge. This "upwash" actually contributes to negative lift, and more air must be diverted down to compensate for it. This is a rather complex area, which falls under the above-mentioned "Circulation Theory," and in the interests of simplicity would be best left out of this discussion. Let it suffice to say that ahead of the leading edge, air is moving *upwards* (upwash), and at the trailing edge, air is diverted downwards (downwash). Over the top the air is accelerated towards the trailing edge. Underneath, the air is accelerated slightly *forward*. This should give the reader a sense of why aerodynamicists refer to this phenomenon as "circulation."

So, why does the air follow this pattern? First, we have to bear in mind that air is considered an incompressible fluid for low-speed flight. That means that it cannot change its volume and that there is a resistance to the formation of voids. Now the air has been accelerated over the top of the wing by of the reduction in pressure. This draws air from in front of the wing and expels if back and down behind the wing. This air must be compensated for, so the air shifts around the wing to 'fill in.' If one is able to determine the "circulation" around a wing, the lift of the wing can be calculated. Lift and circulation are proportional to each other, and are calculated mathematically.

It is a fact the top surface of the wing does much more to move the air than the bottom. So, the top is the more critical surface. Thus, airplanes can carry external stores, such as drop tanks, ordnance, etc., under the wings but not on top where they would normally interfere with lift. That is also why wing struts under the wing are common but struts on the top of the wing have been historically rare. A strut, or any obstruction, on the top of the wing would usually interfere with its lift. [*NB: There some aircraft, such as the new HondaJet, that have their engines mounted on top of the wings, but these are exceptions with special design considerations.*]

Coanda Effect

A natural question is, "how does the wing divert the air downwards?"

When a moving fluid, such as air or water, comes into contact with a curved surface *it will try to follow that surface.*

To demonstrate this effect, hold a water glass horizontally under a faucet such that a small stream of water just touches the side of the glass. Instead of flowing straight down, the presence of the glass causes the water to wrap around the glass. This tendency of fluids to follow a curved surface is known as the Coanda Effect. From Newton's first law we know that for the fluid to bend there must be a force acting upon it. From Newton's third law we know that the fluid must exert an equal and opposite force on the glass.

So why should a fluid follow a curved surface? The answer is *viscosity*, the resistance to flow, which also gives air (which is a fluid) a kind of "stickiness". Viscosity in air is very small but it is enough for the air molecules to want to stick to the surface. At the surface the relative velocity between the surface and the nearest air molecules is exactly zero. (That is why one cannot hose the dust off of a car.) Just above the surface the fluid has some small velocity component. The farther one goes from the surface the faster the fluid is moving until the external full stream velocity is reached. Because the fluid near the surface has a change in velocity, the fluid flow is bent towards the surface by shear forces. Unless the bend is too tight, the fluid will follow the surface. This volume of air around the wing that appears to be partially 'stuck' to the wing is called the "boundary layer" and is less than one inch thick, even for a large wing.

The magnitude of the forces on the air (and on the wing) is proportional to the "tightness" of the bend (called "camber" in an airfoil). The tighter the air bends, the greater the force on it. This is why most of the lift is concentrated at the forward portion of the wing, at its region of maximum curvature. In fact, half of the total lift on a wing is typically produced in the first 1/4 of the chord length.

Lift (and therefore Downwash and Ground Effect) as a function of angle of attack

There are many types of wing: conventional, symmetric, conventional in inverted flight, early biplane wings that looked like warped boards, and even the proverbial "barn door". In all cases, *the wing is forcing the air downwards*, or more accurately, pulling air down from above (though the early wings did have a significant contribution from the bottom). What each of these wings has in common is an *angle of attack* with respect to the oncoming air.

Angle-of-attack is the primary parameter in determining lift.

To better understand the role of the angle-of-attack (AOA) it is useful to introduce an "effective" AOA, defined such that the angle of the wing to the oncoming air *that gives zero lift* is defined to be zero degrees. If one then changes the AOA both up (positive) and down (negative), one finds that the lift is proportional to the angle. A similar lift versus AOA relationship is found for all wings, independent of their design. This is true for the wing of a 757, an inverted wing, or your hand out the car window. The inverted wing can be explained by its AOA, despite the apparent contradiction with the popular Bernoullian explanation of lift!

A pilot adjusts the AOA to adjust the lift for the speed and load.

The role of the AOA is more important than the details of the wing's shape in understanding lift.

The shape comes into play in the understanding of stall characteristics and drag at high speed.

Typically, the lift begins to decrease at a "critical" AOA of about 15 degrees. The forces necessary to bend the air to such a steep angle are greater than the viscosity of the air will support, and the air begins to separate from the wing.

This separation of the airflow from the top of the wing is called a "stall".

Newtonian ("Physical") Description of Lift

So, how, then, does a wing generate lift? To begin to understand lift we must review Newton's first and third laws. (Newton's second law will be introduced a little later.) Newton's first law states *a body at rest will remain at rest, or a body in motion will continue in straight-line motion unless subjected to an external applied force.* That means, if one sees a bend in the flow of air, or if air originally at rest is accelerated into motion, *a force is acting upon it.* Newton's third law states that *for every action there is an equal and opposite reaction.* As an example, an object sitting on a table exerts a force on the table (its weight) and the table exerts an equal and opposite force on the object to hold it up.

Similarly, in order to generate lift *a wing must do something to the air.*

What the wing does to the air is the *action,* while lift is the *reaction.*

In the "classic" diagram that everyone is familiar with, the air comes straight at the wing, bends around its shape and then leaves in a straight 'slipstream' behind the wing. We see these kinds of pictures even in flight manuals. The air leaves the wing exactly as it appeared ahead of the wing. In such a situation, *there is no net action on the air.* Therefore, there can be no lift!

In reality, the air passes over the wing and is deflected *downwards.* Newton's first law says there must be a force on the air to bend it downwards (the action). Newton's third law says that there must be an equal and opposite (upward) force on the wing (the reaction).

In order to generate lift, a wing must divert a large mass of air downwards.

The lift that a wing generates is equal to the change in momentum of the air it diverts downwards. Momentum is the product of mass and velocity (mv). The most common form of Newton's second law is F= ma, or force equal mass times acceleration. The law in this form gives the force necessary to accelerate an object of a certain mass. An alternate form of Newton's second law can be written thus:

The lift a wing produces is directly proportional to the amount of air diverted downward, times the vertical velocity of that air.

It's that simple.

For more lift the wing can either divert more air (mass), or increase the vertical velocity of a given mass of air. This vertical velocity behind the wing is the vertical component of the "downwash".

The greater the AOA of the wing, the greater the vertical velocity of the air. Likewise, for a given AOA, the greater the *speed* of the wing the greater the vertical velocity of the air. Both the increase in the speed and the increase of the AOA increase the vertical velocity of the deflected air. It is this **vertical velocity** imparted to the air mass that gives the wing lift.

When the aircraft is near to the ground, it is this deflected sheet of air that is the principal cause of ground effect.

Wingtip vortices (induced drag) and their own energy systems do not directly enter into this equation.

If one could actually "see" air, an observer on the ground would see the air traveling almost *straight down* behind the aircraft! This can be demonstrated by observing the tight column of air behind a propeller, a household fan, or under the rotors of a helicopter; all of which are "rotating wings." If the air were coming off the blades at an angle the air would produce an extremely wide cone rather than a tight column!

The wing develops lift by transferring momentum to the air. For straight and level flight very near to the ground (E.g., the alleged Boeing 757 at the Pentagon) this momentum eventually strikes the earth. That is why, as mentioned earlier, if an airplane were to fly over a very large weighing scale, the scale would momentarily "weigh" the airplane.

And this is why when you stand under a ceiling fan, the air blows DOWN on you — even though its blades are almost horizontal (small angle of attack), the generated airflow certainly does not scatter radially sideways. It is this same "downwash" that exists beneath Air Cushion Vehicles (ACVs, or hovercraft, as they're commonly called). This highly energized cushion of air is what keeps a hovercraft aloft.

Consider the following little thought experiment: Imagine a small radio-controlled model hovercraft. Let's imagine you have the craft hovering right in front of you, a few inches above the ground. Now, imagine placing your hand atop the craft, attempting it to push it *down*, against the cushion of air beneath it. What would happen? The craft would react by *resisting* the applied force, pushing back against your hand — behaving much like a compressed air "spring."

If you continued to push it even further, the resisting force would increase to where, eventually, the craft would begin to struggle, all on its own, *fighting* to revert to its original position. Continue to push downwards, and the craft will actually thwart your efforts and escape the constraints of your hand by slipping sideways and away from your hands!

This is precisely what happens when a pilot attempts to 'push' an airplane too close to the ground while flying at high speed. It is the same downwash present in the hovercraft that also prevents fixed-wing aircraft from getting too close to the ground at high speed.

Ground Effect becomes appreciable at a height above the ground of about one half the aircraft's wingspan, and increases in intensity in inverse proportion to that distance.

To summarize:

To make a hovercraft settle down to earth, the operator must reduce power, which in turn reduces the force of the down-blast (downwash). Similarly, to bring an airplane down to earth, the pilot must reduce power, which reduces airspeed, which in turn reduces lift, and thereby reduces the down-wash, which allows the craft to settle upon the ground during landing.

The amount of air diverted by the wing is proportional to the speed of the wing and the air density;

The vertical velocity of the diverted air (downwash) is proportional to the speed of the wing and the angle of attack;

The lift is proportional to the amount of air diverted (downwash) times the vertical velocity of the air;

The vertical component of the diverted air, when in close proximity to the ground, is the primary cause of "ground effect", and occurs along the entire wingspan. Ground effect has nothing to do with, induced drag, tip vortices, or wake turbulence.

The energy within the ground effect layer ('cushion') is directly proportional to the aircraft's weight, its airspeed, and angle-of-attack.

Conclusion

In order to better understand the forces inherent in the downwash sheet, and the effect these forces have on ground effect, it is important that Lift be understood in terms of the physical (Newtonian) description as opposed to the more common Bernoullian explanation.

When these spanwise downwash forces and effects are considered separately from the forces inherent in wingtip vortices (wake turbulence), it becomes clear why the alleged Boeing 757 could not have flown in a flat trajectory at 400 MPH for a distance of nearly a mile at a height lower that about half its wingspan, or approximately 60 feet.

The energy generated by its downwash would have prevented the aircraft from getting any closer to the ground.

The only way the craft could have got any closer to the ground would have been through a reduction in power, which, according to all available data, did not occur in the instance of "Flight 77".

Epilogue "Flight 77"

The US Department of Defense could easily end all conjecture, speculation, and rumors about this highly controversial event by releasing one clear photograph of a Boeing 757 approaching the Pentagon.

Since there were 96 — ninety-six — outwardly aimed CCTV cameras ringing the Pentagon, it is entirely reasonable to assume there must exist at least *one* clear frame of this world-changing event. Pentagon officials claim all ninety-six cameras mysteriously malfunctioned simultaneously just prior to the incident, and as a result no photographs are available.

The ONLY photograph released by the Pentagon to date is a solitary video frame captured from a security camera located in a parking lot.

The release of *one* clear photo of an inbound AA Flight 77 in a ground-hugging approach to the Pentagon would summarily end this interminable argument once and for all, and render all further debate on the subject moot.

However, given that in thirteen years the government has produced no such evidence, it can be safely assumed none shall be forthcoming in the future. That being the case, independent investigators seeking conclusive proof of the real events of that day are left with few, if any, avenues of recourse.

That being said, the following two possibilities bear potential to effectively nullify the official narrative and offer an alternative hypothesis; they are offered for the reader's consideration:

1. Extend a challenge to any pilot in the world (*any* pilot — fighter ace, test pilot, astronaut…) to replicate the alleged maneuver in an actual airliner. For that matter, replicate it in *any* powered fixed-wing airplane regardless of size — from a fabric-covered Ultralight to a multi-ton jumbo jet. A videotaped account of the feat (recorded from inside the cockpit as well as by a ground-based observer) would conclusively prove everything presented in this paper, and summarily end all argument.

2. Watch the Italian production ***Zero: An Investigation into 9/11***. In this excellent documentary, a veteran *Alitalia* captain lucidly explains the phenomenon of 'ground effect' by attempting to perform an ultra-low-level maneuver in a Boeing 757 flight simulator. He proves beyond a doubt what this paper strives to explain: When an aircraft gets in very close proximity to the ground at high speed, ground effect begins to aggressively resist further descent into this highly energized domain. This resistance actually causes the simulated aircraft to vigorously *fight* the pilot's control inputs, violently rock its wings, pitch its nose UP, and literally *climb* out of the ground effect region, seeking relief from the extraordinary loads, in order to reestablish aerodynamic equilibrium.

3. NB: The writer has actually attempted this maneuver in three different types of aircraft, and proved beyond any doubt that it is practically impossible to force an aircraft any closer to the ground than a height of approximately half its wingspan when operating at full power.

All three aircraft demonstrated a surprisingly powerful tendency to want to climb — even under forced application of full forward stick – thereby confirming the tests performed in a flight simulator in the above-mentioned video. Obviously, this is an extremely unusual flight domain, and thus one that is rarely — if ever — experienced by any civilian pilot (and very few, if any, military pilots), and explains why such counter-intuitive aircraft behavior under these abnormal conditions remains unknown to most aviators.

Source note: This chapter originally appeared as "An Aeronautical Engineer: No Boeing 757 Hit the Pentagon", *jamesfetzer.blogspot.com* (28 September 2015).

Part VI

The 9/11 Crash Sites

16

Planes/No Planes and 'Video Fakery'

by Jim Fetzer

Perhaps no question within the scope of 9/11 research generates as much heat and as little light as questions that have arisen over the role of the aircraft on 9/11, which has come to be known by the name of "planes/no planes" and of "video fakery". While I had long since concluded that no plane had crashed in Shanksville and that, while a Boeing 757 appears to have flown toward and then over the Pentagon, I was personally unable to bring myself to take the idea that no real airplanes had hit the North or the South Tower until nearly two years of being verbally assailed by Morgan Reynolds, who understood these issues far better than I, where his studies can be found on his web site, nomoregames.net, especially a response to criticism he has received for raising the issue during a FOX News appearance.

Morgan has also authored excellent critiques of alternative theories of how the Twin Towers were destroyed. It was the dawning realization that video fakery and real planes were logically consistent, since video fakery could have been used to conceal features of the planes or of their entry into the buildings, that enabled me to take a

serious look to sort out what was going on here. Even I initially thought the very idea was quite bizarre.

During the research I have done on this question, some of the most important reasons to question the use of planes on 9/11 are (1) that Flights 11 and 77 were not even scheduled to fly that day and, (2) that, according to FAA Registration records I have in hand, the planes corresponding to Flights 93 and 175 were not deregistered until 28 September 2005, which raises the questions, "How can planes that were not in the air have crashed on 9/11?" and "How can planes that crashed on 9/11 have still been in the air four years later?"

We have studies (3) by Elias Davidsson demonstrating that the government has never been able to prove that any of the alleged "hijackers" were aboard any of those planes and research (4) by A.K. Dewdney and by David Ray Griffin demonstrating that the purported phone calls from those planes were faked. And (5), as Col. George Nelson, USAF (ret.) has observed, although there are millions of uniquely identifiable components of those four planes, the government has yet to produce even one.

My purpose here is not to persuade anyone to believe the 9/11 planes were phantom flights on 9/11, but simply to lay out some of the evidence that supports that conclusion, even though I myself was initially unwilling to take it seriously.

Flights 11 and 77: The BTS Tables

ORIGINAL Bureau of Transportation Statistics Chart Showing No American Airlines (AA) Flight 77 Scheduled to Depart Washington Dulles Airport on 9-11-2001

The first to notice that American Airlines Flights 11 and 77 were not even scheduled to fly on 9/11 was the brilliant Australian jazz musician, Gerard Holmgren, who was interviewed by David West on 27 June 2005.

Others, such as Nick Kollerstrom, "9 Keys to 9/11", have also reported the same difficulty with the government's official account.

If AA Flight 11 did not even take off from Boston's Logan Airport on the morning of 9/11, then it cannot possibly have hit the North Tower around the 96th floor at 0846 hours and thereby brought about the death of its 92 passengers.

And if AA Flight 77 did not take off from Dulles International on the morning of 9/11, then it, also, cannot have crashed into the Pentagon at 0940 hours and thereby brought about the death of its 64 passengers.

Yet that is what the data that Holmgren discovered in the Bureau of Transportation Statistics shows to have been the case. In his new book, 9/11: ENEMIES FOREIGN AND DOMESTIC (2011), Edward Hendrie has published the data tables for both of these alleged flights, where it turns out that the BTS subsequently revised their tables with partial data in order to cover up their absence. For Flight 77, for example:

REVISED Bureau of Transportation Statistics Chart Showing American Airlines (AA) Flight 77 But Without Tail Number or a Departure From Washington Dulles Airport on 9-11-2001

The tables for AA Flight 77 can be found in Hendrie's book on pages 9 and 11, while similar tables for AA Flight 11 can be found on pages 8 and

10. The case against the use of planes becomes even more powerful when we realized that, as David Ray Griffin, THE 9/11 COMMISSION REPORT: OMISSIONS AND DISTORTIONS (2005), explains, Waleed al-Shehri, whom the government claims was aboard AA Flight 11, was interviewed after 9/11 by a London-based newspaper and spoke with the US Embassy in Morocco on 22 September, which would have been remarkable for someone who had died when the plane he allegedly helped to hijack hit the North Tower.

And the same is true of Ahmed al-Nami and Saeed al-Ghamdi, both alleged to have been aboard Flight 93 and were interviewed by multiple sources, while the Saudi Embassy in Washington, D.C., reported that three other alleged hijackers, Mohand al-Shehri, Salem al-Hazmi, and Abdulzaiz al-Omairi, were all alive and well and living in Saudia Arabia (page 19). Salem al-Hazmi was supposed to have been aboard AA Flight 77 and al-Nami to have piloted AA Flight 11 (page 20), which reinforces the BTS data.

Flight 11: On-Site Evidence

If AA Flight 77 was not even in the air on 9/11, then we should expect to find indications of one or another kind of video fakery in the evidence. As the term should be properly understood, "video fakery" encompasses any use of video to convey a false impression to mislead a target audience.

Although Hollywood specializes in the presentation of impossible events, its films do not generally qualify as "video fakery", insofar as they are not intended to mislead their audience.

The situation on 9/11, however, appears to qualify. Indeed, remarkably enough, Jules Naudet, a French filmmaker, just happened to be in the vicinity doing a modest documentary about New York firemen out looking for a "gas leak".

First Hit Flash Frame

Indeed, as Leslie Raphael has explained, that a cameraman should have been in precisely the right position to film this event depended upon a rather large number of conditions—either as a matter of coincidence, as the government would have us believe, or by design.

If this occurred by chance, it's improbability is astonishingly small. An odd flash occurs just as the flying object makes contact with the building, which may have been the trigger for a prearranged explosion to create a pattern of damage to the side of the building, which turns out to have anomalies of its own.

Both AA Flight 11 and United Flight 175, which is alleged to have hit the South Tower, were Boeing 767s, while AA Flight 77 and United Flight 93 were both Boeing 757s. While individual images are too blurry and indistinct to be even be identifiable as a commercial carrier, much less as a Boeing 767, a time-sequence of the image in motion as it approaches the 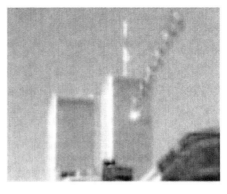 tower—which was prepared by Rosalee Grable—reveals that it does not bear even a faint resemblance. She has speculated that it might be an arrangement of unmanned aerial vehicles (UAVs).

And when you compare the pattern at the time of impact with what we see subsequently, there does not seem to be lot of room for doubt that they do not appear to be the same. How can four impact points–which suggest that it may be four UAVs–that constitute an extended "Z" have 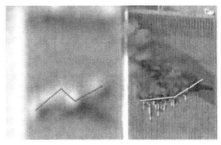 been turned into an impression in the side of the building that has now become an elongated "V"? That video fakery was involved here appears to be difficult to deny.

Flight 77: On-Site Evidence

There appear to be more than a half-dozen arguments against the official account that a 757 hit the Pentagon, which appears to be a fantasy. This "hit point" was too small to accommodate a 100-ton airliner with a 125' wingspan and a tail that stands 44' above the ground. The debris is wrong for a Boeing 757: no wings, no fuselage, no seats, no bodies, no luggage, no tail! Not even the engines, which are made of titanium and steel, were recovered.

According to the official account, AA Flight 77 approached the Pentagon on an acute north-east trajectory, barely skimming the ground at over 500 mph and taking out multiple lampposts, which would have ripped the wing off and caused the plane to burst into flame.

The aerodynamics of flight, including "downdraft", moreover, would have made the official trajectory–flying at high speed barely above ground level–physically impossible, because a Boeing 757 flying over 500 mph could not have come closer than 60 or more feet to the ground, which means that the official account is neither physically nor aerodynamically possible. And the only image that the Pentagon has ever produced of an aircraft approaching the building cannot possibly be a 757:

Russ Wittenburg in the DVD "Zero", an experienced pilot who flew the planes alleged to have been used on 9/11, states that the Boeing 757 can't go 500 mph hour at sea level because the air is too dense. Robin Hordon, an air traffic controller, in the same film, explains that the Boeing 757 cannot do the maneuvers attributed to it.

The official story thus appears to entail violations of laws of physics, of engineering, and of aerodynamics, insofar as the damage to the building, the absence of debris, the clear, smooth, unblemished lawn and now its alleged performance are incompatible with a Boeing 757.

Moreover, if a Boeing 757 could have traveled at 500 mph at ground level, it would have caused enormous damage to the grass and the ground, including producing substantial furrows from the low hanging engines. At this point, it appears to be "pilling on" to observe that data from a flight recorder provided to Pilots for 9/11 Truth by the National Transportation Safety Board corresponds to a plane with a different approach and higher altitude, which would have precluded its hitting lampposts or even the building itself, which means that, if the NTSB's own data corresponds to the Boeing 757 that is alleged to have been flown toward the building, it would have flown over the Pentagon rather than hit it.

For more, see Pilot's video studies, "Pandora's Black Box" and "Pentacon", which offer additional substantiation.

What about Flights 93 and 175?

As Greg Szymanki observed, "Two 9/11 Airliners, Flight 93 and 175, Were Only Just Recently Taken Off The FAA 'Active' List" (26 November 2005), both of the United airplanes that were supposed to have crashed on 9/11 were only 'deregistered' in September "after snoopy 9/11 researchers questioned FAA officials a month earlier".

And, indeed, Szymanki had it right. FAA Registration data shows that they were not officially reported to have been taken out of service until 28 September 2005, which is more than four years after they had "official" crashing in Shanksville (United Flight 93) and crashed into the South Tower (United Flight 175):

```
Next is United Flight 175, tail number N612UA, which hit the South Tower
of the WTC.  Please note the same details

Deregistered Aircraft 1 of 1

   Aircraft Description
      Serial Number      21833                   Type Registration
Corporation    Manufacturer Name      BOEING      Certificate Issue Date
01/18/1984     Model      767-222     Mode S Code   51773757      Year
Manufacturer   1983       Cancel Date   09/28/2005    Reason for
Cancellation   Cancelled      Exported To

   Hmmm.  What?  Cancelled registration on 9/28/05?  Not destroyed and
deregisterd in early 2002?  What about the last flight, United Flight 93,
tail number N591UA, the one that allegedly crashed near Shanksville,
Pennsylvania.

Deregistered Aircraft 1 of 1

   Aircraft Description
      Serial Number      28142                   Type Registration
Corporation    Manufacturer Name      BOEING      Certificate Issue Date
07/01/1996     Model      757-222     Mode S Code   51721341      Year
Manufacturer   1996       Cancel Date   09/28/2005    Reason for
Cancellation   Cancelled      Exported To
```

united 175
WTC-2
(South)

united 93
Pennsylvania

Notice the "Reason for Cancellation" in each case is simply "Cancelled". No pretense that they might have been destroyed in crashes four years earlier. Just as we discovered in the case of the BTS data for American Flights 11 and 77, where replacement records were created to add those flights to the data based where they were previously missing, that form of documentary fakery was also perpetrated in the case of the FAA Registration records, where both of the planes that were associated with those flights also appear, but with deregistration dates of 14 January 2002 and the purported "Reason for Cancellation" in their case of "Destroyed" *(see top of next page):*

As we found in the case of AA Flight 11 at the North Tower and AA Flight 77 at the Pentagon, the on-site evidence does not confirm that United Flight 93 actually crashed in Shanksville or that United Flight 175 hit the South Tower, which, as we are going to discover, is far and way the most interesting of the forms of fakery surrounding the planes that are supposed to have been "hijacked" on 9/11.

Aircraft Description
    Serial Number   22332   Type Registration
Corporation   Manufacturer Name   BOEING   Certificate Issue Date
01/06/2000   Model   767-223   Mode S Code   50722254   Year
Manufacturer   1987   Cancel Date   01/14/2002   Reason for
Cancellation   Destroyed   Exported To

Next is American Flight 77, tail number N644AA, which hit the Pentagon.
Please note the same details, reason for cancellation and cancellation date.

FAA Registry
N-Number Inquiry Results

N644AA is Deregistered

Deregistered Aircraft i u 2

    Aircraft Description
    Serial Number   24602   Type Registration
Corporation   Manufacturer Name   BOEING   Certificate Issue Date
05/09/1991   Model   757-223   Mode S Code   52072030   Year
Manufacturer   1991   Cancel Date   01/14/2002   Reason for
Cancellation   Destroyed   Exported To

Pilots for 9/11 Truth Corroboration

IT IS CONCLUSIVE - 9/11 AIRCRAFT AIRBORNE WELL AFTER CRASH
UNITED 93 IN THE VICINITY OF FORT WAYNE, INDIANA AND CHAMPAIGN, ILLINOIS AT TIME OF SHANKSVILLE ALLEGED CRASH

[PilotsFor911Truth.org] 12/06/11 - More information has surfaced which conclusively demonstrates the aircraft reportedly used on 9/11, were airborne well after their alleged crashes. This article supplements our last, 'ACARS CONFIRMED - 9/11 AIRCRAFT AIRBORNE LONG AFTER CRASH' in which the ACARS system is explained as well as how to determine if a message were received by the aircraft, along with how ground stations are selected through Flight Tracking Protocol based on messages routed to United 175, N612UA. We now have further evidence which places United 93, N591UA, in the vicinity of Champaign, IL, 500+ miles away from the alleged crash site in Shanksville, PA. This information is further corroborated by a [now former] United Airlines Manager of Flight Dispatch Michael J. Winter. read more...

Indeed, the evidence that United Flight 93 did not crash in Shanksville and that United Flight 175 did not hit the South Tower has been considerably strengthened by new discoveries from Pilots for 9/11 Truth. By means of meticulous research on electronic communications between those aircraft and air traffic controllers, they have been able to establish that United Flight 93 was in the air in the vicinity of Fort Wayne, IN, and Champaign, IL, at the time of the alleged Shanksville crash. Since no aircraft can be in two places at one time, it is difficult to imagine more conclusive proof that the Shanksville crash of Flight 93 was another fabricated event:

ACARS CONFIRMED - 9/11 AIRCRAFT AIRBORNE LONG AFTER CRASH
UNITED 175 IN THE VICINITY OF HARRISBURG AND PITTSBURGH, PA

[PilotsFor911Truth.org] 12/01/11 - Aircraft Communications Addressing and Reporting System (ACARS) is a device used to send messages to and from an aircraft. Very similar to text messages and email we use today, Air Traffic Control, the airline itself, and other airplanes can communicate with each other via this 'texting' system. ACARS was developed in 1978 and is still used today. Similar to cell phone networks, the ACARS network has remote ground stations installed around the world to route messages from ATC, the airline, etc. to the aircraft depending on its location and vice versa. ACARS Messages have been provided through the Freedom Of Information Act (FOIA) which demonstrate that the aircraft received messages through ground stations located in Harrisburg, PA, and then later routed through a ground station in Pittsburgh, 20 minutes after the aircraft allegedly impacted the South Tower in New York. How can messages be routed through such remote locations if the aircraft was in NY, not to mention how can messages be routed to an aircraft which allegedly crashed 20 minutes earlier? Pilots For 9/11 Truth have briefly touched on this subject in 9/11: Intercepted through the excellent research of "Woody Box", who initially discovered such alarming information in the released FOIA document(s). We now have further information which confirms the aircraft was not in the vicinity of New York City when the attacks occurred. read more....

281

Even more surprisingly, however, Pilots has also determined that United Flight 175 was in the air in the vicinity of Harrisburg and Pittsburgh, PA, at the time it was purportedly crashing into the South Tower in New York City. This may come as quite a shock to those who watched as it entered the South Tower on television. Indeed, when an FBI official was asked why the NTSB, for the first time in its history, had not investigated any of these four crashes, he replied that it wasn't necessary "because we saw them on television". Well, we didn't see the Shanksville crash or the Pentagon crash on TV, which leaves us wondering what we did see on television on 9/11.

Flight 93: On-Site Evidence

Just as American Airlines planes were supposed to be Boeing 767s, both of these United planes were supposed to be Boeing 757s. A Boeing 757 weighs about 100 tons with a wingspan of about 125' and a tail that stands 44' above the ground.

It would have been overwhelmingly larger than the trucks in this photograph, where the alleged crater from the crash was situated. Compare this crash site with those from bona fide crash sites to begin to appreciate the enormity of the deception involved. "This is the most eerie thing", the coroner observed at the scene. "I have not, to this day, seen a single drop of blood. Not a drop."

FOX News reporter: It looks like there's nothing there, except for a hole in the ground.

Photographer Chris Konicki: Ah, basically that's right. The only thing you can see from where we where, ah, was a big gouge in the earth and some broken trees. We could see some people working, walking around in the area, but from where we could see it, there wasn't much left.

Reporter: Any large pieces of debris at all?

Konicki: Na, there was nothing, nothing that you could distinguish that a plane had crashed there.

Reporter: Smoke? Fire?

Konicki: Nothing. It was absolutely quite. It was, uh, actually very quiet. Um, nothing going on down there. No smoke. No fire. Just a couple of people walking around. They looked like part of the NTSB crew walking around, looking at the pieces..." – FOX (09/11/01)

An alleged eyewitness, Val McClatchey, who resides less than two miles from the purported crash site, claims to have taken a photo showing a plume of smoke from the crash site. There are good reasons to suspect that her photo was faked, however, and that Ms. McClatchey has to have had reasons of her own for taking such a deceptive public stance.

The plume resembles those from detonation explosions more than it does fires from crash sites, for example, and estimates of the location of the plume from the location the photo was allegedly taken place it over a pond, which suggests that this is yet another fake photograph in the 9/11 inventory. Indeed, there are many good reasons to suspect that 9/11 was staged with Hollywood-style special effects.

The virtually complete absence of any debris from the Shanksville "crash site" was explained on the basis of the claim that the ground had been used for mining in the past and was therefore "very soft", *where the plane simply disappeared into the ground.* Some accounts even have it that the plane disappeared into an abandoned mind shaft. But we know what to do with miners trapped in mine shafts: we bring out the heavy equipment and the bright lights and dig 24/7 in the hope that, by some miracle, someone might have survived.

But that was not done in Shanksville, where no effort was made to save anyone or even recover the bodies–and for good reason. There were none.

Flight 175: On-Site Evidence

The footage of the South Tower hit exemplifies several anomalies, including a Boeing 767 flying at an impossible speed, an impossible entry into the building (in violation of Newton's laws), and even passing through its own length into the building in the same number of frames it passes through its own length in air—which is impossible, unless this 500,000 ton, steel and concrete building posed no more resistance to its trajectory in flight than air.

Some have claimed that this was a "special plane" that could fly faster than a standard Boeing 767, but no real plane could violate Newton's laws. The structure of the building, moreover, meant that it actually intersected with eight different floors as follows:

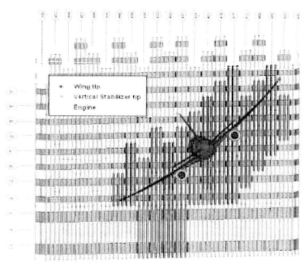

Figure 6–8. Orientation and trajectory of UAL 175 that matches the impact pattern (vertical approach angle = 6°, lateral approach angle = 13°).

Each of those floors consisted of steel trusses connected at one end to the core columns and at the other to the steel support columns. They were filled with 4-8" of concrete (deeper in the v-shaped grooves) and posed enormous horizontal resistance. (Imagine what would happen to a plane encountering one of them suspended in space!) The windows were 18" wide and the support columns one meter apart, while there were no windows between floors, which means far less than 50% if the plane should have entered via them. But as Jack White has shown here, that is not what the videos display:

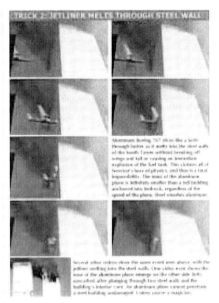

Notice that the plane completely enters the building before its jet fuel explodes, when one would have thought that, insofar as most of its fuel is stored in its wings, they should have exploded on entry—which is comparable to the failure of the 757 at the Pentagon to have its fuel explode when its wings hit those lampposts.

And while some have sought to support the claim that this was a real 767 based upon the engine found at Church & Murray, those who were fabricating evidence in this case did not get it right: the engine component did not come from a 767 and, if this FOX News footage is authentic, appears to be a plant, as another of Jack's studies reveals:

Pickup or delivery?

Indeed, as John Lear, perhaps our nation's most distinguished pilot, has observed, the plane in these videos does not even have strobe lights, which are required of every commercial carrier.

But how can a Boeing 767 possibly travel at an impossible speed (as Pilots for 9/11 Truth has confirmed), enter a steel and concrete building in violation of Newton's laws, pass through its own length into the building in the same number of frames that it passes through its own length in air, and not have its fuel explode as it makes contact with that massive edifice?

Even the frames from the Pentagon show a huge fireball upon impact. If that was true of the 757 there, why is it not also true of the 767 here?

It looks as though, in this respect, the fabrication of Flight 77 fakery was just a bit better than the fabrication of Flight 175 fakery.

The Use of Video Fakery

Since we all saw United Flight 175 hit the South Tower on television–and many also claim to have watched it happen with their own eyes–what was actually going on in New York City? What did we see on television or, assuming we take the witnesses at face value, with their own eyes?

There are three alternative theories, which involve the use of computer generated images (CGIs), the use of video compositing (VC), or the use of a sophisticated hologram, respectively.

That third alternative may sound "far out" until you realize that *many witnesses claim to have seen a plane hit the South Tower with their own eyes*, which would have been impossible if VC or CGIs had been the method that was used. Since we are dealing with visual phenomena, here are some videos that illustrate what I have been talking about in relation to "video fakery":

The serious question that has to arise at this point, of course, is "Why?" *Would it not have been far simpler just to fly a real plane into the North Tower and another into the South?* Where the answer turns out to be, "No".

Pilots for 9/11 Truth discovered that it is extremely difficult to hit an edifice 208′ across at more than 500 mph. After 20 or more tried it repeatedly, only one was able to hit it once. In addition, a real plane could not enter all the way into the building before it would explode.

But that was a requirement of the mission, since otherwise there would have been no pseudo-explanation for the subsequent "collapse" of the buildings due to fire.

And equally important, the explosions that were planned for the subbasements to drain the towers' sprinkler systems of water so they could not extinguish the relatively modest fires that would remain after the pre-positioned jet fuel was consumed in those spectacular fireballs.

The plan was to explain them away effects of jet fuel falling through the elevator shafts–a flawed theory, but good enough for a gullible public.

The mission required something that looked like a real plane but could perform feats that no real plane could perform by entering the building before it would explode, which would have been impossible with a real plane. And that had to be timed to coincide with explosions in the

subbasements that, even with the most meticulous planning, would inadvertently take place 14 and 17 seconds before the planes officially hit the buildings.

It was an audacious plan, brilliant in design, and nearly perfect in execution. But those who were working this out did not realize that they were also creating the image of a plane that would turn out to be traveling faster than a Boeing 767, violating Newton's laws, and passing through its own length into the building in the same number of frames it passed through its own length in air.

As in the case of the Pentagon, they thereby violated laws of aerodynamics and of physics that gave their game away. And those blemishes, subtle as they may have been, have provided the opportunity to expose a fantastic fraud, which has been used to justify wars of aggression and constraints upon civil rights that our nation continues to endure to this day.

Source note:This chapter originally appeared as "9/11: Planes / No Planes and "video fakery"", *veteranstoday.com* (20 February 2012).

17

9/11 Truth will out:
The Vancouver Hearings

by Jim Fetzer

"And ye shall know the truth and the truth shall make you free" — the motto of the CIA, taken from the Gospel according to St. John, which was inscribed on the facade of its Headquarters Building in 1959.

The array of ongoing attacks on the 9/11 Truth movement has reached astonishing proportions. A "10th anniversary 9/11 Truth 'Hit Piece' Roundup" published on 12 September 2011, a year and a day after 9/11, included excerpts from and links to no less than 32 attacks, where the majority emphasize the psychological needs of those who embrace "conspiracy theories" to give meaning, coherence and security to their lives—as though the belief that your government has perpetrated crimes of such magnitude could enhance your sense of security!

But logic and reason are not their strong suits, where these articles are largely bereft of considerations about photographic, witness and physical proof substantiating the conclusions that many within the movement have drawn, where those who study the evidence tend to become truthers themselves.

Attacks upon the movement from the outside, however, pale in comparison with those that arise from groups that are within the movement itself. Richard Gage, head of Architects and Engineers for 9/11 Truth, reportedly tried to convince 9/11 Vancouver

that it should not support the hearings that would be held there on 15-17 June 2012. Rob Balsamo, the head of Pilots for 9/11 Truth, has denounced "No Plane Theory" (NPT), virtually without regard for the evidence that supports it, to which Pilots itself has made major contributions. And the Judy Wood clique (which displays the behavioral characteristics of a cult), denounces anyone who has even the least doubt of her theory of the destruction of the Twin Towers, while paradoxically denying that she even has "a theory"!

In spite of efforts to undermine them, which even included a death threat directed against those who organized the conference, The Vancouver Hearings have made a powerful contribution to understanding the events of 9/11. The quality of the 19 presentations was uniformly excellent—clearly organized, well-reasoned, and thought-provoking—where the most controversial issues within the 9/11 Truth community were addressed— and effectively settled—in an effort to expose falsehoods and reveal truths.

The most important outcome was the resolution of several of the major 9/11 controversies that have divided the research community, which represents an enormous step forward in bringing these factions within the movement together—provided that reason and rationality are going to prevail in lieu of ego-centric and defensive attempts to save face when confronted with overwhelming evidence to the contrary.

The Vancouver Hearings were designed to compensate for perceived weaknesses in The Toronto Hearings, which were held with great fanfare across the continent nine months earlier. As Joshua Blakeney explained, there was a noticeable failure in Toronto to address who was responsible for 9/11 and why.

And as I accented in my critique of those hearings, alternative theories about the destruction of the Twin Towers, including the possible use of mini or micro nukes, much less directed energy weapons, were not even considered, which meant that *no comparative judgments could be rendered about which among the alternative accounts provides the best explanation of the available data because no alternatives were discussed.* That is not a scientific attitude.

The desire to avoid controversial questions, such as whether a Boeing 757 hit the Pentagon, whether all four of the crash sites had been fabricated or faked, much less who was responsible and why, were not addressed, even though there is a powerful and growing body of evidence that makes their resolution possible. The Vancouver Hearings were intended to compensate for those shortcomings.

The "Official Account"

One commentator who attended the hearings, Ernst Rodin, has suggested that the difference between these events is that the Toronto Hearings were devoted to establishing that the "official account" of 9/11 cannot be sustained on the basis of the available relevant evidence, while The Vancouver Hearings were focused upon the question of who was responsible and why. But another student of 9/11, Craig McKee, has come decidedly closer to the heart of the matter by observing that, unlike Toronto, there was no "partly line" in Vancouver, where the presentations were diverse and some speakers openly disagreed with others, which is right on the mark.

The Vancouver Hearings were intended to confront and resolve the issues that divide us, which invited not only their discussion but even, as it turned out, open differences between speakers themselves. While Ernst Rodin implies the Toronto Hearings were more objective and scientific, frequently talking about what can be "verified" and what cannot, he minimizes the science at the Vancouver and, rather oddly, does not even bother to report our research on "No Plane Theory" (NPT) or to explain our findings about who was responsible and why. In this part, I am going to address issues related to NPT and, in part II, those related to the destruction of the Twin Towers and who was responsible and why 9/11 was produced.

The "official" 9/11 flight paths

While Ernst Rodin contends that he is only going to focus on "a few presentations that provided, at least for [him], new information", he not only does no more by way of discussing who was responsible and why than to mention in passing" government circles here and/or in 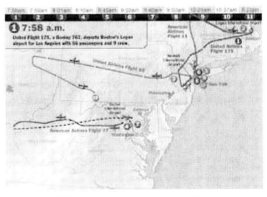 Israel" but has nothing to say about NPT, even though several of the speakers, including Nick Kollerstrom, Christopher Holmes, and I, presented extensive, detailed, and scientific evidence in its support.

Moreover, since Israeli complicity in 9/11 and evidence that all four of the 9/11 crash sites appear to have been fabricated had never been addressed during previous 9/11 conferences—with the exception of Morgan Reynolds during the Madison Conference in 2007—it is difficult to believe that this did not come as "new information" for Rodin.

In order to appreciate the historic significance of The Vancouver Hearings, however, it may be appropriate to review the "official account" of what happened on 9/11. According to The 9/11 Commission Report (2004)—with support from the National Institute of Standards and Technology (NIST)—the key events were:

That 19 Islamic fundamentalists hijacked four commercial carriers–Flight AA 11, AA 77, United 93, and United 175–outfoxed the most sophisticated air defense system in the world and perpetrated these atrocities under the control of Osama bin Laden, from a cave in Afghanistan.

That two of those planes, Flights 11 and 175, both Boeing 767s, were flown into the Twin Towers, where the combination of damage from their impacts, the jet-fuel based fires and those that endured, weakened the steel and caused both of them to collapse in about 10 seconds apiece.

That at 5:20 PM that afternoon, another enormous building in the World Trade Center complex, WTC-7 (also known as "Building 7", a 47-story skyscraper, also collapsed due to fires inside the building, even though it had not been hit by any plane and had no jet-fuel-based fires.

That the Pentagon was hit by Flight 77, a Boeing 757 that approached on a northeastern trajectory at around 500 mph and, just skimming the ground and taking out multiple lampposts, created a spectacular fireball and extensive damage, with 125 casualties at the building itself.

That another Boeing 757, Flight 93, crashed in Shanksville, after the passengers heroically attempted to regain control, which we know from phone calls they made–as others had made from other planes–where this plane virtually completely disappeared into the very soft earth.

That the government identified the 19 hijackers almost immediately, where 15 were from Saudi Arabia and the number from Iraq was none, where these events were used to justify wars of aggression in Iraq and Afghanistan, the passage of the PATRIOT ACT, and the on-going "War on Terror".

We have long known that every element of this account is riddled with claims that are not only false but even impossible, which I have summarized in "20 reasons the official account of 9/11 is wrong", where Elias Davidson has shown that the government has never been able to prove that any of those alleged "hijackers" were aboard any of those planes; David Ray Griffin and A.K. Dewdney have shown that all of the alleged "phone calls" from all four flights were faked; and Col. George Nelson, USAF (ret.), has observed that, even though there are millions of uniquely identifiable component parts from those four planes, the government has yet to produce even one!

And while an FBI spokesman explained why the NTSB had not conducted investigations of any of the four plane crashes for the first time in its history on the ground that "it wasn't necessary because we saw what happened on television", we did not see what happened in Shanksville on television and the only frame purporting to show what happened at the Pentagon features a plane that is too small by half to have been a Boeing 757.

What we did see on TV of events in New York is laden with anomalies.

Proving False Claims True

The title of Col. Nelson's study, "Impossible to Prove a Falsehood True", is relevant here, because *falsehoods can mistakenly seem to have been proven true when their premises are false because of suppressed evidence, manufactured evidence, or other forms of fakery and fabrication.*

A great deal of the proceedings that took place during The Vancouver Hearings, therefore, had the function of a formal certification of the deceit and deception that characterizes the official account of 9/11, not because we did not know that it was riddled with false claims and was based upon fabricated evidence but because of the importance of further certifying that to be the case with qualified experts, who confirmed that:

The 19 9/11 "patsies"

(1) *Flights 11 and 77 were not even scheduled that day and the planes corresponding to Flights 93 and 175 were not formally taken out of service until 28 September 2005;*

(2) *no Boeing 757 hit the Pentagon, but one appears to have been flown toward the building and swerved over it as explosives were set off to simulate a plane crash;*

(3) *Flight 93 was over Urbana, IL, after its alleged crash in Shanksville, PA, and Flight 175 was over Pittsburgh, PA, long after its alleged hit on the South Tower;*

(4) *all four of the alleged "crash sites" were fabricated, where different*

forms of fakery were used in each instance in an effort to conceal how had been done; where,

(5) *the Twin Towers appear to have been destroyed by a sophisticated arrangement of mini or micro nukes exploded in a sequence intended to simulate a collapse;*

(6) *9/11 appears to have been a "national security event" approved at the highest levels of the U.S. government and executed with the assistance of the Israeli Mossad.*

These conclusions—with the possible exception of how the Twin Towers were destroyed—now appear to have been established beyond a reasonable doubt, because there are no reasonable alternatives. The solitary exception (regarding how the Twin Towers were destroyed) is that the use of nukes may have been complemented by one or another kind of directed energy weapon.

But any alternatives that posit the primacy of conventional weapons, thermite/thermate/nanothermite—which could have been used for limited special purposes—or continue to maintain a collapse of any kind, after The Vancouver Hearings, no longer deserve serious consideration within the 9/11 Truth movement. Those theories have been defeated. They are not even physically possible. Indeed, the "official account" of 9/11 is littered with violations of the laws of aerodynamics, engineering and physics, which means that it is not only false but cannot possibly be true.

An unusual aspect of The Vancouver Hearings is that they were conducted within a quasi-judicial framework in which each of the speakers was sworn in by one of the hearing's panel of two judges, with the expectation of subsequently submitting evidentiary statements for the panel to use as the foundation for the preparation of formal indictments of those who appear to have been responsible for these atrocities, comparable to the Kuala Lumpur Tribunal's indictments of George W. Bush and Anthony "Tony" Blair.

The evidentiary submissions and indictments that are based upon them, some of which have recently appeared on Veterans Today, including Susan Lindauer's "Confessions of a former CIA Asset", may well become the most enduring legacy of the hearings. Let us begin with events at the Pentagon and follow up with the fabrication of the four "crash sites", then turn to how the Twin Towers were destroyed and who was responsible (including Israeli complicity) and why, which no other 9/11 conference has ever addressed.

(1) What didn't happen at the Pentagon

According to the "official account" of 9/11, the Pentagon was hit by a Boeing 757 that approached on a northeastern trajectory at around 500 mph and, just skimming the ground and taking out multiple lampposts, created a spectacular fireball and extensive damage, which caused 125 fatalities within the building itself.

The public needs to understand that events that violate the laws of aerodynamics and of physics are scientific impossibilities, where ground effect—the accumulation of a pocket of compressed gas —would make it impossible for a Boeing 757 to fly closer than 60-80' feet of the ground and that the effects of a plane traveling at 500 mph hitting stationary lampposts would be the same as a stationary plane being hit by lampposts traveling 500 mph: they would rip through the wing, the fuel stored there would burst into flames, the plane would twist around and its tail would have broken off, while the plane cartwheeled into the ground.

The "official account" is not even aerodynamically or physically possible, where arguments that are based upon scientific laws among their premises properly qualify as "scientific reasoning".

The first speaker to address the Pentagon was Enver Masud, founder and CEO of The Wisdom Fund, recipient of the 2002 Gold Award for THE WAR ON ISLAM, now in its 5th edition. An engineer by profession, he was

Where's the Boeing 757?

residing near the Pentagon and observed its condition immediately after the hit, which he wrote about in 9/11 UNVEILED (2nd edition), perhaps the best brief introduction to 9/11.

Enver Masud not only explained that Hani Hanjour, the alleged pilot, could not have executed the flight path of "Flight 77" into the Pentagon, but that the plane itself would have undergone G-forces that would have caused it to crash into the lawn. He offers the witness testimony of personnel inside the building, including April Gallup, but that other witnesses outside the building, such as CNN's Jamie McIntrye, also contradict the "official account". Among his other important points, he explains that the Pentagon Damage Assessment Report does not comport with the crash of a Boeing 757 and that the Flight Data Recorded provided to Pilots for 9/11 Truth by the NTSB does not show the plane leveling off for its approach to hit the Pentagon.

Barbara Honegger, Former White House Policy Analyst and, for more than a decade, Senior Military Affairs Journalist at DoD's science, technology and national security affairs graduate university, she authored OCTOBER SURPRISE (1989) and "The Scarlet A: Anthrax Links to 9/11", presents compelling evidence that the central fact of the Pentagon attack on 11 September 2001 is the same as at the World Trade Center: inside-the-building explosives, which no foreign terrorists could have had the access to plant, which, by itself, makes the "official account" of the Pentagon attack a fabrication on its face.

Physical evidence and eyewitness testimony converge to show that internal as well as external explosions went off just after 9:30 a.m., when the official narrative maintains that Flight 77 was still miles from Washington and did not approach the building until 9:37:46, where these primary explosions went off at locations far removed from the official "plane penetration path" in Wedge One, including in Wedge Two, and in the innermost rings well beyond the alleged C Ring "exit" hole. Honegger's study thus confirms and reinforces the presentation by Enver Masud.

Dennis Cimino, who spoke on Sunday morning, addressed issues related to the FDR data, which, according to the NTSB, was from Flight 77. With an A.A. in electrical engineering, 35-years in EMI/EMC testing and field engineering; FDR testing and certifications specialist; Navy Combat Systems Specialist; 2,000 hours, Pilot in Command, Commercial Instrument Single and Multi-Engine Land Pilot, Eastern Airlines 727-200, Second Officer, his presentation fit with others about the Pentagon. As Rodin accurately reports, "the most interesting aspect was his analysis of the AA77 FDR. It revealed that there could not have been a struggle in the cockpit because at no time was the autopilot disengaged which would have inevitably happened under those circumstances."

Furthermore, the preamble of the FDR file, which normally carries identifying information of the plane it came from, had 000. This indicated that the file did not originate from AA77." Dennis and I co-authored a study, 'The 'official account' of the Pentagon attack is a fantasy", which he asked me to move to my blog after it unexpectedly disappeared from Veterans Today.

Dean Hartwell, who holds a Bachelor's Degree in Political Science, Masters in Public Administration, and law degree, J.D., is also the author of DEAD MEN TALKING: CONSEQUENCES OF GOVERNMENT LIES (2009) on JFK, RFK and 9/11 and of PLANES WITHOUT PASSENGERS: THE FAKED HIJACKINGS OF 9/11 (2011). If Flight 77 did not hit the Pentagon, after all, then what became of its passengers? As Dean observes, Bureau of Transportation Statistics records, which were first discovered by Gerard Holmgren, reveal that neither Flight 11 nor Flight 77 were scheduled to fly that day.

But if those flights were phantoms, then the passengers were imaginary, too. As he illustrates in his evidentiary submission, the most famous passenger alleged to have been killed that day was the popular right-wing political commentator, Barbara Olson. Her husband, Ted, then the Solicitor General of the United States, gave three different versions of his claim that she had called him twice from the airplane, even though we know from the research of A.K. Dewdney and David Ray Griffin that calls from those planes would have been impossible in 2001. Even the FBI would eventually confirm that Barbara Olson had not had any conversation with her husband during 9/11. Dean's study removes a psychological obstacle to concluding that Flight 77 did not hit the Pentagon and that the "official account" is a fraud.

(2) The fabrication of all four crash sites

Since the presentations by Nick Kollerstrom (on Saturday morning) and by Christoper Holmes (on Sunday morning) can perhaps be best appreciated within the more general framework of how we know that all four of the "official crash sites" were fabrication, I shall begin with my own presentation, "Fraud and Fakery in the 'official account' of 9/11". As Dean observed, BTS records show neither Flight 11 (which officially hit the North Tower) nor Flight 77 (the Pentagon) was scheduled to fly that day. FAA Registration records, which I also display, show that the planes associated with Flights 93 (the Shanksville crash) and Flight 175 (the South Tower hit) were not de-registered (or formally taken out of service) until 28 September 2005.

Which raise the following questions: How could planes that were not even in the air have crashed on 9/11? And how could planes that crashed on 9/11 have still been in the air four years later? In addition, Pilots for 9/11 Truth has established (on the basis of studies of air/ground communications) that Flight 93 was in the air but was over Champaign-Urbana, IL, after its alleged crash in Shanksville and that Flight 175 was also in the air but, long after its alleged hit on the South Tower, was over Harrisburg and Pittsburgh, PA. All four crash sites involved forms of fakery.

This is such stunning information, which completely pulls the rug out from under the "official account" of 9/11, that I am in a state of disbelief that Ernst Rodin does not even mention, much less discuss, these findings. It also clarifies and establishes the position known as "No Planes Theory" (NPT), which might be better described as "No 'official plane crashes' theory" or, as Morgan Reynolds has proposed, "No Big Boeing's Theory". Properly understood, NPT consists of the conjunction of the following four propositions:

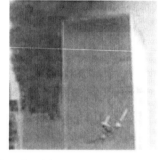

(1) Flight 11 did not hit the North Tower;

(2) Flight 77 did not hit the Pentagon;

(3) Flight 93 did not crash in Shanksville;

(4) Flight 175 did not hit the South Tower.

NPT does not mean that no planes were involved in 9/11, since Pilots' study of the FDR data suggests and CIT's witness research has confirmed that a large plane—presumably, a Boeing 757—flew toward the Pentagon on a due east trajectory (as opposed to the acute northeast trajectory of the "official account"), far too high to have hit any lampposts and, instead of hitting the building, swooped over it, as the trucker buddy of a friend of mine from JFK research had told him, while explosives were set off to simulate the crash of a plane. They appear to have left nothing to chance, where 125 casualties died when these events took place in the West Wing.

Shanksville is a relatively trivial case, but New York is another story. Christopher Holmes, Ph.D., who is a clinical and forensic psychologist, the director of the Zero Point Institute and author of THE MADNESS OF HUMANITY (2011), gave a presentation inspired by a psychological and forensic examination of Simon Shack's "September Clues" studies, which he elaborates upon in "Fabled Airplanes". Christopher began with a searching exploration of a blow-up of the alleged entry hole in the facade of the South

Tower, observing that features are present that should not be present and that other features are absent that should have been present if a real plane had entered the building. It was a stunning and effective discussion. He amplified with an analysis of other indications of video fakery — which could include fake videos of real or fake planes but also real footage of fake planes — which provided powerful proof that no real plane had actually entered the building on 9/11. In fact, given the laws of physics, that would have been an impossible event.

This is such a remarkable situation—where many, even within the 9/11 Truth community, remain convinced that violations of the laws of physics occurred on 9/11—it may be worth expanding upon this issue. As Pilots has confirmed, the plane was traveling faster than a standard Boeing 767 could fly. That has inspired some to infer that it must have been a "special plane". But no plane, no matter how "special", could have made the effortless entry shown in these videos, especially when it was intersecting eight (8) floors consisting of steel trusses connected at one end to the core columns and at the other to the external steel support columns, where each floor was filled with 4-8″ of concrete and, at 208′ on a side, represented an acre of concrete apiece.

Imagine the effects were a commercial carrier to encounter *just one of those floors in flight!* A real plane would have crumpled, its wings and tail broken off, with bodies, seats and luggage falling to the ground. Instead, it effortlessly passes through its own length into the building in the same number of frames that it passes through its own length in air. Its jet fuel should have exploded during its collision with the facade. How could a 160′ plane traveling over 500 mph have possibly come to a screeching halt within 48′ and not blown out the other side? The answer is, "It could not!", which is one more indication that we are viewing videos that record a fantasy encounter.

The question thus becomes not whether we are witnessing some kind of video fakery but how it was done. Nick Kollerstrom, Ph.D., an historian of science, who has published on Sir Isaac Newton, and Fellow of the Royal Astronomical Society, founding member of the UK's 9/11 Truth movement, member of the New York Academy of Sciences and author of 7/7: TERROR ON THE TUBE (3rd edition, 2012), in his presentation, "Did a Phantom Plane hit the 2nd Tower?", may have answered that question. Consistent with the BTS and FAA records that I have cited, Kollerstrom discusses the research of Richard Hall, who conducted a 3-D study of the flight path found in the videos of the plane, where he was able to establish locations and times for its approach toward the South Tower.

He subsequently discovered the existence of a RADES military radar track of (what he presumed to be) the same plane, except that its trajectory was 1,400′ to the right of the video image. He discovered that the same phenomenon occurred in relation to the Naudet Brothers film of the North Tower hit, where the RADES radar track was again 1,400′ to the right and, as in the first instance, missed the tower.

His account, which I believe to be correct, is that a real plane (probably cloaked) was used to project a holographic image of "the plane", where the sound of the real plane was taken to be coming from the projected image, which could be flown faster than a Boeing 767, could enter the towers in violation of Newton's laws and without exploding and come to a screeching halt, virtually instantaneously.

9/11 Truth Will Out

Ernst Rodin's repeated insinuations that The Toronto Hearings were objective and scientific, while The Vancouver Hearings were not, is palpably false. *The difference is we were willing to consider the alternative theories that have caused so much division and distress within the 9/11 community and they were not. The Toronto Hearings were less scientific and objective precisely on that basis, since it is logically impossible to establish what happened in cases of these kinds without comparing alternatives.*

While it is entirely appropriate for Rodin to compare and contrast the backgrounds of David Ray Griffin and me, where David is a theologian and philosopher of religion, he could not find the words to report that I had earned my Ph.D. in the history and the philosophy of science, in which I have published more than 20 books and 100 articles, that I taught logic, critical thinking and scientific reasoning for 35 years or that I was selected to be a Distinguished McKnight University Professor by the University of Minnesota in 1996.

That he places so much emphasis on science but suppresses my qualifications with regard to scientific methods suggests he was not on the up-and-up but was performing a subtle smear of The Vancouver Hearings by minimizing both its science (with regard to faking the crash sites) and its politics (by barely mentioning Israel's role in 9/11). Reasoning

that is based upon laws of aerodynamics, of engineering and of physics is scientific reasoning. And that is the kind of reasoning that was pervasive at The Vancouver Hearings.

A few lesser bones to pick with Ernst Rodin: he belittles Splitting the Sky (STS), who is one of Canada's most famous and admired human beings. When I read his comparison of this magnificent Native American to "a somewhat elderly rather agitated hippie on the stage addressing the audience in what is best described as a rant", I became concerned that this man was not going to give The Vancouver Hearings a fair shake.

In my opinion, STS has more integrity in his least digit than Ernst Rodin in his whole being. For all of his deference to The Toronto Hearings as adopting the better strategy of staying with less encompassing and (what he takes to be) more firmly supported positions, implying that they were "empirically based" while our hearings were "speculative", he went out of his way to minimize the scientific findings that prevailed during The Vancouver Hearings, not only with respect to alternative theories of how the Twin Tower were destroyed but meticulous and detailed studies of what didn't happen at the Pentagon and extensive and scientific documentation of the fabrication of all four "crash sites", which anyone can judge for themselves.

The closest that I can come to a charitable interpretation of his remarks is that Rodin understands the nature of scientific reasoning no better than those who ran The Toronto Hearings, who displayed their disposition for controlling debate and by restricting the discussion of alternatives.

Since reasoning involving laws of aerodynamics, of engineering and of physics qualifies as "scientific" and these studies were chock full of empirical data with observations and measurements as well as thought experiments, there appears to be no good reason for Ernst Rodin to have completely ignored these historic findings.

If the four crash sites were fabricated or faked (albeit each in its own different way), where two planes were not even in the air and the other two remained in the air four years later, then not only the American people but the nations of the world have been subjected to an enormous scam. And we demonstrated that all four crash sites were fabricated or faked. The dimensions of the hoax are almost impossible to exaggerate, where Hollywood-style special effects were combined with pseudo-flights and imaginary passengers.

Bear in mind: *if none of these planes crashed, then there were no dead passengers; and if there were no dead passengers, then there were no Islamic terrorists to hijack the planes; and if there were no Islamic terrorists to hijack the planes, then there was no justification for the "war on terror", the invasion of Afghanistan, the destruction of Iraq, or the passage of the PATRIOT Act, the creation of the Department of Homeland Security and the Transportation Security Agency.*

They are part and parcel of the massive scamming of the world that is known as "9/11".

Source note: This chapter originally appeared as "9/11 Truth will out: The Vancouver Hearings I", *veteranstoday.com* (7 July 2012).

18

Reason and Rationality in Public Debate: The Case of Rob Balsamo

by Jim Fetzer

"I would like to make it clear that Pilots For 9/11 Truth do not endorse the No Plane Theory nor the article mentioned in the OP. I personally have not read the article in detail, nor do I intend to. People are free to make their own choices". – Rob Balsamo

Those words might seem to be a peculiar way for the co-founder of Pilots for 9/11 Truth to introduce a thread about an article written by a core member of his own organization, but that is indeed the case.

The article in question, "The official account of the 9/11 attack on the Pentagon is a fantasy", by Dennis Cimino, was the third of a series on the four crash sites that are the foundation for what the government has told us about 9/11. Since the Pilots home page declares that,

"Our main focus concentrates on the four flights, maneuvers performed and the reported pilots. <u>We do not offer theory or point blame</u> at this point in time. However, we are focused on determining the truth of that fateful day based on solid data and facts — since 9/11/2001

ROB BALSAMO   JOHN LEAR

PILOTSFOR9IITRUTH.ORG/CORE

is the catalyst for many of the events shaping our world today — and the United States Government doesn't seem to be very forthcoming with answers or facts."

> *It might have seemed appropriate for Rob Balsamo to have actually read—even repeatedly, but certainly carefully and in detail—studies that advance extensive and detailed proof that all four of these crash sites were faked and fabricated, especially when the organization he heads "concentrates on the four flights, maneuvers performed and the reported pilots".*

> *But that was not his attitude or approach, which in the course of this thread led him to commit serious blunders that, in my opinion, raise serious doubts about his competence for his role. It grieves me to say this, but this conclusion appears to be inescapable.*

In particular, as I shall demonstrate, while declaring that Pilots does not and will never accept "NPT" ("No Planes Theory") and "video fakery", it becomes clear that he does not understand either concept, where the positions he asserts to be his and Pilots are logically inconsistent with this stance. The place to begin, no doubt, is with definitions of the concepts that matter to this inquiry, beginning with the nature of rationality, which requires distinguishing between "rationality of belief" and "rationality of action". Those concepts in turn provide a framework for analyzing the arguments that Rob Balsamo has advanced in the course of this thread and the extent to which they properly qualify as rational or not.

Reason and Rationality

As a professional philosopher and student of the theory of knowledge (also known as "epistemology"), the distinction between "rationality of belief" and "rationality of action" deserves preliminary consideration. The first involves accepting beliefs that are well-founded in relation to the available evidence, where the acquisition of new evidence (which may include new hypotheses) may lead to the acceptance of beliefs previously rejected, the rejection of beliefs previously accepted, or the suspension of beliefs that were previously accepted, rejected, or not.

The second involved adopting courses of actions that are effective, efficient, or reliable in attaining our aims, objectives, or goals. Human failings regarding rationality of belief sometimes fall into the category of psychoses but those of rationality of action are more like neuroses.

Persons can be high in one and low in the other, where even those who are high in rationality of both kinds can display actions that do not reflect their actual beliefs, as in the case of politicians, editorial writers, and used car salesmen. The concept of primary interest here is the first (of rationality of belief), which I have explored in *Scientific Knowledge* (1981), *AI: Its Scope and Limits* (1990), and other works. I have found that the most defensible conditions for a set of beliefs B to qualify as "knowledge" (for an individual x at a time t in relation to a body of evidence e) are the following four conditions for x at t given e:

(CA-1) the set of beliefs B held by x at t, given e, must be *logically consistent*, which means that they could be true together and are not contradictory;

(CA-2) the set of beliefs B held by x at t, given e, must be *deductively closed*, where consequences of those beliefs must also be included in set B;

(CA-3) the set of beliefs B held by x at t, given e, must satisfy *partial evidence* requirements, which means their acceptance is rationally justified by e at t, given suitable rules of reasoning R; and,

(CA-4) the set of beliefs B held by x at t, given e, must also satisfy *total evidence* requirements, which means that, as more evidence e* becomes available, suitable adjustments must be made in the new set of beliefs B* in conformity with rules (CA-1), (CA-2), and (CA-3).

What this means is that the conditions of consistency, closure and partial evidence characterize a set of beliefs B at a specific time t for those beliefs to qualify as *rational beliefs* or as "knowledge". These conditions thus define "rationality of belief" (for a person x at a time t in relation to a given body of evidence e). The rules of reasoning that apply include familiar principles of deductive and of inductive logic, which includes adductive reasoning in the form of "inference to the best explanation", which I have addressed relative to 9/11 and JFK.

"No Planes" Theory

In order to evaluate the rationality of beliefs about "NPT", of course, it needs to be well defined, where it can be taken to be the position that *all four of the "9/11 crash sites" the government has identified were fabricated or faked, where none of the planes that the government claims to have crashed on 9/11 actually crashed on 9/11*. "No Planes Theory" can therefore be defined as these beliefs:

Those who deny "no planes theory", therefore, are committed to the belief that EITHER Flight 11 hit the North Tower OR Flight 77 hit the Pentagon

OR Flight 93 crashed in Shanksville OR Flight 175 hit the South Tower. They do not need to deny all four crash sites are fake but only need to affirm that at least one of those crash sites was

real. Some have acknowledged that the crash sites for Flight 77 and Flight 93 were fabricated or faked, but denied that to be the case for Flight 175, especially, which, as we shall see, is the case of paramount interest.

Since we have videos that purport to show Flight 11 hitting the North Tower and Flight 175 hitting the South, which would otherwise qualify as partial evidence undermining NPT, those who accept NPT must, in order to preserve the rationality of their beliefs, reject that evidence as one or another forum of "video fakery", which as I have defined it in "Planes/ No Planes and 'Video Fakery'"— and reiterated repeatedly in the course of the thread on the Pilots' forum—is a phrase covering any use of video to convey a false impression of the events of 9/11, especially those videos that are supposed to show Flight 11 hitting the North Tower and Flight 175 hitting the South.

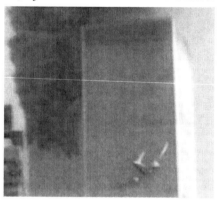

Thus, there are four possibilities, where only the first (real/real) is not video fakery:

So, for video fakery to have taken place, either the planes must have been faked or the videos must have been manipulated in the videos that have been used to support the "official account" of 9/11. Real videos of fake planes are just as much video fakery as fake videos of real planes, where features of the planes or of their interaction with those buildings might have been obfuscated or removed to insure the public did not have access to the evidence that would have "given the game away".

Logic and "Video Fakery"

There are four possible combinations:

Planes	Videos
Real	Real
Fake	Real
Real	Fake
Fake	Fake

Only real planes and real videos circumvent the charge of "video fakery", where those planes have to be Flights 11 and 175.

The Pilots' Forum

After having publishing three articles on the fabricated plane crashes of 9/11 ("Planes/No Planes and 'Video Fakery'", "9/11: The 'official account of the Pentagon attack is a fantasy" with Dennis Cimino, and "The Passenger Paradox: What Happened to Flight 93?" with Dean Hartwell), It came as a rather surprising that Pilots for 9/11 Truth was featuring a new thread on its forum entitled, "Debunkers respond to Dennis Cimino", which was dedicated to attacking ("debunking") the article we had published, 90% of which had been written by Dennis Cimino, who has impressive credentials, as his signature reflected:

Dennis Cimino, A.A., EE; 35-years EMI/EMC testing, field engineering; FDR testing and certifications specialist; Navy Combat Systems Specialist; 2,000 hours, Pilot in Command, Commercial Instrument Single and Multi-Engine Land Pilot, Eastern Airlines 727-200, Second Officer

I thought the article was very substantial and provided a devastating refutation of those who endorse the official account of a Boeing 757 approaching the Pentagon on an acute north-east trajectory, flying very low to the ground at more than 500 mph and taking out a series of lampposts before impacting with the building and producing some spectacular fireballs, which were included in the five frames that were originally released, one of which was conveniently labeled "plane", but which turned out to be too small to be a Boeing 757 as follows:

That the plane itself cannot possibly be a Boeing 757 counts as only one among a wide array of evidence that the official account cannot possibly be true, including that no Boeing 757 could have flown that fast at that altitude because of "ground effect" and that, had such a plane hit stationary lampposts at 500 mph, the effects would have been the same as had a lamppost traveling at 500 mph had hit the stationary plane: its wing would have been ripped off, the fuel stored in the wing would have exploded, its trajectory would have changed and its tail broken off, with immense damage to the lawn and parts of the plane strewn across it.

But none of that happened, as I explained in other articles and as Dennis, who was also a core member of Pilots for 9/11 Truth, had confirmed in this one about the Pentagon, where the use of that frame qualifies as a mini-case of "video fakery".

The Pentagon Approach Path

While Dennis had composed most of the study, I had added photos and diagrams, including one of the approach that Hani Hanjour, the purported pilot of Flight 77, had taken, which even experienced pilots regarded as extremely difficult, if not impossible, especially for a pilot who had difficulty handling a Cessna. The one that I posted was this:

American Airlines Flight 77
(Topographical Map Background)

Among the first criticisms raised (in post #14) was that this was an early analysis, which had been superseded by another as follows:

where I made an immediate substitution. At that point in time, I had the impression that this was a collaborative enterprise in the search for the truth about 9/11, an impression of which I would be disabused.

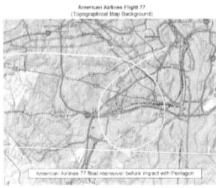

American Airlines 77 final maneuver before impact with Pentagon

Figure 3 – DC Area Flight Path

Pilots on Flights 93 and 175

As "Planes/No Planes and 'Video Fakery'" makes clear, the evidence that Flight 93 did not crash in Shanksville and that Flight 175 did not hit the South Tower includes that FAA Registration records show that the planes corresponding to Flights 93 and 175 had not been "de-registered" until 28 September 2005, which raised the interesting question of how two planes that crashed on 9/11 could have still been in the air four years later. On the top of next page is a copy of the FAA records thereof:

As though that were not impressive enough, the on-site evidence that no plane had crashed in Shanksville was extensive and compelling. I was therefore ecstatic when I discovered Pilots had determined that Flight 93 had been in the air on 9/11 but over Urbana, IL, far removed from Shanksville, PA, thus confirming that element of NPT as follows:

and, in addition, that Pilots had also determined that Flight 175 had been in the air on 9/11, but over Pittsburgh, PA, again far removed from the South Tower. So, unless the same planes could be in two places at the same time, Pilots had also confirmed another element of NPT. I therefore assumed that we were in sync about what had and had not happened on 911 in relation to both Flights 93 and 175.

Insofar as Pilots had published about Flight 77 at the Pentagon and established that the FDR data provided to Pilots by the NTSB did not correspond to the official trajectory but instead to plane on a due east approach that was too high in the air to have hit any lampposts and a second from impact was 100' above the building, I had presumed that Pilots maintained that no Boeing 757 had hit the Pentagon and wrote about it in a Scholars' press release, which was qualified by Rob in a note that appeared on the Pilots home page, which confirmed their analysis of the data but disavowed the inference no plane had not hit.

As an example of Pilots' concerns, they offered the following caveat, suggesting they were parsing some language:

* Pilotsfor911truth.org does not make the claim that "No Boeing 757 hit the Pentagon". We have analyzed the Flight Data Recorder data provided by the NTSB and have shown factual analysis of that data. We do not offer theory. While we do not make this claim in these words, the analysis we present on the basis of the NTSB's own data factually contradicts the official account that Flight 77 hit the Pentagon–if trends are continued beyond end of data records–and therefore supports the inference that American Airlines Flight 77 did not hit the building based upon that data.

[NOTE: The first of these paragraphs was originally authored by Rob Balsamo, which I thought required some clarification. So I submitted the second to him, which he adopted. He now claims that I am misrepresenting the position of Pilots, but I am quoting from its web site, which includes the prefatory note, *"Official Comment / corrections. Please use this link if anyone has questions regarding the article. Jim Fetzer and I worked on this together."* So I am having a hard time appreciating why he now contends that this is a misrepresentation.]

Presumably, this meant that, even though their study implied that Flight 77 had not hit the Pentagon, they were leaving it open that some other Boeing 757 might have hit the building, which I personally thought was most unlikely. I thought the use of the word "theory" in this context was the least bit odd, but attributed that to my having a great deal more experience with concepts like that as a professional philosopher of science, while they were professional pilots, instead.

Anyone can verify the matter for themselves, but I had thought that I had offered an objective summary of the Pilots' study and only drawn obvious inferences from what they had discovered. I even ended the Scholars' press release with these observations, which draw upon the distinction the between "rationality of belief" and "rationality of action":

"The Pentagon has become a kind of litmus test for rationality in the study of 9/11," Fetzer said. "Those who persist in maintaining that a Boeing

757 hit the building are either unfamiliar with the evidence or cognitively impaired. Unless," he added, "they want to mislead the American people. The evidence is beyond clear and compelling. It places this issue 'beyond a reasonable doubt'. No Boeing 757 hit the Pentagon."

Our Previous Correspondence

When I discovered that Rob had posted a disavowal of NPT and of "video fakery", therefore, I was completely dumbfounded. Not only had their own study of the NTSB data supported the conclusion that Flight 77 had not hit the Pentagon but, I thought, *what could be more obvious than that, if Flight 175 had been over Pittsburgh at the time, it could not have also been entering the South Tower, which meant that some kind of video fakery had to have taken place in New York.* So I wrote to him on 29 February 2012, to seek clarification of his position and, in response to questions I posed to him, he wrote back with the following explanation of Pilots' positions, which he said I could quote:

(1) Pilots has established that Flight 93 was over Urbana, IL, at the time that it purportedly crashed in Shanksville. Is it Pilots' position that Flight 93 was BOTH over Urbana, IL, AND crashed in Shanksville, PA, AT THE SAME TIME?

"Absolutely not. There isn't any evidence which has been provided by government agencies that proves UAL93 crashed in Shanksville. In fact, all data and information provided by government agencies conflicts with their story. We want to know why, others are free to speculate."

(2) Pilots has established that Flight 175 was over Pittsburgh, PA, at the time it purportedly hit the South Tower. Is it Pilots' position that Flight 175 was BOTH over Pittsburgh, PA, AND hit the South Tower AT THE SAME TIME?

"According to ACARS data and statements made by UAL Dispatchers, UAL175 was in the vicinity between MDT and PIT, PA during the events taking place in NYC at the South Tower. Since the aircraft observed to hit the South tower was flying at a speed impossible for a standard 767, combined with the numerous targets converging and then diverging from the alleged UA175 target prior to the impact, the govt has not proven that UA175, N612UA, caused the damage to the south tower. If fact, the data provided conflicts with the govt story.

"For clarity, this does not mean that some other aircraft may have caused the damage considering the aircraft observed to cause the damage has never

been positively identified (nor any of the other 3 aircraft allegedly used on 9/11). When we say "Impossible speed", this does not mean the speeds are impossible for all aircraft. The speeds are impossible for a <u>standard</u> 767-200. The speeds reported are not impossible if the aircraft were modified. This is covered thoroughly in our presentation 9/11: World Trade Center Attack. *"*

Flight 175 Anomalies

At this point in time, I still took for granted that we were on the same page with regard to the official account, where I supposed that we both agreed that Flight 93 had not crashed in Shanksville and that Flight 175 had not hit the South Tower. (Since Flight 11 has not come up, I tentatively assumed that he did not contest that the weight of the evidence supported the inference that it also had not hit the North Tower, given oddities in the Naudet Brothers' video, which I explained in "Planes/No Planes and 'Video Fakery'".) But it would be Flight 175 that would strain my credulity, since Rob appeared to deny what his own findings implied, namely: that since Flight 175 was not in New York City at the time, the videos we have had to entail video fakery of one kind or another—either a fake plane or manipulated videos, or both.

There are several dimensions to proofs of video fakery involving Flight 175, including that the plane is traveling at a speed that is aerodynamically impossible for a standard Boeing 767—which Pilots itself had confirmed—and had made an impossible entry into the building, in violation of Newton's laws, where it passes through its own length into the building in the same number of frames that it passes through its own length in air, which would have been impossible unless this massive 500,000-ton building posed no more resistance to the flight of an aircraft than air!

Consider this diagram:

What it shows is that Flight 175 was intersecting with eight (8) floors that consisted of steel trusses connected at one end to the core columns and to the external

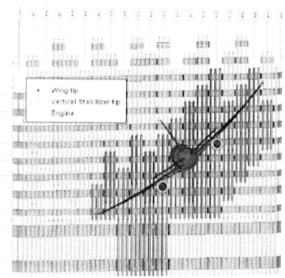

support columns at the other, where each floor was covered with 4-8" of concrete, representing an acre of concrete apiece and posing enormous horizontal resistance to any airplane's penetration into the building. Other points that have been made include John Lear's observation that the plane has no strobe lights, Ben Collet's notice that it casts no shadow, and videos showing its left wing disappearing before it enters the South Tower, which strongly suggests we have to be dealing with something that looks like a real plane but cannot be one. No real plane could done these feats.

Since Pilots had previously confirmed that the plane shown in these videos is traveling at an aerodynamically impossible speed for a standard Boeing, I rather took for granted that Rob would be on board with video fakery in this case, since given Pilots' own study, it cannot be Flight 175 and must therefore be some other plane, where these videos have been used to sell the "official account" of 9/11 to the American people.

Speeds Reported For World Trade Center Attack Aircraft Analyzed
For Immediate Release

Supplement to "9/11 World Trade Center Attack"

(PilotsFor911Truth.org) - Much controversy has surrounded the speeds reported for the World Trade Center attack aircraft. However, none of the arguments for either side of the debate have been properly based on actual data, until now. Pilots For 9/11 Truth have recently analyzed data provided by the National Transportation Safety Board in terms of a "Radar Data Impact Speed Study" in which the NTSB concludes 510 knots and 430 knots for United 175 (South Tower) and American 11 (North Tower), respectively. A benchmark has been set by the October 1999 crash of Egypt Air 990, a 767 which exceeded it's maximum operating limits causing in-flight structural failure, of which data is available to compare to the WTC Attack Aircraft. read more...

Since Pilots already confirmed that Flight 175 was over Pittsburgh at the time, either the plane in the video has to be faked or the videos have to have been manipulated as a matter of consistency and closure with regard to rationality of belief. I was therefore stunned to discover that Rob continued to deny **both** NPT **and** video fakery several times in the course of its thread attacking Dennis.

Rob Balsamo's Position

Here, for example, is a post in which Rob had faulted me for comparing an airliner to an empty coke can, while he insisted that it was more like a full coke can. He made that claim that on the basis of the consideration that a Boeing 767, for example, has a complex internal structure, but a coke can has its own internal structure. And the behavior that would have been expected of a commercial carrier hitting a massive building like the South Tower would have been more like that of an empty coke can hitting a brick wall (or a car hitting an enormous tree) than a can full of coke.

I thought it was peculiar that he was resisting my analogies, but that would turn out to be far from the only problems I discerned in his reasoning about Flight 175.

As Balsamo makes clear, he believes that a "modified" aircraft could have performed the feats—of flying at a speed that is impossible for a standard Boeing 767 and of making its effortless entry into the South Tower, for example, in violation of Newton's laws—on the basis of suppositions about "modification" and reliance upon an animation of the planes "entry" into the building—which, as I shall explain, are question begging and cannot be sustained.

After all, if the plane shown in these videos was not Flight 175, yet the videos are being presented as proof that Flight 175 hit the South Tower, we are confronted with a perfect illustration of video fakery, thus defined, even though he categorically asserts that, "Pilots for 9/11 Truth will never endorse NPT nor video fakery", in the final sentence at the end:

So if he were right about the use of a modified plane, he would be wrong about video fakery, insofar as his position implies the use of videos to convey a fake plane to simulate Flight 175. His twin claims are therefore logically inconsistent: they cannot possibly be true together. He relies upon an animation produced by Purdue University, which he features in this post, to support his claim that the entry shown in the videos is not in violation of Newton's laws.

But, as I shall explain, the plane is shown intersecting with too-few floors, where the façade of the South Tower and the internal structure of the building are grossly distorted, especially by completely ignoring the 4-8" of concrete on each floor. But this means that this animation offers a provably false account of the entry into the building, from which it follows that Rob has not only relied upon a "fake video" from Purdue to discount video fakery—but that, as I shall explain, he is also thereby embracing the theory that is implicit in this animation in doing so.

Rob's "Modified Plane" Scenario

Rob Balsamo's insistence that a "modified plane" could have performed the feats observed in these videos is not only peculiar because he still insists that Pilots will never accept "video fakery", even though his own position implies it, but that he cites Dennis Cimino as someone else who rejects NPT and "video fakery". But when I consulted with Dennis about this, he offered a wide ranging critique of Rob's position about the plane, since a constraint on the "modification" would have to be that it still looked like a Boeing 767 and closely resembled the image of the plane shown in these videos. According to Dennis, however, that is virtually impossible, where Rob has produced no evidence to support any such modifications:

"I think that the amalgamation of all that I had stated about the obvious 'lack' of engine and structural modifications to these planes (if the VIDEOS are any indication to the planes used) is pretty on target: the compressor stall issue, the drag coefficient issue, and the clear lack of ANY meaningful visible clues that would support that these planes were re-engined and structurally modified in a way to decrease form drag and parasite drag, seems to indicate that you can scream MODIFIED all day long but how so? The question remains to Rob is this: "IF these planes were modified, show where and in what fashion. . . .

"These nacelles still had high bypass turbofans in them. Very fuel efficient engines but not as capable of speed as PURE JET types which are much more fuel hungry, in the speed department area–and LONG LONG LONG nacelles are needed for afterburning to be possible, as the exhaust section is extremely long on those types of engines. As far as I can tell there is NO EXTERNAL EVIDENCE of any the following:

1) wing aspect ratio and or other MAC 'mean area chord' changes to these aircraft's wing structures;

2) wing or vertical stabilizer sweep angle changes;

3) fuselage tapering to decrease drag; or,

4) augmented thrust of any kind in form of JATO or other assists.

"In light of these simple truths that are SELF EVIDENT if you look at those videos which we are pretty sure are FAKE, there is no empirical evidence to support the requisite modifications needed to allow these planes to achieve these speeds and maintain them to their targets at these altitudes in STRAIGHT AND LEVEL FLIGHT.

"And without extreme modifications, it's highly UNLIKELY if not pretty damned impossible for these planes to fly at 515 KTAS at such a low altitude, below 1,000 feet msl, without a lot of major problems due to COMPRESSOR

STALLS and engine inlet blockages, as well as structural failures, especially as the one aircraft abruptly SNAP ROLLS just before going into the building. At that speed and at that roll rate, that most likely would have broken the plane up. So I'm still firmly in the VIDEO FAKERY and NO REAL PLANES department here for sure."

To the extent to which Rob's conjecture is testable, therefore, it appears to be false; beyond that, it is simply speculative. What that means is that he is offering a guess, speculation or conjecture, which is an example of the weak sense of the term "theory", which stands in contrast to the strong sense of an empirically-testable explanatory hypothesis, as in the cases of Newton's theory of gravitation, Darwin's theory of evolution, or Einstein's theory of relativity. I discuss the distinction in "Thinking about 'Conspiracy Theories': 9/11 and JFK", which Rob, as with my articles on planes/no planes, does not appear to have read or, at best, simply skimmed. But I would observe that, during an email exchange on 3 January 2012,

Rob reiterated his position that Pilots does not deal with theories. When I mentioned I was planning to cite Pilots' research in some of my own, he replied with these remarks:

Sure...

Feel free to use anything from our site if you would like to present it... but if you add your own conclusions based on our work, be sure to make the distinction in the presentation. Keep in mind, P4T does not endorse any theory.

Regards,
Rob Balsamo
Co-Founder pilotsfor911truth.org

The "impossible entry"

It is the least ironic that, while Rob Balsamo has combined a photo of him and a photo of John Lear, perhaps our nation's most distinguished pilot (which is the featured photograph for this article), John supports NPT and the use of a hologram in New York to simulate a real plane, which sets him at odds with Rob. John Friend has published a blog about John Lear's view, "No planes on 9/11?", in which he included an excerpt from John's affidavit, which is archived in its totality at Scholars for 9/11 Truth forum:

"The debris of the Boeing 767, as found after the collapse, was not consistent with actual debris had there really been a crash. Massive forgings, spars from both the wing and horizontal and vertical stabilizers, landing

gear retract cylinders, landing gear struts, hydraulic reservoirs and bogeys oxygen bottles, a massive keel beam, bulkheads and the wing box itself cold not possibly have 'evaporated' even in a high intensity fire. The debris of the collapse should have contained massive sections of the Boeing 767, including 3 (sic: 2) engine cores weighing approximately 9000 pounds apiece, which could not have been hidden. Yet there is no evidence of any of these massive structural components from either 767 at the WTC. Such complete disappearance of 767s is impossible. [Part II, Section H, pg. 6]"

The Purdue Animation

Notice that Rob advances the Purdue animation in support of his position that the plane could have made an effortless entry into the building, which was therefore not in violation of Newton's laws. But he commits the major blunder of simply assuming that the Purdue animation was well-founded, when it is easily shown that it was not. But the Purdue simulation does not even show 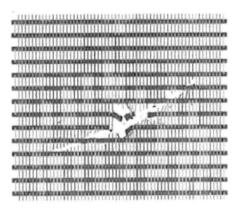 the plane intersecting with eight (8) floors, the correct number, but instead shows it intersecting with only six (6) as this diagram displays:

In addition, it grossly misrepresents the façade of the building, which is only faintly shown, but where most of the façade consists of the external support columns, which are made of steel, and concrete framing around the windows, which are substantially less that 50% of the surface area, and ignores the consideration that each of those floors was covered with 4-8" of concrete, which would have posed massive horizontal resistance: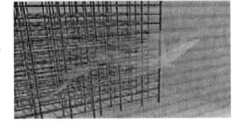

As though that were not enough, the video effects the subtle distortion of turning the plane toward the vertical, thereby creating the impression that it is entering the building effortlessly because most of the floor it entered was open space, as though it were only one, again ignoring that it should have been intersecting with eight (8) floors consisting of steel trusses connection to the core columns at one end and external support columns at the other, where Rob features the simulation in his post #198:

Most importantly, Rob overlooks that every computer simulation is constructed on the basis of assumptions, which may or may not be well founded. In this case, he begs the question by taking for granted that its assumptions are appropriate, ignoring the "GI/GO" principle of computer science, "Garbage In/Garbage Out", which fits this animation to a "t". Once again, therefore, he commits himself to a theory about the design and engineering of the Twin Towers but which, unlike his commitment to a "modified plane", is easily testable by the comparison of the actual structure with its simulation, which is provably inadequate.

Witnesses and "Video Fakery"

During the exchange on the Pilots' forum, I discovered that Rob Balsamo was rejecting video fakery on the twin grounds that witnesses, including some he knows personally, had reported seeing "a plane", as well as the Purdue animation. But "video fakery" does not mean that no witnesses saw something they took to be a plane. It means that, if they reported seeing "a plane", it had to have been something that looked like a plane but was not a real plane, since it was performing feats no real plane could perform, as I repeatedly explained.

Indeed, as I also explained repeatedly, there are three hypotheses (or "theories") about how this ("video fakery") was done, including the use of computer-generated images (CGI) and of video compositing, where both would only affect the images being broadcast but not those seen in real time. Although others participating in the thread did not understand my point, the more weight we give to witness reports, the greater the support for the use

Mar 28 2012, 09:39 AM

This post is wrong on so many counts that it is itself a piece of fakery.

(1) Since it shows the intersection with only six (6) and not seven (7) at the North Tower or eight (8) at the South, this is sloppy research from scratch and does not accurately represent either "hit" in New York City.

(2) I consider three alternatives: the use of CGIs, of video compositing, and of a sophisticated hologram. CGIs and video compositing would only apply to the broadcast footage, however, and not what witnesses saw.

(3) Not only do I take into account the eyewitness reports, but I accent that, the more seriously we take their reports, the greater the weight for a hologram, since otherwise "the plane" would not have been observable.

(4) There is no evidence for a "mini-demolition" of the inside of the North or of the South Tower. Notice that the plane is completely inside the South Tower BEFORE IT EXPLODES and there are no indications of prior explosion.

(5) The "obstacles" that would have impeded the penetration of "the plane" into the building included those eight (8) floors of steel trusses covered with 4-8" of concrete. Their removal would have created major explosive effects.

(6) The Purdue simulation was an animation that has been widely discounted as "work for hire". It does not show the plane intersecting with eight (8) floors, where an explosion of its fuel would have occurred before was inside the tower.

of a sophisticated hologram, about which Tambourine man was the most informed and appreciative. Rob's "witnesses" are not evidence against video fakery but provide support for the use of a sophisticated hologram:

(7) No such effects are visible, which means that this is an hypothesis which has no evidence to support it. The author introduces a misleading version of my position and then simply disregards the absence of any proof for his own.

(8) Killtown has done excellent work on the "plane crashes", including this one as a critique of a fake video that was actually broadcast over CBS News, "How not to fake plane crash videos", http://fake-plane-crash-videos.blogspot.com/

(9) The obvious reason that paranoia has not convinced anyone of this theory is that there is no evidence to support it. All the evidence is on my side, once you separate contrived versions of my position from misleading ones like his.

My Ultimate Disappointment

(10) Among the experts I have interviewed about the use of a hologram was Stephen Brown, who had just completed a course of holography at Cambridge and confirmed that the technology for such a project had been available then.

Anyone who studies the evidence as I have explained it SHOULD arrive at the same or similar conclusions, as is the case with the very nice Barry Berman blog. My first article on this, "New Proof of Video Fakery on 9/11", appeared in 2008.

Because Pilots mission statement includes these sentences, "Our main focus concentrates on the four flights, maneuvers performed and the reported pilots" and that "Pilots

See "No Planes Theory", which exposes the apparent use of actors on 9/11, and includes a link to one of his interviews with me on "The Dynamic Duo" on 19 August 2008 (with graphics), in which he explains why they had to fake it.

This is an especially excellent interview with the most important footage you need to know to understand how we know that 'video fakery' was employed in New York on 9/11. It should leave no room for any serious doubt about it.

for 9/11 Truth is an organization of aviation professionals and pilots throughout the globe who have gathered together for one purpose. We are committed to seeking the truth surrounding the events of the 11th of September 2001", I have been very enthusiastic over its accomplishments, which I have often cited and used to substantiate my arguments about NPT and video fakery. It therefore came as a surprise and bitter disappointment to discover that Rob was adamantly opposed to NPT and video fakery, which, I thought, he could not possibly understand and maintain his position with consistency and closure, much less satisfy the partial and total evidence conditions as more proof becomes available.

My confidence in his competence was further shaken when he offered an image of the Twin Towers that created the initial impression that they were flimsy in their construction, when they were actually extremely robust. The interesting question about this photograph, of course, concerns the date on which it was taken, which appears to have been before their construction was complete.

Recall that I mentioned that more than 50% of the façade of each building was steel and concrete, yet there is a stunning amount of light that comes shining through. Rob tried to capitalize on this image, but in the process he was virtually emulating the Purdue animation, because a construction crane still sits on top the South Tower.

The Engine at Church & Murray

Among his final arguments for the reality of the plane that had hit the South Tower was that he had performed his own calculation and had determined that an engine component found at Church & Murray "ended up right where it is supposed to be based on simple High School physics", thus:

But what he does not appear to realize is that that component had been planted and did not come from a Boeing 767. The evidence he cites in support of his theory of a "modified plane", therefore, once again shows that the government went to extraordinary lengths to deceive the public:

Not only had this been published in "Planes/No Planes and 'video fakery'" but I had also even pointed out in an earlier post that it had been planted:

Pickup or delivery?

Newsworthy things were happening on 9-11 at Church and Murray, so Fox News was there. An FBI van is parked on Murray at the Church intersection, door open. An FBI agent stands guard over something not seen in other photos at this location. Blue-clad FBI agents appear beside the van and seem to struggle with something heavy. There appear to be six FBI agents and a photographer in the video frames. Another image taken at the deserted corner, right, shows a dolly used for moving something. What does the complete video show...a pickup or delivery?

What this told me was that Rob Balsamo had not only not read carefully the post that was the overt target of the thread on the Pilots' forum, but that he had not read the other related articles and didn't know any better than to commit one gaff after another. Moreover, for raising the objections that I had during the course of this thread, he had me classified as a "troll" and, if you look carefully, you can see that designation in some of my posts here.

When I tried to respond to this one, which claims that I had falsely named Rob Balsamo, Anthony Lawson, and Dennis Cimino as "supporters of NPT", when I attempted to set the record straight by explaining that, while Anthony was a lost cause, Dennis does and Rob *should* support NPT, I discovered I had been, without public notice, cut off from posting there.

Concluding Reflections

While convergence in conclusions depends upon having the same body of evidence, the same set of alternative hypotheses, and the same rules of reasoning, it is difficult for me to see how Rob Balsamo can continue to be the spokesman for an organization when his capacity to reason has so clearly been warped. My most charitable interpretation is that, even though he actually knew better, he was so intent upon putting me in my place that he began to emulate politicians, editorial writers, and used-car salesmen by violating the conditions of rationality of belief by actions that were at odds with his own *bona fide* understanding. If that is not the case, however, and he really has no greater competence for reasoning that he has displayed here, then he really is unqualified to head up such an important society for 9/11 Truth.

This case illustrates the importance of the total evidence requirement for rational beliefs, since partial evidence could at least initially appear to be supportive of planes as well as no planes. But once the totality of what we have available is taken into consideration, it becomes apparent that the "no planes" position exemplifies the maxim that, "When you have eliminated the impossible, whatever remains, no matter how INITIALLY improbable, must be the case", which I offer here in a modified form. Dennis has given this exchange considerable consideration and offers his final reflections:

"My position, per THEIR hard and fast stance, puts me in the 'NPT' corner because by NO PLANES, my assertions go in that direction, given the definition laid out by a host of people other than just Rob Balsamo. He and those who attempt to debunk NPT assert indefensible claims such as:

a) that modified Boeing jetliners of the B-767-200 family were involved in the WTC attacks, when no signs of such modifications can be seen in any of the photographic evidence, which means they are wrong to conclude this as being the case;

b) that the speeds and building entries, particularly the SOUTH TOWER hit are possible, when they fly in the face of physics, aerodynamics, and Boeing speed limitations, up to the engine manufacturers guidelines for such incredibly HIGH speeds at such incredibly LOW altitudes; and,

c) that the buildings' reactions to the strikes by these 90 tons of hurtling metal were 'nominal' and or 'in line with Newtonian physics", which is also an enormous stretch.

If being "non-NPT" means accepting contentions like these three, then I into the category that in the Veitch diagram subset defines me rather unequivocally as a "NPT". I also have to say that treating a) through c) as though they were facts is, in my professional opinion, far from adequate justification to "discredit" or "malign" or "impugn" those of us in the aviation community as a whole who decry these very kinds of irregularities as purely nonsensical and unreal."

What this means is that NPT and video fakery are well-founded in relation to the available relevant evidence and the criteria for rational belief, where those who have understood the kinds of fakery that were involved in all four crash sites are committed to moving the boundaries of 9/11 Truth closer to their proper scope and depth in the pursuit of justice for every American, especially those who died on 9/11, whose relatives and loved ones as well as the American people deserve to know how and why their lives were taken on that tragic and fateful day.

Source note: This chapter originally appeared as "Reason and Rationality in Public Debate: The Case of Rob Balsano", *veteranstoday.com* (1 April 2012).

In Memoriam: Jack White

The author of Ch. 8, "A Photographic Portfolio of Death and Devastation", and of Ch. 9, "9/11 Illusions, Special Effects and Other Magic Tricks", was a dear friend of the editor of this book, with whom he collaborated on research in relation to the assassination of JFK, the atrocities of 9/11 and the moon landing hoax, where his research on moon photos is archived at aulis.com/ jackstudies_index1.html. The following is adapted from his biography at *www.spartacus-educational.com:*

Jack D. White was born on 17 January 1927, in San Angelo, Texas. His parents, John Nathan White and Billie Lorena Dumas White, moved the family to Fort Worth shortly after his birth and he was raised and educated there. After graduation from Amon Carter Riverside High School in 1944, White worked briefly for the Fort Worth Press as a sports writer covering high school sports under legendary sports editor H. H. "Pop" Boone.

During the Second World War White enlisted in the U.S. Navy. After his discharge in 1946, White returned to Fort Worth to pursue his interest in journalism, art, and history. He graduated from Texas Christian University in 1949, with a B.A. in journalism and began an advertising career as copywriter and art director at Yates Advertising Agency in Fort Worth. In 1954, he joined the Witherspoon and Ridings Public Relations Agency in Fort Worth, which later became Witherspoon and Associates.

White began as the firm's first art director and during his twenty-seven years with the agency rose to vice-president, executive art director, personnel manager, and part owner. He specialized in design, type management, and photography and developed their in-house facilities for darkroom work, studio photography, and slide show presentations.

Although White had photographed the city since the 1950s, he only began collecting Fort Worth-photographs seriously in 1972, when Witherspoon was planning the 100th anniversary of one of its clients, the Fort Worth National Bank. He was in charge of acquiring copies of historical prints of Fort Worth for the bank's annual report, a historical booklet, and an exhibit for the bank lobby. Another of White's areas of expertise and collecting interests is the assassination of President John F. Kennedy in Dallas, Texas, in 1963. He is nationally known as an expert on the assassination and served as a photographic consultant to the House Select Committee on Assassinations during the hearings. He was also a consultant on the Oliver Stone film, JFK.

As a result of his interest in the Kennedy assassination, White published two videotapes on his photographic studies of the assassination. He has developed a slide lecture, which he presents to classes and symposia on the JFK assassination and also contributes his research to professional journals.

White, along with David Mantik, Charles Crenshaw, Robert Livingston and Ronald F. White, contributed to Assassination Science (edited by James H. Fetzer). He also contributed several articles for Murder in Dealey Plaza (2000) and The Great Zapruder Film Hoax (2003).

White retired from Witherspoon and Associates in 1981, and formed his own company, Jack White Enterprises, which specialized in free-lance art and photography. In 1984, as business increased, he took on partners. The firm's name changed to VJS Companies, and the company added new services, including typography and photostats.

The firm closed for a brief period in 1991, following several setbacks, but reopened later in the year as Jack White Graphic Arts. Now retired, White lives in the White Lake Hills addition in east Fort Worth with his wife the former Sue Benningfield. Their home, built in 1970, was designed to focus on a view of the downtown Fort Worth skyline.

Jack D. White died, aged 85, on 18 June 2012.

Part VII

The Myth of Nanothermite

20

Has nanothermite been oversold to the 9/11 Truth community?

by Mark Hightower with Jim Fetzer

*"It's not what we don't know that hurts us,
it's what we know that ain't so."* – Will Rogers

Architects & Engineers for 9/11 Truth is heavily promoting the theory that "explosive nanothermite" was used to bring down the Twin Towers on September 11th, 2001, and that microscopic chips of a fused compound containing unignited nanothermite were found in the World Trade Center dust. This discovery is now considered a "smoking gun" by most members of the 9/11 Truth community, even though a good many serious researchers and 9/11 activists remain unconvinced.

Let's take a look at what is supposed to be the current best evidence in the controlled-demolition theory of the World Trade Center's tallest buildings. Steven Jones, a physicist who joined the 9/11 Truth movement from Brigham Young University during 2005, introduced the theory that thermite/thermate played a role in the destruction of the towers; and in 2006, he refined this theory to propose that nanothermite or "superthermite" – a finely granulated form of thermite – was in fact the substance used, and its high reactivity served to pulverize the steel, concrete and many additional tons of skyscraper material, including the buildings' contents.

In an effort to confirm the claims being made about thermite and nanothermite, T. Mark Hightower, a chemical engineer from both the space program and chemical industry, decided to investigate its use as an explosive. In addition to doing his own study, he has repeatedly written to leading 9/11 researchers who champion the use of nanothermite as the principal (if not exclusive) mechanism for bringing about the destruction of the Twin Towers, probing them on the explosive capabilities of nanothermite. The replies he has received suggest that this is an issue they are unwilling to examine fully and openly.

Hightower wrote directly to Richard Gage, the founder of Architects and Engineers for 9/11 Truth, citing a frequently referenced March 2005 LLNL paper on thermite, which can be downloaded from the Reference 2 link at the bottom of *http://911research.wtc7.net/wtc/analysis/theories/thermitetech.html.*

This paper explains what nanocomposites are, focusing on thermite mixtures and how they are produced. It also includes some experimental results.

As Hightower observed to Gage, however: "This paper offers no evidence to me that explosive velocities anywhere near that of TNT (22,600 feet per second) can be produced by the nanothermites as described and presented. On page 10, it states, 'One limitation inherent in any thermite energetic material is the inability of the energetic material to do pressure/volume work on an object. Thermites release energy in the form of heat and light, but are unable to move objects.'"

What Hightower was asking Gage was: "How can a substance be an explosive and not be able to do pressure/volume work on an object – that is, move an object?" Gage responded: "The nanothermite was set in a bed of organic silica, which I believe the authors suggest may provide the explosive pressure/volume work. In addition, I believe that the authors are quite open to the possibility that other more high-energy explosives may have been used."

Without further characterization, the "bed of organic silica" is not a sufficient explanation, so the possibility is raised that "other more high-energy explosives may have been used." Surely thermite or nanothermite would become explosive if combined with bona fide explosives. Hightower decided to take an even closer look at the claims advanced on behalf of nanothermite, and has spent several months researching everything he could find in the open literature. Again and again, he found that thermite, even in its nano form, unless combined with high explosives or another high-explosive mechanism, cannot be a high explosive.

So if nanothermite is to be the "smoking gun" of 9/11, it would have had to have been combined with some form of high-power explosives or other high-explosive mechanism to do the job of bringing the buildings down. What was it combined with? By itself, nanothermite cannot have been the sole agent of demolition – it was only another "helper." By itself, therefore, nanothermite cannot be "explosive evidence," as AE911 Truth maintains.

There are reasons to believe that the 9/11 movement's nanothermite experts are actually aware of this problem. For example, during a recent interview ("9/11: Explosive Testimony Exclusive" http://www.youtube.com/watch?v=0lU-vu2JvZY), Niels Harrit explains that nanothermite is built from the atom scale up, which allows for the option of adding other chemicals to make it explosive. He states that the role played by the red-gray chips found in the dust is unknown. But he is convinced, based on observation of the towers' destruction and the molten metal present, that both explosives and incendiaries were used. It's just that he and his fellow researchers have not been able to prove that the nanothermitic material they found in the dust has the explosive properties he believes were necessary to accomplish the destruction.

Harrit suggests the use of "a modern military material which is unknown to the general public" as an explanation for the missing pieces to the 9/11 nanothermite puzzle. He urges a new investigation, whereby NIST will test WTC dust samples for remaining explosives and thermitic material. But he also seems to be saying that he and his fellow 9/11 researchers do not consider it worthwhile to pursue further analysis beyond their current findings.

9/11 truthers may agree that (1) if unignited nanothermite was in the WTC dust after the event, it proves a demolition plan of some kind; or (2) if unignited nanothermite was found in the dust after the event, it only proves that nanothermite played some role either on 9/11 or in its aftermath – including the cleanup, which was overseen by the federal and city governments. Those who believe (1) may in fact be satisfied with the lack of conclusive evidence of explosives the discovery of nanothermite presents. Those who agree with

(2) are most likely to be unsatisfied by the current state of affairs, and may indeed argue, "We still have no real 'hard evidence' proving that the Twin Towers were brought down by explosives."

We do have visual evidence (videos) that strongly indicate to any discerning viewer that the Twin Towers did not come down by gravitational collapse. However, apart from that, we are still where we started – pursuing different inquiries into how and why the buildings fell the way they did. "Explosive nanothermite" is no firmer a theory than conventional explosives demolition, nuclear demolition, or directed free-energy technology; in fact, it is somewhat misleading and – for that reason alone – probably not the best horse for us to be betting on.

HOW INDEED CAN NANOTHERMITE BE EXPLOSIVE? & THE NANOTHERMITE CHALLENGE

by T Mark Hightower, B.S., M.S., Chemical Engineering

Introduction

This paper explores the explosiveness of nanothermite.

Steven E. Jones made the error early in his research, of classifying nanothermite as an explosive in the same category as the high explosive RDX, with no published science to back up his claim. The 911 truth movement has never recovered from this error, for to this day nearly everyone in the movement refers to "explosive nanothermite," as even this clever cover for a fictitious "For Dummies" book illustrates. (1)

Examples of Jones confusing these issues are cited and commented upon. Two technical papers on nanothermite are cited to support my contention that nanothermite is not anywhere near being an explosive in the sense of a high explosive like RDX. These two papers are also cited on the issue of adding organics to nanothermites to produce gas generating nano-thermites (GGNT) and I maintain that these papers suggest that the only way to make a nanothermite truly explosive is to combine it with an explosive or other high-explosive mechanism. "It's not the "nano" that makes it explosive. It's the explosive that makes it explosive."

Finally, I make recommendations of what those who advocate the nanothermite theory for WTC destruction can do to clarify their position, and I announce The Nanothermite Challenge.

EXAMPLES OF JONES CONFUSING THERMITE AND NANO-THERMITE WITH EXPLOSIVES

Here is a two-paragraph quote from Steven Jones' first paper. (2)

"Thus, molten metal was repeatedly observed and formally reported in the rubble piles of the WTC Towers and WTC 7, metal that looked like molten steel or perhaps iron. Scientific analysis would be needed to conclusively ascertain the composition of the molten metal in detail."

"I maintain that these observations are consistent with the use of high-temperature cutter-charges such as thermite, HMX or RDX or some combination thereof, routinely used to melt/cut/demolish steel." (2)

Here Jones puts thermite, HMX, and RDX in the same category. But thermite is totally different than HMX and RDX. Thermite is an incendiary. It gets very hot, it produces molten iron, it can melt steel, and it can catch things on fire, but it is absolutely not an explosive. It is not even a low explosive. On the other hand, HMX and RDX are high explosives. HMX detonates at 9,100 m/s (meters per second) and RDX detonates at 8,750 m/s.

He also lumps all three under the category of cutter-charges, but a cutter-charge with thermite would be totally different than a cutter-charge with a high explosive. A thermite cutter-charge would cut by melting the steel with the high-temperature molten iron it produces (an extremely low velocity and slow process compared to high explosives), whereas an RDX cutter-charge would cut by the supersonic detonation of high explosives in what is known as a shaped charge, which essentially produces a supersonic projectile of molten metal (copper is often used in shaped charges) that instantly penetrates and severs the member.

Later in the paper Jones says

""Superthermites" use tiny particles of aluminum known as "nanoaluminum" (<120 nanometers) in order to increase their reactivity. Explosive superthermites are formed by mixing nanoaluminum powder with fine metal oxide particles such as micron-scale iron oxide dust." (2) And further down he says "Highly exothermic reactions other than jet-fuel or office-material fires, such as thermite reactions which produce white-hot molten metal as an end product, are clearly implied by the data.

In addition, the use of explosives such as HMX or RDX should be considered. "Superthermites" are also explosive as must be remembered in any in-depth investigation which considers hypotheses suggested by the available data." (2) From page 85 of a presentation that Jones gave early in his work (3), he says "Gel explosives: Tiny aluminum particles in iron oxide, in a sol-gel: "High energy density and extremely powerful" and "can be cast to shape". *http:// www.llnl.gov/str/RSimpson. html* (Livermore Nat'l Lab, 2000) I have read the LLNL web page that Jones cites above (4) very carefully and I cannot find anything in it that implies that the "thermitic nanocomposite energetic material" referred to is an explosive.

It refers to the result as a thermite pyrotechnic, releasing an enormous amount of heat, but it does not say that it is an explosive. In the web page another class is explained briefly, energetic nanocrystalline composites. "The Livermore team synthesized nanocrystalline composites in a silica matrix with pores containing the high explosive RDX or PETN." No mention is made here of thermite, so this wouldn't apply to Jones claiming that nanothermite is an explosive.

COMPARING NANOTHERMITE REACTION VELOCITIES TO EXPLOSIVE VELOCITIES

The explanation given for claiming that nanothermite is an explosive goes something like this. The thermite reaction is

$$Fe2O3 + 2\ Al \text{ ---> } 2\ Fe + Al2O3.$$

By making the particle sizes of the reactants smaller, down to the nanosize (approximately 30 nm to 60 nm) and mixing them well, the reaction takes place so fast that it becomes explosive. Let's look at some data from technical papers where the reaction velocity of nanothermites were measured and compare these values with the reaction velocities of explosives to see if it seems reasonable to call nanothermite an explosive.

A paper by Spitzer et al. published in the Journal of Physics and Chemistry of Solids in 2010 presents a variety of research on energetic nano-materials. (5) In one section they deal with nano-thermites made with tungsten trioxide (WO3) and aluminum nano-particles. They experimented with different particle sizes, but they highlight the mixture made with the smallest nano-particles of both WO3 and Al for its impressive performance.

"WO3/Al nano-thermites, which contain only nano-particles have an impressive reactivity. The fireball generated by the deflagration is so hot that a slamming due to overpressure is heard. The combustion rate can reach 7.3 m/s. This value is extremely high compared to classical energetic materials." (5)

A paper by Clapsaddle et al. published by Lawrence Livermore National Laboratory in 2005 also contains some reaction rate data for nanothermite composed of nano-particles of Fe2O3 and aluminum. (6) In Figure 2. in the paper the combustion velocity is plotted versus percent SiO2 content. The highest values were obtained at zero percent SiO2, so those are the only values I am going to cite. The nanothermite produced by a sol gel process had the highest velocity of 40.5 m/s, compared to the one produced by a simple mixing of the nano-particles with a combustion velocity of 8.8 m/s. (6)

Compare the above combustion velocities of nanothermite with the detonation velocities of high explosives HMX and RDX of 9,100 m/s and 8,750 m/s, respectively, and they are dwarfed by the velocities of the conventional high explosives. Steven Jones appears to be calling the nanothermite reaction explosive only in the sense that it is reacting much faster than regular thermite, but not in the sense that it is anywhere near as explosive as a conventional high explosive.

By failing to make this distinction Jones has misled nearly the entire 911 truth movement into believing that nanothermite is a super explosive, possibly even more powerful than conventional high explosives.

From the above, it is quite clear that the "nano" in nanothermite does not make the thermite explosive anywhere near the degree of a high explosive like RDX.

In addition to saying that nano-izing thermite makes it explosive, I have heard Jones say that adding organics to nanothermite also makes it explosive. This issue is explored in the next section.

CAN ANYTHING BE DONE TO MAKE A NANOTHERMITE EXPLOSIVE?

First I would like to quote an entire two paragraph section, with its title, from the LLNL paper. (6)

"Gas generating Al-Fe2O3-SiO3/2-R (R = –(CH2)2(CF2)7CF3) nanocomposites."

"One limitation inherent in any thermite energetic material is the inability of the energetic material to do pressure/volume-work on an object. Thermites release energy in the form of heat and light, but are unable to move objects. Typically, work can be done by a rapidly produced gas that is released during the energetic reaction.

Towards this end, the silica phase of sol-gel prepared oxidizers, in addition to modifying the burning velocities, has also been used to incorporate organic functionality that will decompose and generate gas upon ignition of the energetic composite [3-4,7]. Phenomenological burn observations of these materials indicate that the Al-Fe2O3-SiO3/2-R nanocomposites burn very rapidly and violently, essentially to completion, with the generation of significant amounts of gas. Figure 5 shows a comparison of the ignition of an energetic nanocomposite oxidizer mixed with 2 μm aluminum metal without (left) and with (middle) organic functionalization.

The still image of the energetic nanocomposite without organic functionalization exhibits rapid ignition and emission of light and heat. The still image of the energetic nanocomposite with organic functionalization also exhibits these characteristics, but it also exhibits hot particle ejection due to the production of gas upon ignition. This reaction is very exothermic and results in the production of very high temperatures, intense light, and pressure from the generation of the gaseous byproducts resulting from the decomposition of the organic moieties."

"These materials were also mixed with nanometer aluminum. Figure 5 (right) shows a still image of the ignition of the Al-Fe2O3-SiO3/2-R nanocomposite mixed with 40 nm aluminum. This composite is much more reactive than the same oxidizing phase mixed with 2 μm aluminum metal; the burning of the composite with 40 nm aluminum occurs much too quickly to be able to observe the hot particle ejection.

This observation is a good example of the importance mixing and the size scale of the reactants can have on the physical properties of the final energetic composite material. When the degree of mixing is on the nanoscale, the material is observed to react much more quickly, presumably due to the increase in mass transport rates of the reactants, as discussed above." (6)

Note that in the title of the section quoted above, the symbol R is used to represent the organic functionality added to the nanothermite. In this case it is a 10 carbon atom straight chain functional group fully saturated, with hydrogen atoms on the first two carbon atoms of the chain and fluorine atoms on all the rest. I have not explored the precise energy level of this functional group, but I can tell by just looking at it that it will consume energy (from the thermite reaction) in order to break it down into multiple smaller molecules in order to get the expanding gases necessary to make it behave as explained.

This is not an efficient way to make an explosive. I wouldn›t expect the explosiveness to be anywhere near that of a conventional high explosive, and the qualitative description given in the paper certainly does not seem to support it being a true explosive, but unfortunately the paper does not give data on what its reaction rate would be. Wouldn't it be better if the organic added to the nanothermite was a molecule that, instead of consuming energy to drive its decomposition, actually produces energy as it decomposes? Such a molecule could be the RDX molecule. This leads to the quoted two-paragraph section below from the Spitzer et al. paper. (5)

"3. Gas generating nano-thermites "

"Thermites are energetic materials, which do not release gaseous species when they decompose. However, explosives can be blended in thermites to give them blasting properties. The idea developed at ISL is to solidify explosives in porous inorganic matrixes described previously. Gas generating nano-thermites (GGNT) are prepared by mixing Cr_2O_3/RDX and MnO_2/RDX materials with aluminium nano-particles. The combustion mechanisms of these nano-thermites were investigated by DSC and high-speed video. In the case of Cr_2O_3-based GGNT, the decomposition of RDX induces the expansion and the fragmentation of the oxide matrix.

The resulting Cr_2O_3 nano-particles, which are preheated by the combustion of the explosive, react violently with aluminium nano-particles. In the case of MnO_2-based GGNT, the mechanism of combustion is somewhat different because the decomposition of RDX induces the melting of oxide particles. The droplets of molten MnO_2 react with aluminium nano-particles."

"The non-confined combustion of GGNT is rather slow (1-11 cm/s) in comparison with other nano-thermites presented here. However, in a confined environment their combustion rate is expected to be significantly higher. Indeed, the thermal decomposition of GGNT produces gaseous species, which contribute to increase the pressure and the combustion rate in accordance with the Vieille's law. The thermal decomposition of miscellaneous GGNT compositions was studied in a closed vessel equipped with a pressure gauge. The GGNT were fired with a laser beam through a quartz window. The pressure signal was recorded along time for each material (Fig. 7). The pressure released by the combustion of a GGNT is directly linked to the RDX content of the nano-composite used to elaborate it. Depending on its formulation, a GGNT can provide a pressure ranging from a few bars to nearly three thousand bars." (5)

I am surprised by the low number given for the reaction velocity, only 1-11 cm/s. Also, it does not say what percent RDX resulted in this low velocity. Maybe it was a very low content of RDX. But the main point I want to make about the above quoted section does not depend on this velocity anyway. The key point is that you have to blend explosives (like RDX) into nanothermite to make it an explosive ("give them blasting properties").

WHAT NANOTHERMITE ADVOCATES NEED TO DO TO CLARIFY THEIR THEORY

Steven E. Jones and other nanothermite theory advocates should be upfront and truthful about these issues, and clearly elaborate upon the factors missing from their theory that need further fleshing out. It is not good enough to just say "explosive nanothermite" over and over again without explaining exactly what is meant by the term. If they think that incendiary thermite or incendiary nanothermite or low explosive nanothermite or high explosive nanothermite were used in cutter-charges, or some combination, then they should say so.

The lack of or degree of explosiveness claimed, whether incendiary, low explosive, or high explosive, is key, because the type of cutter-charge used would depend on this. Once they clarify what they mean by their use of the term "nanothermite", then they should start describing the quantities of thermite that would have been necessary for the destruction. Only by adding these details to their theory can it be fairly evaluated against alternative theories of the destruction of the buildings of the World Trade Center for the benefit of the wider 9/11 truth community.

Source note: This chapter originally appeared as "Has Nanothermite been Oversold to the 9/11 Truth Community?", *jamesfetzer.blogspot.com* (1 May 2011).

19

Is "9/11 Truth" based upon a false theory?

by Jim Fetzer with Mark Hightower

Given my background in the history and the philosophy of science and as a professional scholar, I founded Scholars for 9/11 Truth for the purpose of promoting collaborative research on the events of 9/11 by creating a web site, issuing press releases, archiving old research and supporting new research, sponsoring conferences, announcing public presentations, and making efforts to reach out to the public with the results of our investigations.

The most intense conflicts in relation to the 9/11 Truth movement, however, turn out to come from within and between research groups, which have all too often found themselves at odds and severely attacked and even denounced one another.

Based upon my experience, I can report with confidence that the three most controversial issues within the 9/11 Truth movement are these:

(1) the Pentagon attack, especially, whether a Boeing 757 hit the Pentagon, which I have addressed in "What didn't happen at the Pentagon" and in "Inside Job: Seven Questions about 9/11";

(2) the planes in New York, especially, whether video fakery was used there, which I have addressed in "New Proof of Video Fakery on 9/11" and "Inside Job: More Proof of 9/11 Duplicity"; and,

(3) the demolition of the Twin Towers, especially, how it was done, the dominant theory being that they were destroyed using nanothermite as the principal mechanism, which I address here.

These are questions that can be investigated using scientific reasoning to evaluate alternative hypotheses.

The benefits from this appear to be considerable, since, if my efforts are successful, (a) we will have a better understanding of what happened, (b) there will be fewer, less intense conflicts between us, and (c) we will become more cohesive and effective in promoting our objectives and goals. A "9/11 Truth" movement, after all, has to be based on truth, where science is our most reliable method for distinguishing between what is true and what is false, where I can apply my background and the 35 years I spent offering courses in logic, critical thinking and scientific reasoning.

The evidence presented in those studies about (1) the Pentagon attack and (2) the planes in New York and (3) the demolition of the Twin Towers here not only falsifies the official account of 9/11 but also implicates the Department of Defense in the case of (1) and the national media in the case of (2) with its deceit and deception in perpetrating fraud on the American people. While I have no doubt that the Mossad was involved, it could not have been responsible for the "stand down" of the US Air Force on 9/11 nor for the failure of the Pentagon to take measures to protect itself from an aircraft, whose approach was known to Dick Cheney and to the pilot of a C-130, who was circling the building at the time.

The Mossad is far more likely to have been deeply involved in (3) the destruction of the Twin Towers.

The Nanothermite Theory

While there are many points of agreement within the 9/11 Truth community, which include that the North Tower was hit first but "collapsed" second'; that the fires burned neither long enough nor hot enough for the steel to have weakened, much less melted; that collapse scenarios were not even physically possible; and that NIST has never been able to justify a "point of initiation", much less present a serious collapse simulation, there has been ongoing controversy over how it was done, where the prevalent theory is that nanothermite was the principal ingredient. If any single event could be said to have inspired the 9/11 Truth community, it was the publication of an article in the Bentham Open Science journal:

The Open Chemical Physics Journal

ISSN: 1874-4125

BENTHAM OPEN

[DOI: 10.2174/1874412500902010007]

Active Thermitic Material Discovered in Dust from the 9/11 World Trade Center Catastrophe

Niels H. Harrit, Jeffrey Farrer, Steven E. Jones, Kevin R. Ryan, Frank M. Legge, Daniel Farnsworth, Gregg Roberts, James R. Gourley and Bradley R. Larsen Pp 7-31

We have discovered distinctive red/gray chips in all the samples we have studied of the dust produced by the destruction of the World Trade Center. Examination of four of these samples, collected from separate sites, is reported in this paper. These red/gray chips show marked similarities in all four samples. One sample was collected by a Manhattan resident about ten minutes after the collapse of the second WTC Tower, two the next day, and a fourth about a week later. The properties of these chips were analyzed using optical microscopy, scanning electron microscopy (SEM), X-ray energy dispersive spectroscopy (XEDS), and differential scanning calorimetry (DSC). The red material contains grains approximately 100 nm across which are largely iron oxide, while aluminum is contained in tiny plate-like structures. Separation of components using methyl ethyl ketone demonstrated that elemental aluminum is present. The iron oxide and aluminum are intimately mixed in the red material. When ignited in a DSC device the chips exhibit large but narrow exotherms occurring at approximately 430 °C, far below the normal ignition temperature for conventional thermite. Numerous iron-rich spheres are clearly observed in the residue following the ignition of these peculiar red/gray chips. The red portion of these chips is found to be an unreacted thermitic material and highly energetic.

Bolstered in their belief by this article by Niels Harrit, Jeffrey Farrer, Steven Jones, Kevin Ryan, and others, "Active Thermitic Material Discovered in Dust from the 9/11 World Trade Center Catastrophe", in The Open Chemical Physics Journal 2 (2009), pp. 7-31, the theory has become dominant in 9/11 research. And this has remained the case even though the Editor-in-Chief of the journal, Marie-Paule Pileni, who specializes in nano-materials research at the Université Pierre et Marie Curie in France, resigned her position in protest of its publication, which she regarded as very inappropriate.

The article itself, which was based upon studies of dust that was collected from the immediate vicinity of "Ground Zero", maintains that nanothermite residue was found in the dust and suggests that this finding holds the key to understanding the means by which the Twin Towers were blown apart. It was done using "explosive nanothermite". The article asserts, for example,

"The feature of 'impulse management' may be significant. It is possible that formulations may be chosen to have just sufficient percussive effect to achieve the desired fragmentation while minimizing the noise level" (page 26);

And concludes with the following (somewhat ambiguous) declaration:

"Based on these observations, we conclude that the red layer of the red/ gray chips we have discovered in the WTC dust is active, unreacted thermitic material, incorporating nanotechnology, and is a highly energetic pyrotechnic or explosive material" (page 31);

. . . which has been widely construed to have established scientifically that nanothermite was found in the dust, that nanothermite is explosive, and that nanothermite was the crucial ingredient in bringing about the conversion of the Twin Towers into a few large pieces and millions of cubic yards of very fine dust, which appears to have been critical for the preservation of the bathtub, the shattering of which would have allowed Hudson River water to flood beneath Lower Manhattan, the subway and the PATH train tunnels, causing monumental damage to the most valuable real estate in the world, which the conspirators, it appears, wanted to preclude by employing a novel mode of demolition.

Enthusiastic Endorsements

The widespread acceptance of nanothermite as the crucial component of the demolition of the Twin Towers has become a matter of common knowledge within the 9/11 Truth community. But here are samples of the extent to which it has become embedded in reasoning about 9/11. On April 5, 2009, for example, Architects & Engineers for 9/11 Truth published "Exotic High Tech Explosives Positively Identified in World Trade Center Dust", presenting its ringing endorsement of its findings:

"A ground-breaking scientific paper confirmed this week that red-gray flakes found throughout multiple samples of WTC dust are actually unexploded fragments of nanothermite, an exotic high-tech explosive.

"The samples were taken from far-separated locations in Manhattan, some as early as 10 minutes after the second tower (WTC 1) collapsed, ruling out any possible contamination from cleanup operations. . . .

"Ordinary thermite burns quickly and can melt through steel, but it is not explosive. Nanothermite, however, can be formulated as a high explosive. It is stable when wet and can be applied like paint."

During an interview in RUSSIA TODAY (July 2009), Neils Harrit, the paper's first author, offers observations that are rather more qualified by suggesting that, while thermite was "used for melting the steel beams", he is certain that conventional explosives were also used:

"There is very solid evidence for that some thermite has been used for melting the steel beams. We should not, I do not know, we do not know if the thermite that we have found is the same thermite which has been used for melting the beams. It's very very possible that different varieties was used and I personally am certain that conventional explosives were used too in abundance." When asked what he meant by the phrase, "in abundance," he said "tons, hundred tons, many many many tons."

In his admirable "Left-Leaning Despisers of the 9/11 Truth Movement: Do You Really Believe in Miracles?", GLOBAL RESEARCH (6 July 2010), David Ray Griffin, the dean of 9/11 research, expressed his emphatic support for nanothermite as a powerful explosive capable of exerting enormous force and ejecting large sections of steel hundreds of feet:

"NIST thereby admitted that debris had been thrown out horizontally from the North Tower at least 350 feet.84 NIST's report also stated:

"When WTC 1 collapsed at 10:28:22 AM, . . . some fragments [of debris] were forcibly ejected and traveled distances up to hundreds of meters. Pieces of WTC 1 hit WTC 7, severing six columns on Floors 7 through 17 on the south face and one column on the west face near the southwest corner. The debris also caused structural damage between Floor 44 and the roof.85

"Debris that caused such extensive damage, including the severing of seven steel columns, had to be quite heavy. NIST seemed to be granting, therefore, that sections of steel columns had been hurled at least 650 feet (because "hundreds of meters" would mean at least 200 meters, which would be about 650 feet). Enormous force would be needed to eject large sections of steel that far out.

"What could have produced this force? According to NIST, as we saw earlier, there were only three causal factors in the collapse of the Twin Towers: the airplane impacts, the fires, and gravitational attraction. The airplane impacts had occurred 56 minutes (South Tower) and 102 minutes (North Tower) earlier, and gravitational attraction pulls things straight downward. Fire could, to be sure, produce horizontal ejections by causing

jet fuel to explode, but the jet fuel had, NIST pointed out, burned up within "a few minutes."86 Therefore, although NIST admitted that these horizontal ejections occurred, it suggested no energy source to explain them.

"High explosives, such as RDX or nanothermite, could explain these horizontal ejections. According to NIST, however, explosives did not contribute to the destruction of the Twin Towers. Those who accept NIST's account must, therefore, regard these horizontal ejections as constituting yet another miracle."

And there can be scant room for doubt that Griffin's characterization has become the dominant view within the 9/11 Truth community, where it has assumed a standing akin to that of a religious dogma, where those who challenge that belief have been subject to severe reactions from within the community, including forms of banishment and blackballing, very much on the order of heretics in theological disputes of the past, many of whom were even burned at the stake.

The Split in Scholars

And I have been among them. When I founded Scholars for 9/11 Truth, I invited Steven Jones, a physicist from BYU, to serve as my co-chair, on the advice of David Ray Griffin, whom I invited first. I would later learn from David that, at that time, he had no confidence that a society could make a difference, which was an opinion he would later retract.

In the months between founding the society in December of 2005 and the American Scholars Conference in Los Angeles in June of 2006, I had heard a lot about thermite, thermate, and nanothermite, but was skeptical that it could perform the feats of blowing massive assemblies of steel hundreds of yards and converting two 500,000 ton buildings into millions of cubic yards of very fine dust. On Saturday of the conference, I approached Steve in the lobby and asked him if he was confident that nanothermite could bring about these effects—and was not entirely persuaded when he assured me that, *"Yes, it could!"*

By the end of the year, I had become convinced that it was necessary to broaden the range of hypotheses that were under consideration as candidates to explain the destruction of the Twin Towers. None of us had any problems with WTC-7, which exhibited all the characteristics of a classic controlled demolition: the explosion began at the base, ran up the side of the building with a kink in the roof, where all the floors fell at the same time into the buildings foundation at the approximate rate of free fall and a stack of debris about 12% of its original height remained.

The Twin Towers were different, where all of their floors remained stationary until they were "blown to kingdom come" (in the memorable phrase of Morgan Reynolds), where they were destroyed at the approximate rate of free fall, too, but where, as Fr. Frank Morales from St. Mark's Episcopal Church observed during two interviews on a radio program I co-hosted with Kevin Barrett, "The Dynamic Duo", both buildings, unlike WTC-7, were destroyed below ground level!

The differences between us were exacerbated when I interviewed Dr. Judy Wood, a former professor of mechanical engineering, who was promoting the alternative theory that directed energy weapons might have been used to destroy the buildings rather than thermite in any of its guises, which took place on November 11, 2006. What I liked the most about Judy's work was that it offered a fresh perspective about how it could have been done, where she asked me to guess where a directed energy device could have been located and, when I offered WTC-7 as a guess, she corrected me and said, "In space!"

I would bet that this interview caused more division in the 9/11 Truth community than any other event before or after. Judy began being attacked for advocating "space beams" and "death rays", while I was castigated for supporting her. That I was SUPPORTING RESEARCH on her theory as opposed to ENDORSING IT was a subtlety that was lost on the crowd, where it has become part of the presumptive history of the 9/11 movement.

Critique of Steven Jones

Perhaps my strongest critique of Steve's work occurred by accident. On May 17, 2007, my scheduled guest on "The Dynamic Duo", Don Paul, was a no-show and I had to wing it for two hours. So for the first part of the show, I talked about my collaborative research on the death of Sen. Paul Wellstone and on the assassination of JFK. During the second part, however, I focused my attention on a new paper he had just published, "Why indeed did the World Trade Center buildings completely collapse?" A copy can be found on the Journal of 9/11 Studies 3 (2006), which I suppose is a close facsimile of the paper I discussed, although Steve has sometimes revised his work on-line without formal notice.

In my critique, I pointed out that the title was wrong, since the buildings had not "collapsed" and that he was talking about the Twin Towers, but my more serious criticisms concerned his deeply flawed conception of the scientific method and what I regarded as inadequate support for his thermite/ thermate/nanothermite theory, "On the Manipulation of the 9/11 Research Community". Here are a few passages for the flavor:

"Don't forget that eleven hundred bodies were never recovered. Eleven hundred bodies were never recovered. Those were bodies that were turned into very fine dust. Never recovered. That's completely inconsistent with a "collapse". Even involving explosive, you would expect to find body parts, even if they were detached from bodies. And you'd find lots of skulls and torsos and arms and legs, but here we're talking eleven hundred bodies, no parts of which were recovered. This is stunning stuff. And it certainly implies that something was going on here far beyond the use of any merely conventional explosives.

"But what's going on in the research community is an attempt to constrain research that would actually have the capacity potentially to explain what's going on. By reaching beyond conventional weaponry in to the range of unconventional weaponry, such as lasers, masers, plasmoids, mini-nukes. I mean, who knows in advance of actually conducting an investigation that theories or hypotheses about the use of lasers or masers or mini-nukes are wrong? You can't know that without investigation. And I'm going to suggest that a gigantic hoax is being perpetrated on the research community by the claim that [the] scientific method supports this very narrow definition of the use of thermite and thermate . . . .

". . . where I have now taken a look at the latest paper of the leading proponent of that view, Steven Jones, and it doesn't add up. I mean it may be impressive to those who are naïve about the nature of science and who are incapable of reading a paper that has the least degree of technical sophistication to it, but I'm going to suggest to you as we go through this paper that what we have here is a rather elaborate "snow job", where the most important points made are actually concessions that the evidence he has found is merely consistent with the use of thermite or thermate but doesn't prove it was produced by thermite or thermate, where, provided that there are multiple alternative possible explanations, he has not done the job. And I'm going to claim that he has not done the job because he has a commitment to a conception of scientific method that is hopelessly inadequate. Hopelessly inadequate. And that while he talks a lot about science, he is, alas, not practicing it."

Jones' maintains that the scientific method is a process of observation, formulating an hypothesis, performing tests and experiments, and then publishing the results in a peer-reviewed journal. That's wrong, because science cannot simply begin with observation (since there is too much we could observe) and it cannot proceed by studying one hypothesis at a time. Science is a process of puzzlement (because something doesn't fit into your background knowledge), speculation (by identifying the alternative hypotheses that might explain the data), adaptation (of hypotheses to data by calculating and comparing their likelihoods), and explanation (by accepting the hypothesis with the highest likelihood when the evidence has "settled down", in the tentative and fallible fashion of science).

His inadequate methodology derives from the failure to grasp that scientific research requires the comparison of alternative hypotheses and cannot focus only on one.

"Houston, we have a problem!"

The most glaring empirical failure of the then-current version of his paper is that he finally gets around to talking about **barium nitrate**, and by the time you reach the final page, he has acknowledged that what he is talking about is not actually thermite but what he calls a "thermite analog", which he does not actually define, and he admits that thermite, which he now calls "TH3", is an analog of thermite that contains sulfur and *barium nitrate* and now he talks about thermite "as defined here". It turns out this *barium-nitrate-containing thermite* is the military

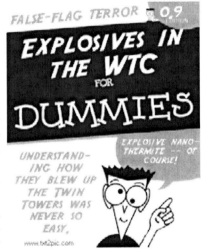

grade thermite that he has been using to demonstrate the effectiveness of thermite, illustrated by the use of a thermite grenade on the top of an engine block.

But no *barium nitrate* has been found in the analysis of the chemical residue in the analysis of the dust by Steven Jones or by the US Geological Survey. So in this version, he has pulled a bait-and-switch. Looking at the current version on-line, however, *barium nitrate* is mentioned on page 19 but not at the end of his paper, which means that it has been revised since I critiqued it.

I am not the only one to have evaluated that version of his paper in caustic, negative terms, since a complementary critique comes from Stephen Phillips, "A Physicist Critiques Steven Jones' New Paper" (May 21, 2007), where the present version is clearly not the same as the one he and I were addressing—a reflection of which may be that he actually includes my name in the acknowledgements!

So let's look at the conclusion of the current version and consider what he says there:

"Remarkably, the controlled-demolition hypothesis accounts for all the available data rather easily. The core columns (and corner perimeter columns) on floors damaged by the planes are cut near-simultaneously using radio-signaled explosives/incendiary-cutters. In this scenario, cutter-charges were set every two or three floors during routine "maintenance" of elevator shafts, etc., so that the cutting sequence could be matched in a controlling computer to begin at the level where the plane entered each Tower.

Next cutter-charges were detonated from the top downward for the Towers, ejecting beams and material long distances horizontally as observed during the destruction. The "collapses" are thus near-symmetrical, complete, at near-free-fall speeds with accompanying "squibs". Thermite analogs (whose end product is molten iron) including the explosive form, nano-thermite, may account for the molten metal which then pooled beneath the rubble piles as well as the sulfidation observed in steel from both the WTC 7 and Towers rubble piles (points 1 and 2 above). WTC 7 evidently proceeded in a more conventional fashion for controlled demolition, with collapse-initiating explosions starting on lower floors (rather than at high-floor levels as for the Towers)."

Notice that, like Architects & Engineers and David Ray Griffin, Steve is attributing vast powers to thermite in its "explosive" nanothermite form, including the capacity to eject steel beams and materials long distances horizontally "as observed during the destruction". He appeals to "thermite analogs" whose end product is molten iron—"including the explosive form, nanothermite"—may account for the molten metal that pooled beneath the rubble piles, where WTC-7, he acknowledges, "evidently proceeded in a more conventional fashion for controlled demolition", beginning on the lower floors rather than from the top. This is well and good and moves in the right direction. But can even these claims for nanothermite be sustained? It appears that they cannot.

Nanothermite: A Feeble Explosive

I has been my great pleasure over the past twelve months or more to participate in a research group focusing on the properties of thermite in all its original, thermate and nanothemite forms. We were aided and abetted in this process by contributions from Daniel Fairchild, a Vietnam veteran experienced in dealing with explosives, who was my guest on "The Real Deal" on an interview that stimulated our thinking about how explosives work and how they might have been employed on 9/11. While some of his numbers struck us as faulty, Dan's work motivated T. Mark Hightower, an engineer who has worked in the chemical industry and the space program—including with NASA for 21 years—to undertake a search of the open technical literature on nanothermite to determine its explosive potential in comparison to other explosives.

Explosive, Grade ⊠	Density (g/cm³) ⊠	Detonation Vel. (m/s) ⊠	R.E. ⊠
Ammonium nitrate (AN)	1.123	5270	0.42
Black Powder, 75%KNO₃+15%C+10%S	1.700	400	0.55
ANFO, 94.3% AN + 5.7% Fuel Oil	0.840	5270	0.80
Erythritol tetranitrate	1.6	8100	1.60
TNT	**1.654**	**6900**	**1.00**
Amatol, 80% TNT + 20% AN	1.548	6570	1.17
Tetrytol, 70% Tetryl + 30% TNT	1.707	7370	1.20
Tetryl	1.73	7570	1.25
C-4, 91% RDX	1.737	8040	1.34
C-3 (old RDX based)		7924	1.35
Composition B, 63% RDX + 36% TNT	1.751	7800	1.35
Nitroglycerin	1.6	7700	1.50
RDX	1.82	8750	1.60
Semtex, 94.3 %PETN + 5.7% RDX	1.776	8420	1.66
PETN	1.773	8400	1.66
HMX	1.91	9100	1.70
HNIW (CL-20)		9380	
DDF (4,4'-Dinitro-3,3'-diazenofuroxan)	2.02	10000	
Heptanitrocubane			
Octanitrocubane	1.98	10100	2.70
Nuclear weapon yield (variable; see note)	19.1	>100000	5.2M

What Mark discovered was surprising, especially given the extent to which leading figures of the 9/11 Truth movement have promoted it. The highest degree of explosiveness for iron oxide/aluminum nanothermite—the chemical form claimed to have been involved in WTC destruction—that Mark could find documented in the technical literature has a detonation velocity of only 895 m/s (or meters per second). Since TNT, the universal standard for comparison, has a detonation velocity of 6,900 m/s, the explosive potential of thermite in its most potent form of nanothermite is acutely disappointing. When we divide the velocity of nanothermite by that for TNT (895/6,900), it turns out nanothermite is not even 13% as powerful as TNT. (See "Table of Explosive Velocities" from Wikipedia.)

As Mark has explained in a blog, "Has nanothermite been oversold to the 9/11 Truth community?", and an interview on "The Real Deal", 895 m/s is obviously too low of a value to account for the explosive effects observed in the catastrophic destruction of the WTC Twin Towers, including turning concrete and other materials into dust or separating and propelling steel members and other materials outward. Comparisons with the detonation velocities of conventional high explosives, such as 8,750 m/s for RDX or 9,100 m/x for HMX (not to mention 8,040 m/s for C-4 and 8,400 m/s for PETN), it is clear that nanothermite is not even in the same ballpark.

While thermite in one or another of its guises as a rapid incendiary could have been used to sever or pre-weaken steel members, this low velocity melting process is a totally different mechanism for the cutting of steel than the shock wave method that requires detonation velocities of at least 3,200 m/s for concrete and 6,100 m/s for steel.

With respect to the demolition of the Twin Towers and blowing them to bits, low-explosive nanothermite, which does exist, can be eliminated as an hypothesis because it is ineffective. High-explosive nanothermite as an alternative can be eliminated because it simply does not exist. Mark therefore concludes that the phrase, "explosive nanothermite", when used to describe the causal mechanism for demolishing the Twin Towers is either seriously misleading under a charitable interpretation and at worst deliberately deceptive under an uncharitable one. Either way, conventional or unconventional explosives would have had to be combined with thermite, even in its nanothermite form. And if such a blend had been employed, the nanothermite would function more as an additive to high explosives rather than as the main ingredient itself.

The Nanothermite Challenge

On May 1, 2011, Hightower published, "The Nanothermite Challenge", as part of a longer study, "Has nanothermite been oversold to the 9/11 Truth community?". The challenge comes to this:

"Find and document peer-reviewed scientific research [publications] that demonstrate that a gas-generating nanothermite (GGNT) based upon iron (III) oxide (Fe_2O_3) and aluminum (Al), where the gas-generating chemical

added to the nanothermite is not itself a high explosive, can be made to be a high explosive with at least a detonation velocity of 2000 m/s. The author of this paper will donate [to AE911Truth] $100 for every 1000 m/s of detonation velocity that can be documented, the donation not to exceed $1,000."

The deadline date of June 20, 2011 passed with not even one entry to this contest. Interestingly, Kevin Ryan posted an article at 911blogger that very day entitled "The explosive nature of nanothermite". In this article, Ryan admits that they know very little about the role that nanothermite played in 9/11.

"Although we know that nanothermite has been found in the WTC dust, we do not know what purpose it served in the deceptive demolition of the WTC buildings. It could be that the nanothermite was used simply to drive fires in the impact zones and elevator areas – fires which would otherwise have gone out too early or not been present at all – and thereby create the deception that jet fuel-induced fires could wreak the havoc seen. Nanothermite might also have been used to produce the explosions necessary to destroy the structural integrity of the buildings."

In Ryan's paper he cites (what he claims to be) "ten references to the fact that nanothermites can be made to be explosive." During my interview with Mark Hightower on "The Real Deal", however, Mark refuted every one of Ryan's ten references. Let me document just one especially interesting example of those refutations here. Ryan's reference 4 states,

"A high explosive creates a shockwave that always travels at high, supersonic velocity from the point of origin. This paper describes how – 'the reaction of the low density nanothermite composite leads to a fast propagating combustion, generating shock waves with Mach numbers up to 3.'"

All you need to do is go to the title of this paper to see that it is not relevant to the nanothermite hypothesis advanced by Jones, Ryan, Griffin and Harrit, among others, *because it is for the wrong chemical form of thermite.* The Twin Towers destruction allegedly involved the use of *iron oxide/aluminum nanothermite,* but in this paper, "Generation of fast propagating combustion and shock waves with copper oxide/aluminum nanothermite composites", *Applied Physics Letters* (2007), we have *copper oxide/aluminum nanothermite.* Although not the main thrust of the paper, it gives a qualified reference to *iron oxide/aluminum nanothermite* research.

It says, *"Recently, we reported that higher combustion wave speeds were achieved for the composites of ordered porous Fe_2O_3 oxidizer and Al nanoparticles (5) as compared with the one containing porous oxidizer with no ordering of the pores and Al nanoparticles."*

Unfortunately no velocities are given, so it was necessary to go to the reference (5) cited in this paper to find more data, which Mark has done. The information for the reference (5) paper is as follows: Mehendale, Bhushan , Shende, Rajesh , Subramanian, Senthil, Gangopadhyay, Shubhra, Redner, Paul , Kapoor, Deepak and Nicolich, Steven(2006) 'Nanoenergetic Composite of Mesoporous Iron Oxide and Aluminum Nanoparticles', *Journal of Energetic Materials*, 24: 4, 341 — 360.

On page 357, there is a graph, where the highest velocities (referred to as "burn rates" on the graph) are reported for the specified *iron oxide/aluminum nanothermites*. Those velocities are all less than 300 m/s, which is *even less than* the 895 m/s that Mark Hightower has established for *iron/oxide aluminum nanothermite*. It is safe to say that nothing revealed by Kevin Ryan provides an adequate response to "the nanothermite challenge".

Replies from Researchers

In retrospect, it should have been obvious that nanothermite could not live up to its capabilities as they have been advanced by Steven Jones, Kevin Ryan, and others, who regard themselves as the custodians and only true practitioners of the scientific method in 9/11 research. Thus, Denis Spitzer et al., "Energetic nano-materials: Opportunities for enhanced performances", Journal of Physics and Chemistry of Solids (2010), where, given the crucial role of the rapid expansion of gases to perform work by explosives, states, "Gas generating nano-thermites: Thermites are energetic materials, which do not release gaseous species when they decompose. However, explosives can be blended in thermites to give them blasting properties", which implies that, unless supplemented with explosives, nanothermites are not explosive.

In his efforts to inform prominent researchers about his discoveries, Mark wrote to Steven Jones, Richard Gage, and others. Dwain Deets, the former Chief of Research Engineering and Director for Aeronautical Projects at NASA Dryden Flight Research Center, wrote to Mark and told him that he had listened to our interview on "The Real Deal" and said: "Excellent interview. A step toward trimming back claims that overshoot the evidence." He also sent a diagram illustrating certain detonation velocities as well as the sonic (speed of sound) velocities in various materials. Thus, *for a high explosive to significantly*

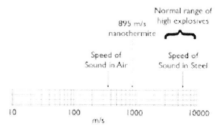

350

fragment a material, its detonation velocity has to be greater than the speed of sound in that material, which requires a detonation velocity of at least 3,200 m/s to fragment concrete and 6,100 m/s to fragment steel–far beyond 895 m/s for nanothermite.

On July 7, 2011, Hightower received emails from both David Ray Griffin and Richard Gage. Gage wrote back that "it [nanothermite] should not be called a 'high' explosive". Griffin made a similar suggestion and, in reply, Mark observed that calling it simply "an explosive" would convey to most members of the public that it is "a high explosive" or, given it's invocation by the "hard evidence" crowd, at least, has the ability to disintegrate concrete and even steel. Since that is the impression that has been indelibly implanted in the consciousness of the public, within and without the 9/11 Truth movement, until that claim is corrected, the 9/11 Truth movement will be based upon a provably false theory.

Griffin himself, of course, is not a scientist and is relying upon the work of Jones, Ryan, and others. But when he wrote back, "We are happy with our formulation, that it can be tailored to work as an incendiary or [as] an explosive. We cannot be responsible for the fact that many people may equate 'explosive' with 'high explosive'", his answer raised a number of rather disturbing questions about the ethical implications of allowing these enormously misleading impressions to linger:

(1) Will Architects & Engineers for 9/11 Truth inform the public that it has misrepresented the potential for "explosive nanothermite"?; and,

(2) If nanothermite only exists as a low explosive, that it cannot "hold the key" to the destruction of the Twin Towers, as has been claimed?; and,

(3) Will A&E admit that nanothermite cannot possibly be the "smoking gun" of 9/11 research, when the hard evidence contradicts that claim?

The 9/11 Truth Dilemma

Once again, as in the case of the Pentagon crash site and the question of "planes/no planes", serious students of 9/11 are placed in a dilemma. If they are committed to truth, as the name "9/11 Truth" implies, then they have to confront the fact that claims advanced on behalf the nanothermite hypothesis—*that the scientific key to understanding the demolition of the Twin Towers is the use of the nano-version of thermite*—cannot be sustained. When the detonation velocity of nanothermite is only 895 m/s, while TNT has a detonation velocity of 6,900 m/s, the explosive potential of thermite—even in its most potent form as nanothermite—is more than acutely disappointing.

When it turns out nanothermite is not even 13% as powerful as TNT, the very idea that nanothermite should "hold the scientific key to understanding what happened to the Twin Towers" is simply absurd.

But shouldn't the leaders of a self-proclaimed 9/11 "scientific research" group have sorted this out before they proclaimed that nanothermite was "the key"? As Mark has observed in his study, Steve Jones made a mistake early in his 9/11 research career by classifying nanothermite as an explosive in the same category with RDX, HMX, and others, whose detonation velocities are overwhelmingly greater. Alas, "The 9/11 truth movement has never recovered from this error, for to this day nearly everyone in the 9/11 movement refers to 'explosive nanothermite', as even this clever cover for a fictitious 'For Dummies' book [above] illustrates." And shouldn't those who were promoting it to the community have discovered their blunder and taken steps to correct the false impression that they were thereby conveying?

My critique of Steve Jones' research, "On the manipulation of the 9/11 Truth Community", in which I observed, for example, that "the most important points [he has] made are actually concessions that the evidence he has found is merely consistent with the use of thermite or thermate but doesn't prove it was produced by thermite or thermate, where, provided that there are multiple alternative possible explanations, he has not done the job. And I'm going to claim that he has not done the job because he has a commitment to a conception of scientific method that is hopelessly inadequate. . . .

And that while he talks a lot about science, he is, alas, not practicing it", was presented on the air on on May 17, 2007. It was even published on 911blogger, but met with derision and hostility, where the comments were extremely revealing.

As critical thinkers,   Login to post comments

As critical thinkers, members of the 9/11 community weren't taken in, but they aren't so sophisticated in scientific reasoning, now to be taken in by narrow channeling within the 9/11 research community. And that narrow channeling is being enforced by 911blogger, by Loose Change (I'm sorry to say), by Jack Blood's forum, but especially by Steve Jones, Alex Jones, Kevin Ryan, Jim Hoffman. This is very distressing. Very distressing. If you care about truth, you have to follow science. You have to entertain all the possible hypotheses. You have to look for the ones that confer the highest probability on the evidence. You have to become familiar with the evidence. You have to sort out the authentic evidence from the inauthentic evidence.

For the record, this site isn't intended to be a 'research' site, it is intended to be a news and activism site. Research sites are typically forums whereby data collection and discussions can take place over longer periods of time rather than sporadically across various blog entries - that is not the intention of this site, nor has it ever been. The intention of this site was to unify those in action and news rather than divide over points of contention - which at the time of the start of this website were surrounding the Pentagon crash and the 'pod theory'. People are welcome to whatever views they wish, but discussions (or more typically arguments) on various theories are better suited elsewhere, and are typically counter productive to what our collaborative goals should be - paying attention to 9/11 related news (and responding to it directly), and taking action. If you are looking for a 'research site', then this is not it - nor will it be. My suggestion to those who wish to have more active debates over subjects is to start a website devoted to that where moderators can be around 24/7 to ensure that the debates stay social - and seeing as how we all work full time jobs that is not within our abilities - no one site can be everything to everybody. As for the assertion that everyone here buys into some mantra regarding thermate/thermite, that is a false dichotomy suggesting that there are only two groups of thought regarding the destruction of the WTC buildings - each of us have our own thoughts on how that might have occurred, and support for any given theory or researcher is on an individual level, not site wide.

And there were other signs of trouble brewing. The Rock Creek Free Press (May 2009), for example, published a piece about nanothermite, which offered a more reasonable assessment of its explosive capabilities, explaining that even if it has the potential to be a low grade explosive, its use as a high explosive—which might be capable of doing the work required to bring about (at least a major part of) the destruction of the Twin Towers—would require that it be combined with a high explosive. Surely this front-page article, which featured photos of Neils Harrit, Jeffrey Farrer, Kevin Ryan, and Steve Jones, ought to have caught the attention of the leaders of the "hard-evidence" research group.

Even now, after the publication of "Has nanothermite been oversold to the 9/11 Truth community?", some of its most important advocates, such as Steven Jones, Kevin Ryan, and Neils Harrit, remain its obdurate supporters. There are signs that others may be more appreciative of the significance of these considerations, where recent handouts from Architects & Engineers for 9/11 Truth advance the slightly more modest claim, "WTC dust samples contain chips of highly energetic nano-thermite composite materials – uniformly nano-sized, proportioned in an organic gas-generating (explosive) matrix", which appears to be the fallback position: *nanothermite may not be explosive, but it can be combined with explosives to make it explosive.*

The same, alas, can also be said of toothpaste. At some point, therefore, these "leaders" of the 9/11 Truth movement have to concede that a mistake was made and that they have misled the movement: nanothermite cannot possibly hold the key to understanding the demolition of the Twin Towers on 9/11.

Source note: This chapter originally appeared as "Is '9/11 Truth' Based upon a False Theory?", *veteranstoday.com* (17 July 2011).

21

Nanothermite: If it doesn't fit, you must acquit

by Mark Hightower

Those who remember the 1995 O.J. Simpson trial will recall the gloves that turned out to be "too small" for O.J.'s hands when the long-awaited day of trying them on in the courtroom finally arrived.

The blood-soaked gloves (one found at the crime scene and the other outside O.J.'s house in Brentwood the morning after his former wife was murdered) were gloated over as "hard evidence" by the prosecution and the media, very comparable to how the discovery of unignited nanothermite chips in the WTC dust is considered to be "hard evidence" of the explosive demolition of the Twin Towers on September 11th, 2001

Although some have expressed skepticism about what is often called the "smoking gun" of 9/11, the great majority of 9/11 Truthers have accepted – and many have celebrated – this discovery, confident that it will lead to "a new, independent investigation" of the event and bring the perpetrators to justice. But precisely how did the resulting "nanothermite theory" of destruction of the Twin Towers come about – and how well does it stand up to critical scrutiny?

Why Nanothermite?

Observations by first responders of apparent molten metal – thought to be molten iron – could be explained by thermite reactions, which, in turn, could possibly explain the severing of steel columns through a process of melting. However, the explosive effects observed in the destruction call for some further explanation. Nanothermite has been identified as a candidate, being faster-reacting and alleged to be "an explosive form" of thermite.

In a paper titled "Why Indeed Did the WTC Buildings Completely Collapse?" (2006), physicist Dr. Steven E. Jones cited thermite to explain the molten metal and first started raising the possibility that nanothermite could explain the additional explosive effects observed. Then four dust samples collected in the aftermath of the towers' collapse by different individuals were sent to Dr. Jones, and upon testing, they were found to contain unreacted red chips of a nanothermitic material.

Prof. Steven E. Jones

Those results were reported in a later paper titled "Active Thermitic Material Discovered in the Dust from the 9/11 World Trade Center Catastrophe" by Niels Harrit, et al. (April, 2009), and because of this many assumed that nanothermite had been definitively identified as the prime candidate destructive agent. The paper, said to have been peer-reviewed, came out in the *Open Chemical Physics Journal* (Bentham Science Publishers), causing 9/11 Truthers to run with the news that explosive nanothermite blew up the Twin Towers, proclaiming what soon became a form of gospel in the 9/11 community. The Gospel of Nanothermite has given the incendiary properties of thermite a set of new miraculous powers: in its nano-state it becomes "Super Thermite" – a high-explosive that pulverized hundreds of thousands of tons of building materials in no more than 10 seconds.

A Literature Search

A scientific person, or one who prefers to use logic, might wonder about such claims and proceed by examining the scientific literature on nanothermite as well as the principle of how explosives achieve destructive force through generating shock waves that produce fragmentation. This might be a good time to note that the *Rock Creek Free Press* made a very important point in its May 2009 article on nanothermite: "To be a high explosive, the reaction speed must exceed the speed of sound in the material, which is unlikely in the case of thermitic materials, but nano-thermitic material may act as a low explosive in a manner similar to gunpowder."

Few who have carefully watched video footage of the Twin Towers coming down could fail to notice what might appropriately be called "explosive effects" in the nature of the destruction. The question then would be: Were conventional explosives or some other kind of destructive energy source employed? If nanothermite is indeed a high explosive, then was it *also necessary* to use conventional explosives to

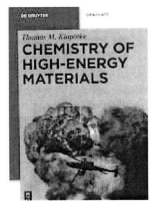

The Thermite Reaction

$$Fe_2O_3 + 2Al \rightarrow Al_2O_3 + 2Fe$$

achieve the demolition of the towers? The more sophisticated believer might agree that conventional explosives also could have been employed, but for the scientifically less sophisticated 9/11 Truther, the "Thermite/Nanothermite Gospel" says it all – and has been "conclusively proven" by the nine authors of the 2009 published and peer-reviewed paper.

But what does other peer-reviewed scientific literature actually have to say about nanothermite? "Nanoscale Aluminum-Metal Oxide (Thermite) Reactions for Application in Energetic Materials," *Central European Journal of Energetic Materials* (2010), authored by Davin G. Piercey and Thomas M. Klapötke, identifies the fastest known combustion velocity for a mixture of metal oxide and aluminum: 2,400 meters per second (m/s), in a type of nanothermite made of *copper oxide* and aluminum. Remember that what Steven Jones found in the dust was *iron-oxide/aluminum nanothermite*. The authors of this paper make it clear that *copper-oxide/ aluminum nanothermite* is significantly more reactive than the *iron-oxide* version, and cite a combustion velocity of 895 m/s for an *iron-oxide/aluminum nanothermite aerogel. So 895 m/s is the highest velocity yet to be found for an* iron-oxide/aluminum nanothermite *in the scientific literature*, where this velocity is far too low to have played a significant role in the destruction of the Twin Towers by means of its shock waves.

Not Powerful Enough

Let's examine the reason for that important last statement. The "destructive fragmentation effect" of an explosive is its *detonation velocity, or the speed of the shock wave through the substance it is traveling in.* To significantly fragment a substance, *the detonation velocity of the explosive must equal or exceed the sonic velocity (the speed of sound) in the material.* For example, the speed of sound in concrete is 3,200 m/s. In steel, the speed of sound is 6,100 m/s. Conventional high explosives such as TNT and RDX have detonation velocities of 6,900 and 8,750 m/s respectively, and are therefore capable of fragmenting concrete and steel, because both 6,900 and 8,750 exceed the sonic velocities of 3,200 m/s required to shatter concrete and 6,100 m/s required to shatter steel. As Dwain Deets has diagrammed, at only 895 m/s, *iron-oxide/ aluminum nanothermite* does not come close to TNT and RDX.

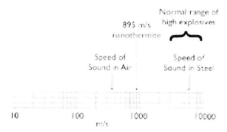

However, prominent 9/11 researchers have nonetheless termed nanothermite to be a powerful explosive. The very highly respected David Ray Griffin, Ph.D. calls nanothermite a "high explosive" in his July 6, 2010 article entitled "Left-Leaning Despisers of the 9/11 Truth Movement: Do You Really Believe in Miracles?", which was published in the online journal, Global Research. "High explosives, such as RDX or nanothermite," wrote Griffin, "could explain these horizontal ejections."

Architects and Engineers for 9/11 Truth, the most revered of 9/11 research groups, published a piece called "Exotic High Tech Explosives Positively Identified in World Trade Center Dust" on April 5, 2009. In this they stated, "Ordinary thermite burns quickly and can melt through steel, but it is not explosive. Nanothermite, however, can be formulated as a high explosive."

A "Secret" Technology?

While searching the open scientific literature on nanothermite and establishing the low detonation velocity of its **iron-oxide**/aluminum variety, chemical engineer T. Mark Hightower has been in contact and shared his findings with Dr. Steven Jones and the authors of the highly regarded April 2009 nanothermite paper, as well as with several other well-known 9/11 Truth leaders.

The most recent responses to his challenges fall into two general categories. One response is that the combustion velocity of 895 m/s *is enough* to explain the Twin Towers' destruction. The other is the rather persistent claim that nanothermite can indeed be a high explosive, where this formulation is *a military secret* that is not discussed in the open literature.

Alright. It is true that military explosives' research employs nanotechnology and that applications involving nanothermite are a subset of this research. (The military even connects nanotechnology with mini-nukes, stating that a mini-nuke device the size of a suitcase could destroy an entire building.) But to suggest that the American military has a "secret recipe" that converts *iron-oxide/aluminum nanothermite* into a high explosive when this claim is contradicted by the open literature doesn't make any sense.

Easily found in the open literature is that *copper-oxide/aluminum nanothermite* can have a combustion velocity of 2,400 m/s, compared to 895 m/s for an *iron-oxide/aluminum nanothermite*. If the 2,400 m/s number is not a military secret, why would a velocity greater than 895 m/s (for the *iron-oxide* variety of nanothermite) *have to be kept secret?* It is far more likely that the highest reported value of 895 m/s is due to physical property limitations of *iron-oxide/aluminum nanothermite* rather than a need to keep higher values secret.

Combined" with Explosives?

Additionally – just to be safe, perhaps – 9/11 nanothermite advocates also maintain the fall-back position that, even if nanothermite by itself is not a high explosive, *when combined with an organic substance* (also asserted to not be itself a high explosive), a high-explosive is created. To that T. Mark Hightower responds: "There is *only one sure way* to make nanothermite a high explosive. If you combine enough high explosives with nanothermite, you can get a mixture that is a high explosive. But the same can be said for my breakfast cereal."

Hightower has further calculated that if conventional explosives (such as TNT or RDX) acting alone were used to bring down the Twin Towers, the quantity necessary would have been hundreds of tons of explosives per tower.

On July 27, 2011, Niels Harrit (chief author of the 2009 nanothermite paper)presented a calculation for how much thermitic material would have been necessary to explain the presence of the many tiny iron-rich spheres in the dust (assuming that a thermite reaction was the source of the spheres).

He gave a range of numbers, based on lower and higher concentrations of the thermite formulation. His lowest figure amounted to 29,000 metric tons of thermitic explosive *per tower* – a value hundreds of times greater than the calculation for conventional explosives. His "conservative" estimate (based on 10% *iron-oxide* in the thermitic material) was 143,000 metric tons of thermitic material that would have been placed in each tower. But let's be realistic: *How could the perpetrators drag in and plant over 100,000 tons of explosive without being seen?*

Even 29,000 tons is hard to imagine and would have been rather difficult to put in place unnoticed.

The Missing Element

A side note from the many technical papers on nanothermite studied by Hightower: *nanothermite produces a blinding flash of light when it goes off.* If such immense quantities of nanothermite were used to blow up the Twin Towers, then why didn't we see tremendous bursts of blinding light all over two those buildings as they were destroyed and largely converted into millions of cubic yards of very fine dust?

The Dangers of a False Theory

Architects & Engineers for 9/11 Truth, which is led by Richard Gage, has been ceaselessly promoting the nanothermite discovery as the "smoking gun" of 9/11, and calling the substance a "high

Aero-Sol—Gel Synthesis of Nanoporous Iron-Oxide Particles: A Potential Oxidizer for Nanoenergetic Materials

Anand Prakash, Alon V. McCormick, and Michael R. Zachariah*

Departments of Mechanical and Chemical Engineering, University of Minnesota, Minneapolis, Minnesota 55455

Received August 3, 2003. Revised Manuscript Received January 22, 2004

Figure 11. Photo of thermal ignition of iron oxide/aluminum nanoparticle mixture.

Finally, to access the suitability of these materials as oxidizers, burn tests and in some cases ignition tests to measure the pressurization of an enclosed ignition were performed (at Los Alamos National Laboratories). A simple mixture of oxide-passivated nano-aluminum (primary particle sizes in 40-nm range) and aero-sol–gel derived iron oxide burned vigorously with a propagation speed of about 4 m/s. However, an ultrasonicated stoichiometric mixture (according to the thermite reaction in section I) generated by ultrasonicating the oxide/aluminum mixture (~25 wt % Al and 75 wt % Fe_2O_3 mixed intimately at nanoscale) in ethanol, followed by drying, resulted in a violent explosion as shown in the photograph in Figure 11. A pressure cell[16] test was performed on the aero-sol–gel iron oxide/aluminum nanoscale mixture wherein about 30 mg of the mixture explosive". If there is ever a proper investigation and a lawsuit is filed in a court of law on the "strength" of nanothermite as "hard evidence" of controlled demolition by explosives at the World Trade Center and it is revealed to the court by the opposing side that nanothermite is at best a very weak "explosive" and could not possibly have destroyed the Twin Towers in seconds, the entire case would almost certainly be dismissed and a legal precedent set against future efforts by others.

The danger of promoting a false theory or of overselling a weak hypothesis to millions of people is that it may someday be a convenient way to close the book on the entire issue. That 9/11 nanothermite advocates insist on their position in the face of significant refutations is disturbing. They are clearly unwilling to change their minds or even to discuss facts that expose weaknesses in their statements. What do these refusals really mean? Are some leaders deliberately pushing a flimsy theory with the intent that it will ultimately be shot down? Or is nanothermite a red herring or limited hangout to keep us from looking into what was really used?

The 9/11 Truth community can be confident in its refutations of the official account of 9/11 without having to present a "bullet-proof" alternate theory. It may well be that thermite/thermate/nanothermite was used in its familiar role as an incendiary (or "cutter charge") in destroying the Twin Towers. But that is very different than to claim that it is a "high explosive" that could have destroyed those buildings. The 9/11 Truth movement must not commit itself to a feeble alternative, especially when an honest assessment of the empirical data for that theory does not support its applicability and actually refutes it.

Source note: This chapter originally appeared as "Nanothermite: If it doesn't fit, you must acquit!", *veteranstoday.com* (27 August 2011).

Part VIII

9/11 Limited Hangouts

22

Confessions of a 9/11 Truth Activist

by Steve Fahrney

Jim Fetzer: Steve Fahrney, an activist from 9/11 Truth San Diego, who had worked with Architects and Engineers for 9/11 Truth (A&E) for about a year, contacted me because of his awareness of my research with T. Mark Hightower on the properties of nanothermite, "Is '9/11 Truth' based upon a false theory?" He had a number of issues that he wanted to discuss related to A&E, including that he had discovered during his work with it that research on conventional explosives at the World Trade Center had never been conducted and that communications within the organization did not allow discussion of what happened at the Pentagon or of alternative explanations about how the Twin Towers had been destroyed. I invited him to be my featured guest on "The Real Deal" on Monday, 15 August 2011, an interview archived at *http://radiofetzer.blogspot.com*, and invited him to author the following chapter:

To Test or Not To Test, the Pentagon and "Off Topic" Topics

As much as I respect the work of Richard Gage, AIA, and Architects and Engineers for 9/11 Truth, I decided to publicly address some of my concerns about some of the policies I experienced as a volunteer on the team for a year. Jim Fetzer was kind enough to provide me a public forum to get some of these alarming concerns off of my chest. Most of the Truth movement is aware that NIST shamefully admits to not having tested dust and debris for explosives, despite the overwhelming presence of "high order damage," but what most 9/11 Truthers are largely unaware of is that WE, in the 9/11 Truth movement, have also failed to test for explosives.

I had always assumed that the tests had been done but had yielded no results, which I further assumed was the reason the painstaking nano-thermite research, testing, and publication were carried out. I did not find out until I

Richard Gage and TV Anchor

had been on Richard Gage's staff for nine months, via an e-mail thread, that we had never tested for explosives ourselves. I was alarmed by this revelation and quickly backed the notion of testing as soon as possible. I was even more surprised when a respected team member, Gregg Roberts, a technical writer who co-authored the nano-thermite paper, was arguing adamantly AGAINST testing for conventional explosives and det cord. He argued that we have limited resources, and we already have a "smoking gun" and saw no benefit of testing. He cautioned that since so much time had passed the residues might have broken down, where testing could yield a negative result even if they had been used. He further emphasized that "debunkers" would use a negative result to their advantage.

The Open Chemical Physics Journal

ISSN: 1874-4125

BENTHAM OPEN

[DOI: 10.2174/1874412500902010007]

Active Thermitic Material Discovered in Dust from the 9/11 World Trade Center Catastrophe

Niels H. Harrit, Jeffrey Farrer, Steven E. Jones, Kevin R. Ryan, Frank M. Legge, Daniel Farnsworth, Gregg Roberts, James R. Gourley and Bradley R. Larsen Pp 7-31

We have discovered distinctive red/gray chips in all the samples we have studied of the dust produced by the destruction of the World Trade Center. Examination of four of these samples, collected from separate sites, is reported in this paper. These red/gray chips show marked similarities in all four samples. One sample was collected by a Manhattan resident about ten minutes after the collapse of the second WTC Tower, two the next day, and a fourth about a week later. The properties of these chips were analyzed using optical microscopy, scanning electron microscopy (SEM), X-ray energy dispersive spectroscopy (XEDS), and differential scanning calorimetry (DSC). The red material contains grains approximately 100 nm across which are largely iron oxide, while aluminum is contained in tiny plate-like structures. Separation of components using methyl ethyl ketone demonstrated that elemental aluminum is present. The iron oxide and aluminum are intimately mixed in the red material. When ignited in a DSC device the chips exhibit large but narrow exotherms occurring at approximately 430 °C, far below the normal ignition temperature for conventional thermite. Numerous iron-rich spheres are clearly observed in the residue following the ignition of these peculiar red/gray chips. The red portion of these chips is found to be an unreacted thermitic material and highly energetic.

In regard to the resources, several members of the team had already stepped forth and pledged $200 per person, which would have covered several tests, meaning that A&E's organization funds would be unaffected. In addition to T. Mark Hightower's startling revelation that thermite lacks the explosiveness to be considered as a sole "smoking gun", I had argued at the time that it would greatly benefit the 9/11 Truth movement to empower our outreach specialists with a more easily understood explanation involving conventional explosive, if the results were positive. As an outreach specialist myself for San Diegans for 9/11 Truth, I was using all of the tools at my disposal, including the nano-thermite paper.

Gregg responded to my e-mail, stating it was actually "perverse" to desire different evidence simply because I was having a hard time explaining the evidence I had. I corrected him stating that I could explain it to others, but that I did not feel qualified to do that. How much time might have been saved by the 9/11 Truth movement collectively, if we had simply tested for conventional explosives, gotten a positive result, and been able to state definitively that explosives had been found at the World Trade Center--without having to explain the intricate details of how thermatic material was allegedly engineered to explode?

Gregg Roberts (left) and Dwain Deets

From what I have learned about controlled demolition, I understand that the charges have to be synchronistically timed to go off within a fraction of a second of each other, where any miscalculation could cause the building to fall over instead of straight down. Given the non-explosive character of nanothermite, I find it rather difficult to believe that melting steel by means of an incendiary could achieve the same result. Additionally, I don't see how an incendiary could shatter steel and pulverize concrete to produce those enormous pyroclastic clouds of dust that were so ubiquitous in New York on 9/11.

I additionally pointed out to the team that we were hypocritical to attack NIST for not conducting testing when we at A&E hadn't either. But recently I have realized there is *another* hypocrisy. We ridicule NIST for advancing the unprecedented theory that fire had brought down these massive steel and concrete structures, even while we were advancing our own unprecedented theory that those buildings had instead been destroyed by a controlled demolition using nanothermite. Given Mark Hightower's research and unrefuted "Nanothermite Challenge", I find it rather far-fetched to suppose that nano-thermite could possibly have achieved the symmetrical destruction of the towers.

Gregg's argument that we should not test due to the hypothetical concern of getting a negative result and that the "debunkers" would attack us, in my opinion, is both ethically irresponsible and scientifically irrelevant. Are we supposed to halt the scientific process and continue allow potentially crucial evidence to spoil due to an unsubstantiated irrational fear?

And this brings me to my next concern about the society as a whole. Due to an internal divide on certain issues, A&E had deemed that any discussion of Dr. Judy Wood's theories related to Directed Energy Weapons, lasers, masers, mini-nukes, or anything to do with the Pentagon was "off-topic" and could not be discussed as official business at A&E. I was puzzled to find out that there were people on the team who felt very strongly that Flight 77 had indeed hit the Pentagon, when my experience in the 9/11 Truth movement at large was that most truth advocates agree that the evidence was against it.

Gregg Roberts was one of the advocates of the "Official Conspiracy Theory" (OCT) regarding the Pentagon, as are Justin Keogh and David Chandler, which is one of the reasons that I labeled them as "infiltrators" in my resignation letter to the team when I left. In my interview with Jim Fetzer, I retracted those accusation toward any and all parties. I believe that name-calling and accusations are divisive, but I hope you can understand my skepticism. I challenged all of the members of A&E to go to their local 9/11 Truth groups, and see for themselves that (1) the Pentagon issue is not divisive, as some within A&E have claimed, and that (2) it is largely agreed that the available evidence strongly supports that Flight 77 did not crash there.

Fahrney created this for an event by Toreros for Truth

After leaving the organization, I discovered that the government not only treats the Pentagon as an "on-topic" issue, but even treats it as an architecture and engineering issue as well. In January of 2003, the Pentagon Building Performance Report was generated by the American Society of Civil Engineers (ASCE) due to the structural failure it suffered on 9/11. I asked

Richard Gage why his organization had not critiqued that report, and he said that since its inception, AE911Truth has only focused on WTC-1, 2, and 7. He argued that it is best to promote your strongest most compelling evidence. I realized later, upon reflection, that he had not actually answered my question.

I support the strategy of promoting your best evidence, but we were not discussing strategy. We were discussing policy. Why does A&E have a policy that discourages new discoveries at the Pentagon? Why doesn't A&E critique their peers who generated the Pentagon Building Performance Report about the structural failure at the Pentagon with the same scrutiny they focus on NIST's explanation of the structural failures in the three largest buildings of the World Trade Center?

I would like to point out that the report appears on the website, *fire.nist.gov*. I do not know how much involvement NIST had in the generation of this report, but A&E, which has a "NIST pursuit team" and has collected funds for that cause, should, in my

Fahrney celebrating A&E reaching 1,000 signatures

opinion, find out. Why does NIST get a "bye" on the Pentagon? I offered Jim and his listeners a speculative theory. If indeed we have infiltrators in our midst, by discouraging discoveries at the Pentagon and even promoting the OCT internally in the 9/11 Truth movement, military and government officials could be let off the hook, again.

As Barbara Honneger and CIT have theorized, based on their independent examinations of the evidence, it appears that explosives inside the Pentagon are what caused the destruction. If this theory is correct, it means that there had to be an insider(s). A new investigation could conclude that, even if thermite/explosives were planted in the World Trade Center, the media could still spin it with al CIA-duh involvement -- but not at the Pentagon. You cannot simply sneak explosives into the Headquarters of our Department of Defense without intimate involvement internally.

I previously mentioned that Judy Wood's work is off-topic at A&E, as well as any exotic theories other than nano-thermite. AE911Truth has had many problems with petition signers and volunteers who support Dr. Wood. It is a disqualifier for new members of the team to join if they endorse her work. Anyone who supports "no-plane" theory, laser theory, directed energy theory, or any theory about mini-nukes is disqualified as well. As a Ph.D. and former professor of mechanical engineering, Judy Wood has not been afforded the same dignity and respect of her peers as her counterparts in the nano-thermite realm, particularly by co-authors of the thermite paper.

Created by Steve Fahrney of the San Diego City College 9/11 Truth Club to raise awareness on campus. Note the nano-thermite chips in the display

Gregg Roberts has told me that, in his opinion, Dr. Judy Wood is unscientific when it comes to 9/11. I personally have yet to delve into Dr. Wood's research or into any of the inappropriately ostracized members of our movement; but, after I shared my story with San Diegans for 9/11 Truth, they began looking where A&E and 911blogger have told us not to. As our local NASA engineer, Dwain Deets explained at our last event, after making a presentation about some exotic theories, San Diegans for 9/11 Truth are committed to looking at all the evidence and all the theories, not just those that are approved by "certain groups". Independent of myself, the group decided to buy Judy Wood's book, which compelled them to contact Dr. Wood, has now been invited to give a presentation at our community center.

I would like to make it clear that I still support A&E, but not its policy about "off-topic" subjects and theories. While I retract my accusations of infiltration, I still find it though highly suspicious that the same people who are advocating against testing for explosives are also against looking at the Pentagon, against discussing Dr. Judy Wood's research, in favor of the OCT at the Pentagon, and in favor of nano-thermite as the sole culprit of destruction in the WTC. No subjects or theories about 9/11 should be "off topic". None is "too controversial" to deserve discussion. Science should not be subordinated to politics in the 9/11 movement, which should be dedicated to truth no matter what form it may take.

Source note: This chapter originally appeared as "Confessions of a 9/11 Truth Activist", *veteranstoday.com* (22 August 2011).

23

Judy Wood and DEWs: The Good, the Bad and the Ugly

by Jim Fetzer

On 11 November 2006, I (Jim Fetzer) first interviewed Judy Wood on a program with Republic Broadcasting Network. I was in Tucson, AZ, at the time, and would discuss her ideas about the use of directed energy weapons (or "DEW"s) during lectures I would present in the following days.

I had founded Scholars for 9/11 Truth almost exactly a year earlier and had invited Steve Jones, Ph.D., a physicist from BYU, to be my co-chair as the recommendation of David Ray Griffin.

But I had become increasingly skeptical of the theory that Steve was advancing, according to which nanothermite was responsible for pulverizing the concrete and decimating the steel at the Twin Towers. I believed that Scholars had to cast its net more widely and interviewing Judy was an appropriate step to take in that direction.

The effects were fast and furious. Almost immediately, Steve and his allies, especially Kevin Ryan, began to plan to take over the Scholars web site at http://st911.org, which had become world-famous, even though I had been responsible for selecting every entry that had been made on our site from its conception.

They would fake a phony poll of the members, which they falsely claimed had come from the "Membership Administrator", and freeze me from access to the site.

I had entrusted a member, Alex Floum, to secure the domain name, which he refused to relinquish to me when Steve and others, including from 1/3 to 1/2 of the members, left Scholars for a new group they would name "Scholars for 9/11 Truth and Justice". It was a bleak time for the 9/11 community, where I believed we had to emphasize TRUTH in the search for 9/11 Truth and nanothermite did not advance it, where subsequent research with T. Mark Hightower, a chemical engineer, has demonstrated that I was right.

While the 9/11 Truth community was being feted with such false depictions as, "Nanothermite: What in the world is High-Tech Explosive Material Doing in the Dust Clouds Generated on 9/11?" which was being lauded as "the smoking gun" of 9/11 and described as, "a highly engineered energetic nanocomposite, was conceived around 1990. By 2000 it had been weaponized and manufactured in top secret military laboratories. This nano-engineered form of thermite does not just burn extremely hot, it explodes",

It would turn out that a principle of materials science–which is actually a law of nature–holds that an explosive cannot destroy a material unless its detonation velocity is greater than the speed of sound in that material. The speed of sound in concrete is 3,200 m/s and in steel 6,100 m/s, while the highest know detonation velocity for nanothertmite is 895 m/s, which means you can't get there from there. The claims for nanothermite were therefore greatly exaggerated.

In the meanwhile, I was interviewing Judy Wood on my radio programs and reviewing her web site again and again, topping out with 15 interviews. I published a chapter by her in THE 9/11 CONSPIRACY (2007), and would feature her as the principal speaker at the Madison Conference, "The Science and Politics of 9/11", which was held 3-5 August 2007, during which I gave her an unprecedented 3 hours to speak. Morgan Reynolds, a close associate, and Jerry Leaphart, the attorney for her pro se lawsuit, were also invited and spoke.

When I would later organize The Vancouver Hearings, which were held 15-17 June 2012, I again invited her to speak, in spite of several odd encounters with some of her supporters that transpired in the meanwhile, but I received no response. I invited Morgan Reynolds, who accepted at first and then withdrew, and then asked John Hutchison, who initially agreed, but then would not respond when I asked for him to verify a bio-sketch I had drafted. Clare Kuehn would accept the challenge of presenting Judy's position during the event, but it was a mystery why Judy herself was unwilling to speak up.

I suppose I should have seen it coming. On 26 January 2010, I had published "A Photographic Portfolio of Death and Devastation" on my personal blog, which had been immediately attacked by Andrew Johnson, who may be Judy's closest ally, on the purported grounds that the photos had come from Judy's site. That was very odd, because, with one exception, they had not come from "Judy's site" and even the photos on Judy's site were not taken by Judy and she has no proprietary claim to them.

Moreover, what I published there was a chapter from THE 9/11 CONSPIRACY (2007), namely: the color-photo section, and had been prepared by Jack White, who had long maintained his own photo studies 0f 9/11 as well as of JFK. (Jack died recently, but eventually responded to Andrew's fanciful allegation by sending me an email, which I posted on the blog.)

Ironically, it was the chapter that appeared immediately before the chapter by Judy Wood, "A Refutation of the Official Collapse Theory", where, on the basis of temporal considerations and elementary physics, she showed that a progressive, floor by floor, collapse would have required 96.7 seconds, not the 10 seconds alleged.

I liked her work, but the tempest on my blog would be an early indication I was not dealing with a normal research group.

The Good

As I have often observed, Dr. Judy D. Wood may be the most highly qualified student of the destruction of the Twin Towers in the 9/11 research community. Dr. Wood received her B.S. (Civil Engineering, 1981) (Structural Engineering), M.S. Engineering Mechanics (Applied Physics), 1983), and Ph.D. (Materials Engineering Science, 1992). She is a former professor of mechanical engineering at Clemson University, with research interests in experimental stress analysis, structural mechanics, optical methods, deformation analysis, and the materials characterization of biomaterials and composite materials.

She is also a member of the Society for Experimental Mechanics (SEM), co-founded SEM's Biological Systems and Materials Division, and has served on the SEM Composite Materials Technical Division.

During my interviews with Judy, we frequently visited her web site and surveyed the many photos and studies she has gathered together, which I continue to regard as the most important compilation of evidence about the effects that an adequate theory of the destruction of the WTC has to explain. I have made that point repeatedly during interviews and elsewhere.

Consider, for example, what I wrote about her in the old (and now decimated) version of my Wikipedia entry:

Explaining the explanandum

Fetzer has spoken positively of Judy Wood and Morgan Reynolds, who left Scholars due in part to disagreement with the organization, objecting to the unwillingness of the society to consider 'no big Boeing' theories (conspiracy theories arguing that no large aircraft hit the World Trade Center and that video evidence of the planes hitting the towers have serious inconsistencies showing them to be "doctored").[43] Fetzer has been impressed by their efforts to clarify the extent of devastation at the World Trade Center and mentions a wide range of theories, including that a "satellite-mounted military weapon" may have been used to destroy it, as among those that deserve investigation.

He has written that "the range of alternative explanations that might possibly explain the explanandum must include non-classic controlled demolition from the top-down using mini-nukes, and . . . non-classic controlled demolition from the top-down using directed energy weapons. . . . The specific weapons used to destroy the WTC could have been ground based or space based." [44]

For Fetzer, "Judy [Wood] appears to have done far more to develop her "proof of concept" than has Steven [Jones]".[44] Steven Jones and others claim to have refuted the mini-nuke hypothesis[45][46] Jones has responded to Reynolds and Wood directly, but they have not viewed his remarks as refutations.[47] After featuring fifteen or more students of video fakery as guests on his radio program, Fetzer decided that claims of video fakery and claims that no planes hit the tower are logically distinct issue.

He has become convinced that video fakery took place on 9/11 and has published several articles about it, including "Mounting Evidence of

*Video Fakery on 9/11" [48] and "New Proof of Video Fakery on 9/11".
[49] Wood and Reynolds both contributed chapters to his first book for
Scholars, The 9/11 Conspiracy (2007).*

Judy D. Wood has since published her book, WHERE DID THE TOWERS GO? (2010), which is previewed in this trailer and which I regard as invaluable as a resource for the study of the effects that an adequate theory must explain:

The Bad

While that is all very much to THE GOOD, unfortunately, there has been a down-side to Judy's work, which has extended to some mottos or slogans that have been prominently featured in her work, such the following:

*If you listen to the evidence carefully enough, it will speak to you and tell you exactly what happened.
If you don't know what happened, keep listening to the evidence until you do.
The evidence always tells the truth.
The key is not to allow yourself to be distracted away from seeing what the evidence is telling you.*

Empirical evidence is the truth that theory must mimic.

Unfortunately, for all her good work in displaying the explanandum, what she says here does not do her work justice. For example, the claim that, *"Empirical evidence is the truth that theory must mimic"*, falls short on several grounds. Since truth and falsity are properties of sentences (or propositions), while empirical evidence consists of photographs, remnants of steel and other physical things, including dust samples and the outcome of observations, measurements, and experiments, "empirical evidence" is not the right kind of thing to be either true or false.

Moreover, the idea that "theory mimic" empirical evidence compounds the semantic obstacles to making a claim that makes sense, since "mimicry" is a kind of simulation, replication, or emulation that would, were it successful, produce more of the same: more photographs, more remnants of steel and other physical things.

What she should be saying is, "Empirical evidence is the data that an adequate theory must explain".

Perhaps my background as a philosopher of science makes me more attune to the oddities of her formulations, but others are equally peculiar. To claim that, *"If you listen to the evidence carefully enough, it will speak to you and tell you exactly what happened. . . . The evidence always tells the truth"*, once again, is to make an assertion that may sound appealing but does not make literal sense. Unless the evidence happens to be auditory and consist of sounds, vibrations, or other phenomena capable of being heard, which photographs, remnants of steel and most other physical things are not, the idea of "listening to the evidence" simply does not apply.

I would liken this to a category mistake, such as supposing that geometrical figures, like triangles and squares, are physical things, like metal triangles and square tables, which are physical things in space/time, while the geometrical figures are abstractions, which have ideal properties and are not in space/time. Her confusion is roughly on that order. But to my surprise, she has gone even further by denying that she even has "a theory"!

What makes this so peculiar is that there is a subtitle on her book that baldly states, "Evidence of Directed Free-Energy Technology on 9/11", which, I submit, would lead any rational mind to infer that her theory is that directed free-energy technology was used on 9/11, in particular, to destroy the Twin Towers, which cannot possibly have collapsed, even though the government maintains that indefensible proposition. In a collapse, gravity–operating in only one direction, namely: down–pulls a building toward the ground, which Judy had already shown, in her chapter in THE 9/11 CONSPIRACY (2007), was inconsistent with the time for both collapses, which THE 9/11 COMMISSION REPORT (2004) said had taken place in about 10 seconds apiece.

Not only that, but both towers were blown apart in every direction from the top down and were converted into millions of cubic yards of very fine dust. And, when the dust had settled, moreover, they were actually destroyed below ground level, when there should have been a stack of pancakes (made up of the floors that had presumably "collapsed") equal to about 12% of the original height of the building, which was the outcome of WTC-7, a 47-story building that actually did collapse at 5:20 PM/ET and left a stack of pancakes of around 5-stories high.

The very idea that the government could attempt to peddle such obvious rubbish to the American people–and that many members of the public should be taken in!–has to be one of the most astonishing public relations coups in history. Anyone who compares the features that distinguish the collapse of WTC-7 with the features that distinguish the destruction of the Twin Towers, which are completely different, would recognize the scam, as "This is an orange" and "9/11: The Towers of Dust", so elegantly reveal. In summary form, they include:

	WTC-1 & WTC-2	WTC-7
Sequence:	Top down	Bottom up
Floor motion:	Stationary	Falling together
Mechanism:	Pulverization	Controlled Demolition
Time/Speed:	About 10 secs.	About 6.5 secs.
	(~ free fall)	(~ free fall)
Remnants:	No pancakes	Pancakes
	(below ground level)	(5-7 floors)
Mode:	Explosion	Implosion

As Ace Baker observed some time ago, the term "pulverization" could be viewed as objectionable, since it tends to imply that the process was mechanical, such as by means of grinding, which preempts that it may have been a chemical, a nuclear or an electromagnetic process instead. Judy has been ingenious by introducing words that fit better without taking for granted how it was done. In this case, for example, she has used "dustification" as a term that well describes what we actually see happening on 9/11. It has to be an acknowledgment to the power of verbal repetition by the mass media that the dustification of the Twin Towers, which bears none of the signs of a collapse, could nevertheless be sold to the public as having been a collapse, when it manifestly was not.

The Worse

Judy and I maintained a cordial relationship from our first interview on 11 November 2006 to our last on 28 February 2008, when she appeared with John Hutchison. Because the claims that have been made about John's work and the fact that it is in the domain of electromagnetism, which is among the most complex in physics, I asked (what I thought at the time was) an innocuous question about his background and education, which he had sluffed off by saying he had "flunked crayons and coloring books". That struck me as very odd, since an inquiry about his scientific background was obviously appropriate. But Judy apparently took offense and has refused to respond to any of my communications, including my invitation to her to speak during The Vancouver Hearings, 15-17 June 2012.

An archive of Judy's interviews, which includes both our first and our last, has been created by Andrew Johnson, which reminds me that I also featured many of Judy's closest allies and supporters on my shows, including Morgan Reynolds and Jerry Leaphart, which can be accessed here. They were among the other speakers I invited to participate in the Madison conference, 3-5 August 2007, as I mentioned above, and Morgan would also contribute two chapters to THE 9/11 CONSPIRACY (2007).

The claim that Judy "does not have theory" has struck me as so odd that I have pursued it in several contexts. During an interview she did with Bob Tuskin, I called in to ask how she could deny that she has a theory, when the subtitle of her book declares, "Evidence of directed free-energy technology on 9/11".

To my astonishment, Judy became semi-hysterical and refused to answer. While it may have transpired during a break and not made it onto the air (where what was broadcast can be taken in here), she told Bob that having me call in was *"like a victim having to confront her rapist"*. She probably did not realize I was still connected and overheard this conversation, but I found it so extraordinary and unwarranted that it has made an indelible impression upon me.

Some of her supporters, such as Thomas Potter, have been equally emphatic that she does not have a theory. In an email to Don Fox on 23 July 2012, for example, he wrote, *"The textbook, WHERE DID THE TOWERS GO? by Dr. Judy Wood, B.S., M.S., Ph. D., is not about a conspiracy theory or a theory at all. It is a 540 page textbook about factual evidence, empirical evidence that reveals the truth in a way that is undeniable to anyone who reads it."* The problem is that, if she has no theory, then she has no explanation. She even claimed that I had "threatened" her to not talk about this technology, which is completely false and has no foundation.

There is no doubt that Judy has done more than anyone else to clarify the explanandum (as the evidence that has to be explained by an adequate theory). In technical philosophical language, she needs the explanans (as the premises that can explain the explanandum) in the form of the initial conditions (of the Twin Towers before their destruction) and the causes that transformed them from BEFORE to AFTER. Those causes can take the form of causal mechanisms (such as conventional explosives, thermite or thermate or nanothermite, mini or micro nukes (fission or fusion), or DEWs as directed energy devices), but invoking those mechanisms as THE CAUSES that brought about the transformation of the Twin Towers to a mass of rubble and millions of cubic yards of very fine dust is to advance A THEORY.

The term "theory", as I am using it here, is not simply a guess or a conjecture but a set of laws and corresponding definitions that related those laws to physical things and events in space/time. There is no way around it: If she has no theory, she has no laws; and if she has no laws, she has no explanation.

This business about "having no theory" bothered me enough that I asked myself why in the world she would make such a claim. Part of it appears to be excessive commitment to the ordinary language distinction between "theories" and "facts", as though theories were necessarily either false or at least not known to be true. This, of course, is inconsistent with the use of the term in "Newton's theory of universal gravitation", "Darwin's theory of evolution by natural selection", and "Einstein's theories of special and general relativity", which are–with certain qualifications–generally regarded as *theories that are true.*

But there may be a deeper reason why she and her followers–who are adamant on this point–want to deny that she has "a theory", which includes (a) that the strongest claim she actually makes about how the Twin Towers were destroyed is not that DEWs were responsible but (b) "What I do claim is that the evidence is consistent with the use of energy weapons that go well beyond the capabilities of conventional explosives and can be directed." As Don Fox has observed, "My mini-nuke hypothesis fits in nicely with that definition: mini-nukes can be configured to explode directionally and their capabilities go well beyond those of conventional explosives." So does she rule out mini or micro nukes?

There are at least two important reasons to doubt that she does. The first is that, while she and her followers insist she has, but her "refutations", which are set forth on pages 121-122 of WHERE DID THE TOWERS GO?, are relatively limited to a small number of claims of limited significance:

1. Do they exist? But the problem is, were they used, and would they show these types of signatures?

2. Nuclear weapons explode, but the towers did not explode. They were pulverized and peeled to the ground, almost like a banana peeling.

3. Moreover, the site wasn't "hot", that is, radioactive.

4. The bathtub survived, as has been seen, making it highly unlikely that nukes of any kind were used.

5. Additionally, the Richter reading did not show the use of a nuclear weapon. If a nuke large enough to destroy the WTC had been used, it would have registered a seismic signal greater than if the building had fallen to the ground. What the seismograph showed was that the majority of the WTC did not hit the ground.

6. Finally, the site showed massive amounts of unburned paper, an impossibility if nuclear weapons had been detonated. The "unburned paper" evidence will be discussed subsequently in conjunction with other factors.

Judy's question about the existence of mini or micro nukes suggests a lack of research, since the Department of Defense has been publicly endorsing them at least since 1993. Some of her points count against the idea of 150kt nukes planted at the base of each of the three buildings, which has been advanced by Demitri Khalezov, whom I interviewed on "The Real Deal" on 21 January 2011 on "9/11: Nukes at the WTC?". (I personally have had no doubts about the existence of directed energy weapons, where, in doing research on the plane crash that took the life of Sen. Paul Wellstone, I had discovered the existence of the Directed Energy Professional Society, which was then in 2004 holding its eighth annual meeting in Honolulu, Hawaii.) But I find it odd to question the existence of mini or micro nukes, whose existence, if anything, is even better known than DEWs, and which her research has not debunked.

I also find it odd she would describe the buildings as having been "pulverized" for the reason that Ace Baker raised. Given her innovative use of language, I would have thought that she would have said "They were dustified", not that they were "pulverized and peeled to the ground". Perhaps even more strikingly, Judy's "conclusions" about the WTC and how it was done are advanced in a series of forty-three (43) propositions about "evidence that must be explained", which are presented on pages 480-483, which qualify more as explanandum than as explanans.

Indeed, I have interviewed Chuck Boldwyn, a retired high-school physics, math and chemistry instructor, about her 43 propositions during 15 interviews, which could be viewed as responses to the 15 I did with her. I thought I would do my best to acknowledge what she has and has not done by posting a review of WHERE DID THE TOWERS GO? on amazon.com. The consequences were not going to be anything like I had expected.

The Ugly

Rather to my astonishment, the 8th post in what has now become more than 1,000 comments on my review would attack me as though I were an enemy of 9/11 Truth, authored by someone using the name "Emmanuel

Goldstein", which many of us have concluded–possibly mistakenly, but probably correctly–is Judy Wood, just as the party who identifies himself as "S. Tiller" appears likely to be her close associate, Andrew Johnson:

> All things considered, I thought this was a rather harsh response to

a 5-star review that is entitled, "Masterful argument by elimination". It exemplifies the fallacy known as the straw man by exaggerating an opponent's position to make it easier to attack. There was no reason to regard me as a "debunker" to begin with. It was one of the first indications that, no matter how carefully I presented my views, how highly I praised her work or how strongly I supported her, it would not be enough for Judy and her followers, where the entire thread would confirm my suspicion that this is not a scientific research group.

Other attacks upon me have been, if anything, even more disgusting and unjustifiable. Several of them have the character or flavor of death threats, which was not exactly what I had expected when I published a 5-star review. Indeed, this thread itself provides further confirmation that what I had said in my review was right and that she had not shown that mini or micro nukes could have been used, as I shall explain below. But her followers were not seriously concerned with the science of 9/11.

Two were so blatant they should have been deleted by *amazon.com* as both offensive and revealing.

The first was:
Posted on May 25, 2012 7:39:19 AM PDT
Last edited by the author on May 25, 2012 7:42:00 AM PDT
Emmanuel Goldstein says:

"The objective of disinformation is not to convince you of one point of view or another, it is to create enough uncertainty so that everything is believable and nothing is knowable." – Philosopher James Fetzer (12/6/1940 to ?)

Should the evidence that is presented by Dr. Judy Wood become a con-tributing factor in the development of cognitive dissonance to the point where your guilt, anger, or embarrassment creates an unmanageable schism, there are other options besides suicide.
Veterans Crisis Line 1-800-273-8255

I thought the use of the date (12/6/1940 to ?) was especially considerate. But the suggestion that I should be contemplating suicide was relatively minor compared to the post that would show up around 2 months later, after I had explained why Judy Wood and her groupies appear to have the characteristics distinctive of a cult. Here is what I wrote as a dissection of the behavior being displayed on this thread and the earlier exchange that took place when I reprinted Jack White's chapter:

Your post, in reply to an earlier post on Jul 21, 2012 11:57:55 AM PDT
Last edited by you on Jul 21, 2012 12:06:36 PM PDT
James H. Fetzer says:

Since I point out the obvious "dustification" of the Twin Towers, which were converted into millions of cubic yards of very find dust–and from the top down–where they were destroyed below ground level (see "New 9/11 Photos Released", for example), but in every other place where I discuss this issue (such as "An Analysis of the WTC on 9/11"), why are my bona fides being questioned again?

Here we have another display of the characteristics of a cult. As I use the word "cult", it refers to a group (formal or informal) typified by (a) core dogmas, (b) mystic leaders, (c) intolerance of criticism, (d) disposi-tion to attack those who question the faith, and (e) devotion to the group even when confronted with well-founded criticism. Examples that come to mind include the Branch Davidians (David Koresh) and, even more appropriately, Scientology (L. Ron Hubbard), with its pretensions toward science. Does any of this sound familiar?

Among their characteristics are their members' excessively zealous, unquestioning commitment to the identity and leadership of the group; the exploitative manipulation of group members; and harm or the threat of harm to those who are perceived to threaten the group, which can be directed inward or directed outward depending on the source of the threat, as Jonestown (Jim Jones) exemplifies. And extremely harsh treatment of anyone who challenges its core beliefs. All of these characteristics have been exhibited on this thread.

Chuck has made a brilliant observation: "The dust samples have only iron or glass spheres. The dust contains no steel dust which would be of highly irregular shapes, not near perfectly round spheres as is actually found in all of the dust samples. This means all of those spheres in the dust of iron and glass had to me liquefied or vaporized in order for surface tension to allow for those spheres to be formed, all from very, very, very high temperatures. There is no steel dust other that the micro and nano sized iron and glass spheres. No other metal particles were found in the dust."

This strikes at the heart of the matter, which is that the defense of their core beliefs is isolated from and treated as though it were immune to criticism or discussion. For true-believing cult members, the question has been sett-led–and those who differ are threats to attack, viciously, repeatedly, and without mercy. I am afraid we have seen this attitude on display here and elsewhere, such as the attacks upon me for publishing "A Photographic Portfolio of Death and Devastation", which is on jamesfetzer.blogspot. com. It is the antithesis of a scientific attitude.

The key point that I have been making, which jbr, S. Tiller, and Emmanuel Goldstein–who are so lacking in confidence in themselves and their own theory that they dare not use their real names–is that the superiority of one theory (DEWs) over alternatives (of mini or micro nukes, fission or fusion, atomic or hydrogen) depends upon their respective clarity of language, comparative explanatory power, degrees of empirical support, and economy/simplicity/elegance, where Chucks observation suggests that, when we get down to the nitty-gritty, the case for the use of DEWs appears to encounter serious problems. Its superiority has yet to be shown.

The suggestion that Judy and her groupies possess the properties of a pseudo-scientific cult was not terribly well received by "Emmanuel Goldstein" and elicited her second especially offensive post, when she ratcheted up the pressure by suggesting that my wife, Jan, might actually shoot me, as though it were an acceptable way to satirize her own failure to understand the meaning of the word "theory", when it is actually extraordinarily revealing for the insight it affords into a perverted mind:

> *In reply to an earlier post on Jul 28, 2012 8:42:41 AM PDT*
> *Last edited by the author 33 minutes ago*
> *Emmanuel Goldstein says:*
>
> *So they find Uncle Fester's body with a bullet hole in his head. When they dig out the slug it matches his wife's gun and she has gun powder residue on her body. When charges are filed against her in a court of law will the prosecutor present evidence to convict her of murder or will they present a theory?*
> *http://i1192.photobucket.com/albums/aa326/Jefffolkman/Still_arguing_K640.jpg*

Not long thereafter, S. Tiller would post an attack upon me that not only falsely suggested that I was defending the theory that thermite / thermate / nanothermite had been the principal cause of the destruction of the Twin Towers but that my dedication to preserving that myth was why I had "thrown them out" of Scholars for 9/11 Truth, when I had done no such thing. Steve Jones, Kevin Ryan and others had split from Scholars *because I was featuring and supporting Judy Wood!*

S. Tiller says:

In reply to your post on Ju

The myth of thermite was refuted by Drs. Wood and Reynolds in the year 2006. This is one of the reasons why Fetzer threw them out of his "Scholars" club. He couldn't get them to stop refuting the thermite myth. So, Fetzer kept the thermite myth alive all this time.

Why?

Dr. Wood also refuted the thermite myth in her book, published in 2010, giving, among other reasons, the speed of various explosives and showing that thermite cannot compete.

So, the question should be why Fetzer promoted the thermite myth for 6 years when he knew thermite was bogus as an explanation for anything to do with the destruction on 9/11.

You replied with a later post

Judy Wood and her groupies clearly satisfy the requirements that define a cult: (a) core dogmas, (b) mystic leaders, (c) intolerance of criticism, (d) disposition to attack those who question the faith, and (e) devotion to the group even when confronted with well-founded criticism. They display their loyalty to the group by excessive zeal in attacking anyone they perceive to threaten it, no matter whether that perception is well-founded or not.

The deification of Judy Wood and her status as the mystical figure at the center of this cult is thus especially well reflected by one of the later posts of S. Tiller:

Where did the Science Go?

On yet another forum, Emmanuel Goldstein has continued the onslaught, maintaining that Judy Wood is being assaulted by Jim Fetzer and by Richard Gage, meant to present her sympathetically as a victim. Not everyone has been taken in, however:

Originally Posted by l4zarus
I'd like to point to your signature which reads:

**Dr. Judy Wood is being attacked on all fronts especially by Jim Fetzer and Richard Gage.
Anybody who attacks Dr. Judy Wood's textbook is, in my opinion, a full fledged disinformation tool. ©
Buy WHERE DID THE TOWERS GO? by Dr. Judy Wood, B.S., M.S. , Ph.D. and empower yourself with
this textbook and its evidence of how the World Trade Center was "dustified".**

It's not accurate. Leaving aside Wood's history with Fetzer which has been documented, I found this review at Amazon by Fetzer praising Judy Wood's book:

Masterful argument by elimination, *May 20, 2012*
By James H. Fetzer
. . . .
–James H. Fetzer, Ph.D., Founder, Scholars for 9/11 Truth
Hardly the words of someone "attacking" Wood.

My question: why are you trying to convince us Fetzer is attacking Wood when that's obviously not true?

Caught with proof demonstrating that what she had been posting was false, she replied, *"Why are you trying to convince us Fetzer is not attacking Dr. Judy Wood when it's obviously true that he is?"*, apparently the best she could do–apart from resorting to cartoon art in which I, Jim Fetzer, am presented as a clown, which is not the first time she has used this motif:

Indeed, Judy and her followers constructed a YouTube in which they presented me explaining the views of someone else, Phil Jayhan, who had appeared on one of my shows. They attributed Jayhan's views to me and then attacked me as a clown, where Judy was attacking me even though she had to know that what I was saying was a report about the views of Jayhan and not mine. I have tried to find it on YouTube, but it was so outrageous that even Judy and her buddies may have been embarrassed by what they had done. It was about as unethical a form of behavior as I could imagine within this context.

Other students of 9/11 have been less patient than I. Don Fox, for example, who has participated in this lengthy thread has concluded that Judy Wood has stalled the 9/11 Truth Movement for long enough now. While Judy encourages the readers of her book, WHERE DID THE TOWERS GO? to accept the notion that some variety of a Tesla/Hutchison-based technology directed energy weapon was responsible for the destruction of the WTC. *But does Judy believe this herself?*

The material posted on her website at *http://drjudywood.com* might actually lead one to conclude that she does not. Don believes that her primary mission is to undermine and deny that nuclear weapons were used to destroy the WTC complex on 9/11, that she is a gatekeeper and that she most likely works for one of the many intelligence agencies.

I find that ironic, since Judy has implied that about me!

Don came to believe that Judy was pure disinfo when he came across photos she calls, "The Snowball" and "The Bubbler". She shows photos of buildings that are (in Don's view) being nuked and comes up with these cute little catch phrases. The inference we are supposed to draw is that only her conjectured Tesla/Hutchison based DEW weapon could do this sort of damage to the buildings.

But, he observes, Judy Wood NEVER states that a Tesla/Hutchison technology based weapon was used at the WTC. All that she EVER commits to is: "What I do claim is that the evidence is consistent with the use of energy weapons that go well beyond the capabilities of conventional explosives and can be directed. "Notice, especially, that Don's mini-nuke hypothesis also fits in nicely with that definition: *mini-nukes can be configured to explode directionally and their capabilities go well beyond those of conventional explosives.* And Don has raised some rather telling questions:

(a) What Tesla or Hutchison effect will produce a fission process that otherwise would only be found from exploding advanced nuclear devices? What Tesla or Hutchison effect will cause elevated tritium levels that otherwise would only be found from exploding advanced thermonuclear devices?

(b) What Tesla or Hutchison effect will eject debris from the middle of WTC-1 up at a 45 degree angle and out into the Winter Garden 600 feet away? What Tesla or Hutchison effect could produce the China Syndrome at Ground Zero? Nukes fit ALL of these phenomena to a "t".

(c) If Goldstein, Potter, Johnson, Reynolds and Wood were after the truth, they would conduct themselves in a completely different manner. Instead I see baseless attacks on other researchers, veiled intimidation/death threats and a coordination of efforts that smacks of an intelligence operation.

Don believes there is a pattern here that reflects the standard script they follow is more about toeing the party line than to contributing to scientific discussion. Whoever goes off of the script gets attacked. Even if you support Judy Wood as much as 95%, that is not good enough. I wish I could say that Don is wrong, but my fear is that he is actually right.

After having interviewed her 15 times, published a chapter by her in THE 9/11 CONSPIRACY, given her three hours to speak during the Madison Conference, inviting her to participate in The Vancouver Hearings and more, the unrelenting and incredibly nasty attacks to which I have been subjected– including the bizarre responses from her and her followers to my 5-star review on amazon.com–I have been forced to conclude that Judy Wood and her followers have lost their way and are displaying the characteristics of a cult.

As I use the word "cult", it refers to a group (formal or informal) typified by (a) core dogmas, (b) mystic leaders, (c) intolerance of criticism, (d) disposition to attack those who question the faith, and (e) devotion to the group even when confronted with well-founded criticism.

Among their characteristics are their members' excessively zealous and unquestioning commitment to the identity and the leadership of the group; the exploitative manipulation of group members; and harm or the threat of harm to those who are perceived to threaten the group, which can be directed inward or directed outward depending on the source of the threat, as the case of Jonestown and Jim Jones chillingly exemplifies.

And notice the extremely harsh treatment dealt out to anyone who challenges its core beliefs. All of these characteristics have been exhibited on this thread and in other venues, as I have documented here.

Don believes that the death threats I received in Seattle and that were sent to the Deman Theatre in an attempt to halt The Vancouver Hearings may have come from her. It is a sad comment on the state of 9/11 research and the factions that have developed that he may be right about that, too. I certainly have no better explanation–and I am sorry to say that it would fit the pattern of harassment and intimidation that I have come to expect from Judy and her gang.

I wish it were not so, but "if you listen to the evidence carefully enough, it will speak to you"!

Source note: This chapter originally appeared as "Judy Wood and DEWs: The Good, the Bad and the Ugly", *veteranstoday.com* (20 August 2012).

24

On C-SPAN, Richard Gage Leaves 9/11 Truth in a Time Warp

by Jim Fetzer

"9/11 was conceived as an elaborate psychological operation to instill fear into the American people in order to manipulate them into supporting the political agenda of the Bush/Cheney administration"–Jim Fetzer

Everyone who's committed to 9/11 Truth should welcome more coverage from C-SPAN. Perhaps the greatest coverage to reach the public in the past was also from C-SPAN, when it covered the panel discussion of the American Scholars Conference, Los Angeles, 24-25 June 2006. But this one might be an exception.

We heard then about nanothermite from Steve Jones, Co-Chair of Scholars for 9/11 Truth. And we heard it again from the founder of A&E911.

But a major division has arisen between those who claim that nanothermite can have blown the buildings apart and those who maintain that it isn't even theoretically possible. Recent intel dumps confirm the use of nukes and explain those small iron spheres as a consequence of the use of special (iron jacketed) high-tech nukes.

So what's with Richard Gage and A&E911 that they are still promoting a theory that T. Mark Hightower and I proved was indefensible in three articles published on 1 May 2011, on 17 July 2011 and on 27 August 2011? Why did Gage squander this precious opportunity to advance 9/11 Truth on C-SPAN by endorsing a provably false theory?

The "big three" questions

Not only that, but there are three major questions in the public mind about 9/11, which are these:

(a) what happened on 9/11?

(b) how was it done?

(c) who was responsible and why?

We know the before and after of the World Trade Center in relation to 9/11, so the answer to (a) is trivial. But Richard Gage had no answer to (c), even though he was asked it several times, and his answer to (b) was false and misleading. Is this the best that Richard Gage and A&E911 can do? It was embarrassing when he was asked the all too obvious question and could not answer it:

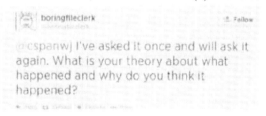

A&E911 is not alone in attempting to place *the how* ahead of *the who* and *the why*, where Judy Wood and her DEW supporters adopt the very same stance. But the American public has limited patience with those who can't produce answers to such obvious questions, especially more than a decade after the event. And that is why "Operation Terror", Art Olivier's reconstruction of the events of 9/11, is a more powerful instrument for opening the mind to what may have happened than the appeal to an obscure causal mechanism—especially when it is misconceived.

All three questions have justifiable answers, but Richard Gage did not deliver them. It was much worse than that, because the host had prepared to defeat any appeal he would make to "thermite", using NIST as his authority and thereby begging the question, by assuming the position of NIST that is the position in doubt:

14. Is it possible that thermite or thermate contributed to the collapse of WTC 7?

NIST has looked at the application and use of thermite and has determined that it was highly unlikely that it could have been used to sever columns in WTC 7 on Sept. 11, 2001.

Thermite is a combination of aluminum powder and a metal oxide that releases a tremendous amount of heat when ignited. It is typically used to weld railroad rails together by melting a small quantity of steel and pouring the melted steel into a form between the two rails. Thermate also contains sulfur and sometimes barium nitrate, both of which increase the compound's thermal effect, create flame in burning, and significantly reduce the ignition temperature.

To apply thermite to a large steel column, approximately 0.13 lb. of thermite would be needed to heat and melt each pound of steel. For a steel column that weighs approximately 1,000 lbs. per foot, at least 100 lbs. of thermite would need to be placed around the column, ignited, and remain in contact with the vertical steel surface as the thermite reaction took place. This is for one column; presumably, more than one column would have been prepared with thermite, if this approach were to be used.

It is unlikely that 100 lbs. of thermite, or more, could have been carried into WTC 7 and placed around columns without being detected, either prior to Sept. 11, 2001, or during that day.

Given the fires that were observed that day, and the demonstrated structural response to the fires, NIST does not believe that thermite or thermate was used to fail any columns in WTC 7.

Analysis of the WTC steel for the elements in thermite/thermate would not necessarily have been conclusive. The metal compounds also would have been present in the construction materials making up the WTC buildings, and sulfur is present in the gypsum wallboard used for interior partitions.

Most Americans are too gullible to realize that this is citing the very source that Gage is disputing. But it could have been worse. He could have pointed out that Neils Harrit, a proponent of the nanothermite hypothesis, has estimated that it would have required "hundreds of tons" to do the job (where Harrit has also offered the more precise calculation of from 29,000 metric tons to 143,000 metric tons for each tower) or that the lab Christopher Bollyn has cited Los Alamos as his source for "explosive nanothermite" told Gordon Duff "they couldn't produce anything smaller than 10 microns and it couldn't blow a hole in a piece of paper".

Why nanothermite can't cut it

If this had been an episode of "The Twilight Zone", it might have made more sense where 9/11 Truth is caught in a time warp. Richard Gage must know by now that nanothermite cannot live up to its capabilities as advanced by Steven Jones, Kevin Ryan, and others, who regard themselves as the custodians and only true practitioners of the scientific method in 9/11 research. Nanothermite (or even "thermite", which is the term Gage used) has only 1/13 the explosive force of TNT and, whatever contribution it may have made to the collapse of Building 7, cannot possibly have been responsible for blowing apart the Twin Towers.

As Denis Spitzer et al., "Energetic nano-materials: Opportunities for enhanced performances", *Journal of Physics and Chemistry of Solids* (2010), observes, given the crucial role of the rapid expansion of gases to perform work by explosives, states, "Gas generating nano-thermites: Thermites are energetic materials, which do not release gaseous species when they decompose.

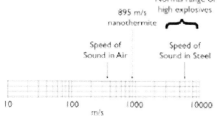

However, explosives can be blended in thermites to give them blasting properties", which implies that, unless supplemented with explosives, nanothermites are non-explosive. So Mark and I may have been overly generous.

Having published three articles explaining that nanothermite cannot have done it and to inform prominent researchers about this discovery, Mark wrote to Steven Jones, Richard Gage, and others. Dwain Deets, the former Chief of Research Engineering and Director for Aeronautical Projects at NASA Dryden Flight Research Center, wrote to Mark and told him that he had listened to our interview on "The Real Deal" and said: "Excellent interview. A step toward trimming back claims that overshoot the evidence."

Dwain also sent a diagram illustrating certain detonation velocities as well as the sonic (speed of sound) velocities in various materials. Thus, for a high explosive to significantly fragment a material, its detonation velocity must be equal to or greater than the speed of sound in that material. This law requires a detonation velocity of at least 3,200 m/s to fragment concrete and 6,100 m/s to fragment steel, which is far beyond the highest recorded detonation velocity of 895 m/s for nanothermite.

"Explosive Evidence"

It came as no surprise when Richard Gage recommended "Explosive Evidence", the A&E911 documentary about what happened to the World Trade Center, especially to WTC-7. Since it was published on 12 September

2012, while Mark and I published our studies in May-August 2011, A&E911 must have known that the theory they were presenting had already been shown to be indefensible on scientific grounds. While nanothermite proponents claim to be "scientific", they violate the canons of science by not revising their views when new evidence or new hypotheses become available.

Indeed, during The Midwest 9/11 Truth Conference, which was held in Urbana, IL, on 22 September 2013, we presented "Explosive Evidence" as the first hour of the conference, where I advanced a critique of its limitations and shortcomings during the second hour as follows and explained why the currently available evidence now supports the conclusion that the Twin Towers were taken out using a sophisticated arrangement of micro or mini nukes, which appear to have been attached to the core columns of each:

Indeed, ample substantiation had already been presented during The Vancouver Hearings, which were held there 15-17 June 2012, including several presentations that supported the use of nukes on 9/11, the most significant of which was made by Jeff Prager (where Don Fox presented on his behalf). Jeff explained that, in 2002, he set out to prove that, on 9/11, 19 Muslims had hijacked four planes and attacked us. But by 2005, he realized this was false, sold his business, left the US and began to investigate 9/11 full-time. (See his 9/11 America Nuked.)

How it was done

In "Proof of Ternary Fission in New York City on 9/11" he observes (1) that dust samples are the best evidence of what happened on 9/11; (2) that the USGS samples taken over a dozen locations show how various elements interacted prove that fission reaction(s) had taken place; (3) that Multiple Myeloma in the general population at a rate of 3-9 incidents per 100,000 people, but the rate was 18 per 100,000 among first responders; (4) that other cancers relatively unusual cancers have appeared among the responders, including non-Hodgkins lymphoma, leukemia, thyroid, pancreatic, brain, prostate, esophageal and blood and plasma cancers; and (5) that, as of March 2011, no less than 1,003 first responders died from various cancers. The elements found in the USGS dust samples provide a rather astonishing array of proof of nukes:

*Barium and Strontium: Neither of these elements should ever appear in building debris **in these quantities**. The levels never fall below 400ppm for Barium and they never drop below 700ppm for Strontium and reach over 3000ppm for both in the dust sample taken at Broadway and John Streets.*

Thorium and Uranium: These elements only exist in radioactive form. Thorium is a radioactive element formed from Uranium by decay. It's very rare and should not be present in building rubble, ever. So once again we have verifiable evidence that a nuclear fission event has taken place.

Lithium: With the presence of lithium we have compelling evidence that this fission pathway of Uranium to Thorium and Helium, with subsequent decay of the Helium into Lithium has taken place.

Lanthanum: Lanthanum is the next element in the disintegration pathway of the element Barium.

Yttrium: The next decay element after Strontium, which further confirms the presence of Barium.

Chromium: The presence of Chromium is one more "tell tale" signature of a nuclear detonation.

Tritium: A very rare element and should not be found at concentrations 55 times normal the basement of WTC-6 no less than 11 days after 9/11, which is another "tell tale" sign of nukes.

New research on the use of nukes has provided further confirmation, including studies by Don Fox, Dr. Ed Ward and Jeff Prager, show these elements occur in patterns of correlation that make the hypothesis virtually undeniable (not that Steve Jones, Kevin Ryan and Richard Gage, among others, will not continue to deny it), where Gordon Duff has recently published that the actual number of New Yorkers who have incurred these unusual 9/11-related cancers has now increased to more than 70,000.

And this is not a new issue. In his analysis of "The Pros and Cons of the Toronto Hearings", for example, which was published 20 September 2011, Joshua Blakeney observed that Judge Richard Lee was concerned about Kevin Ryan's appeals to nanothermite and

asked whether it had ever been used to demolish a building. If there was ever "an embarrassing moment" in the history of the 9/11 Truth movement, this must have been it. So why was Richard Gage repeating the blunder on C-SPAN? *Wasn't once bad enough?*

It is ironic that the nanothermite theory, which was based on dust samples, has been superseded by new research based on more comprehensive dust samples, but that is characteristic of scientific research: the discovery of new data or of new alternatives can lead to the rejection of hypotheses previously accepted, to the acceptance of hypotheses previously rejected and to leaving others in suspense, which is characteristic not only of science specifically but of rationality of belief in general.

What about Planes/No Planes?

If the impossibility of nanothermite having blown apart the Twin Towers drives Richard Gage, Steve Jones and Neils Harritt up the wall, questions that have arisen about the 9/11 crash sites and evidence suggests that all four of them were fabricated or faked (albeit in different ways). It was profoundly disturbing, therefore, when Richard Gage implied the 9/11 plane crashes were real, which contradicts the available evidence. But we have documentary proof that Flights 11 (North Tower) and 77 (Pentagon) were not even scheduled that day, where FAA registration records show that the planes used for Flights 93 (Shanksville) and 175 (South Tower) were not taken out of service ("deregistered") until 28 September 2005. So how could planes that were not even in the air have crashed on 9/11? and how could planes that crashed on 9/11 have still been in the air four years later?

United 93 Still Airborne After Alleged Crash - According To ATC/Radar

04/28/09 (PilotsFor911Truth.org) - Recently it has been brought to our attention that Air Traffic Control (ATC) transcripts reveal United 93 as being airborne after it's alleged crash. Similar scenarios have been offered with regard to American 77 and American 11 showing an aircraft target continuing past its alleged crash point in the case of American 11, or past the turn-around point in the case of American 77. However, both these issues can be easily explained by "Coast Mode" radar tracking. This is not the case with United 93.

Radar Coast Mode activates when a transponder is inoperative (or turned off) and primary radar tracking is lost, which enables ATC to have some sort of reference of the flight after losing radar coverage of the physical aircraft. When an aircraft target enters 'Coast Mode', ATC is alerted in the form of a blue tag on the target as well as the tag letters switching to CST. ATC will readily recognize when an aircraft enters 'Coast Mode'.

ACARS CONFIRMED - 9/11 AIRCRAFT AIRBORNE LONG AFTER CRASH

UNITED 175 IN THE VICINITY OF HARRISBURG AND PITTSBURGH, PA

(PilotsFor911Truth.org) - Aircraft Communications Addressing and Reporting System (ACARS) is a device used to send messages to and from an aircraft. Very similar to text messages and email we use today, Air Traffic Control, the airline itself, and other airplanes can communicate with each other via this "texting" system. ACARS was developed in 1978 and it still used today. Similar to cell phone networks, the ACARS network has remote ground stations installed around the world to route messages from ATC, the airline, etc, to the aircraft depending on it's location and vice versa. ACARS Messages have been provided through the Freedom Of Information Act (FOIA) which demonstrate that the aircraft received messages through ground stations located in Harrisburg, PA, and then later routed through a ground station in Pittsburgh. 20 minutes after the aircraft allegedly impacted the South Tower in New York. How can messages be routed through such remote locations if the aircraft was in NY, not to mention how can messages be routed to an aircraft which allegedly crashed 20 minutes earlier? Pilots For 9/11 Truth have briefly touched on this subject in 9/11: Intercepted through the excellent research of "Woody Box", who initially discovered such alarming information in the released FOIA document(s). We now have further information which confirms the aircraft was not in the vicinity of New York City when the attacks occurred. read more...

For many students of 9/11, their brains shut off at the very idea, even though Pilots for 9/11 Truth have established that Flight 93 was in the air that day, but that it was over Champaign-Urbana, IL, after it had allegedly crashed in Shanksville; and that Flight 175 was also in the air that day, but that it was over Harrisburg and Pittsburgh, PA, long after it had purportedly hit the South Tower. This means that the videos we have seen of the planes hitting the North and the South Towers involved some form of fakery, as I have repeatedly explained.

It won't do to suggest that real planes of any kind–such as drones or special military aircraft–were used for that purpose, since their entry involved no loss in velocity in violation of Newton's third law. And, as Jack White, a legendary student of JFK, who turned his attention to 9/11, discovered, the engine component found at Church & Murray was under a steel scaffolding, sitting on a relatively undamaged sidewalk, and was the wrong make to have come from a Boeing 767. He also found FOX NEWS footage of men in FBI vests unloading something heavy from a white van, which would have come as sensational news, had Richard Gage made observations of this kind on C-SPAN:

Pickup or delivery?

Newsworthy things were happening on 9-11 at Church and Murray, so Fox News was there. An FBI van is parked on Murray at the Church intersection, door open. An FBI agent stands guard over something not seen in other photos at this location. Blue-clad FBI agents appear beside the van and seem to struggle with something heavy. There appear to be six FBI agents and a photographer in the video frames. Another image taken at the deserted corner, right, shows a dolly used for moving something. What does the complete video show...a pickup or delivery?

That no plane crashed in Shanksville should be apparent to anyone who has seen what a real plane crash looks like, such as the downing of the

"Malaysian 17" in Ukraine. While that case is fascinating in its own right, the proof that we were mislead about the Pentagon extends from violation of laws of aerodynamics and physics entailed by the official flight trajectory to the more obvious consideration that the plane shown in the one frame that the Pentagon claims to show "the plane", when compared to the image of a Boeing 757 (properly sized for comparison) was far too small to have been a Boeing 757:

Issues about the planes would be overwhelmingly more interesting to the public than talking about red-and-grey chips found in the dust, especially when–even if they were *bona fide* nanothermite–cannot possibly explain how the Twin Towers were destroyed. That none of the 9/11 aircraft actually crashed and none of the passengers aboard them died is an entirely different matter, because it proves the entire "War on Terror" was a fabrication. Too many in the movement seem to forget that a half-dozen or more of the "suicide hijackers" turned up alive and well the following day. Gage not only made none of the obvious points made here but implied that the 9/11 aircraft were real. Either way, issues are raised about his competence or his integrity.

Who was responsible and why?

More disturbing than his failure to discuss the planes that did not crash– and to imply that they were real–was his utter incapacity to answer simple, direct questions about who and why. 9/11 dates from the collapse of the Soviet Union in 1990-91, which left the military-industrial complex without a boogie man to pacify the American public with regard to the "peace dividend" it would never see and a new threat to keep the taxpayer's billions coming into their coffers. It involved collusion between the CIA, the Neocons in the Department of Defense and the Mossad, where Israel would come out of 9/11 as "the big winner".

During The Vancouver Hearings, Susan Lindauer revealed inside infor-mation that 9/11 was an "inside job." She served as the liaison between the CIA and Saddam Hussein, who was so eager to avoid war with the U.S. that he offered to purchase 1,000,000 cars per year for the next ten years. If that was not enough, he said, make it the next twenty! Imagine where the U.S. would be economically if we had only taken up his propo-

sal? Instead, when Susan learned of plans to attack Iraq, she protested vigorously to President Bush. For taking that step, for speaking out about her concerns over the injustice of it all, she was harassed, intimidated, imprisoned and tortured.

9/11 was conceived as an elaborate psychological operation to instill fear into the American people in order to manipulate them into supporting the political agenda of the Bush/Cheney administration, which included the invasion of several nations in the Middle East to bring about the creation of a new century of American domination of the world for the next 100 years. The evidence supports the inference that 9/11 was a "national security event" which was authorized at the highest levels of the American government–the CIA, the NSA, the Pentagon and The White House. It facilitated a reversal of US foreign policy and extraordinary constraints on the Constitution of the United States, which have dramatically increased the centralization of political power in the executive branch and dominating the legislative and judicial branches of government.

The creation of the Department of Homeland Security has been especially ominous, where DHS has now requisitioned more than 2 billion rounds of .40 caliber hollow point ammo, which is not even permissible in the conduct of warfare under The Geneva Conventions. Combined with more than 300 FEMA camps around the country, every American should be alarmed at the parallels with the rise of The Third Reich in Germany before WWII. As a former Marine Corps officer, I am extremely apprehensive over the future of my country, which has been transformed from the most admired and respected nation in the world–along with our "gallant ally"' in the Middle East, Israel–to being the most despised and reviled. By 2014, Richard Gage should have known these things, which makes his silence about them all the more telling.

Source note: This chapter originally appeared as "On C-SPAN, Richard Gage leaves 9/11 Truth in a 'time-warp'", *veteranstoday.com* (4 August 2014).

Epilogue

Richard Gage, A&E911 and the *Journal of 9/11 Studies*

by Jim Fetzer and Dennis Cimino

Ryan's book ... confirm(s) my impression that Steve Jones, Kevin Ryan and Richard Gage are the core of a limited hang-out designed to contain the breadth and depth of 9/11 research"–Jim Fetzer

In my critique of Richard Gage on C-SPAN, I faulted him especially for offering an answer to the question of HOW that was provably false–the myth of explosive nanothermite.

I also faulted A&E911 for its failure to address the WHO and the WHY, which are ingredients that are essential to constructing a narrative about 9/11 for the American public.

There are going to be those who respond that I have overlooked Kevin Ryan's recent book, *Another Nineteen* (2013) and, on that basis, claim that it proves I am wrong.

But the meaning and implications of Ryan's book, including its own subtitle, "Investigating Legitimate 9/11 Suspects", instead confirm my impression that Steve Jones, Kevin Ryan and Richard Gage are the core of a limited hang-out designed to contain the breadth and depth of 9/11 research.

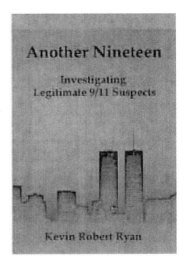

399

As the author's bio explains, *Kevin Ryan is co-editor of the Journal of 9/11 Studies and a whistleblower from Underwriters Laboratories. He has contributed to many books and scientific articles on the subject of 9/11, and has made presentations around the U.S. and Canada. He has appeared on National Public Radio, Air America Radio, Pacifica Radio, C-SPAN Book TV, Free Speech TV, and Colorado Public Television.* His views are taken seriously by a large percent of the 9/11 Truth community. The question is whether they ought to be.

The original nineteen

Wikipedia summarizes the official account, where "the hijackers in the September 11 attacks were 19 men affiliated with al-Qaeda, and 15 of the 19 were citizens of Saudi Arabia. The others were from the United Arab Emirates (2), Egypt and Lebanon. The hijackers were organized into four teams, each led by a pilot-trained hijacker with four 'muscle hijackers' who were trained to help subdue the pilots, passengers, and crew". Their images have been widely published in many places, even though their identities have never been confirmed:

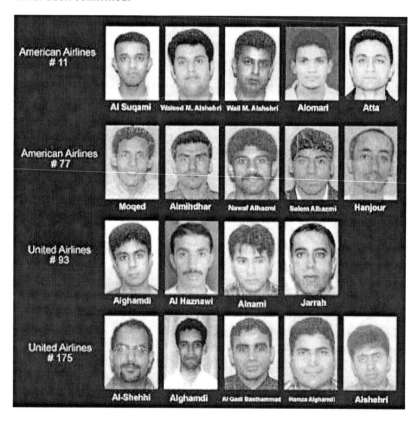

Their names were released by the FBI on 27 September 2001, by the FBI Director, Robert Mueller, allegedly based upon the passenger manifests. But that claim is indefensible on multiple grounds, including that, as David Ray Griffin has observed in The 9/11 Commission Report: Omissions and Distortions (2005), page 23, no Arab name appears on the manifests published by CNN and the airlines have refused to release the originals. Efforts to explain this away are transparently contrived, suggesting, for example, that they were "victims lists" rather than "passenger lists", when the airlines would only have known who was aboard their planes, not their roles.

The names almost certainly originated with the Mossad since, as Wayne Madsen has reported, the Mossad was running the "hijackers" to make sure their whereabouts were known and to lay a trail of evidence implicating them in the crimes of 9/11. Moreover, since a half-dozen or more of the alleged "hijackers" turned up alive and well–but scared out of their minds– the following day, as Griffin also observes (pages 19-23), claims about any "suicide hijackers" are dubious *unless they could survive their own death and then appear the following day!*

The "other" nineteen

Since the "original" nineteen are clearly fabrications (where the evidence suggests that none of those aircraft actually crashed on 9/11), it would be a good thing if Kevin Ryan were to point us in the direction of the real perps who brought us 9/11. It could not have been Osama bin Laden, no matter how many times it may benefit an administration to revive a man who died on 15 December 2001 for the sake of promoting a political agenda. Thus, David Chandler, who publishes in the Journal of 9/11 Studies, offers this concise summary overview:

Most Helpful Customer Reviews

145 of 152 people found the following review helpful

☆☆☆☆☆ **A Masterpiece of Deep Reporting** July 3, 2013

By David Chandler

Format: Paperback

How much do you know about Vice President Dick Cheney, Secretary of Defense Donald Rumsfeld, Frank Carlucci of the Carlyle Group, Deputy Secretary of State Richard Armitage, FBI Director Louis Freeh, CIA Director George Tenet, "Counterterrorism Czar" Richard Clarke, FAA hijack coordinator Michael Canavan, FAA Command Center operations manager Benedict Sliney, General Ralph Eberhart of NORAD, Carl Truscott of the Secret Service, former CIA Director John Deutch, Undersecretary of Defense John Hamre, Deputy Secretary of Defense Paul Wolfowitz, Peter Janson of AMEC Construction, Iraq Occupation Governor L. Paul Bremer, National Commission on Terrorism Advisor Brian Michael Jenkins, Wirt Walker of KuwAm Corp., Barry McDaniel of Stratesec, New York Mayor Rudy Giuliani, Duane Andrews of SAIC, Congressman Porter Goss (That's more than 19, and there are actually more mentioned in the book.)

Do you know about Richard Clarke's close ties with the United Arab Emirates? Did you know that L. Paul Bremer's parent company occupied the exact floors where the North Tower was struck by Flight 11, or that another company Bremer directed patented a thermite demolition device? This book provides extensive background on many key individuals and connects the dots. A common objection to the idea of insider participation in 9/11 is that people cannot imagine Americans who would actually do such a thing. This book makes insider participation much more understandable and believable. The result is not to close the book on who did 9/11; it rather opens the book, exposes the players, and calls for a real investigation. It is a masterpiece of deep reporting.

While I am not disputing that many of those Ryan names appear to have played key roles on 9/11, especially in the Pentagon (to make sure that there would be no military response by attempting to intercept the four "hijacked" airlines), there is a conspicuous absence of those who arranged for the transfer of the World Trade Center into private hands for the first time since it was opened in 1970–*where the events of 9/11 would take place just six weeks later*–and of those "managing" the hijackers, which means that he excludes some of the other most important players. But Dick Cheney and Donald Rumsfeld *are* among the most important few.

A mountain of evidence substantiates that 9/11 was a national security event, which involved collusion between the CIA, the Neocons in the Pentagon and the Mossad. Given the crucial role of the Mossad in looking after the "original nineteen", *Kevin Ryan seems to be oblivious to the role of Israel in 9/11*. Many military/intel experts have observed there were only two agencies in the world capable of pulling this off: the CIA and the Mossad, which were collaborating in this instance. The indications of complicity by American Zionists and other agents of Israel is simply overwhelming, but you would not know that from Kevin Ryan's book on "another nineteen".

The Kevin Ryan "Paradox"

Adam Syed has published a fascinating study of (what he refers to as) "the Kevin Ryan paradox", namely: the stance that the way to show the 9/11 official story is false is by accepting as much of it as possible as true. Right off the bat, it should be apparent that something is wrong. After all, if The 9/11 Commission Report (2004) or NIST has anything right, then it would be indefensible to claim that its true claims are untrue. What he seems to be implying is that, in any case where there is room for doubt, the benefit should go to the government account.

That ignores the difference between *accepting a conclusion, rejecting a conclusion* and *leaving it in suspense* (by neither accepting it as true nor rejecting it as false). What could be more obvious? Moreover, it is essential to do your own research in order to be in the position to appraise what you are being told in a document such as The *9/11 Commission Report* (2004). For an appropriate parallel, consider *The Warren Commission Report* (1964) of 40 years earlier. Lee Harvey Oswald was not only not "the lone assassin" but wasn't even a shooter!

The Kevin Ryan paradox: the way to show the 9/11 official story is false is by accepting as much of it as possible

By Adam Syed (Special to Truth and Shadows)

As Syed reports, Ryan says he favors this strategy for the sake of "simplicity" and to avoid "adding unnecessary complications." The problem is that he often achieves just the opposite – adding complications and muddying the waters. My first tinge of alarm came upon reading the book's introduction: "For simplicity, this alternative conspiracy should accept as much of the official account as possible, *including that the alleged hijackers were on the planes.*" This is extremely disturbing and is an excuse to beg serious questions about 9/11.

Problems with the Planes

Syed continues, "This is not the book's only such passage. On the first page of Chapter 10, which deals with the Pentagon portion of 9/11, he says: "Considering means, motive and opportunity might allow us to propose a possible insider conspiracy *while maintaining much of the official account as well.*" But the evidence is all against the hijackers being real, the planes having been commandeered or even having actually crashed. Consider some of the most important research on these questions, which Ryan attempts to finesse:

(1) Elias Davidsson has demonstrated that the government has never been able to show that any of the alleged hijackers was aboard any of those planes in "There is no evidence that Muslims committed the crime of 9/11";

(2) A.K. Dewdney has established that then-available cell phones were useless above 2,000' altitude and speeds over 200 mph: the towers transmitted horizontally and could not relay the messages rapidly enough;

(3) Dewdney and David Ray Griffin have demonstrated that all of the

phone calls allegedly made from the 9/11 aircraft were fabricated or faked, where none of them was authentic: "Phone Calls from the 9/11 Airliners";

(4) Col. George Nelson, USAF (ret.), has observed that, of the millions of uniquely identifiable component parts of those four airplanes, the government has yet to produce even one: "Impossible to Prove a Falsehood True";

(5) Leslie Raphael has demonstrated that, for the "French film crew" to have been in the right position to film the first strike, a hundred improbable factors had to have converged: "Jules Naudet's 9/11 Film was Staged";

(6) Killtown, among other, has shown the virtual absence of any proof that Flight 93 crashed in Shanksville, where Pilots for 9/11 Truth have established it was over Champaign-Urbana, IL, after it had allegedly crashed;

(7) the videos of Flight 175 entering the South Tower display feats that no real plane could perform, while Pilots have established that it was over Harrisburg and Pittsburgh, PA, long after it had allegedly hit the tower; and,

(8) FAA Registration Records show that the planes used for Flight 93 and 175 were not formally taken out of service (or "deregistered") until 28 September 2005, which would be impossible had they crashed in 2001.

Indeed, since Bureau of Transportation Statistics records show that Flight 11 (North Tower) and Flight 93 (the Pentagon) were not even scheduled that day, how could planes that were not in the air have crashed on 9/11? and how could planes that crashed on 9/11 have still be in the air four years later?

Ryan is not only begging the question by taking for granted the answer to crucial questions about 9/11 but has ignored a mountain of proof that his position is wholly and hopelessly untenable because it has already been proven to be false.

The box that Didn't Squawk

Adam Syed has done a masterful job of debunking Kevin Ryan's position, including, for example, the issue of precisely why, if real hijackers really were aboard those planes, none of the pilots had signaled that their planes were in the process of being commandeered by hijackers, for which there are well-established procedures. Here is his critique of how he attempts to explain the inexplicable by adding complications and muddying the water:

> *Some 9/11 researchers, particularly David Ray Griffin, have provided strong cumulative evidence that there were no hijackers on the alleged planes. One example that shows Griffin to be superior to Ryan as an analyst of evidence involves the issue of "hijack codes," namely, the code that a pilot would "squawk" back to the FAA in the event of an actual hijacking.*

> *In his New Pearl Harbor Revisited, Griffin addresses this issue. He quotes a passage from the 9/11 Commission Report that says: "FAA... assumed that the aircraft pilot would notify the controller via radio or by "squawking" a transponder code of "7500" – the universal code for a hijack in progress."*

> *Griffin then goes on to explain how all four planes did not squawk the hijack code. He then alludes to a famous Sherlock Holmes mystery story, "Silver Blaze," in which a famous racehorse disappeared the night before a big race. Holmes disputed a police investigator's belief that an outside intruder had stolen the horse: the guard dog never barked during the night. Had an outside intruder stolen the horse, the dog would have barked.*

> *Griffin then concludes: "Just as the intruder theory was disproved by the dog that didn't bark, the hijacker theory is disproved by the pilots who didn't squawk." (NPHR, p. 178) (It is important to remember that while I am isolating this issue of the hijack codes, it is just one of many pieces of evidence presented in Griffin's research which points to a "no hijacker" scenario.)*

> *So how does Kevin Ryan address this same issue? Looking at the index of Another Nineteen, we find one mention of the hijack codes on page 125. On this page, the issue is mentioned in the context of a list of facts as to why NORAD commander Ralph Eberhart should be a prime suspect for 9/11 culpability:*

> *8. For whatever reasons, Eberhart also gave false information about the NORAD response to others. General Richard Meyers, acting CJCS that*

morning, said that Eberhart told him there were "several hijack codes in the system." Yet none of the four planes had squawked the hijack code on 9/11 and therefore it is not clear how such codes could have been in the system.

While Griffin's analysis makes perfect logical sense (and in so doing, achieves the kind of "simplicity" that Ryan professes to desire), Ryan's analysis muddies the waters and leaves the readers scratching their heads in confusion.

Ryan's analysis seems to hinge on the idea that real hijackings were taking place, and that of course the hapless pilots would indeed have squawked the codes if only they were in the system.

While Ryan stated at the book's outset that we should accept that "the alleged hijackers" were on the planes, passages like the above go further, and promote the idea that these Middle Eastern men were conducting a genuine terrorist hijacking. (Without stating it explicitly, Ryan's analysis seems to insinuate that the hijack codes might have been disabled or removed from the four flights in question so that the hijackings could be successful; in other words, a "LIHOP" [let it happen on purpose] scenario, whereby US officials took steps to allow a terrorist hijacking to take place.)

As Syed observes, Kevin Ryan's scenario is not only confusing in attributing far more sophistication to the purported hijackers than anyone would suppose they deserve (in light of their modest experience with piloting aircraft) but implies that they gained access to the planes (including those that were not scheduled that day) and that they successfully hijacked them and caused them to crash, in spite of a mountain of proof to the contrary.

The Journal of 9/11 Studies

Kevin Ryan is also co-editor of the Journal of 9/11 Studies, as I have previously observed. But the journal has published a series of studies that support the conclusion that the Pentagon was hit by a large aircraft, which of course is supposed to be Flight 77 (even though BTS records initially showed that neither it nor Flight 11 were scheduled to fly that day). Here is a sample of articles from the Journal, including several on the Pentagon:

The Pentagon Attack: Problems with Theories Alternative to Large Plane Impact John D. Wyndham, December 2011

Why Australia's Presence in Afghanistan is Untenable James O'Neill, February 2011

Flight AA77 on 9/11: New FDR Analysis Supports the Official Flight Path
Leading to Impact with the Pentagon Frank Legge and Warren Stutt,
January 2011

Falsifiability and the NIST WTC Report: A Study in Theoretical Adequacy
Anonymous and F. Legge, March 2010

Destruction of the World Trade Center North Tower and Fundamental
Physics David Chandler, February 2010

Material Termítico Activo Descubierto en el Polvo Originado en la
Catástrofe del World Trade Center el 11 de Septiembre Spanish
Translation of the Harrit et al. Article, December 2009

Nachweis von reaktionsfähigem thermitischen Material im Staub der
World Trade Center- Katastrophe vom 11. September 2001 German
Translation of the Harrit et al. Article, December 2009

What Hit the Pentagon? Misinformation and its Effect on the Credibility of
9/11 Truth Dr. Frank Legge, July 2009

What are we to make of this? Here we have several on the discovery of those red-and-grey chips that are said to be nanothermite, which cannot possibly explain how the Twin Towers were blown apart in every direction but appear to function as a massive distraction to keep the 9/11 Truth community from asking, "What was used to blow them apart?", where it won't do to claim, "They never said that only nanothermite was involved!" *If the heaving lifting was done by other sources of massive energy, what were they?* For that, they have no answer.

The Pentagon is an excellent test case of the authenticity of the professed commitment of the *Journal of 9/11 Studies*, whose subtitle is "Truth matters". But when it comes to the Pentagon, there appears to be very little truth in the *Journal of 9/11 Studies*. The "official account" is neither aerodynamically nor physically possible, as I have explained many places, but that has not inhibited the *Journal of 9/11 Studies* from publishing articles that support it. Here I take just one example from the three about the Pentagon included in the sampler above:

1) In *What Hit the Pentagon? Misinformation and its Effect on the Credibility of 9/11 Truth* Dr. Frank Legge talks about "the hit point" but he does not include any photographs that display it, for the obvious reason that it makes the theory that a 100-ton airliner with a 125′ wingspan and a tail standing 40′ above the ground hit there look ridiculous. Notice the clear, green and unblemished lawn, which displays neither wings nor tail nor bodies nor seats nor luggage. Not even the engines, virtually indestructible, were recovered from the Pentagon:

(2) In *Flight AA77 on 9/11: New FDR Analysis Supports the Official Flight Path Leading to Impact with the Pentagon,* Frank Legge and Warren Stutt support the theory that a Boeing 757 struck a series of lamp posts en route to "the hit point" (above). But the effect of a plane flying over 500 mph hitting a stationary lamp post would be the same as the effect of a lamp post flying over 500 mph hitting a stationary plane: it would have ripped the wing open, the fuel would have burst into flame, and the plane would have careened on fire across the lawn, see top image on the opposite page:

(3) In *The Pentagon Attack: Problems with Theories Alternative to Large Plane Impact,* Dr. John D. Wyndham offers his summary of the evidence in this case, which does not take into account that virtually all the witness testimony appears to be fabricated and that no alleged "evidence" can overcome the laws of aerodynamics and of physics, which means that the official account cannot possibly be true, no matter how many articles *Journal of 9/11 Studies* might publish to the contrary. No competent "peer review" process could have endorsed them.

Table 1: Theory and Observation Summary

Do the Observations Support the Theory?

Observation	Large Plane Impact	Flyover and Impossible Maneuver	Flyover and North of CITGO	Small Plane Impact	Missile Impact	Bombs, Explosives
Eyewitness testimony	YES	NO	NO	NO to very little	NO	NO
Airplane debris	YES	NO	NO	NO to very unlikely	NO	NO
Overall damage path	YES	NO	NO	NO	NO	NO
Downed light poles	YES	NO	NO	NO	NO	NO
Concrete wall and trailer damage	YES	NO	NO	NO	NO	NO
Building façade damage	YES	NO	NO	NO to unlikely	NO	Possibly
Interior columns damage & debris	YES	NO	NO	NO to unlikely	NO	NO
C Ring hole	YES	NO	NO	Possibly	Possibly	Possibly

The alleged "witnesses" at the Pentagon–more than 80 in number–are fascinating subjects of analysis on their own, where Mike Sparks, who has an extensive background in military and defense matters, and I went through the list and appraised their credibility.

The overwhelming majority were either not in the position to have seen what they claim to have seen or offered testimony that was either too vague or too ambiguous to be of forensic value.

And how can Wyndham remotely reasonably dismiss the very significant findings of CIT? Unbelievable!

It took six hours for Mike and me to cover them all on 4 January, 18 January, and 1 February 2010.

On capturing the public's attention

Suppose that, instead of talking about a non-explosive incendiary that emits bright light and high temperatures but has virtually no explosive force, Richard Gage had explained that, on 9/11, Israel nuked New York; or that the evidence confirms that no plane crashed in Shanksville or hit the Pentagon; and that, what was shown on television across the nation was images of planes hitting the North and South Tower, which were performing feats that no real plane could perform? Or that 9/11 was brought to us by the CIA, Neocons in the Department of Defense and the Mossad?

One of the most surprising discoveries in relation to those three Pentagon studies is that Frank Legge actually includes a photograph of the most interesting piece of debris, which actually came from a Boeing 757. But the crash in this case occurred in Buga, Columbia, which some refer to as Cali. The plane hit the side of a mountain and passed through jungle terrain, during which it was ripped from the fuselage and entangled a piece of vine. I have published about this many times, but this journal's authors apparently only read each other's articles :

What can be said about Richard Gage, A&E911 and the *Journal of 9/11 Studies*? Even on C-SPAN, Richard Gage is promoting a false theory about explosive nanothermite, which has been indefensible at least since 2011

when T. Mark Hightower and I began publishing about it. A&E911, in its documentary, "Explosive Evidence", strikes the same note, where they allow for the use of "other explosives" but have shown no inclination to pursue them, perhaps because they appear to have been micro or mini nukes, which might excite the attention of the public.

So they do a poor job with respect to the question, "HOW was it done?" In relation to the questions of WHO and WHY, which Gage and A&E911 tend to eschew altogether, Kevin Ryan has published, Another Nineteen (2013), which invited attention to some worthy suspects. But he does not explain that 9/11 was brought to us with the compliments of the CIA, the Neocons and the Mossad. It is difficult to avoid the inference that all is not well with respect to 9/11 Truth, because its ostensive leaders do not seem to be aggressively pursuing truth.

The Pentagon serves as an appropriate litmus test. Dennis Cimino and I have published a number of articles on what did and did not happen there (some as early as 2009), where proof that no Boeing 757 hit the building is abundant and compelling. While I am not surprised when the BBC produces a documentary that supports the "official account" of the Pentagon, it simply astounds me that the Journal of 9/11 Truth publishes articles that could have come from the government itself. Truth *does* matter, but we are not getting truth from any of these sources, who, I regret to say, appear to have an agenda that diverges substantially from advancing 9/11 Truth.

Source note: This chapter originally appeared as "Limited Hangouts: Richard Gage, A&E911 and the Journal of 9/11 Studies", *veteranstoday.com* (14 August 2014).

Afterword

The BBC's instrument of 9/11 misinformation

by Jim Fetzer and Joshua Blakeney

For a second time, the BBC television network has produced a documentary about 9/11 featuring Dylan Avery, the producer of "Loose Change"'; Alex Jones, the talk show host; and me, the Founder of Scholars  for 9/11 Truth—this time accompanied by Neils Harrit, a chemistry professor from Denmark.

The program is part of the BBC's "Conspiracy Files" series. The first installment is available here. This one, now entitled, "The Conspiracy Files: '9/11: Ten Years On'", was initially accessible at the following link: *http:// www.youtube.com/watch?v=oV_R70Qo8Zc&feature=share*

Interestingly, not long after it had been posted, the "user" had it removed from YouTube, which is not an effective method for disseminating your message. Presumably, it will soon be up and running again, which we will archive and then link to this column.

The inclusion of Neils Harrit is especially striking, since he was the lead author on the nanothermite study published in the *Bentham Science Open Chemical Physics Journal*, which T. Mark Hightower and I have discussed in several articles here at VT, including "Is '9/11 Truth' based upon a false theory?" and "Nanothermite: If it doesn't fit, you must acquit".

413

Since I believe there are real problems with (what Mark Hightower and I have called) "the myth of explosive nanothermite", the BBC may have missed an opportunity to pit us against one another. Neil's statements about the use of nanothermite, however, have

actually been more responsible than those that have come from and been supported by the "hard science" group.

So the focus of this discussion will be on some of the more blatant problems with "9/11: Ten Years On". Here I (and Joshua Blakeney) will offer several striking illustrations of the BBC's "sleight-of-hand" in misrepresenting key points that I explained to Guy Smith and to Mike Rudin, which they cannot possibly have misunderstood, where cases like these leave no doubt of that the BBC in its "Conspiracy Files" series functions as an instrument of disinformation.

We will also cite examples that exemplify other especially notable demonstrations that the BBC's duplicity is not limited to its presentation of ersatz documentaries like these but extends into its reporting of news as it happens, which we illustrate with Jane Standley's premature reporting of the collapse of WTC-7 on 9/11 and the introduction of Richard Clarke's efforts to revive the indefensible theory that "9/11 was due to incompetence".

[NOTE: I use the first-person pronoun to accent that "I was there" and know these things based upon my "up close and personal" experience, but I am grateful to Joshua Blakeney for his contributions here, especially relative to the so-called "Global War on Terror".

Joshua recently drew to my attention a seminal text edited by Benjamin Netanyahu entitled *Terrorism: How the West Can Win* (1986), which we discussed during our two-hour interview on my 31 August 2011 radio show (and will be archived at *http://radiofetzer.blogspot.com/*).

I agree with Joshua that this book appears to be offering a blueprint for the "Global War on Terror" already in 1986, which should quality as a central piece of evidence about the true origins of that war and a hint of whom it most benefits. (A version of this article with active links can be found here.)]

BBC's "Conspiracy Files"

This was my second encounter with the BBC, whose director, Guy Smith, came to Madison and interviewed me for eight hours for its previous segment on 9/11, which also featured Dylan, Alex, and me. This segment has also been archived at *http://www.youtube.com/watch?v=lMyKhVwj6GI &feature=related*, where there can be little doubt that the BBC is attempting to trade in stereotypes and that Dylan is supposed to be the obnoxious kid, Alex a messianic preacher, and me the kooky professor.

While some may even agree, especially about me, this is an obvious attempt to suggest the only possible reasons that anyone would dissent from the "official account" of 9/11 are emotional needs or cognitive impairments. The 9/11 movement is actually highly eclectic with members of varied backgrounds and qualifications. That we might actually be right and the official account wrong was tacitly denied.

During both interviews, I presented literally dozens and dozens of arguments about why the "official account" of 9/11 is not only indefensible but actually violates laws of physics, engineering and aerodynamics. The fires burned neither hot enough nor long enough to have caused the steel to weaken, much less melt. WTC-7 displays all the features of a classic "controlled demolition".

There is no evidence that a Boeing 757 crashed in Pennsylvania and clear and convincing proof that the Pentagon "hit" was a fabrication, which appears to include the flyover by a plane simulating Flight 77 at the same time as the detonation of explosions. Later in the day, the Hollywood-style production of billowing black smoke from fires deliberately set in a series of dumpsters was deployed in order to intimidate the members of Congress. (See "Seven Questions about 9/11", *Veterans Today.*)

For the first show, the BBC extracted about 7.5 minutes they wanted to use from my interview, which it combined with about 4 minutes of Alex and 3.5 minutes of Dylan. The rest of the program was used to misrepresent and undermine what we had told them, where logic and evidence were not their concern.

By offering psychoanalyses of 9/11 skeptics, rather than engaging the evidence that refutes the official story of 9/11, the makers of the BBC's 9/11 documentary harnessed the same tactics employed by journalist Jonathan Kay, author of *Among the Truthers* (2011), and by Michael Shermer, an ersatz-professor, who was exposed for having mischaracterized his credentials by Anthony Hall and Joshua Blakeney.

Their focus was upon the psychology of beliefs that are, according to their point of view, not merely weird but even bizarre—which is certainly true, unless you take a serious look at the evidence. (See "Why doubt 9/11?" for 20 counter-examples.)

The Ground Floor "Hit"

The Pentagon is an especially nice example, where I explained in both interviews that the alleged "hit" point is on the ground floor and not the second as has often been alleged. *Both programs, nevertheless, misrepresented its location by using photos of the*

second floor, which has to have been intentional, given that I had explained this point to Guy Smith and to Mike Rudin during their separate visits. They even use animations of this inaccurate location in their animations of its occurrence, which is inconsistent with the photos that are presented correctly in both "What didn't happen at the Pentagon" and in "Seven Questions about 9/11".

It makes an enormous difference to understanding what happened there, since, at the ground-floor location, we find a chain-link fence, two huge spools of cable, two somewhat damaged cars and unbroken windows beside and above the entry hole, which is only about 10' high and 16-17' wide—far too small for a 100-ton airliner that is 155' long with a 125' wingspan, and a tail that stands 44' above the ground. There is no debris: no wings, no tail, no fuselage, no bodies, seats or luggage. Neither of the virtually indestructible engines was recovered. But the fact that this mass of debris is missing is

obfuscated by the simple but effective technique of presenting the wrong photos. You have to admire the elegance of the plan.

It has been said that the absence of evidence is not evidence of absence, which is true—*except in those cases where it is false.* If you were to inspect the living room of your home, for example, the absence of evidence of the presence of an elephant would properly qualify as evidence of the absence of an elephant from your living room. Similarly, *the absence of evidence that a plane—in particular, a Boeing 757—crashed at the Pentagon is evidence that no Boeing 757 crashed there.* So one of the most important indications of BBC duplicity is that, although I had explained to Guy Smith and to Mike Rudin that the actual "hit point" was on the ground floor, they continued to use images of the second floor in their work.

The clear, green lawn

Think of the simplicity of the deception involved here. Have your target speak about the hit point (where he is talking about the ground floor "hit") but present images of another location (as if that were what he was actually discussing). And it is a technique that can be used again and again. During both interviews, I also  emphasized a photo that was taken even as the civilian lime-green fire trucks were extinguishing the very modest fires, which shows a completely clear, green, unblemished lawn, entirely free from debris of any kind. You can see that the upper portion of the building has not yet collapsed, which means it was not the effect of the alleged impact. This collapse appears to have been contrived to enhance the apparent damage to resemble more like what a hit might have caused.

In this case, the BBC contracted the time line and claimed that the upper floors had collapsed "within minutes" of the hit, *showing images of building AFTER the collapse.* Since 25-30 minutes is "within minutes", there was a flimsy

pretext to justify using that phrase. But there is now considerable debris in the foreground and *the lawn is no longer pristine.* The effect, once again, was to use my voice explaining what is visible in the photo that I was discussing but juxtaposed with film from the subsequent collapse of the upper floors that I was not discussing, which was clearly intended to convey the impression that I did not know what I was talking about—a simple but effective technique, which they employed repeatedly.

Ironically, some of the BBC's own footage substantiated my observations about the completely clear, green, unblemished lawn, entirely free from debris of any kind.

But it would have taken a discerning viewer to overcome the emphasis imparted by the soothing, confident voice of the BBC's commentator, who conveyed the impression of objectivity and impartiality while nevertheless debunking what I had said in nuanced and subtle ways. That this footage actually appeared in this documentary came as a surprise to me, once I had sorted out their technique of implicitly contradicting what I had to say by the presentation of images other than those that I was addressing, since this one actually confirmed what I had explained.

Lt. Col. O'Brien and the C-130

The difference between the originally clear, green and unblemished lawn, which was free from debris, and the subsequent appearance of debris across a broad swath of the Pentagon lawn led me to speculate as to its origins. It would have been awkward and obvious to have enlisted men and officers carry debris out onto the lawn. It had to have been done in a more subtle fashion.

A C-130 had been circling the building, which led me to consider the possibility that perhaps the debris had been dropped from the plane, where its settling down from above would be something that many observers might regard as an effect from the hit, where it would not be unexpected for at least some debris to have been airborne.

So the BBC featured Lt. Col. O'Brien, USAF, who was presented as the captain of the C-130, who feigned to be disgusted with the implication that he could have been involved in the cover-up by having debris dropped from his plane. Since it was circling

as the allegedly hijacked plane approached the building, it appears to be a good question why the Pentagon was surprised by the hit.

Surely the Lt. Colonel could have warned them, insofar as he reported that he had watched its approach. Apparently, the evidential value of his claiming to have seen the plane outweighed the implied admission that he had failed to warn his superiors, since all sides alleged that the Pentagon had no idea it was going to be hit—when the plane would most certainly have been shot down, had such a warning occurred.

If there is a better explanation of the source of the debris, what could it possibly be? Those who harbor lingering doubts about the role of the BBC as a purveyor of disinformation should study these photographs and compare them to "What didn't happen at the Pentagon?" and "Seven Questions about 9/11". Then watch the show, when it is accessible again— perhaps in a new version in response to the public's reaction to the original, which I am discussing here. We all have to appreciate the role of the mass media in distorting 9/11, where the phrase "info wars" has been used by Alex Jones to convey exactly the right impression. And this is not the first time that the BBC has been "caught with its pants down", since an earlier and possibly even more spectacular illustration occurred on 9/11 itself.

Jane Standley on WTC-7

One of the most remarkable events of the day of 9/11 was the premature report by Jane Standley of the BBC that "the Solomon Brothers Building"— another name for WTC-7—had collapsed, which of course did happen that day, but she claimed it had happened at 4:57 PM/ET, when in fact that did not occur until 5:20 PM/ET, 23 minutes later!

This has to be one of the most stunning illustrations of the dual role of the mass media in presenting news as it happens but with a spin dictated by the intelligence assets and the government agencies who control access to what the public is going to see and hear.

Since WTC-7 can actually be seen over her left shoulder (to the right as a viewer watches her presentation), there can be no doubt that the BBC got "ahead of the script", which may even be the single most glaring example of complicity between MI-5 and the BBC in the nation's history.

Another example of the spin that the BBC was offering in its "Conspiracy Files: '9/11: Ten Years On'" program, is that, toward its conclusion, Richard Clarke, the Bush/Cheney administration's "anti-terrorism" expert, attempts to revive the long-discounted theory that these attacks occurred only because of incompetence by the agencies who were responsible for protecting the country from terrorist attacks like these, including communication and cooperation failures by the CIA and the FBI.

But this theory cannot account for the physical impossibility of the Twin Towers to have been destroyed by the purported plane crashes, the resulting (very modest) fires, and the weakening of the steel, none of which—even had they happened as the official account proclaims—could have brought about the complete, total, and abrupt demolition sequence that would occur, which can be viewed relative to the North Tower in "New 9/11 Photos Released", for example, on my blog.

9/11 was clearly cleverly planned, including a variety of false leads, some of which were discernible in the original broadcasts from the networks that day. As Preston James and I explain in "Peeling the 9/11 Onion: Layers of Plots within Plots", the first suggestions presented by the media were intended to lay blame on Palestinians, of which we have three major indications: the image of cheering Palestinians broadcast as these events were unfolding; anchors reporting that "The Democratic Front for the Liberation of Palestine" was claiming credit; and the statements to the officers arresting the "Dancing Israelis" in their white van from Urban Moving Systems, a Mossad asset, whose driver said,

"We are Israelis. We are not your problem. Your problems are our problems. The Palestinians are your problem."

That was hokum then and remains hokum now, where three of the five would return to Israel and explain on TV that they were there "to document" the destruction of the Twin Towers, which obviously implies prior knowledge that it was going to occur.

The "Global War on Terrorism"

The BBC's propaganda for the 9/11 wars largely rests on the empirically flawed-assumption that there is a disproportionate threat posed to citizens of the U.S., Britain, Canada and elsewhere by Islamist terrorists. Yet, data posted on the FBI's official website demonstrates that actual cases of Islamic terrorism are rare, making it a virtually negligible phenomenon. According to FBI statistics, between 1980 and 2005, for example, only 6% of reported terrorist acts in the U.S. were committed by Muslims, compared to 7% by Jewish extremists, 42% by Latino extremists, and 24% by extreme right-wing groups (sometimes misidentified as "left wing", but including local and state-wide militias).

The BBC has been highly instrumental in reinforcing the falsehood that Islamists were responsible for the events of 9/11, which in turn justifies their scrutinizing of Muslims at home and abroad. Bear in mind that, if there were no planes to hijack, there would have been no hijackers, and if there were no Islamic hijackers, then 9/11 could not have been used to justify the "War on Terror" and a "clash of civilizations" pitting the Judeo-Christian West against radical Islam.

Elias Davidsson has demonstrated that the American government has not been able to prove that any of the alleged hijackers were aboard any of these planes, where Flight 11 and Flight 77 were not even scheduled to fly that day. The BBC has done its part by persistently covering-up evidence demonstrating that those alleged hijackers engaged in egregiously un-Islamic activities in the months prior to 9/11, including snorting cocaine, attending strip clubs, eating pork and drinking Vodka.

These activities imply that either they were not Muslim at all or, at least, if they were, they were not devote Muslims and therefore most unlikely to engage in fanatical acts on behalf of their religion. Suicidal hijackings are not the kind of actions we would expect from Muslims who take pleasure in strip shows, eating pork and snorting coke! As the phrase has it, "What's wrong with this picture?"

Wayne Madsen has released British intelligence documents purporting to prove that "the Israeli Mossad ran the Arab hijacker cells that were later blamed by the U.S. government's 9/11 Commission for carrying out the aerial attacks on the World Trade Center and Pentagon", which is very plausible, given what we know about the motives that appear to have contributed to its planning and execution, which involve oil, Israel, and ideology, which were interrelated. Reconfiguring the Middle East through the implementation of the Sharon Doctrine could then result in the construction of a pipeline through Israel to the Mediterranean Sea — which it could tap to solve its energy needs— and facilitate the despoliation of Iraqi oil.

Taking out Saddam Hussein and converting Iraq into smaller states (or "statelets") based on ethnic and religious sectarianism, moreover, appears to be part and parcel of a master plan for the destabilization of the Middle East to create a new reign of Israeli supremacy and domination.

What does it mean?

Reluctance to report well-documented Israeli involvement in 9/11 may explain the metamorphosis of the once highly respected BBC into a propaganda organ of the Likudnik right and its allies. The network, officially an agency of the British state, lost many of its best reporters as a consequence of the BBC's role in dealing with reports about and the subsequent death of Dr. David Kelley. Its erstwhile Director General (DG), Greg Dyke, appears to have been ousted and replaced in 2004 by the highly pro-Israel Mark Thompson, who, upon assuming office, made a trip to Israel with his Jewish wife to work out with Ariel Sharon the "softening" of the BBC's editorial line about the State of Israel.

A nice indication of the BBC's pro-Israel bias, by the way, was its refusal to allow a "Gaza Appeal" phone-line number to be broadcast during the 2008-2009 massacre in Gaza. With 9/11 being used primarily to facilitate the epochal process identified by sociologist James Petras as "The Globalization of Zionist Power", the BBC's infiltration by likely Mossad affiliates makes perfect sense. Thompson is now the highest paid public servant in Britain— and he influences the BBC to support the "Global War on Terror".

In doing research about the BBC and its "Conspiracy Files" series, I discovered a web page devoted to "Conspiracy Theories", in which five familiar arguments are presented and then "debunked". To offer one instructive example, it dismisses concerns about WTC-7 arising from Larry Silverstein's use of the phrase, "pull it", and the alleged ground that he was actually requesting that firemen be "pulled" from the building. Not only were there no firemen in the building at the time, but "pull it" is a term of art in the construction business.

Barry Jennings was actually in the building that morning and witnessed explosions taking place to prime it for demolition. It appears to me that any source that promotes falsehoods as blatant as these about 9/11 is unworthy of belief—which we now know includes the BBC!

The BBC's own attempt to debunk "conspiracy theories" has had an unexpected and mildly encouraging effect. More than 700 comments were posted before the comments were closed, where I found many reflecting genuine understanding of the role of the BBC in promoting false information about 9/11.

As we have found, in its biased documentaries about 9/11, its live reporting at the time, and even on a web page it has published to debunk those who are speaking the truth, the BBC has abandoned its commitment to objective and independent journalism and has become a shill for false theories and government ops. More is the pity, because it once stood as a beacon of truth that was widely admired around the world, which, as we have seen, can no longer be said on behalf of this once-great UK institution.

Source note: This chapter originally appeared as "The BBC's instrument of 9/11 misinformation", *veteranstoday.com* (3 September 2014).

INDEX

American Society of Civil Engineers (ASCE) 368
American Zionists 402
American/Israeli Public Affairs Committee (AIPAC) 74
Among the Truthers 415
"Angel is next" 75
angle-of-attack (AOA) 264
Anonymous 407
Anonymous Physicist 175, 183-184
Another Nineteen 399, 405
anti-Semitism 101, 97-106
"anti-Semitism" 101
"anti-Zionism" 101, 104
AOA (angle-of-attack) 264
Apollo 11 193
Applied Physics Letters 349
are shills covering up nukes at the WTC?
Argentine attacks 1992 and 1994 21
Armstrong, Neil 193
arrested under the PATRIOT Act 25
ASCE (American Society of Civil Engineers 368
Ashcroft, John 26, 36, 46, 56, 99
Assad, Bashar 21, 172
Assassination Science 133, 135
Atta, Mohammed 69-70
attacks on 9/11 Truth movement 289
Avery, Dylan 413, 415
Avraham, Alora 71
"Axis of Evil" 78

B

Baker, Ace 380
Balsamo claims "modified aircraft" could have performed these feats 314
Balsamo if right on plane, wrong about video fakery 314
Balsamo, Rob 290, 303-322
Balsamo's "modified plane" scenario 314-316
Balz, Dan 86
Barak, Ehud 73
Barium 7
Barium and Strontium 153-154, 157-158, 172, 394
barium nitrate 345
Barrett, Kevin 343

"Basic Point Defense" 206, 208
"bathtub" 129
BBC 233, 413-423
Beck, Glenn 98
before and after alleged impact point 130
Ben-Gurion, David 178
Bentham Science Open Chemical Physics Journal 413
Berg, Phil 40
Bernoullian theory 259-261
Biden, Joe 124
big nuke theory 175
Bin Laden, Osama 20, 32, 35, 52, 72, 76, 401
Blair, Anthony "Tony" 294
Blakeney, Joshua xv, 394, 413-423
blinding flash of light 360
blood and plasma cancers 173
Boeing 757 8, 15, 26, 106, 112, 128-130, 137, 141, 149, 205-229, 269, 271, 273, 275, 277, 279, 281, 283, 285, 287, 310, 328-329, 435
Boeing 767 28, 83, 128, 134-135, 137, 149, 310, 330, 334-335
Boldwyn, Charles 5, 102-104, 120, 199, 380
Bolton, John 100
Booker Elementary School 90-91
brain cancer 173
Bregman, Zeev 72
Bremsstrahlung 198
BTS (Bureau of Transportation Statistics) 83, 209, 404
BTS original records showing no flights scheduled 274
BTS records 297
BTS revised records showing flights scheduled 275
Buga, Columbia 225, 229, 233, 240, 410
Building 7 3
Bureau of Transportation Statistics (BTS) 83, 209, 404
Burlingame, Chuck 206
Bush, George W. 13, 23, 28, 30, 35-37, 71, 75, 82, 85, 87, 90-93, 294, 398
Buswell, Donald 101
"By way of deception shall you make war" 78

426

C

C-130 112, 227, 233, 338, 418-419
C-130H 93-94
C-SPAN 389-390, 395, 400
(CA-1) logical consistency 305
(CA-2) deductive closure 305
(CA-3) partial evidence 305
(CA-4) total evidence 305
Cali, Columbia 110, 113, 233, 410
can a nanothermite be made explosive?
334
Card, Andy 37
Carswell Air Force Base 45
Carter, Jimmy 175
Castro, Fidel 47
"Catcher's Mitt" 225, 235, 240, 244,
249, 267
*Central European Journal of Energetic
Materials* 357
Central Intelligence Agency (CIA) 76
CGI (computer generated images)
286-287
CGI fakery 187-189
CGI vs. video compositing vs.
hologram 10
Chandler, David 401-402, 407
Cheney, Dick 13, 23-24, 28, 73, 75,
92, 102, 227, 338, 402
Cheney, Richard 26, 82, 85-87, 90, 93
Chertoff, Michael 56, 73, 78, 100
Chomsky, Noam 24
Chromium 7, 161, 173, 394
Church & Murray 396
Church & Murray, wrong engine type
at 187
CIA (Central Intelligence Agency) 2,
20, 31, 55-56, 77, 397, 402, 410-411,
CIA-sponsored boogey-men 19
CIA's advanced knowledge of 9/11 27
Ciminio, Dennis xv-xvi, 109, 112,
183-202, 206-229, 231-250, 252,
296-297, 303, 307, 315, 321, 399-411
Circulation theory 255, 258
CIT (Citizen Investigation Team) 8,
247, 249, 252, 298, 369, 410
Clark, Richard 32
Clark, Wesley 12-13
Clarke, Richard 55-57, 77-78, 414

clash of civilizations 421
classic controlled demolition 173-174, 342
clear, green, unblemished Pentagon lawn 8
CNN 401
Coanda Effect 263-265
Cohen, Eliot 72, 100
collapse not even possible 4
collapse of Soviet Union 387
"collapse" 104
Collet, Ben 313
Colony Beach and Tennis Resort 91
command failure 26
comparison of explosive potential of
nanothermite with explosives 346
complicity between MI-5 and the BBC 420
computer generated images (CGI) 286-287
computer simulations (GI/GO) 318
"Confessions of a Former CIA Asset"
294-295
Conspiracy Files 233, 413, 423
"Conspiracy Files: 9/11 Ten Years On" 95
Copper and Zinc 158-161
copper oxide 357
copper-oxide/aluminum nanothermite 359
Council on Foreign Relations 72
Cover Story #1: Palestinians did it! 49-50
Cover Story #2: Arab hijackers did it! 50-51
Cover Story #3: The Pakistanis did it! 51-52
Cover Story #4: It was allowed to happen!
53-54
CPM 222-223
Crenshaw, Charles 135
cruise-type missiles 253
Cuba 24

D

Dancing Israelis 420-421
Dancing Israels 99-100
dangers of a false theory 360-361
Danner, John 246
Dave Clark aviation headset 188
Davidsson, Elias 105, 274, 292-293, 403,
421
DEA (Drug Enforcement Agency) 76
*Dead Men Talking: Consequences of
Government Lies* 297
Deagle, Bill 175
death of JFK vs. 9/11 184

Griffin, David Ray 2, 20, 51, 78, 84, 98, 105, 206, 274, 276, 293, 297, 300, 341-342, 346, 349, 351, 358, 371, 401, 403, 405

Grossman, Marc 52, 73

Ground effect 218

ground effect vs. induced drag 252-270

"Ground Zero" 339

ground-attack fighter-bombers 254

H

Haas, Richard 73

Hall, Anthony 415

Hall, Richard 299-300

Hamilton, Lee 86

hand-truck left behind 188

Hanjour, Hani 217

"Hannity & Colmes" 86

Hanson, James 113m 233

Harrit, Neils 341, 329, 339, 349, 353, 359, 391, 395, 413

Hartwell, Dean 297

"Has nanothermite been oversold to the 9/11 community?" 146, 181, 348, 353

Headroom, Max 185

Hemmer, Bill 24-25

Hendrie, Edward 84, 275

Heyman, Charles 172

Hezerkhani, Michale 9

high-speed flight in close proximity to the ground impossible in fixed-wing aircraft 251

Hightower, T. Mark xvi-xvii, 34-35, 146, 181, 327-336, 337-353, 355-361, 367-368, 372, 392-393, 411, 414

hijackers turned up alive and well the following day 12

History Will Not Absolve Us 47

HMX 331-333, 348, 352

Hoffman, Jim 205

Hollywood special effects 9

Holmes, Christopher 291, 297-298

Holmes, Sherlock 405

Holmgren, Gerard 187, 275, 297

Holocaust 105

Honegger, Barbara 296, 369

Hoover, Gregg 98

House Select Committee on

Assassinations (HSCSA) 19, 134, 174

HSCA (House Select Committee on Assassinations 19, 134, 174

Hubbard, L. Ron 383

Hussein, Saddam 18, 23, 397, 422

Hutchison effect 386-387

Hutchison, John 181, 373, 377

I

IAEA (International Atomic Energy Agency) 177

ICTS 25

Identification "Friend or Foe" (IFF) 207

IFF (Identification "Friend or Foe") 207

importance of "HOW" 3

Impossible entry 284-285

"Impossible to Prove a False Claim True" 293

inference to the best explanation 305-306

inside job 27

International Atomic Energy Agency (IAEA) 177

International bankers 18

Iraq 18, 23, 26

Iraq and Afghanistan were invaded on that basis 292

Iraqi Embassy at the United Nations 27

iron oxide/aluminum 358

iron oxide/aluminum nanothermite 350, 359

Irving, David 71

"Is '9/11 Truth' based upon a false theory?" 146, 181, 413

ISIL (Islamic State and the Levant) 21

Islamic State and the Levant (ISIL) 21

Israel 13, 18, 73

Israel as an undeclared nuclear state 176-179

Israel nuked the WTC on 9/11 171

Israeli terrorism 21

J

Jack White Enterprises 135

James, Preston 420

James, Preston 47-58

Jayhan, Phil 385

Jennings, Barry 122, 196, 423

430

CPSIA information can be obtained at www.ICGtesting.com
Printed in the USA
LVOW08s0523140816

500201LV00003B/3/P